THE ARCHAEOLOGY OF MEDITERRANEAN LANDSCAPES

This volume presents a comprehensive review of palaeoenvironmental evidence and its incorporation with landscape archaeology from across the Mediterranean. A fundamental aim of this book is to bridge the intellectual and methodological gaps between those with a background in archaeology and ancient history, and those who work in the palaeoenvironmental sciences. The aim of this volume is twofold: first, to provide archaeologists and landscape historians with a comprehensive overview of recent palaeoenvironmental research across the Mediterranean, and second, to consider ways in which this type of research can be integrated with what might be considered 'mainstream' or 'cultural' archaeology. This volume takes a thematic approach, assessing the ways in which environmental evidence is employed in different landscape types, from coastal zones via rivers and wetlands to islands and mountainous areas. This volume also presents analyses of how people have interacted with soils and vegetation, and revisits the key questions of human culpability in the creation of so-called degraded landscapes in the Mediterranean. It covers chronological periods from the Early Neolithic to the end of the Roman period.

Kevin Walsh is senior lecturer in the Department of Archaeology at the University of York. He has completed research in the Southern French Alps, the Roman mill at Barbegal near the Camargue, the Sainte Victoire Mountain near Aix-en-Provence, and at Stymphalos in the northern Peloponnese. He is co-editor of two books: *Interpretation of Sites and Material Culture from Mid-High Altitude Mountain Environments* and *Mediterranean Landscape Archaeology 2: Environmental Reconstruction in Mediterranean Landscape Archaeology.*

THE ARCHAEOLOGY OF MEDITERRANEAN LANDSCAPES

Human–Environment
Interaction from the Neolithic
to the Roman Period

KEVIN WALSH
University of York

CAMBRIDGE
UNIVERSITY PRESS

32 Avenue of the Americas, New York, NY 10013–2473, USA

Cambridge University Press is part of the University of Cambridge.

It furthers the University's mission by disseminating knowledge in the pursuit of
education, learning, and research at the highest international levels of excellence.

www.cambridge.org
Information on this title: www.cambridge.org/9780521853019

First published 2014

Printed in the United States of America

A catalog record for this publication is available from the British Library.

Library of Congress Cataloging in Publication data

Walsh, Kevin, 1963–
The archaeology of Mediterranean landscapes : human–environment interaction from the
Neolithic to the Roman period / Kevin Walsh, University of York.
    pages   cm
Includes bibliographical references and index.
ISBN 978-0-521-85301-9 (hardback)
1. Human ecology – Mediterranean Region.   2. Landscape archaeology – Mediterranean
Region.   3. Human geography – Mediterranean Region.   4. Excavations
(Archaeology) – Mediterranean Region.   5. Mediterranean Region –
Civilization.   6. Civilization, Ancient.   I. Title.
GF541.W35   2014
937–dc23   2013007621

ISBN 978-0-521-85301-9 Hardback

For Flo, who opened my eyes to so much ... and kept me going by regularly asking, 'C'est quand que tu termines ce livre...?'

Contents

Acknowledgements

Special thanks are due to several people for reading draft chapters. In particular, Tony (A. G.) Brown for reading an entire draft, and the following for their invaluable comments on various chapters: Eleni Asouti, Geoff Bailey, Andrew Bevan, John Bintliff, Will Fletcher, Helen Goodchild, Allan Hall, Bruce Hitchner, Bernard Knapp, Caroline Malone, Christophe Morhange, and Terry O'Connor.

I am indebted to friends and colleagues in the Department of Archaeology at the University of York for their support over the years, and also to the University of York for awarding me an anniversary lectureship grant that permitted extended research leave for the initial research for this book.

I would also like to thank friends and colleagues in the Centre Camille Jullian (Aix-en-Provence) for their continuing support; in particular the Bibliothèque d'Antiquité d'Aix has been one of the key resources for the research for this volume. I am also indebted to Philippe Leveau who directed my postdoctoral research at the Centre Camille Jullian and has continued to support me ever since.

Thank you to the following for providing and/or helping with figures and photos: Greg Aldrete, Jean-Francois Berger, Andrew Bevan, Philippe Boissinot, Tony (A. G.) Brown, Karl Butzer, Shirley Cefai, Gaëtan Congès, Jacques-Louis de Beaulieu, Carlo Giraudi, Itamar Greenberg and Ehud Galili, Fred Guiter, Bruce Hitchner, Nick Marriner, Anne Mather, Berengere Perez, Lisa Rayar-Bregou, Santiagio Riera-Mora, Dorit Sivan, Cynthianne Spiteri, Iain Stewart, Stathis C Stiros, Jon Swogger (and the Çatalhöyük Research Project), Sebastian Vogel, Jamie Woodward, and Eberhard Zangger. I would particularly like to thank Kieron Nieven for his work on many of the figures in this volume, and Gordon Wallace for help with copy-editing.

Special thanks go to Jean-Marie Gassend for allowing me to use (and convert) his watercolours into black-and-white images. I would also like to thank my copy editor, Luane Hutchinson, for her work on the manuscript.

Introduction

One motivation for writing this book is to bridge the conceptual and methodological gaps for those with a background in archaeology and ancient history, and those who work in the palaeoenvironmental sciences; different groups of researchers who all share a passion for Mediterranean landscapes. Therefore, the aim is twofold: to provide archaeologists and historians with a comprehensive overview of recent palaeoenvironmental research across the Mediterranean, and second, to consider ways in which this research can be integrated with what might be considered 'mainstream' or 'cultural' archaeology. This synthesis is structured in such a way that readers can 'jump' to the geographical or thematic sections that are of particular interest to them. In addition, the landscape thematic approach (with each chapter addressing a landscape type or connected themes) is designed to provide readers working in or researching a given landscape type access to modern environmental studies in those areas. Therefore, most of the chapters in this book follow a similar form. The first section in each chapter provides an overview of how each landscape/environment type has been studied, followed by a resumé (which is largely descriptive) of the principal findings of this research. Finally, latter sections of most chapters provide integrated assessments of some archaeological and palaeoenvironmental projects from across the region. The aim is not to define a sequential development of the Mediterranean environment and its peoples; this book is more concerned with the ways in which different peoples have interacted with different landscapes at different times. The examples comprise case studies from the beginning of agriculture to the end of the classical periods. This time span has been chosen, as much archaeological (especially landscape survey) and palaeoenvironmental research focusses on this chronological range. That is not to say that there is a dearth of medieval evidence. In fact, another reason for ending the temporal perspective of this volume at the end of the Roman period is also due to the author's own chronological research interests.

Mediterraneanism

The Mediterranean is the only region in the world that gives its name to a climate type. Although this volume is concerned with the Mediterranean geographical region, Mediterranean environments exist in California, Chile, the Cape (South Africa), as well as South and Western Australia (Allen 2001: ch. 1). Consequently, the cultural significance of studying Mediterranean environments is of global relevance.

There have been many helpful discussions of Mediterraneanism in recent years, most notably in the book edited by William Harris (2005b). The key point is that, after much debate, most people who carry out Mediterranean research believe that a pan-Mediterraneanist framework is reasonable and useful, in part due to the shared environmental characteristics, but also because of the obvious connected histories and cultural developments across the region.

At one level, the sheer variety of landscapes across the Mediterranean (a region where Europe, Africa, and Asia meet) implies that there cannot be a singular Mediterranean. However, there is a set of similar environmental characteristics, in particular, similar geological structures and climatic cycles. There are, of course, important fluctuations in average temperatures, precipitation, and vegetation. However, such variations are not just spread across the region as a whole but can occur within subregions due to considerable local variations in topography. These features are considered in Chapter 2.

If one could provide a straightforward definition of a typical Mediterranean environment, we would emphasise the dramatic differences in landscape forms that exist within relatively small spaces. Between the Alps in the north and the Atlas mountains in the south, there are plains, wetlands, arid zones, forests, barren lands, and, perhaps most importantly, an incredible variation in coastal landforms, and within the sea, there are of course the islands. If we were to draw a transect across any part of the Mediterranean region, most if not all of these landscape types would be available – this sequence or group of landscapes is what

defines the Mediterranean. Most of these environments are dealt with
via thematic chapters. Coastal environments are presented in Chapter 3,
with an assessment of background changes in sea level, and an analysis
of their variation across the Mediterranean. The ways in which different
societies have engaged with coasts and the sea is dealt with in the second part of that chapter. Alluvial and fluvial systems are the subjects of
Chapter 4. Here, descriptions of alluvial processes are presented along
with studies of how Mediterranean people have engaged with rivers
and wetlands. Although a related issue, the problem of aridity and areas
where water supply is restricted or unpredictable is part of the subject
matter of Chapters 5 and 6, where erosion, soils, and wider issues in
Mediterranean geoarchaeology are considered. This analysis incorporates
the assessment of vegetation histories and human engagements with vegetation from the Neolithic through to the Roman period. An overriding
theme (discussed by others, e.g. Grove & Rackham 2001) is the notion
of landscape degradation or the 'Fall from Eden'. This Genesis myth is
founded on the notion that people in the past adopted an instrumental
attitude to the landscape (i.e. exploited it without always caring for it),
and this negligence was punished (in a codified form) via the story of the
expulsion from Eden. Chapters 7 and 8 consider the range of processes
discussed in the preceding chapters, but develop specific assessments
of the 'bounded' and quintessentially Mediterranean islands and then
mountains.

As the chapters unfold, the reader will probably appreciate that
any notion of a single Mediterranean, with homogenous responses to
similar environmental processes and common economic strategies, is
largely misplaced (J. G. Manning & Morris 2007). If we accept that
each environmental niche and its constitutive processes have a role as
a non-human agent (Latour 1997), contributing to the development
and continual reconstitution of cultures, then, on that basis alone,
we cannot argue for a homogenous Mediterranean culture and integrated systems of environmental manipulation. However, it is possible
to idealise a particular type of 'typical' Mediterranean physical geography. This idealised Mediterranean is sometimes conceptualised as a
framework over which variations in cultural development are evident,
but where the environmental framework apparently influences these
variations. As French historian Henry Laurens (2010: 59–60) suggests,
with chronological variations from area to area, Mediterranean peoples

have experienced the same processes that have profoundly transformed the Mediterranean landscape. Agricultural production expresses these shared traits with similar crops (e.g. wheat, olive, and vine) and landscape features (such as terracing). The ways in which people engage with the environment are influenced by the possibilities that occur naturally within a given space. However, the form of human engagement with that space is contingent upon a wide range of cultural processes. Each environmental niche is characterised by its potential and its limitations. The manner in which different peoples impose their layered cultural values on that environment, and develop their awareness of nature, clearly influences the ways in which landscapes evolve. Whilst any kind of environmental determinism is quite understandably frowned upon, we cannot underplay the impact of structural geology (topography), climate, vegetation, and hydrology on settlement, economy, ideology, myths, and culture across the Mediterranean. The complex tectonic processes and extreme topographical variations within relatively small spaces have always had a profound effect on where people can live and work. Anyone who has travelled along the coastline of Italy, Greece, and the larger Mediterranean islands cannot have failed to notice the ever-present mountain ranges in the middle distance, and the sheer cliffs dominating much of the coast. Large portions of these coastlines are uninhabitable or, at best, unsuited for agriculture or even pastoralism. Settlements are nested in the areas adjacent to faults or relatively flat zones that have evolved as rivers and streams, which in turn have deposited sediments and yielded a more 'useful' environment. If we accept that the processes that characterise these heterogeneous environments contribute to the construction of lifeways and culture in their broadest sense, then past human experiences and activities in these landscapes cannot be assessed via material cultural alone; we should also consider environmental processes in the development of a 'symmetrical anthropology' (Latour 1997).

Frameworks for the Assessment of Human–Environment Engagements

When we think about how people have interacted with an environment over time, we often consider the choices that they made regarding settlement location, landscape management (both in terms of the geomorphic system and vegetation), choice of crops, extraction of rocks and minerals, and the impact that these activities had on the landscape. Archaeology and environmental archaeology are often concerned with researching and explaining change in cultural and environmental systems. Quite logically, we are interested in identifying and explaining changes in society and landscape and, most importantly for this volume, changes in the environment. Environmental archaeologists look for impact on the vegetation system or phases of erosion. When we do identify a phase of environmental stability, such a phase is identified because it represents a change or a rupture. However, periods of stability and maintenance of specific activities are just as important. We need to consider why people chose to settle and establish settlements in particular topographic situations within a given landscape. Many settlements have been continually occupied for centuries and even millennia. Briefly abandoned extant settlements often attract reuse; in some landscapes, we may want to consider different forms of inertia, as well as processes of change and adaptation. One relevant notion that has seen much discussion in recent years is 'resilience' (Butzer 2005; Redman 2005). Here, resilience theory does not imply that environments autonomously maintain equilibrium, but that societies who engage with these environments develop strategies for ensuring the persistence and productivity of a given niche.

We are often told that humans adapt to changes in the environment. What do we mean by this, and how can we be sure what adaptations were made? The environmental processes that we measure (eroded sediments, proxy data for vegetation change, etc.) are not necessarily representative of events witnessed by and responded to by past peoples. Whilst evidence for aridification caused by climate change, in the form of a reduction in precipitation, might induce settlement shift over a relatively long period, how do we demonstrate responses to shorter-term events, such as soil erosion? Substantial sedimentary units can be deposited by a few severe storms – events that would have been a common occurrence even within ostensible phases of environmental stability.

Modern, Western notions and perceptions of the environment are regularly informed by instrumental economic philosophies. Modern science, with its roots in the Enlightenment, employs a discourse; a way of interpreting and discussing the world that is so different to the numerous forms of environmental understanding that would have existed in the past. In order to engage with this issue, the final section of most of the core chapters will examine how past societies may have engaged with the environmental processes that we believe are significant and relevant.

The other modern view of nature/landscape is one dominated by a Romantic aesthetic (see Johnson 2007: ch. 2). Again, this is in part a consequence of a disembedded relationship with the natural world: landscapes are places that we visit and engage with at an ideological level where perspectivism is all-important. This relationship with landscape characterises certain postprocessual approaches in landscape archaeology, in particular, phenomenological strands (Tilley 1994); approaches that appear to be underpinned by a Romantic notion of the countryside as destination and distraction, rather than a place of work and engagement with the sometimes harsh realities of the natural environment (Bintliff 2009; Flemming 2006). These approaches are often more detached from the reality of past lifeways than the environmental science that they often attempt to critique. Such approaches are not as common in Mediterranean archaeology (for an exception, see Hamilton et al. 2006), where emphasis is placed on assessing human impact on the environment or the economic potential of a landscape, and how this might have varied with climate change and/or human impact.

As a number of recent works have demonstrated, a significant underlying theme in Mediterranean landscape archaeology is the notion of the 'Fall from Eden', or the culpability of humanity in the destruction of a once supposedly pristine landscape (Grove & Rackham 2001). Recent narratives also attempt to demonstrate how the characterisation of Mediterranean environments as marginal and degraded has been misplaced. Horden and Purcell (2000: ch. V) believe that whilst certain Mediterranean niches are not always productive in isolation (in the sense that they easily generate surpluses), once we see the different niches as nodes within an integrated network of production, the whole is so much greater than the sum of the parts. Whilst these more recent frameworks are useful, we also need to consider how different groups in different societies in the past engaged with these landscapes. For example, some societies saw their relationship with nature as a conflict or battle, such as that which might have been held in Mesopotamian society (Hughes 1994a: 34).

Environmental Knowledge and Cultural Ecologies

Rather than provide a comprehensive overview of the development of cultural and historical ecology (dealt with in a number of publications, e.g. Balée 2006; Crumley 1994b; Meyer & Crumley 2012; Sutton & Anderson 2004), this section identifies some key tenets that underpin the approach adopted in this book.

The origins of most human ecological strands of thought lay with cultural ecology, which is directly associated with functional anthropology (Steward 1955). Cultural possibilists who worked within a cultural ecological framework suggested that certain peoples, in particular, hunter-gatherers, were constrained by their environments. Steward in particular developed these ideas and moved towards assessments of cultural evolution, emphasising adaptation and stability with the investigation of change in hunter-gatherer groups in North America (Bettinger 1991: 44–5). Some of these ideas were then adopted by archaeologists, and the fact its use is often associated with an under-theorised form of processual archaeology should not detract from the value of approaches that adopt a cultural ecological framework. One notion, which was applied by some archaeologists, was the culture-area concept, whereby technologies and human lifeways were apparently correlated with the nature of the environmental context within which societies developed (Clark 1968).

An early example of an unsophisticated cultural ecological interpretation of a historical process was the contention that the fall of Rome was an ecological catastrophe partly caused by a misuse of resources resulting from poor knowledge or information (Sutton & Anderson 2004: 3). As argued at certain points in this volume, what is more likely is that, at certain times and places, the environmental knowledge, articulated via macro-political and economic forces, was at odds with the environmental experiences and concomitant knowledge of the peoples who lived and worked in these different landscapes.

Cultural ecology assesses environmental knowledge, that is, how people understand and engage with their landscape and environment. The notion of adaptive strategies, where groups of people develop technologies that facilitate life and, in particular, food production in a given environment, is important. D. O. Henry's (1994) work in southern Jordan is one example of such an approach. This type of approach does not assume that technologies and human lifeways will be repeated in landscapes characterised by identical or similar sets of environmental characteristics. As noted above, Mediterranean cultures do share certain forms of landscape-management strategies, but these strategies are contingent upon historical, cultural, and economic processes that vary across time and space. Responses to changes in the environment do tend to be controlled by the ability of social institutions to adapt. As Bettinger, Richerson, and Boyd (2009) suggest in their assessment of constraints on the development of agriculture, it was the gradual evolution of certain social institutions that limited the speed of the uptake of farming in some regions. A key question is how was environmental knowledge applied in the past, and by whom? People are not separate from ecological systems; they are participants in environmental processes, and as such, human participation in environmental change is quite natural (Walters & Vayda 2009: 536). At a wider level, a cultural ecological approach can also inform the study of landscapes where there is a dearth of material evidence, or in landscapes that are considered difficult to manage and in some ways 'unattractive', such as arid zones or mountains. Here, the premise is that each society's engagement with the environment is dynamic. Consequently, if we can elucidate the manner in which past peoples manipulated and responded to their environments, then this is an effective scheme for the investigation of past cultures and the transitions or changes in culture across a given landscape. Finally, resilience theory offers a way of conceptualising the relationships between different spatial and temporal scales of cultural processes (Redman 2005). Here, resilience theory presents a scheme for investigations of the relationships between small-scale, localised groups of people (e.g. individual farms) and how they relate to extensive hierarchical structures (e.g. the Roman Empire or its regional authority). Of most interest is the notion that successful environmental exploitation strategies only work if people can adapt. However, if local engagements with environments are controlled by entrenched political forces during periods of environmental change, and local people are unable to respond effectively to these changes, then such a situation might contribute to local and regional societal instability. When local, potentially small-and-fast, adaptive strategies are stifled by slow-responding, large-scale hierarchies, such as certain empires, then environmental problems might ensue. Conversely, certain hierarchical organisations might impose or apply new forms of environmental management that are successful and enthusiastically adopted by local people. It is the appreciation of different forms of human ecology that allows us to move away from the original conceptions of cultural ecology, perhaps best characterised by the definition of 'culture areas' (Steward 2005).

In summary, the discussions developed in some of the following chapters are informed by the frameworks considered in this chapter. The ultimate aim is to identify trends and trajectories in Mediterranean landscapes from the Neolithic to the Roman period, sometimes offering resumés of published environmental research and presenting syntheses of this type of research with related archaeological information. Part of the approach includes the evaluation of the range of human–environment interactions across the Mediterranean, where environmental evidence can be deployed in assessments of human–environment engagements, and, where possible, to consider scenarios where variations in forms of environmental knowledge could have been responsible for stresses, ruptures, and resilience in the wide range of cultures that have lived and worked in these dynamic landscapes.

2

From Geology to Biology: Defining the Mediterranean

This chapter comprises a brief overview of the geological and biogeographical contexts of the Mediterranean. There is also a brief description of catastrophic processes, and some analysis of associated human responses to these phenomena. As the principal aim of this volume is the discussion of more mundane environmental processes, the assessment of catastrophic events is kept to a minimum, partly because there are a number of specialised volumes that deal admirably with these processes, and a single chapter cannot do justice to this increasingly popular area of research (Ambraseys 2009; Balmuth, Chester, & Johnston 2003; Nur & Burgess 2008).

Fundamental Geological and Biological Characteristics

The Mediterranean is defined in part by its geology. The Iberian, Eurasian, Arabian, and African plates; their associated faults; and mountain chains situated within relatively short distances from coastlines explain the enormous variation and complexity of Mediterranean landscapes. This geological crossroads is also important from a biological perspective, as flora and fauna (including humans) have moved from Asia and Africa, and then onwards between the Near East and Europe.

There are many books that provide detailed descriptions of the geological foundations and processes that characterise the Mediterranean (e.g. Dixon & Robertson 1996; Jolivet et al. 2008; Stanley & Wezel 1985). In simple terms, the Mediterranean comprises boundary zones between the Eurasian, African, and Arabian plates (Allen 2001: 48). Consequently, much of the Mediterranean comprises undulating topography and mountainous areas. The eastern half of the Mediterranean possesses a series of active fault lines that also include dormant and active volcanoes (Mather 2009) (Fig. 2.1). This half of the Mediterranean is much more tectonically active than the western half, with Italy and Sicily constituting the boundary. To a certain extent, the distribution of volcanic activity follows this arc, as well as the Calabrian Arc, which includes Vesuvius. This geological configuration leads many authors to characterise the Mediterranean region as inherently unstable, with this instability contributing to degradation processes and the evolution of reputed marginal landscapes or niches. As with the other environmental processes assessed in this book, the relative impact that geological processes have had on human societies in the past has been the subject of much debate in recent years (Grove & Rackham 2001; Horden & Purcell 2000).

Major tectonic events tend to be high-magnitude, low-frequency events, but these processes then determine the conditions for long-term, low-magnitude processes, such as soil erosion. First, there are the characteristics of the solid geological layer, which for the sake of simplification can be divided into alkaline and acidic categories. Despite the fact that limestone is omnipresent, most Mediterranean subregions incorporate a wide range of rocks, including sandstones, granites, lavas, flysch, and shales. Soft rocks, including conglomerates, marls, and clay, are also common. The intrusive igneous and metamorphic rocks comprise minerals or rock types that have been economically valuable in the past, such as marble, jadeite, or obsidian. The geological substrates influence the properties and evolution of soils and their potential for erosion. An erosion pattern is then influenced by climate (phases of relative humidity or aridity), vegetation development, and pedogenesis.

BASIC CLIMATIC AND BIOGEOGRAPHICAL CHARACTERISTICS

The Mediterranean possesses climatic characteristics that are quite rare in that there are relatively few regions on the planet that experience such dramatic seasonal shifts in dominant pressure systems and concomitant weather patterns (Harding, Palutikof, & Holt 2009: 69). There are, of course, variations across the Mediterranean. The western area is influenced by Atlantic systems, and seasonal temperature variations are less severe than in the east, this area being influenced by central European and Asian systems. The south-eastern area is the most arid. Within the Mediterranean, relatively small and localised depressions can develop. This is more common in the central to north-eastern zones, the most famous being the Gulf of Genoa depressions. The important aspects of

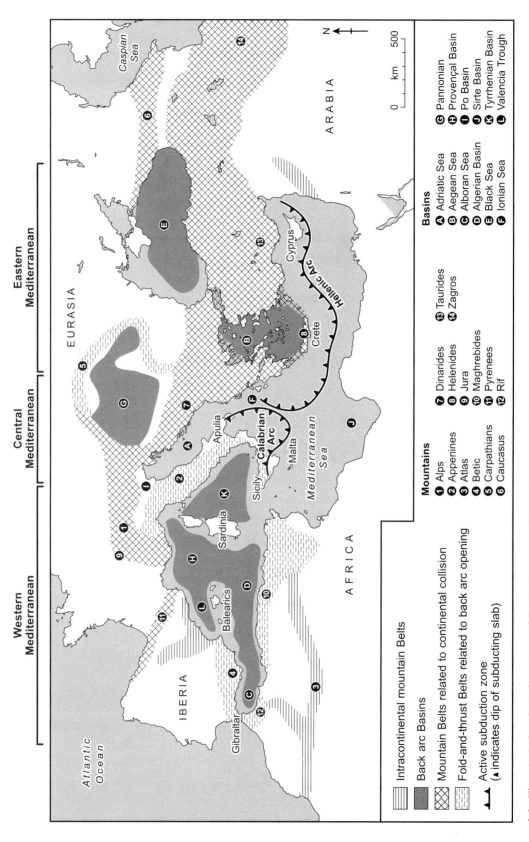

2.1. The principal geological structures of the Mediterranean. (By permission of Oxford University Press, Mather, A. (2009), Tectonic setting and landscape development, in J. Woodward (ed.), *The Physical Geography of the Mediterranean*, fig. 1.1(b), ch. 1, p. 6.)

Western Mediterranean   Central Mediterranean   Eastern Mediterranean

N

0   km   500

EURASIA

ARABIA

AFRICA

IBERIA

Atlantic Ocean

Caspian Sea

Mediterranean Sea

Gibraltar
Balearics
Sardinia
Sicily
Malta
Apulia
Crete
Cyprus

Calabrian Arc
Hellenic Arc

Mountains
❶ Alps
❷ Appenines
❸ Atlas
❹ Betic
❺ Carpathians
❻ Caucasus
❼ Dinarides
❽ Helenides
❾ Jura
❿ Maghrebides
⓫ Pyrenees
⓬ Rif
⓭ Taurides
⓮ Zagros

Basins
Ⓐ Adriatic Sea
Ⓑ Aegean Sea
Ⓒ Alboran Sea
Ⓓ Algerian Basin
Ⓔ Black Sea
Ⓕ Ionian Sea
Ⓖ Pannonian
Ⓗ Provencal Basin
Ⓘ Po Basin
Ⓙ Sirte Basin
Ⓚ Tyrrhenian Basin
Ⓛ Valencia Trough

Intracontinental mountain Belts

Back arc Basins

Mountain Belts related to continental collision

Fold-and-thrust Belts related to back arc opening

Active subduction zone
(▲ indicates dip of subducting slab)

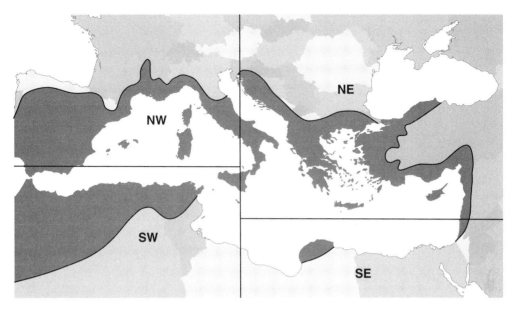

2.2. The biogeographical zones of the Mediterranean (after Blondel et al. 2010).

climate change comprise adjustments in average seasonal temperature and precipitation levels. The Mediterranean climate can be considered as transitional between cold temperate and dry tropical, with the northern part of the region characterised by colder, windier conditions than the south. The other key defining characteristics of the Mediterranean bioclimatic regime are the distribution and timing of rainfall, with the eastern area often experiencing five to six months each year without rainfall, as opposed to two months in the western area (Blondel et al. 2010: 12).

As discussed in the previous chapter, defining the boundaries of the Mediterranean is a difficult task, but the distribution of plants such as olive and holm oak with sclerophyllous leaf structures (thick leaves that preserve moisture) is one widely agreed bioindicator. However, as with all organisms, its geographical distribution has fluctuated. Consequently, the combination of climatic and biological characteristics and the creation of bioclimatic criteria is one of the most useful frameworks for the definition of the region. The intersection of these different features then constitutes the biogeographical characteristics. The four principle biogeographical zones are the four quarters of the Mediterranean, that is, north-west, north-east, south-east, and south-west (Blondel & Aronson 1999; Blondel et al. 2010) (Fig. 2.2). Average temperatures across these biogeographical zones do of course vary. Whilst average summer temperatures across the Mediterranean are usually between

25°C and 30°C, averages are higher and often go above these temperatures in the eastern and southern zones. This trend in higher average temperatures in the eastern and southern zones is also true for average winter temperatures. Topographic situation also effects average temperature, with these averages being lower at higher altitude. For example, Madrid, at 667 m, has mean January temperatures between 2.7°C and 9.7°C, whilst Valencia, at 11 m, has corresponding temperatures of 7°C and 16.1°C (AEMET; Allen 2001). These variations in climate and topographic situation clearly affect soil, plant, and animal distributions. As Blondel et al. (2010: 103–13) have demonstrated, the most effective way of appreciating biogeographic variability within a zone is to examine a transect from the coasts towards the interior high altitudes. In Blondel's north-west transect (the south of France), we move from coastal wetlands (the Camargue; discussed in this volume, Chapter 4), through the hilly zones with the evergreen shrublands (elements in the discussion of Chapters 5 and 6), through to the interior (often mountainous) areas with mixed evergreen vegetation (part of the discussions in Chapters, 4, 5, and 8). In Blondel's south-eastern Quadrant (the Lebanon), the coastal zone (Chapter 3) comprises dune-tufted grasses, then, as we move into the hinterland, evergreen woodlands are present. Then, in the more mountainous zones, the vegetation comprises deciduous oak and pine woodlands, with cedar and juniper above these woodlands. Moving down, towards the east, a more arid-type Mediterranean landscape is evident, comprising shrublands dominated by wormwoods. Lower down, the Beqa'a Valley is a fertile cultivated zone. Even further to the east, we come to desert.

The characterisations presented above refer to current climate data. There have of course been a number of significant climatic fluctuations in the Mediterranean during the Holocene, and these are considered at different points in the book. Most importantly, the recent palaeoclimatic research now allows us to understand the development of these regional climate regimes during the Holocene (Brayshaw, Rambeau, & Smith 2011; Finné et al. 2011; Magny et al. 2011).

Tectonics and the Creation and Destruction of Niches

Although tectonic processes and associated volcanic activity can damage parts of landscapes, render coastal sites unusable, and lead to loss of life, we should not forget that tectonic activity creates the undulating, varied topography that structures the development of numerous environmental niches that are home to an extensive range of flora and fauna. This mosaic characterises many parts of the Mediterranean, and has thus led to the need for people to develop complex forms of environmental knowledge that operate at the local level. This characteristic of Mediterranean landscapes is dealt with in a number of chapters. Here, the immediate consequences of seismic activity are considered (Fig. 2.3).

Catastrophes, in the form of earthquakes and volcanic eruptions, make for good television, popular books, as well as scholarly journals (e.g. Keys 1999; Ryan & Pitman 2000; Silva, Sintubin, & Reicherter 2011; Wilson 2001). Catastrophism became unfashionable for some time in archaeology, but in recent years, its study has taken on a higher profile. The citation of catastrophic events as explanations for ruptures or significant changes in ancient societies, along with attempts to identify the realities behind certain myths such as the Great Flood or destruction of Atlantis, are central themes in such research. More recently, Horden and Purcell (2000: 300) have appropriately observed that 'disaster history continues to fascinate, and needs no misleading promotion by causal association with the language of popular science'. Commenting specifically on the eruption of Vesuvius, they assert that the productive landscape in this area was resilient (ibid.: 306). However, resilience is time dependent in that evidence for people returning to a landscape a generation after the catastrophe may appear swift, but the generation that experienced the event may not have been able to demonstrate resilience. One effect of such an eruption might have been a change in topography as volcanic sediment covered the landscape. However, whilst the volcanic sediments around Vesuvius are up to 15 m deep, the eruption blanketed the AD 79 topography and left a new surface that essentially reflected the original topography (see Fig. 2.4 for a map of sites referred to in this chapter). Despite the fact that the post-AD 79 topography was, in a way, moulded onto the ancient landscape, the volcanic material did have a significant effect on the surrounding environment. These deep deposits would have had an impact on the fluvial and alluvial elements across the landscape (Fig. 2.5) (Vogel & Märker 2010; Vogel, Märker, & Seiler 2011).

One thread running through the following chapters is that of temporal scale and the extent to which we can develop discourses that

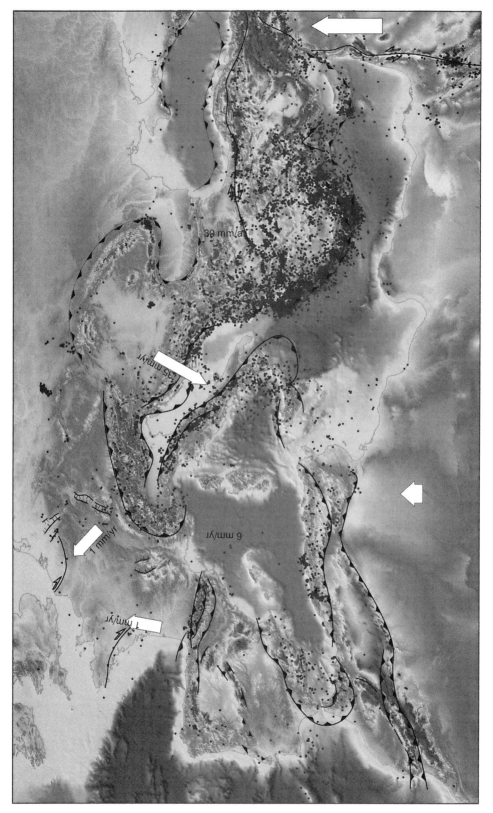

2.3. Major tectonic structures and associated seismicity of the Mediterranean. (By permission of Oxford University Press, Stewart, I., and Morhange, C. (2009), Coastal geomorphology and sea-level change, in J. Woodward (ed.), *The Physical Geography of the Mediterranean*, fig. 13.1a&b, p. 387.)

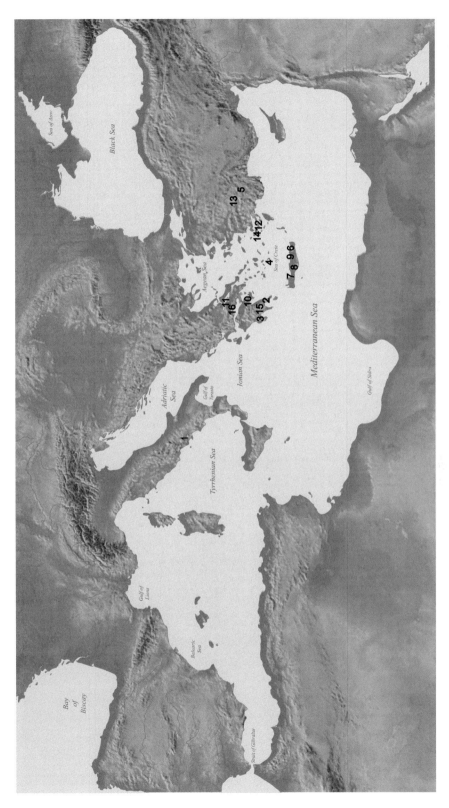

2.4. Map of sites referred to in text. 1: Vesuvius, 2: Ayios Dhimitrios, 3: Voidokilia/Area of Messenia/Pylos, 4: Santorini, 5: Lake Gölhisar, 6: Mochlos, 7: Delphinos, 8: Phaistos, 9: Gouves, 10: Midea/Mycenae/Tiryns, 11: Pyrgos, 12: Cnidus, 13: Pamukkale, 14: Kos, 15: Sparta, 16: Delphi.

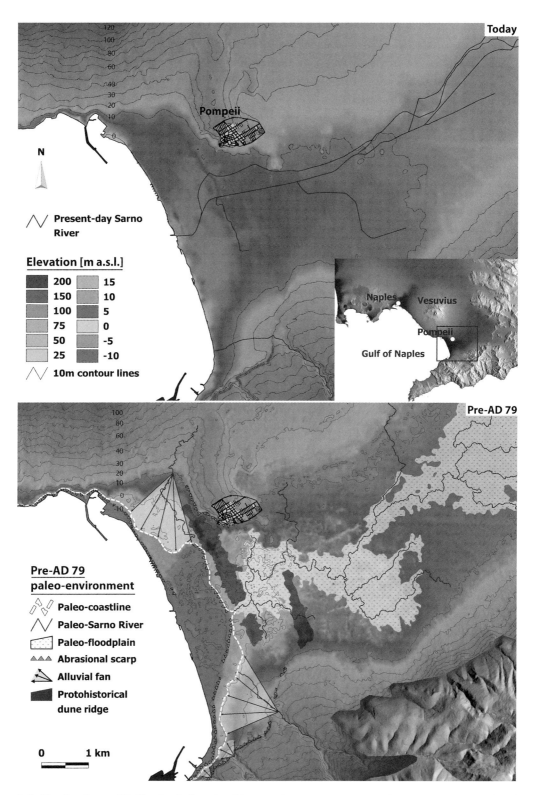

2.5. Vogel et al. post-AD 79 volcanic deposits of Somma-Vesuvius to reconstruct the pre-AD 79 topography of the Sarno River plain (Italy). Top: present-day environment. Bottom: pre-AD 79 environment. (By permission of Geologica Carpathica, Vogel, S., Märker, M., and Seiler, F. (2011), Revised modelling of the post-AD 79 volcanic deposits of Somma-Vesuvius to reconstruct the pre-AD 79 topography of the Sarno River plain (Italy). *Geologica Carpathica* 62(1), 5–16, fig. 5.)

evaluate possible human engagements with various environmental processes. Whilst we should accept that catastrophes cannot usually be
blamed or cited as direct causes of societal and cultural changes, we
cannot reject the notion that certain catastrophic events would have had
profound repercussions for individuals, families, villages, and even towns
at certain points in the past. Despite the fact that average earthquake
magnitudes across the Mediterranean are not large, the Mediterranean
has had a relatively high population density for much of its past, and
therefore the potential hazard/risk has been greater (Mather 2009: 11).
In addition, tectonic processes give rise to certain landscape qualities
that have deeply positive cultural connotations: the 'structural instability' of the Mediterranean also gives rise to features such as thermal
springs and sulphur beds that possess powerful and often-positive cultural associations.

   The historical and archaeological study of seismology and volcanism
is complex (Guidoboni & Ebel 2009; Jones & Stiros 2000), and there
are many problems with the chronologies of these events and thereby the
identification of their impact on specific human communities. Moreover,
the geographical spread of research is patchy, with some areas, such as
Algeria, not having benefited from much detailed study (Benouar 2004).
There is little doubt that some volcanic eruptions have had a profound
impact on communities: the immediate destructive power of high-magnitude eruptions is doubtless. At the Bronze Age site of *Ayios Dhimitrios*
in south-west Greece, it appears that the site's occupants fled without
having time to gather valuable items (Zachos 1996: 169). Some 60 km
away, a similar set of events have also been identified at Voidokilia during
the Early Bronze Age (3200–2050 BC). These sites may represent some
of the earliest evidence that we have for destruction by an earthquake,
including a direct impact on the population (ibid.).

   What is more problematic is an assessment of the longer-term consequences of these events. Even where we have ancient written sources,
in particular for the AD 79 eruption of Vesuvius, we cannot be sure of
the longer-term effects. The eruptions of Vesuvius and Santorini are the
two obvious candidates for discussion within Mediterranean archaeology. Some would argue that the effects of some significant eruptions
were felt on a continental or even a global scale, with ash clouds blocking
solar radiation and reducing temperatures (Grattan & Gilbertson 2000;
LaMoreaux 1995).

The precise definition of the chronological framework is essential for any wider analysis of the relationship of an event with wider sociopolitical and cultural processes. There is probably no other single event in Mediterranean archaeology that has engendered such an extensive and detailed debate regarding its date than the eruption of Santorini/Thera (Thera being one of the islands that constitute the Santorini group) (S. W. Manning 1999; Zielinski & Germani 1998). The issue of chronology is important, as there is the posited high date of 1628 BC for the eruption (Kuniholm 1996; S. W. Manning 1999), and then a low date of around 1520 BC (Warren 1996). The most convincing chronology is that based on the analysis of a series of secure, radiocarbon dates which places the eruption at 1650–1620 BC (possibly c. 1628 BC) (Bruins et al. 2008; S. W. Manning et al. 2002). The eruption itself was a multiphase event comprised of a Plinian explosive phase (an eruption type named after Pliny the Younger's description of the ash and gas column from Vesuvius which reaches the stratosphere), followed by the base-surge phase when seawater connected with the magma. The final phase saw the crater wall giving way and clouds of hot ash and gas sweeping outwards laterally across the island (Friedrich 2004: 75–6). Recent estimates suggest that some 60 km³ of material would have been ejected by the Theran eruption (this is half as big again as earlier estimates) (Sigurdsson et al. 2006).

When we discuss the environmental impact of any phenomenon, whether it is seasonal erosion or the consequences of a 'catastrophic' event such as the eruption on Santorini, we must consider what we mean by 'environmental impact'. Although it has been difficult to demonstrate that Cretan sites were destroyed by tsunamis or even ash fallouts emanating from the Santorini eruption, it was argued that *nuées ardentes* (highly heated gas clouds) could have reached eastern Crete (I. G. Nixon 1985), whilst the tephra fallout may well have covered an area from the Black Sea down to the south-eastern Mediterranean (Gulchard et al. 1996). Santorini ash has been found across the wider region, from the Nile Valley to the Black Sea (ibid.). There is evidence for the creation of homogeneous (redeposited) sediment – 'homogenite' – which has been found in more than 50 deep-sea cores. This layer (up to 10 m thick on the abyssal plains and more than 20 m to the west of the Mediterranean Ridge) must represent a sudden, high-magnitude event (Cita, Camerlenghi, & Rimoldi 1996: 158), which some authors argue to be the Santorini eruption (Cita

& Aloisi 2000). A similar phenomenon has been identified in the central Ionian Sea (Hieke & Werner 2000). The fact that on certain sites, such as Rhodes, there is no break in Minoan activity (Keller, Rehren, & Stadlbauer 1990) suggests that the effects of the Theran eruption were not disastrous in the short term (Minoura et al. 2000: 59). Evidence from Lake Gölhisar in south-west Turkey demonstrates that the eruption had little impact on the vegetation in this part of the Mediterranean (Eastwood et al. 2002). Excavations at the Mochlos site on Crete produced a tephrastratigraphy which demonstrated that the eruption took place towards the end of the Late Minoan IA period, whilst the collapse of Minoan society started somewhat later during the Late Minoan IB period. There is also some doubt as to whether the acidity peaks seen in some of the ice cores directly relate to the Santorini eruption, whilst the reduced growth rings seen in some tree-ring records may have been caused by other environmental processes; in fact, enhanced tree growth may have occurred during this period (Kuniholm 1996).

There is no doubt that the eruption had a profound impact on Santorini itself; the pre-eruption Bronze Age landscape would have been quite different, with greater topographical variation (Heiken, McCoy, & Sheridan 1990; McCoy & Heiken 2000a). In addition, the vegetation on the island would have been far more varied. Charcoal evidence points to the presence of vine, oak, pine, and tamarisk; moreover, tree roots have been found in buried soils. Today, there is remarkably little tree or shrub vegetation on the island (Asouti 2003a: 473). On Crete, there is little evidence to suggest that the Santorini eruption was responsible for vegetation degradation; moreover, there is no sedimentary evidence within the Delphinos (a north-western Cretan coastal marsh) core for a tsunami. In the Delphinos pollen diagram, there is some suggestion that crop cultivation 'stagnated' after the eruption and that olive production levels possibly did decline (Bottema & Sarpaki 2003: 747). Any modifications in vegetation and settlement patterns were more likely the result of socio-economic changes which may have in some small part been influenced by the eruption; an event that possibly 'nudged' an already fragile social system just over the edge. One elegant assessment of the intersection of culture and environment suggests that changes in pottery style after catastrophes articulate a new attitude towards the natural world, in this instance, the sea. Rather than representing the impact of a possible Thera-generated tsunami, one possibility is that the motifs represent maritime life that was lost or damaged by pumice fall, as this would have had a serious impact on the productivity of the sea around Crete. In particular, deep-water cephalopods and gastropods are presented – creatures that require clear, clean water, suggesting that Minoans avoided consuming marine products as a consequence of post-eruption marine pollution (Bicknell 2000: 101).

Despite the lack of evidence for the immediate impact of the Theran eruption on Cretan society, it is possible that a combination of earthquakes and tsunamis (possibly following volcanic activity) did have consequences later on for Crete, at the end of the Neopalatial period (LM IB, fifteenth century BC), and then again during the Late Minoan IIIB period (thirteenth century BC) (Vallianou 1996: 153). Anti-seismic construction methods appear to have been employed at Phaistos (central-southern Crete) from the Old Palace period (phase IB). The building excavated by Vallianou at Pitdiai, just to the south of Phaistos, collapsed and was abandoned during the Late Minoan IB period. Elsewhere in northern and eastern Crete, there were a number of destruction phases recognised on archaeological sites dated to the Late Minoan IB period. Excavations at a Minoan settlement now some 90 m from the present coast and the harbour at Gouves revealed a layer with large quantities of pumice and evidence for flooding. This destruction layer has been dated to the Late Minoan IIIB period (1350/40–1190 BC or 1340/1330–1190 BC) (ibid.). Driessen (1998) considers that the Theran eruption may have damaged food-production systems, thus undermining ruling elites on Crete and leading to the development of decentralised networks of power, which in turn left the way open for an increase in Mycenaean influence. Settlement patterns changed and moved so much during the pre- and proto-historic periods that it seems unlikely that the only (or even dominant) factors were environmental/subsistence criteria (Wallace 2010: 53). These high-magnitude events may well have exposed inherent weaknesses in Minoan society; weaknesses that could not be resolved, perhaps partly because of the nature of insular societies (see Chapter 7) and associated forms of cultural, political, and environmental knowledge. Recent studies suggest that Minoan palatial society was unstable due to its complex hierarchical structure and its dependence on agricultural specialisation and extensive cropping (Driessen 2002; see Hamilakis 1996).

A widespread economic and cultural downturn across the Aegean, and the start of the 'Bronze Age Dark Ages', have been blamed on an earthquake 'storm' – a series of earthquakes in relatively short succession that occurred in the Eastern Mediterranean between c. 1225 and 1175 BC. This research is based on an analysis of modern seismological processes and a reanalysis of evidence for earthquake impact on a series of Late Bronze Age sites in the Aegean (Nur & Cline 2000). There appears to have been a phase of substantial destruction at Midea in the Peloponnese at the end of the Late Helladic IIIB2 period (c. 1190 BC). This is contemporary with destruction events at Mycenae and Tiryns. The authors suggest that the inhabitants of this site may have fled in panic to Tiryns, whilst it is likely that the site was reoccupied during the Late Helladic IIIC period. The west gate of the Acropolis appears to have been destroyed during an earthquake. A young girl was found crushed by fallen stones; she appears to be a victim of an earthquake (Ånstöm & Demakopoulou 1996: 37–9). On the hill of Pyrgos (the Homeric town of Kynos), there is evidence of storerooms that had been damaged by earthquakes. The pottery indicates an early Late Helladic IIIC date for one earthquake followed by a more 'decisive' event later on during this period. The discovery of marine fossils even leads the authors to suggest that these may have been swept in by a tsunami: the building is only 16 m above the present sea level, and some 100 m away from the shoreline. After this destruction phase, the buildings were reused, although the quality of construction was poorer. These new floors also contain baby burials in pits (Dakoronia 1996: 42). A horizon dated to Late Helladic IIIB c. 1250 BC comprised skeletons covered with fallen stones. It is also possible that the preceding construction (heavy terraces to support steep slopes) was a precaution against earthquakes. Repairs after earthquakes do seem possible; for example, mud poured into moulded spaces allows repairs within walls that were still partly standing (E. B. French 1996: 51). There are a number of other sites that comprise similar sequences of events, including the palace at Thebes which was totally destroyed during the thirteenth century BC (LH IIIB) (Sampson 1996; Spondilis 1996).

In the north-east Peloponnese, nearly 100 Bronze Age sites have been found. Many of these sites were destroyed not long after 1200 BC, although some appear to have been evacuated without being destroyed. In Messenia, there were about 150 to 200 Late Helladic IIIB settlements. Most of these were quite small and were abandoned after the burning of the Palace of Nestor at Pylos. Some dismiss the importance of catastrophic natural events, and whilst citing geological catastrophe as the direct cause is problematic, there are also problems in replacing this with another unique cause. However, the possible reasons are varied, and might even include the impact of a new form of warfare employed by invading tribes (Drews 1993). The other fact that might have contributed to the downturn in settlement and economic activity during this period is climate change: the possibility that this region witnessed a phase of relative aridity (L. D. Brandon 2012). Whilst catastrophic events would have affected Bronze Age peoples in the region, they would not have directly led to the destruction of these cultures. These environmental processes may well have tested certain forms of sociocultural resilience. Some food resources may have been affected by catastrophic events combined with a new, relatively arid climate. Ideological and ritual mechanisms may well have emerged that helped mitigate these problems. These ideological mechanisms may well have reinforced the social memory of such disasters and led people to question the ability of social elites, or even the Gods, to moderate the threats posed by the natural world.

HELLENISTIC AND ROMAN CATASTROPHES

Tectonic activity can directly affect buildings (Fig. 2.6) as well landscape structure and concomitant processes, such as soil erosion and watercourse development. An extreme example of the importance of such events comes from Western Anatolia where 12 important cities, along with many minor settlements, were damaged or destroyed by an earthquake in AD 17 (Ambraseys 2009: 105–8). On sites where there is evidence for repeated impact of earthquakes, we have to consider how people responded. It is these sites, where people chose to stay, that probably represent a form of resignation; people accepting that seismic activity is a part of life. Cnidus in south-west Turkey was situated on a fault. Here, two powerful earthquakes took place, the first during the Late Hellenistic Period (late second–third century BC), the second during the fifth century AD (possibly AD 459) (Altunel et al. 2003). This type of scenario is repeated across many sites in the region, including Hierapolis (Pamukkale, Turkey) (Hancock & Altunel 1997). One characteristic of this latter site is the presence of offset irrigation channels, thus revealing how relatively minor events would have damaged the all-important hydraulic elements here.

2.6. Fallen columns at the Temple of Zeus, Olympia, Greece. Probably toppled by a sixth-century AD earthquake (photo: author).

We should not forget the other environmental consequences of seismic activity. Whilst many geoarchaeologists have claimed climatic and/or anthropogenic causes for erosion, there is no doubt that seismic events, with their resultant reconfiguration of topography, would have caused erosion (Papanastassiou, Gaki-Papanastassiou, & Maroukian 2005). In some instances, economic responses to earthquakes might be identified. A series of earthquakes is known to have affected Kos (south-east Aegean) between c. 200 BC and c. AD 200, with a particularly severe and catastrophic event taking place in 198 BC. It seems that this event was followed by a substantial increase in the monetary supply (based on detailed numismatic research), which suggests that this society required new financial resources to support the reconstruction of Kos. The fundamental question asked by Höghammar (2010) is whether these repairs were successfully carried out over a short period, or whether they were protracted, perhaps testing the resilience of this society.

In most instances, individual earthquakes, even if they are very powerful, have had little effect on political and cultural trajectories of past civilisations, unless such an event acts as a catalyst and accentuates an existing political or cultural weakness within a society. However, continued tectonic activity must have had some influence on the ways in which people engaged with the landscape, and in some instances, the cumulative effect of these events would have had some effect on economic and cultural systems.

More often than not, it is felt that earthquakes induce immediate and sometimes calamitous impacts on society, via building collapse or some other dramatic consequence. Earthquakes can also engender medium-term environmental impacts. Subsidence and uplift influence geomorphology and vegetation, and earthquakes will have damaged arid zone irrigation systems, with a change in water supply resulting in vegetation changes. The analyses of pollen from Dead Sea stratigraphic units that include seismites (sedimentary units disturbed by seismic shaking) allow an assessment of post-earthquake vegetation change. After the 31 BC earthquake, there was a reduction in agricultural production, signalled by reductions in olive, *Pistacia*, *Vitis*, and *Juglans* pollen. An increase in the extent of the desert could also have been another result of this event (Leroy et al. 2010).

A key characteristic of effective environmental knowledge is prediction. For example, Sparta experienced a number of earthquakes, but these significant events were separated by many centuries, or even millennia, which was clearly significant in terms of the collective memory and environmental knowledge associated with such processes. Major events are dated to 2500 BC and 464 BC, with relatively minor earthquakes taking place at 3900 BC, 2000 BC, 550 AD, and 1000 AD. Non-periodic events, such as those around Sparta (Finkel et al. 2002), are only predictable if they are recorded and a pattern is recognised, with knowledge of the patterns passed on through collective memory. The 464 BC earthquake in the southern Peloponnese is considered to have been centred on a fault close to Sparta (Armijo, Lyon-Caen, & Papanastassiou 1991), and Thucydides described how the helots took advantage of this event to mount a revolt (Urbainczyk 2008: 24). The unpredictable and powerful nature of the earthquake may well have exposed a weakness in Spartan society, thus creating the ideal moment for revolt. Governing elites may well attempt prediction and mitigation of environmental problems, and if they should fail in these acts, such failures might reveal or accentuate other weaknesses within a society, such as the Spartan Helot conflicts.

Tectonic Legacies

Despite the questions over the relative impact of seismic and volcanic events on Mediterranean civilisations, at the very least we must accept the importance of tectonic processes in the formation of Mediterranean landscapes – not merely in terms of defining a topographic base layer, but also in terms of Holocene tectonic events affecting sea level, fresh-water supplies, sedimentation processes, and, as a product of these processes, vegetation development. Tectonic landscapes are effectively full of surprises; within short distances, spring-fed basins with relatively lush vegetation abut arid, eroded land surfaces (Fig. 2.7). Active fault zones are characterised by varied topography, intermountain basins with springs, and good quality soils that develop on alluvium (Trifonov & Karakhanian 2004: 293–4). Small patches of wheat will grow adjacent to slopes covered in rubble with a few persistent pines. As Trifonov and Karakhanian (2004: 290) suggest, active faults will also comprise elements and natural radioactivity that can have negative consequences for plants, animals, and people, whilst other faults might even furnish unusual conditions, such as the emission of gasses with 'narcotic' effects; a configuration that might explain the location and evolution of Delphi as an Oracle (De Boer & Hale 2000). Technically, active zones can also render water supplies unreliable, with some evidence suggesting earthquakes have been responsible for changes in groundwater supply, leading to the abandonment of certain major sites on Crete (Gorokhovich 2005).

Whilst the *longue durée* has traditionally been employed in the characterisation of environmental process, we should not forget that all human–environment interactions are also constituted by medium and short-term actions. In any assessment of human response to a given process, the analysis must explicitly consider the spatial and temporal scales in which humanity is studied. The great danger with many historical discourses is that the language employed by researchers renders the scales of analysis opaque, even invisible. Horden and Purcell, amongst other recent writers, produce a textual melange that avoids an explicit declaration regarding their scales of interest. There is nothing inherently wrong in writing a history or archaeology that considers societal processes in the *longue*

(a)

(b)

JURASSIQUE

TRIAS

N-E

S.S-O

2.7. (a) Typical Mediterranean limestone topography with geological folds contributing to the creation of multiple niches (Sainte Victoire, nr. Aix-en-Provence) (photo: author). (b) Watercolour of the geological structure of the Sainte Victoire (permission granted by J.-M. Gassend).

durée, in the same way that we should not see fault in those who attempt to write an *histoire événementielle*. However, authors should outline and provide a rationale for their chosen temporal and spatial scales of analysis. Such a declaration, so many decades after the publication of Braudel's histories, may seem unnecessary. However, the articulation of our scales of analysis is primordial if we are to understand the range of possible responses to all environmental processes.

3

Sea-Level Change and Coastal Settlement – Human Engagements with Littoral Environments

Introduction

It is links across the sea that create the very essence of Mediterraneanism (Bresson, 2005). The study of the dynamism of the Mediterranean Sea, environmentally and culturally, is a prerequisite for any historical and archaeological endeavour in the region. The Mediterranean Sea is in itself as important in the minds of people as the lands that abut it (Guilaine 1994). At one point, classical populations seem to have identified 27 component seas within the Mediterranean (V. Burr cited in Harris 2005a: 15). The permeability of the coastline, that is, the ability to move easily between terra firma and the sea, is influenced by environmental change and a society's ability to manipulate access to and from the sea. 'In the relatively tideless Mediterranean, the shore is narrow – a line, a boundary, a margin, a place where opposites meet' (Buxton 1994: 102).

This chapter starts with an overview of the principal environmental processes that contribute to the development of coastlines, and then assesses the development of human use and modification of these areas.

Characterising the Mediterranean

The virtual absence of tides across most of the Mediterranean results in the absence of the diurnal cycles of coastal life that are prevalent in most other regions around the planet. This day-to-day environmental stability in the Mediterranean has its advantages in that the location of settlements, moorings, ports, and harbours is relatively straightforward. However, medium and long-term processes can render life difficult, or even impossible, especially in areas where the increasing progradation (land advance caused by sediment deposition on river deltas) from about 6,000 years ago resulted in significant coastline changes.

Relative sea-level change, whether caused by eustacy or crustal (tectonic and isostatic) movements, are the key processes, but seasonal storms are another problem, and whilst people on the coasts were safer than those at sea, these events would have coloured everyone's perception of the sea and the littoral band. In some ways, the Greek perception of the sea was similar to that held of the mountains; these were environments where specific types of activity such as fishing, trading, and travelling took place (ibid.: 97). The coastline, however, is the interface between two remarkably different worlds; these are environments on the edge – not marginal per se, but zones where a change in one particular environmental parameter or process can test the resilience of any society's engagement with that landscape.

Maritime Processes

The Mediterranean is a small ocean that has a direct connection with the Atlantic Ocean. The characteristics of the outflow and inflow from the Mediterranean towards the Atlantic have changed throughout the Holocene.

The present outflow layers (referred to as Mediterranean Outflow Water (MOW)) are situated at depths of 800 and 1300 m, and were established between 7,500 and 5,500 years ago (Schonfeld & Zahn 2000). On the north-eastern edge of the Mediterranean lies the Black Sea, which is connected to the Mediterranean via the Sea of Marmara (Fig. 3.1). Prior to the Holocene, the Sea of Marmara was a freshwater lake, but it was inundated by the Mediterranean about 12,000 years ago (Cagatay et al. 2000), and in turn, the Black Sea was flooded by Mediterranean/ Marmaran waters. Some have argued that this took place relatively quickly about 7,000 years ago (Ryan et al. 1997). However, the most recent reassessment of the evidence clearly suggests that there was not a catastrophic event (Aksu et al. 2002). More specifically, the absence of underwater archaeological evidence dated to the Late Pleistocene through to the Early Holocene certainly leads us to examine the argument for such a catastrophe at this time (Yanko-Hombach, Mudie, & Gilbert 2011).

Changes in climate, inflows of freshwater, and sediments – all have an impact on the ecological productivity of the regional seas across the

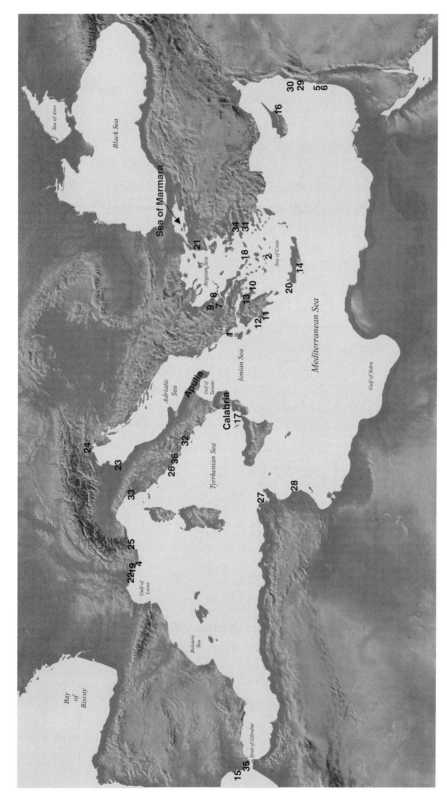

3.1. The Seas of the Mediterranean and map with sites referred to in the chapter. Sea of Marmara, Straits of Gibraltar, Rhodes, Apulia, Calabrian Island arc, Adriatic and Tyrrhenian Sea. 1: Palairos-Pogonia, 2: Santorini, 3: Gouves, 4: Cassis, 5: Atlit-Yam, 6: Tel Nami/Tel Dor/Caesarea, 7: Petromagoula/Pevkakia-Magoula and Lolkos, 8: Dimini bay/Volos, 9: Sesklo, 10: Franchthi Cave, 11: Messenian peninsula, 12: Pylos/Palace of Nestor, 13: Tiryns/Mycenae/Argive plain, 14: Kommos/Matala Bay, 15: Gulf of Cádiz, 16: Kition/Larnaca, 17: Peloro Peninsula/Tindari, 18: Delos, 19: Marseille, 20: Phalasarna, 21: Troy, 22: Fos, 23: Ravenna (North-east Italy), 24: Aquilea, 25: Fréjus, 26: Ostia/Portus, 27: Carthage, 28: Mahdia, 29: Tyre, 30: Beirut, 31: Menderes Delta/Priene/Miletos, 32: Cumae, 33: Pisa, 34: Ephesus, 35: *Baelo Claudia*, 36: Castelporziano, Lazio.

Mediterranean. More specifically, plankton and foraminifera production have always been affected by wider changes in climate (Piva et al. 2008). As with much environmental research, the work carried out on the Mediterranean Sea informs current studies of nutrient problems across the region (e.g. Benoit et al. 2005; Jeftic, Keckes, & Pernetta 1996). The Mediterranean has never been as ecologically productive as other seas and oceans around the world. Very stable strata impede the regeneration of nutrients from lower depths. Consequently, fish catches in the Mediterranean are relatively small compared to the major oceans around the world. For a book that is in part concerned with human impact on the environment, one topic that is missing (due to a dearth of relevant research) is the chronology and nature of human impact on marine ecosystems during the prehistoric and classical periods (Erlandson & Fitzpatrick 2006; Jackson et al. 2001). Changes in sea temperature or even salinity would have affected societies and economies, although specific responses to such processes are difficult to identify.

Within the Mediterranean, the formation of a sapropel (organic-rich dark sediments found across the seabed) took place between 9,000 and 6,000 years ago, this period corresponding with the so-called monsoon maximum. After this, from c. 6500 BC, this deposition was interrupted and resulted in improved deep-water ventilation that coincided with cooling over the Aegean and Adriatic. Another similar cooling event occurred at c. 4000 BC (Rohling et al. 2009: 57). There is some discussion of the precise mechanisms that lead to sapropel formation, with some arguing that climatically controlled stratification of the sea leads to improved preservation of the sapropel organic matter (De Lange et al. 2008). Periods of lower sea level and reduced sediment input seem to correspond to arid periods, which have been identified across the Western Mediterranean from the late fifth millennia BC onwards. There is a two-layered flow of waters in the Strait of Gibraltar: a surface inflow of low-saline water and the deeper outflow of cooler saline (Mediterranean) water (Goy, Zazo, & Dabrio 2003).

Coastal Processes

Many processes and configurations of the different seas are directly affected by tectonic activity (Yaltrak et al. 2000), with geodynamic processes defining many coastlines (see Fig. 2.3) (Stewart & Morhange

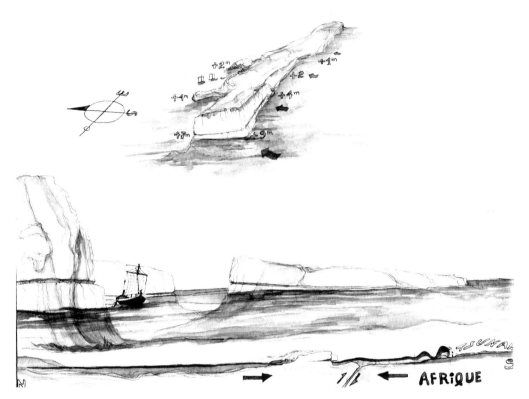

3.2. Watercolour of Crete, illustrating the uplift at the western end of the island (by permission of J.-M. Gassend).

2009). Coastline development is the result of the complex interplay of eustatic, glacio-hydro-isostatic and tectonic processes. This combination results in regionally heterogeneous changes. For example, uplift rates at Taormina and Scilla (the toe of Italy) over the last six millennia were about 100% greater than the long-term average, whilst the last 2,000 years at the Briatico site (on the northern edge of the toe of Italy), eustatic sea level rise has been compensated for by tectonic uplift (Lambeck et al. 2004).

Although the actual coastline is influenced by changes in sea level and sedimentary inputs derived from terrestrial zones, it is of course a complex geological formation, largely dominated by limestone, and highly influenced by crustal processes that structure relative changes in sea level. The most useful general description of Mediterranean coastlines is that they are '…a nested set of marginal-sea coasts – narrow shelves fronting steep hinterlands along the shores of restricted seas enclosed by major land masses and island chains' (Stewart & Morhange 2009: 386).

Whereas eustatic sea-level rise has followed a relatively steady trend, local, relative sea-level changes are specific to each part of the coast. Even across one relatively small island, there will be a variety of sea-level histories.

The input of sediments along river systems is also of profound importance in the development of coastal plains, and even the eruption of volcanoes, such as Vesuvius, can result in shoreline progradation (Pescatore et al. 2001). Whilst eustatic sea-level rise has continued (due to the continued input of glacial and ice-sheet melt waters) throughout the Holocene, tectonic activity can lead to either exaggerated relative sea-level rise, when land moves downwards, or relative sea-level fall, when land moves upwards. In some parts of the Mediterranean, such as across Crete, there is a complex interplay of these processes, with uplift in the west and down-warping in the east occurring across the same island (Fig. 3.2).

Coastlines tend to be characterised by either solid geology or soft geology (clastic coasts where sedimentary processes dominate). These characteristics determine how changes in relative sea level can be studied on a given coastline. However, in both environment types, microscopic and macroscopic floral and faunal species are identified in the assessment of sea-level changes. Soft coasts, with their sedimentary inputs, yield informative environmental records; the sediments themselves, plus the macro- and micro- fossils found therein, along with any chemical signatures, provide a range of useful information regarding natural and cultural processes. However, on coastlines characterised by solid geology, our knowledge of the biological zonation of floral and faunal species across the different littoral zones (from sublittoral to supralittoral) is important (Laborel & Laborel-Deguen 1994). It is necessary to note that the border between midlittoral and sublittoral (or infralittoral) is referred to as the 'biological sea level' (Laborel 1986). The investigation of wave notches is common on rocky coastlines (Fig. 3.3). The measurement of the position/heights of archaeological remains is also noteworthy. For example, some Roman archaeological remains along the coastlines of Croatia and southern Turkey are now about 1.5 m below the present sea level. This demonstrates how regional subsidence has occurred since the Roman period. As we move south to the Ionian Sea, tectonic influences become even more important (Fouache & Dalongeville 2003: 471–6). Subsidence on the north-eastern coast of Crete has been such

3.3. Typical Mediterranean wave notches (characteristic of a tideless sea) on an uplifted coastline (Côte d'Azur, France) that indicate past relative sea-level stands (photo: author).

that wave notches have been erased, and vermitide development has been prevented. It is likely that the overall eustatic rise on the Northern Mediterranean is about 50 cm since the start of the Holocene (Pirazzoli 1976).

Many coastlines have changed their forms as sediments have been transported from inland areas down towards the sea. The processes of aggradation and progradation have been studied across the Mediterranean (Marriner & Morhange 2007). The study of sedimentary facies through boreholes and/or excavated trenches in coastal locales allows us to develop an impression of how land has 'moved' seawards, and relative sea levels have fallen. More specifically, the study of biological sea-level indicators, both macrofauna (marine molluscs) and micro fauna (foraminifera and ostracods) retrieved from sedimentary units permits the analysis of changes in marine environments over time (e.g. from lagoonal, fresh to saline conditions).

Examples of Mediterranean Coastal Change

One common feature of many reports on sea-level change is the use of figures of overall relative sea-level change and, therefore, mean rates of sea-level change. On Gibraltar, one study has demonstrated that tectonic uplift has led to a series of stepped, uplifted marine terraces (Rodriguez-Vidal et al. 2004), and that over the last 200,000 years, the mean uplift rate has been 0.05±0.01 mm. Such statistics are problematic for archaeologists, as these temporal scales have little relevance for understanding human interaction with coastal environments. Mean rates may hide the fact that there have been periods when sea-level change was extremely rapid. Such swift changes are common in the Mediterranean, where tectonic events can have an immediate and dramatic effect on relative sea level. For example, a series of uplifted notches along the north-east east coast of the island of Rhodes were shown to be up to 6,000 years old. A 1-m subsidence occurred as part of an earthquake in 227 BC, which some argue was responsible for the collapse of the giant statue Colossus (Kontogianni, Tsoulos, & Stiros 2002: 301). Slipways in the harbour were also destroyed at this time. Older slipways have been identified which correspond with a sea level between 2.05 and 3.1 m higher than it is today. New slipways were then constructed, possibly built with a view to counteracting seismic land subsidence (Fig. 3.4) (ibid.: 305). This process – and human response to it – clearly differs to that on coastlines where changes are far more gradual. It is, however, important to avoid suggestions that sudden, high-energy events had catastrophic or substantial affects on wider societal and economic processes (Morhange et al. 2013).

As with many environmental processes, the variation in spatial and temporal resolution and the magnitude of the impact of littoral processes vary considerably. Sudden tectonic movements along the coast and concomitant changes in relative sea level would have had an immediate impact on coastal activities, whilst responses to gradual changes in sea level, which lead to the emergence of new coastal topographies, would have been perceived in a different manner. Changes in the coastline thus present archaeologists with an interesting problem in the study of human perception of temporal scales: the *longue durée*, as represented by eustatic sea-level rise, and the short-term (*événementielle*) process constituted by tectonic processes.

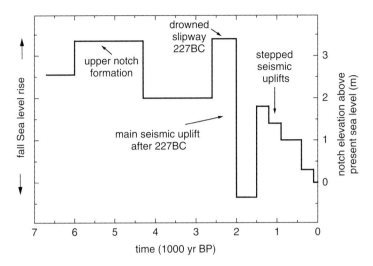

3.4. Conceptual model for the relative sea-level changes responsible for the notch uplift along the north-east Rhodes coast. (By permission of Elsevier BV., Kontogianni, Villy A., Tsoulos, Nikos, Stiros, Stathis C. (2002), Coastal uplift, earthquakes and active faulting of Rhodes Island (Aegean Arc): Modelling based on geodetic inversion, *Marine Geology* 186(3–4), fig. 5, p. 306.)

Higher-Energy Events

One type of high-magnitude event that has taken place across the Mediterranean throughout the Holocene is tsunamis. For example, just within the Sea of Marmara, there is evidence for 30 probable tsunamis having taken place over the last 2,000 years (Yalcner et al. 2002). Tsunamis can be caused by volcanic eruptions as well as submarine slumps (caused by seismic activity). Despite the fact that there is little doubt that tsunamis did take place in the pre- and proto-historic past, the identification of tsunami deposits is notoriously difficult, as they are very similar to sediments deposited by storm-surge flooding (Stewart & Morhange 2009: 400). Accumulations of large boulders can be deposited by high-powered waves, such as those studied on the Apulian coast (Mastronuzzi & Sansò 2000, 2004). Despite the inherent problems in the accurate identification of tsunami deposits, there are places where tsunami sediments have been identified. Several have been identified from sedimentary units in the Huelva Estuary (Gulf of Cadiz, south-western Spain), a zone that is not strictly Mediterranean, as it is situated to the west of the Straits of Gibraltar. The tsunami deposits comprise coarse material (especially marine molluscs) and heavy metals that were clearly derived from outer coastal or continental shelf environments. A mid-to-late fourth century

AD event is the earliest in the sequence of tsunamis identified here (Morales et al. 2008). Not all parts of the Mediterranean are exposed to the same level of tsunami risk. As Soloviev's (2000: 15) analyses of Mediterranean tsunamis demonstrates, recorded tsunamis are more common in the northern half of the region, with a concentration in the Aegean, around the Calabrian Island arc, and other higher-risk areas in the Eastern Mediterranean, the Adriatic, and Tyrrhenian Sea.

Evidence for the Santorini tsunami (a direct consequence of the c. 1620 BC eruption) has been identified on the seabed between Santorini and Crete (McCoy & Heiken 2000a, 2000b). The tsunami may have been some 40 m high (Monaghan, Bicknell, & Humble 1994). One simulation suggests that the impact of the wave would have been restricted to the South Aegean, although a low wave would have arrived in other areas (Pareschi, Favalli, & Boschi 2006). A number of numerical models of the pyroclastic flow from the eruption and ensuing tsunami have been produced (Monaghan et al. 1994). Another simulation, based on the presence of tsunami deposits around the Aegean and Eastern Mediterranean, suggests that Crete and the coast of western Turkey may have experienced tsunami waves with heights of 5 m and above. A layer of sediment was also found at Gouves (30–90 m inland from a Minoan harbour), 15 km to the east of Knossos (Minoura et al. 2000: 60).

Pre- and Proto-Historic Coastal Exploitation

Mediterranean coasts could be considered as *the* most significant environment for the study and understanding of Mediterranean Early Neolithic societies. Some consider that the majority of Neolithic colonisation took place via the sea; the large number of Cardial Neolithic sites along Mediterranean coastlines might support such a hypothesis (Guilaine 2003: 161, 181) (Fig. 3.5), whilst the movement of farming (associated with Impressed Ware) along the eastern Adriatic up to northern Dalmatia is also evident (Forenbaher & Miracle 2005).

Lower sea levels would have reduced the distances between continental landmasses, the archipelagos, and their islands. We should remember that many sites that could represent the movement of people would have been lost or masked by sedimentation. For example, Thrace, which some consider to have been a 'missing link' in the story of the movement of agriculture around the Mediterranean, was subject to a marine

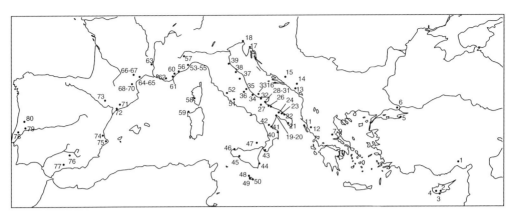

1: Mersin; 2: Parekklisha-*Shillourokambos*; 3: Akrotiri-*Aetokremnos*; 4: Kissonerga-*Mylouthkia*; 5: Ilipinar; 6: Yarimburgaz; 7: Nessonis; 8: Achilleion; 9: Theopetra; 10: Franchthi; 11: Sidari; 12: Konispol Cave; 13: Crvena Stijena; 14: Odmut; 15: Obre; 16: Vela Špila; 17: Pupićina; 18: Edera; 19-20: Neolithic villages at Matera including Trasano; 21: Torre Sabea; 22: Torre Canne; 23: Ostuni; 24: Grotta del Guardiano; 25: Balsignano; 26: Pulo di Molfetta; 27: Rendina; 28: Lagnano da Piede; 29: Masseria La Quercia; 30: Coppa Nevigata; 31: Masseria Candelaro; 32: Guadone; 33: Prato Don Michele; 34: Torre Sinello; 35: Fontanelle; 36: Tricalle; 37: Maddalena di Muccia; 38: Ripabianca di Monterado; 39: Fornace Cappuccini; 40: Capo Alfiere; 41: Favella; 42: Grotta San Michele di Saracena; 43: Umbro; 44: Stentinello; 45: Grotta del Kronio; 46: Grotta dell'Uzzo; 47: Castellaro Vecchio; 48: Ghajn Abdul; 49: Skorba; 50: Ghar Dalam; 51: Le Caprine di Montecelio; 52: La Marmotta; 53: Arma dello Stefanini; 54: Grotta Pollera; 55: Arene Candide; 56: Riparo Mochi; 57: Alba; 58: Basi; 59: Grotta Verde; 60: Pendimoun; 61: Caucade; 62: Chateauneuf; 63: Grotta l'Aigle; 64: Peiro Signado; 65: Pont-de-Roque-Haute; 66: Camprafaud; 67: Grotte Gazel; 68: Jean Cros; 69: Dourgne; 70: Leucate; 71: Les Guixeres de Vilobi; 72: L'Esquerda Roques del Pany; 73: Chaves; 74: Cova de l'Or; 75: Cova de les Cendres; 76: Cariguela; 77: Los Castillejos de Montefrió; 78: Almonda; 79: Calderião; 80: Eira Pedrinha.

3.5. Many of the key Cardial sites from across the Mediterranean. (Figure produced by Cynthianne Spiteri. By permission of Debono Spiteri, C. (2012), *The transition to agriculture in the Western Mediterranean: Evidence from pots*, Unpublished PhD thesis, University of York; p. 28, fig. 2.3.)

transgression about 2,900 years ago, and consequently, any Neolithic sites would have been destroyed (Ammerman et al. 2008).

For coastal communities, the impact of sea-temperature change could have had serious consequences. Although it is difficult to model palaeo-marine resource changes, there is no doubt that temperature changes and concomitant affects on water circulation (in all dimensions) would have led to changes in marine animal presence, abundance, and seasonal movement. Research around the Mediterranean clearly demonstrates that sea-surface temperature changes did take place, one example being the winter cooling in the southern Adriatic at c. 4000 BC (Sangiorgi et al. 2003). Such a change could have been an impetus for increased emphasis on terrestrial resource production.

Whilst the transition to agriculture was taking place across much of the Mediterranean, sea levels had not achieved the point (and *relative* stability) that characterises the modern Mediterranean coastline. Substantial eustatic sea-level rise continued until about 6,000 years ago. During the Early Neolithic, islands continued to be drowned, and coastlines were gradually submerged. At about 6000 BC, the distance between Corsica and Sardinia was only about 6 or 7 km, whereas today it is about 12 km. Settling in an area susceptible to marine inundation is a potential risk if the benefits of locating in such a zone are outweighed by the threats posed by the hazard.

For all periods, the use of archaeological sites as sea-level markers has enormous potential, in that such phenomenon not only serve as an (indirect) record of sea-level change, but they also represent human interaction with littoral environments. However, we should be aware that the chronological resolution offered by such markers is often imprecise (Auriemma & Solinas 2009). One project that has investigated some of the most enigmatic underwater sites is that at Atlit-Yam. The growth of fishing villages was undoubtedly one of the most significant developments along the Neolithic coastline. The Pre-Pottery Neolithic site of Atlit-Yam is now situated about 300–400 m off the Carmel coast under 8–12 m of sea (Galili, Zviely, & Weinstein-Evron 2005; Galili et al. 1993). During the sixth to fifth millennia BC, a particular economic system developed on the coastal plain where hunting, fishing, and gathering were practiced alongside agriculture and grazing (Gopher 1993: 62). A fishing-farming settlement should not necessarily be located adjacent to the sea, as sea spray would reduce the productivity of the land for agriculture. Therefore, in order to maximise the productive capacity of the area around the village, it should be located a few hundred metres inland. However, if fishing is productive, and the village is not reliant on agricultural produce, then a coastal location might make more sense. Another possibility would be a split community. At Atlit-Yam, evidence for fishing comes from artefactual remains (bone points, hooks, and possible net gauges) and some 6,000 fish remains (Galili et al. 2002: 180). Across the Eastern Mediterranean, inland agro-pastoral sites predate the development of the first fishing villages. A few centuries after the development of sites such as Atlit-Yam, similar villages developed on Cyprus and in parts of the Aegean. Galili et al. (2002: 190) believe that the spread of fishing villages (and the combination of agricultural with marine resource gathering) may be a consequence of certain groups exhausting the agricultural capacity of their lands, or '…it may have been the natural outcome of the meeting and merging of agriculture and husbandry with a well-developed local Mesolithic-Early Neolithic maritime subsistence system'.

The earliest known well in the world was found at Atlit-Yam. When established, the sea level adjacent to the village was some 17 m below its present height; within four centuries, it had risen by about 9 m (Nir 1997: 148). The rate of rise then decreased, with stabilisation at its present level

3.6. The now-submerged Neolithic well at Atlit Yam. (By permission of photographer, Mr. Itamar Greenberg; excavator, Ehud Galili. The Institution Israel Antiquities Authority.)

taking place during the latter half of the sixth millennium BC. The rapid sea-level rise that occurred during the early phases of activity at Atlit-Yam must have been apparent within a human generation. As sea levels rose, storms may have deposited sand into the well, with the well then used as a refuse pit, with seeds from spices, pistachio nuts, grape seeds, and also specimens of the granary weevil (*Sitophilus granarius*) found therein (Kislev, Hartmann, & Galili 2004: 1302).

Coastal wells must not be dug too deep in order to avoid the incursion of saline waters. This operation is complex, as at least 30–40 cm of water was required in the well if water was to be drawn using jars. Consequently, it is assumed that the depth of the wells was some 0.3–0.4 m below the water table. Moreover, the base of the well should have been between 0.1 and 0.2 m above the average sea level when the well was in use (Fig. 3.6). The excavation of the well at the Tel Nami site on the Carmel coast (early second millennium BC) demonstrated that the lowest course of this well is at 0.7 m below the present sea level. This well is now some 100 m inland from the present coastline (Sivan et al. 2001: 107–8) (Fig.3.7). Despite these apparently successful attempts to deal

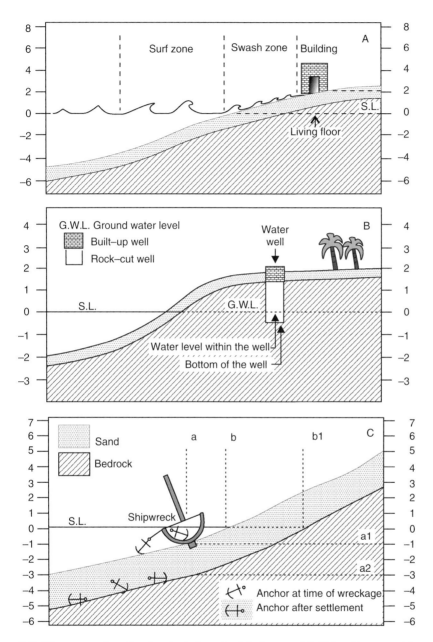

3.7. Three examples of archaeological sea-level indicators. (a) Living floors provide upper bound. In this research, palaeo sea level is assumed to have stood at least 2 m below the floor levels so as to be beyond the swash zone. (b) Ancient wells provide upper and lower bounds at sea level. Coastal wells have to be dug to a minimal depth in order to avoid salinisation, but they still have to be effective at the lowest water levels. The inferred bottom depth of ancient coastal wells along the Israeli coast was 0.3±0.4 m below the water table (in order to draw clear water when using jars). This implies that the base of the well was about 0.1±0.2 m above mean sea level at the usage period. For lower bound, we adopt a level of 1 m below sea level. (c) The dispersion line of shipwrecks and heavy objects from the wreckage approximates the palaeocoastline. Analogous to modern observations, we assume that approximately 1.5±2 m of sand covered the wrecked objects, and their present dispersion at water depths not shallower than 23 m imply that palaeo sea level at the time of the wreckage was close to the present level. (By permission of Elsevier, Sivan, D., Wdowinski, S., Lambeck, K., Galili, E., and Raban A. (2001), Holocene sea-level changes along the Mediterranean coast of Israel, based on archaeological observations and numerical model. *Palaeogeography, Palaeoclimatology, Palaeoecology* 167(1–2), fig. 2, p. 105.)

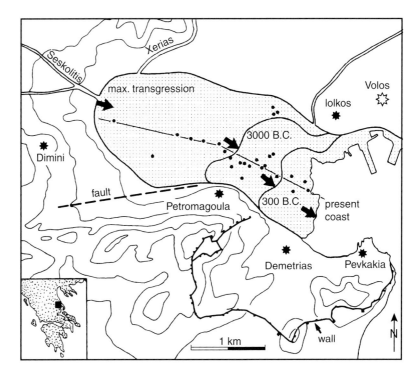

3.8. Coastline advancement at Volos – an area where settlements appear to have 'followed' the advancing coastline (by permission of E. Zangger).

with changing sea levels, these settlements did fall out of use and were even destroyed. The reasons were perhaps political, military, or perhaps the result of technical problems with the wells, such as wall collapse and salinisation (Nir 1997).

At Petromagoula, located on what would have been the coastline between Pefkakia and Dimini (Andreou, Fotiadis, & Kotsakis 1996: 549), activity increased during the Late and Final Neolithic. New activity in the hinterland of Volos Bay may have caused alluviation that had an impact on the Dimini bay (Halstead 1984, cited in Andreou et al. 1996). Later on, sites migrated, following the prograding coastline – thus maintaining direct links with the sea. Zangger considers that this explains the presence of single-phase sites in this zone. For example, the Neolithic site of Sesklo (6000–4400 BC) is now 8 km from the coast. During the Early Bronze Age (3000 BC), the shoreline had advanced by almost 2 km, and the site of Petromagoula would have been on the coast at that time (Zangger 1991: 3) (Fig. 3.8). The sites at Pevkakia-Magoula and Lolkos were located on higher ground, either side of the embayment, and their relationship with the coast has not changed over the last three-and-half millennia. Consequently, there was variation in the choice of settlement locations in this coastal area; the combination of fixed settlements, such as those at Pevkakia-Magoula and Lolkos, compared to the single-phase settlements that followed the prograding shoreline. Here, we see how people responded to gradual coastal change, a process that may have had a generational or multigenerational resolution (ibid.).

Perhaps the most famous prehistoric coastal site in the Mediterranean is Franchthi Cave. This area has largely been influenced by eustatic rather than crustal processes, any possible effects of tectonic activity are either minor or not apparent given the time range and time scale of the Franchthi sequence and local topography. From about 13,000 BP, the rate of sea-level rise was as high as 5 cm/year. Therefore, during a lifetime of 40 years, the sea level would have risen by about 2 m – a significant change in the coastal landscape. This rate of sea-level rise slowed during the Early Holocene, although 20 m of eustatic rise has occurred during the last seven millennia (van Andel 1987: 33). However, these estimations are based on regional or global models; there is no complete local curve for the southern Argolid.

The sea around Franchthi was probably more productive between 9,000 and 7,000 years ago, when marine resources were heavily exploited. Sapropel deposition at this time supports such a conclusion (ibid.: 53) in that sapropels possess higher concentrations of organic carbon and appear to enhance productivity due to nitrogen fixation (Katsouras et al. 2010).

The beach, or 'Paralia' site, at Franchthi was first occupied during the Early Neolithic. Between 6500 and 5000 BC, sea levels in front of Franchthi Cave were 11 m lower than they are today (van Andel 1987: 34). Therefore, a more extensive beach was exposed during the Early Neolithic, with the sea between 1 and 2 km further out, thus increasing the possibility of aeolian deposition across the site (Wilkinson & Duhon 1990: 77). Most of the beach site appears to have been abandoned by the end of the Middle Neolithic, although occupation at the cave site continued into the Late Neolithic.

The changes in sea level at Franchthi and other Neolithic sites were varied in their rate and nature. However, eustatic sea-level rise was a feature of Neolithic coastal life, and would have affected settlement infrastructures, as well as the range of resources available to early farmers – farmers who undoubtedly continued to exploit marine resources. We know that shellfish use at Franchthi continued up until the end of the Neolithic at c. 3000 BC (Shackleton & van Andel 1986: 130). Here and elsewhere, these changes in sea level may well have helped push Neolithic farmers towards a greater reliance on terrestrial foods. However, there is little doubt that Neolithic exploitation of coastlines did encompass the continuation of earlier food gathering strategies, including the intensification of fishing. The concomitant development of coastal villages, with specific forms of environmental knowledge, such as well digging, might have been threatened by the continuing eustatic sea-level rise (which was still relatively rapid for the earlier Neolithic) as well as variations in marine productivity.

Coastal Exploitation: The Development of Ports and Harbours (Bronze Age Onwards)

Whilst there is plenty of evidence for mixed coastal economies, evidence for early boat mooring or beaching is negligible. Although movement of people and materials undoubtedly took place via the sea during the Neolithic, the assessment of the harbouring or beaching of boats is inferred rather than demonstrated. As we move into the Bronze Age, the first conclusive evidence for technological intervention along coastlines appears.

The late third and second millennia witnessed a fundamental change in some societies' relationships with the coast. The emergence of deep-hulled sailing ships during the late third millennium BC would have changed the way in which the sea was perceived (Broodbank 2000: 341). The development of complex trading networks and the need for permanent ports and harbours led to an intensification of the management of coastal environmental processes.

The coastal geomorphology of many parts of the Northern Mediterranean provides a number of natural harbours (protected inlets, estuaries, and lagoons). On the other hand, the Southern Mediterranean has far fewer natural ports and harbours, and therefore these facilities tend to be constructed. Fortunately, such construction is relatively straightforward compared to Atlantic coasts due to the absence of tides. Moreover, in many places (including Tunisia and Libya), relative sea levels were quite stable during the later Holocene (Anzidei et al. 2011).

However, one fundamental problem was sedimentation and the infilling of harbours. If a port or harbour was built near a river delta, it was often located to the west of the delta, as long-shore action in the Mediterranean often moves in a broadly west–east (counterclockwise) direction.

There were obviously certain types of coast that were deemed unsuitable for ports and harbours. For example, the Messenian peninsula (south-west Peloponnese), comprises for the most part a rugged and treacherous coastline, and this probably explains the relative lack of Mycenaean sites here (Higgins 1966: 23). However, the easily erodible coastline in this area may have been lost as sea levels rose, thus destroying any harbours (Higgins 1966). One notable harbour that does exist in this area is Pylos (Messenia, Peloponnese) (Davis 2007). Located 5 km to the south-west of the Palace of Nestor, the harbour was situated 500 m inland and comprised a rectangular basin, along with a reservoir that was created through the damming of a river. Clean water from this reservoir passed through an artificial channel, and this helped prevent the reservoir from silting up (Zangger 2001; Zangger et al. 1997) (Fig. 3.9). Tiryns, a Late Bronze Age citadel on the Argive plain in the Peloponnese, possesses extant foundations that date to c. 1250 BC (LH IIIB) (Zangger 1994). As with many low-lying plains, the Argive Plain has undergone dramatic changes during the Holocene. At about 2500 BC, the sea-level transgression achieved its maximum, and the coast was some 1.5 km further inland than it is today, only 300 m from the early site at Tiryns. Large quantities of alluvial material just to the south of Tiryns led to coastal progradation, and by the Late Bronze Age, 1 km separated the palace from the coast (Fig. 3.9). During the Early Bronze Age, a lower town at the south-western foot of the palace knoll was traversed by a stream. An artificial levee was built to protect part of the town from flooding. Eventually, this area was abandoned and covered by thick alluvial deposits (ibid.: 196–8). During the Late Holocene (IIIB2–IIIC periods), there were significant changes in the alluvial system that affected the lower town on the plain below the palace at Tiryns. A stream that once flowed to the south moved to the north of the palace knoll, and about 4 m of sediment was deposited to the north and east of the citadel. Houses were then built in the ancient stream bed, and a dam was built, possibly in response to these dramatic flooding and erosional events. The dam and a canal served to divert the stream to the south, away from Tiryns (ibid.). At Tiryns, this early example of environmental

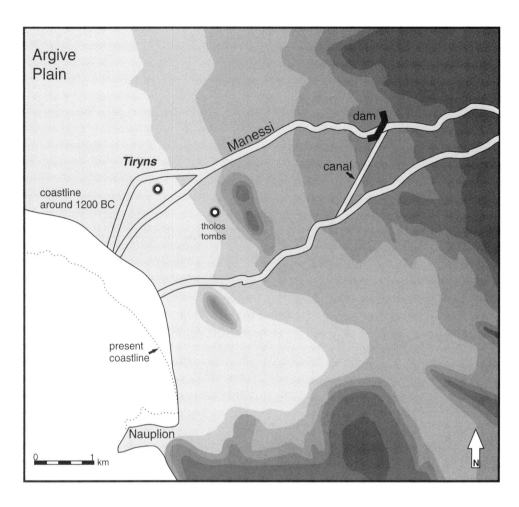

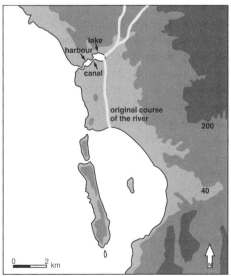
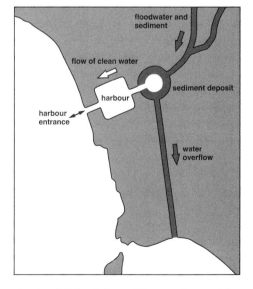

3.9. Bronze Age coastal management systems at Tiryns (top) and Pylos (Palace of Nestor) (bottom) (by permission of E. Zangger).

management, which endeavoured to reduce the ever-present problem of sedimentation and coastal alluvial processes, is in some ways a precursor to the complex marine engineering that developed during the classical and Roman periods.

Early Ports and Harbours

The development of ports on Mediterranean islands during the Bronze Age was essential for integration into wider Mediterranean networks, and in some cases, this led to islands such as Crete establishing themselves as regional economic powers (Gkiasta 2010). Crete comprises a wide range of coastal environment types and related environmental processes, from progradation to tectonic uplift and downwarping. These environmental complexities lead to the development of diverse responses. One coastal process which is relatively rare across the Mediterranean is sand-dune development. At the Minoan harbour town of Kommos (southern Crete), sand dunes developed during the second and first millennium BC. Eventually, the Greek sanctuary here was covered with sand after it went out of use at c. AD 150 (Gifford 1995: 49). Sand-dune development is initiated by the exposure of a large expanse of sand to wind. In this instance, tectonic activity was the key to a change in environmental processes. A rapid tectonic uplift event may well have exposed sand to aeolian action across a previously submerged beach.

Others suggest that this part of Crete has experienced an uninterrupted sea-level rise. The presence of now submerged Roman fish tanks and tombs implies that the sea level was 1.2 m lower 2,000 years ago than it is today, and that between the fifth and the end of the first millennia BC, relative sea levels changed on two occasions, moving from 3.8 m to 2.5 m below the present sea level (Watrous et al. 1993: 204–5). At its greatest extent, the shoreline would have been a further 90 m out to the west. The fact that these measurements come from Matala Bay, a rocky embayment just to the south of the Masara Plain, suggests that quite distinct processes were taking place. Kommos was potentially subject to a variety of different destructive processes. A large portion of one of the major buildings at Kommos (building-T) seems to have been destroyed by the sea. However, it is possible that a more immediate threat (during LM I) was an earthquake, which may have damaged much of this impressive building (J. W. Shaw 2006: 33–5). Moreover, sea levels could have risen significantly during the occupation of Kommos. Floor levels in building-T (J. W. Shaw & Shaw 1993) were raised by more than 1 m, most likely a response to the rising sea level, or rather the highest reach of the waves (J. W. Shaw 2006: 56). Much of the cultural interest associated with the assessment of these natural processes relies on a tight chronology, that is, proof that these environmental events were actually witnessed and responded to by the people living on the site. The research at Kommos and its environs, perhaps more than most other sites, allows us to assess the intersection of cultural and environmental processes. Whilst the environmental processes demanded technological and cultural responses, the environment did not seem to have an adverse impact on the settlement and its people. A series of actions mitigated changes in sea level and the movement of sand, in particular, the architectural modifications mentioned above.

Unsurprisingly, where possible, ports and harbours exploited natural littoral topography. A major harbour on the south-eastern coast of Cyprus – Kition – lay within a large protected bay. Established by the Late Bronze Age, activity continued up until the end of the Phoenician period. There are at least two harbours in this area; the first, in the northern part of this area, is associated with the Late Bronze Age town, whilst the second, to the east, is associated with the classical town. The choice of location is explained by the fact that this area is protected from strong winds, and is the closest point to Egypt and the Levantine coast (Collombier 1988: 35–7). From 4000 to 2100 BC, the deposition of fine sediments ultimately led to the development of a coastal spit that seems to have been in place at about 600 BC. The main archaeological site is now some 500–600 m from the shore, and an earthquake towards the end of the eleventh century BC seems to have been responsible for the temporary demise of the Late Bronze Age town. The town then developed again by the ninth century BC, expanding across a much wider area (ibid.: 40–1). Adjacent to Larnaca on Cyprus, the inner harbour of Bamboula (now 400 m inland) was connected to Lichines (an ancient marine embayment) during the Phoenician period (eighth to fourth centuries BC). The lagoon area was gradually isolated from the sea, although the bay at Larnaca was still connected. Ultimately, the lagoon was isolated from the sea, and uplift in this area prevented access to the harbour (Morhange et al. 2000: 223).

The uplifted Peloro Peninsula on the north-east coast of Sicily is another area that has witnessed significant changes during the Holocene.

Today, there is no natural harbour, although in the past, and in particular during the fifth century BC, the Pantano Piccolo was connected to the Tyrrhenian Sea via a 120-m wide, 1-m deep channel. This harbour was probably adequate for 320 ships (Bottari & Carveni 2009). A similar situation was also observed to the east at Tindari, where palaeotopographic reconstruction has identified the probable location of a sheltered inlet that would have been used during the fourth century BC (Bottari et al. 2009).

One example of a response to sea-level rise which is verifiable archaeologically comes from the Tel Dor site (Israel), dated to c. late thirteenth century BC. This site included slipways and flushing channels that fed seawater into an industrial area. Solution notches on these features were used to infer past sea levels. Three phases of construction might indicate how people responded to the rising sea level through the construction of higher courses of stonework at +1.04, +1.57, and +2.53 m (Sivan et al. 2001: 108). Here, we see how cultural and environmental temporalities did intersect, with a society responding to a specific change in their landscape. As stated earlier, it does seem that, in some cases, we can identify landscapes or sites where societies were not only aware of a risk, but were willing and able to negotiate the risk, as the benefits of remaining on a site, or indeed cultural attachment to a site, led them to manage the environmental hazard. These Bronze Age examples represent a range of opportunistic exploitations of naturally occurring harbour locations, as well as the early development of technological interventions in the coastal landscape – engineering works that became all important during the classical and Roman periods.

Classical Coasts and Harbours

The creation of artificial ports and harbours developed apace during the classical periods, these installations forming the nodes in the quintessential 'connected' Mediterranean (Horden & Purcell 2000: 391–5); a space where everything Mediterranean (economy, culture, myths, flora, and fauna) transited via ports and harbours. Whilst many Bronze Age ports and harbours merely modified existing natural emplacements, the classical and Roman periods saw the emergence of complex engineering and management of harbour facilities. As with all periods, Mediterranean sites were subject to a variety of environmental processes, and one

3.10. Relative sea-level rise at the harbour at Kenchreai (Peloponnese, Greece) (photo: author).

notable characteristic that we should not forget is that sea level at a number of Graeco-Roman sites was lower than it is today (Fig. 3.10); for example, the sea was some 2 m lower when Delos was active (Duchêne, Dalongeville, & Bernier 2001: 174). However, despite this rise, relative sea levels in a number of regions, including Sardinia and parts of the Adriatic coast (Florido et al. 2011) would have been comparatively stable. In some areas, the last 2,000 years has seen subsidence ranging from about 1.5 m to between 0.63 and 0.89 mm per year (Antonioli et al. 2007). As stated earlier, this rate of subsidence might not have been stable and linear. Moreover, subsidence may have been less than this, with some suggesting a figure for the Roman sea level of about –50 cm (Evelpidou et al. 2012).

We can categorise a range of environment types within which different ports and harbours were situated in the past (Fig. 3.11). The first category comprises protected estuarine inlets that are usually at the mouth of drainage basins (e.g. Marseille and Phalasarna), or more open bays such

Unstable coasts		Stable coasts				
Submerged harbours	Uplifted harbours	Buried urban harbours	Buried landlocked harbours	Buried fluvial harbours	Buried lagoonal harbours	Eroded harbours
-Alexandria - Baia - Eastern Canopus - Egnazia - Helike - Herakleion - Kenchreai - Megisti - Miseno - Pozzuoli	-Aigeira - Lechaion - Phalasarna - Seleucia Pierea	- Acre - Beirut - Byzantium/Istanbul - Cartagena - Kition Bamboula - Marseilles - Naples - Olbia - Piraeus - Sidon -Toulon -Tyre	- Enkomi - Ephesus - Kalopsidha - Leptis Magna - Miletos - Malta - Priene -Troy - Salamina	- Antioch - Aquileia - Gaza - Minturnae - Narbonne - Naucratis - Ostia (Sardinia) - Pelusium - Rome - Sevilla - Schedia - Thebes - Valencia - Zaragoza	- Coppa Nevigata - Cuma - Frejus - Lattara	- Ampurias - Caesarea (outer harbour)

3.11. Non-exhaustive list of harbours classed into seven groups. Categories of coastline types vis-à-vis important Mediterranean harbours. (By permission of Elsevier. Marriner, N., and Morhange, C. (2007), Geoscience of ancient Mediterranean harbours. *Earth-Science Reviews* 80(3–4), fig. 8.)

as at Troy. Some harbours or ports are built on the edges of deltas, such as Fos (south of France), Ravenna (north-east Italy), and Aquileia; others at the mouths of rivers and wetlands, with Fréjus (south of France), Ostia (close to Rome), and Carthage (Tunisia) falling into this category. These different environments have a direct effect on the preservation potential of environmental and archaeological materials (Marriner & Morhange 2007) (Fig. 3.12). Those harbours built on rocky coasts often have Greek or Phoenician origins. From the fourth century BC onwards, the Greeks and Romans used less favourable environments for their harbours as the technology for managing these environments developed (ibid.). This technology included dredging, empoldering, and actually moving docks (Morhange et al. 1999: 147–8). For example, at Phalasarna, on the western part of Crete, where fortifications were built during the second half of the fourth century BC, the harbour started to silt up at c. 67 BC, thus resulting in the possible blocking of the harbour entrance. However, this low-magnitude process could have been managed; it was the uplift event attributed to AD 365 that ensured the demise of this harbour (Pirazzoli et al. 1992). The presence of solution notches on this part of the coast does suggest that the sea level was stable for relatively long periods. The uplift event probably occurred over an extremely short period (either minutes or days) (Hadjidaki 1988: 466). Two canals that once connected the harbour to the sea are now on dry land. On the side of one of the channels, solution notches indicate that the sea level was

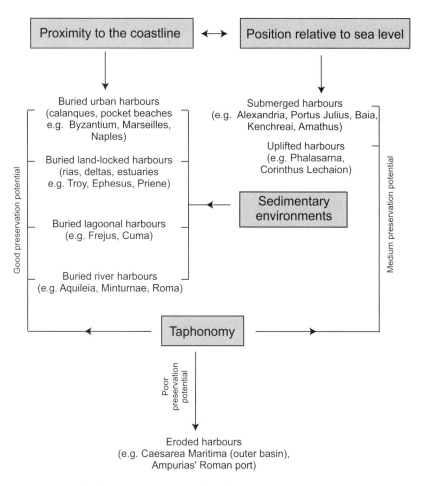

3.12. Ancient harbour classification based on four variables: (1) proximity to the coast-
line, (2) position relative to sea level, (3) sedimentary environments, and (4) taphonomy.
(By permission of Elsevier. Marriner, N., and Morhange, C. (2007), Geoscience of ancient
Mediterranean harbours. *Earth-Science Reviews* 80(3–4), fig. 7.)

6.6 m higher when the channel was in use. It is possible that the Romans
deliberately blocked the channel in 67 BC, as some consider Phalasarna
to have been a port used by pirates (Hadjidaki 1988: 476). Some interpret the Hellenistic port here as a 'cothon', dug in zones where natural,
sheltered harbours did not exist (Blackman 1982a, 1982b; Frost 1995).
These were often dug behind the coast in soft sedimentary environments,
such as lagoons, as was the case at Carthage. A channel would then be
excavated linking the cothon to the open sea. It is likely that the primary
aim was to create a port that was located within a town's protective walls
(Carayon 2005: 11). Perhaps it is more reasonable to suggest that such

towns would have developed on or adjacent to natural sheltered ports if such places had existed. As noted earlier, there are more natural harbours in the Northern Mediterranean, whilst the southern coastlines (where many of the cothon lie) tend not to provide such favourable environments (ibid.).

The term 'cothon' is particularly associated with Carthage, where a channel linked a rectangular basin with the open sea. The area around Carthage was initially covered with a dune blanket at the start of the Holocene, from the Middle to the Late Holocene eustatic sea-level rise eroded the headland. This was followed by the reworking of these sediments and the development of a spit, and the emergence of a lagoon which was to become the setting for the Late Punic circular harbour (Gifford, Rapp, & Vitali 1992: 585). Carthage also comprises a circular basin. A similar configuration existed at the port of Mahdia to the south of Carthage. The analysis of sedimentological (abiotic and biotic) data demonstrated that the sediments beneath the Late Punic cothon were from a lagoonal environment that could have provided a useable natural site for a harbour, thus demonstrating the probability that the Cothon was not the first harbour on this site (Vitali et al. 1992).

One of the tasks of modern coastal geoarchaeology in the Mediterranean is to verify or question ancient descriptions of specific ports, harbours, and their settings. For example, much work has been done on the harbour of the Phoenician city of Tyre. Tyre, which was once an island, is connected to the mainland by a tombolo (a sand isthmus), which was certainly formed by the nineth century BC, attested to by the presence of the Phoenician necropolis of Al Bass (Carmona & Ruiz 2008). However, Marriner, Goiran, and Morhange (2008) suggest a later date of 332 BC, although the conditions for tombolo development existed before this date. Ancient texts implied the existence of four harbours at Tyre (Marriner, Morhange, & Carayon 2008). The central area of Tyre's seaport is now buried beneath the modern and medieval city centres (ibid.: 1282). The northern harbour had Bronze Age origins, and was protected by an aeolianite ridge system. The harbour continued to develop during the Iron Age, and then the Hellenistic and Roman artificially closed harbours were developed, as suggested by the fine texture of sedimentary units dated to this period (ibid.: 1292). As we have already seen, the silting up of harbours is one of the most serious environmental problems across the Mediterranean, and extensive dredging of the harbour at Tyre took place during the Greco-Roman periods (Marriner & Morhange 2006). Sedimentary evidence from Beirut also demonstrates the development of a managed Roman harbour (Marriner Morhange, & Saghieh-Beydoun 2008: 2510). Using controlled currents was one method employed for de-silting. Such a system existed for the inner south harbour at Tyre (Blackman 1982b: 199). In fact, harbours are themselves sedimentary traps to the extent that accumulation rates within harbours can be as much as 10 to 20 times higher than on naturally prograding coasts (Marriner & Morhange 2007: 175).

On a regional scale, similar processes were also seen on the Menderes Delta in western Turkey (Aegean coast) where the ancient ports of Priene and Miletos suffered from silting. Whilst Priene's harbour was moved, Miletos appears to have lost its importance (Brückner 2001: 124). Geophysical work has shown how the harbour possessed a shallow mouth with a deeper inner area.

In some areas, which may have been perceived as potentially dangerous for navigation, harbours were not necessarily built, and we should not forget the importance of small 'sheltering' islands that could be used as a refuge by sailors during storms (Greaves 2000). The exploitation and manipulation of littoral zones that possess natural characteristics ideal for the development of ports and harbours is quite understandable. However, it is essential that geoarchaeologists verify the development of such installations, and the nature of any interaction between people and the littoral environment. For example, it was once argued that a Roman harbour at Cumae lay within a lagoon (Paget 1968). However, recent geoarchaeological research demonstrates that during the Roman period, this part of the coast would have been far from ideal for the installation of a harbour. From the second century BC through to the second century AD, sandbars would have rendered navigation along this part of the coast quite dangerous. Therefore, this area was characterised by a large and potentially useful beach, but with difficult access. The substantial quantities of pottery and structural remains indicate that the area was exploited, but probably not as a port (Stefaniuk et al. 2005: 58).

The development of complex forms of environmental knowledge is nowhere more evident than in the field of harbour and port construction and maintenance. Possibly the most significant development in ancient harbour construction was the Roman invention of hydraulic cement (pozzolana). This could set under water, thus facilitating the construction of harbours in areas where people had been unable to build before (Blackman 1982b: 185). Unsurprisingly, ancient engineers had a clear grasp of the processes that could undermine port and harbour structures. The use of rubble cushions to protect sea walls that were built on sand from under trenching caused by wave currents is known at Caesarea (Raban 1988: 187). Moreover, Roman engineers used poz-zolana concrete to build moles in order to create an offshore harbour (Oleson et al. 2004; Raban 1992).

We have to ask if the palaeoenvironmental record always implies 'improvement' or rather 'maintenance' in the face of hostile environ-mental processes. The rate of silting in ports at the mouths of rivers or in sheltered natural coves (such as Marseille) obviously varies. As colonies developed during the proto-historic periods, centres such as Marseille became home to a wide variety of peoples – some, permanent residents, others, itinerant traders. These different groups would have possessed different attitudes to and understandings of the natural environment, but would have had an expectation that major ports and harbours would be accessible and operational. The management and maintenance of a port environment in some ways represents a step towards the professionalisa-tion of environmental management and the direct engagement with the natural processes that contribute to riskiness in such a milieu. However, there are certain processes affecting ports and coastal settlement, such as tectonic movement and extreme sedimentation, that no society can manage, and the only form of possible 'improvement' is mobility and rebuilding.

The courses and sedimentary regimes of the rivers Arno and Auser around Pisa changed a great deal during the later Holocene (Bruni & Cosci 2003). Catastrophic floods on the Pisan coast seem to have resulted in the movement of harbour activity to the north during the Roman period (Lippi et al. 2007). During the second and first centuries BC, the coastline was 7 km landward of its current position; prograda-tion is thought to have started towards the end of the first century BC (Pasquinucci & Rossetti 1988: 137). During the late Republican and Early Imperial periods, it is likely that Pisa's port was attached to the city itself, and landing areas for boats have been hypothesised in the city and along the River Arno at San Piero a Grado. As ships increased in size, and the Arno and its delta prograded, the relocation of the port just to the north of Livorno took place (ibid.: 139). A similar difficulty

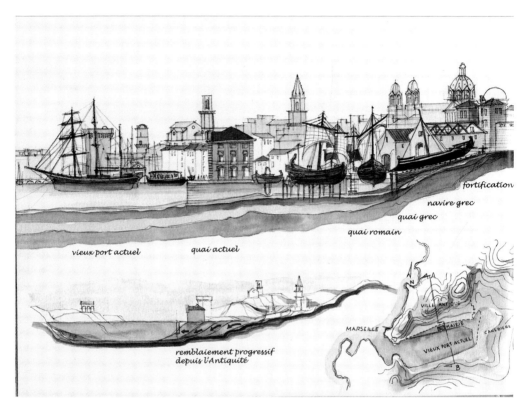

vieux port actuel

quai actuel

quai romain

quai grec

navire grec

fortification

remblaiement progressif depuis l'Antiquité

MARSEILLE

VILLE ANTIQUE

MAIRIE

VIEUX PORT ACTUEL

CANEBIERE

3.13. Watercolour reconstruction of the development of the port at Marseille. Note how the ancient Greek and Roman port is now inland, with the silting up of the port area having caused coastal advance, thus forcing the development of the modern port out towards the south (by permission of J.-M. Gassend).

was experienced at the harbours of Ephesus and Smyrna, which were also built near river mouths, where the silting up of the harbours forced the seaward migration of these cities (Brückner 1997). Ephesus actually went out of use during the Late Roman period (Blackman 1982b: 186). Other sites suffered similar problems, including Aquileia, which may have been replaced by Grado, situated on a coastal bar at the mouth of a lagoon; Ravenna and Narbo were also subject to such processes. Silting also affected Ostia, with a new port built about 3 km to the north of the Tiber's mouth. However, southerly winds and currents moved sediments towards the harbour, and resulted in its eventual closure, despite the construction of a mole designed to protect the area (ibid.: 187).

One of the most studied harbours in the Mediterranean is that at Marseille. Founded by the Phoceans during the seventh century BC, it is still in use today (albeit in a different form and environment) (Fig. 3.13), whilst the harbour at Fos, to the west, was established some five centuries later, and went out of use during the Middle Ages (Morhange et al. 2003; Morhange et al. 1999: 145).

The ancient harbour at Marseille is now on dry land. Silting up of the area has 'forced' the modern harbour to move seaward, whilst the harbour at Fos is now under water. In order to understand these early urban ports, we need to consider the impact that people had on the landscape around the port. One of the most critical processes is erosion, which leads to the silting of harbours. The earliest evidence in the port area at Marseille includes Late Neolithic shell middens, but there is little evidence for Neolithic erosion into what became the harbour zone. The first 'environmental event' took place during Early to Mid-Bronze Age (2020–1681 BC) when there appears to have been some silting up of the area. Also, at about 1390–1043 BC, a shell midden was created. The next major process took place from 600 BC onwards, when erosion from the surrounding slopes seems to have become a problem. These sediments included 'urban refuse', and are clearly indicative of an anthropogenically induced process, with pollution tolerant species of marine mollusc appearing in these units. During the Roman period, soil erosion into the harbour area continued. It seems that the Greek (Phocean) sediments were derived from unpaved urban surfaces, whilst the Roman units were the result of run-off across paved or cemented areas in the city. Although there was some reduction in sedimentation at about AD 50, the Romans were forced to dredge the harbour, cutting into the existing Greek sedimentary units (Morhange et al. 1999: 151). This environmental history of a specific port presents a series of environmental processes, or even problems, that ancient peoples had to manage. Whilst these processes were extremely difficult to control, they were probably just accepted as a 'natural' consequence of activity in this type of environment, and environmental managers were resigned to the need for mitigation.

A markedly different situation existed just to the west of Marseille at Fos-sur-Mer. Underwater archaeological research has revealed a complex series of remains comprising a necropolis with stele and objects dated to the end of the second or the beginning of the third century AD. These sites were situated on two different sandbars that ran parallel to the coast with a lagoon between the sandbars; both bars are now submerged. The closest bar to the coast supported the boat construction yard, whilst a necropolis was situated in a literally liminal position on the second sandbar. Cores from this area demonstrate that the ancient sea level (represented by a layer of pebbles dated to between 410 BC and 180 AD) was about 2 m lower than it is today (Gassends & Maillet 2004).

On the Spanish littoral, relatively few Roman port constructions have been found on the coast of Roman Baetica (Andalucia, Spain). Either remains have disappeared because of coastal change, or alternative methods and locations for loading and unloading ships were employed. For example, geoarchaeological investigations at the possible harbour bay associated with the Phoenician site of Toscanos demonstrated that, during the eighth century BC, the bay was partially filled, and the centre of the bay was about 6–7 m deep. At c. 400 AD, a sand barrier existed on the shore of the bay, with the coastal delta prograding since the Roman period (Hoffman & Schulz 1988: 60–2). It is possible that the Romans did not choose to employ their harbour-building technology in this area, as sand beaches and navigable rivers may well have provided the simplest solution. In certain situations where ships could not be beached, slaves may well have waded and brought goods ashore, as is suggested for the beach at Belo (Hohlfelder 1976: 467–8). Harbour installations were only built where they were needed for economic or environmental reasons. Manageable, natural landing places would probably have been quite common, but they are perhaps not always easy to identify. We should not assume that Rome imposed technology for technology's sake; technological solutions were only employed in locations where the environment did not proffer a natural solution within given economically instrumental parameters.

Whilst Rome's original port was at Ostia, a new port to the north was inaugurated a little before AD 64. Named Portus, it would serve as the port of Imperial Rome, and would remain in use well into the Late Antique period. From a geoarchaeological perspective, perhaps the most intriguing characteristic of the sediments on the delta is the fact that Roman structures are often covered with a clayey unit which implies that sediments accumulated at quite a slow rate (Keay et al. 2006: 18). Moreover, some geomorphological evidence points to the establishment of the Republican settlement on a stable shoreline. Nevertheless, any activity in this area had to negotiate incredibly complex and persistent alluvial sedimentation (Bellotti et al. 1994; Mikhailova et al. 1998). Coastal advance did not begin until the Imperial period (Keay et al. 2006: 26–9). This sequence demonstrates that the potential hazard for

Roman sites was not necessarily extreme, and this would have influenced the manner in which Roman engineers responded to this landscape. In fact, the engineering works themselves might have exacerbated any environmental risk; once the harbour was established, its moles would have had a dramatic effect on the deposition of sand from long-shore drift. In fact, it is possible that the difference in coastal advance (400 m to the north, 1400 m to the south) was a result of the moles disrupting this process (ibid.: 30).

The northern quay of the Claudian harbour was situated in a landscape comprised of sand dunes, with salt and freshwater lagoons between these dunes. Artificial wells were dug along the first line of dunes and lagoons, and this evidence is taken to indicate activity in this zone from the second century BC onwards.

There clearly comes a point in time when people, and engineers in particular, are aware of the potential environmental problems, such as sedimentation within a harbour (Figs. 3.14 & 3.15) (Morelli, Paroli, & Verduchi 2006: 247). Either it was accepted that this would happen, or the intensity and even the nature of the process was not understood. Trajan modified the harbour during the second century AD, and it is clear from the sedimentary evidence that this harbour was immediately vulnerable to silting (Giraudi, Tata, & Paroli 2009), with the connection between the sea and port basins only remaining open until AD 230–450 (Goiran et al. 2009).

The Roman investment in harbours was entirely logical, and we should not forget that the imperative for the management of the interface between land and sea resulted in the most impressive engineering works in the ancient Mediterranean. It was not just the scale of the sites, but innovations such as hydraulic concrete seen on a number of sites, including Baiae and Portus Iulius in Italy (C. J. Brandon, Robert, & John 2008).

Up until this point, emphasis has been placed on the study of harbour/port installations, with no consideration of other uses of the coast. Specific niche resources, such as saltings, were present across much of the Mediterranean, and variations in sea level would have affected the ability to control the drying process. Salt production would have been important from quite early on. The ancient Greek word for salt was the same as for sea (Powell 1996: 12). In addition, people in coastal towns (or vicus) would have embraced a variety of coastal economic activities.

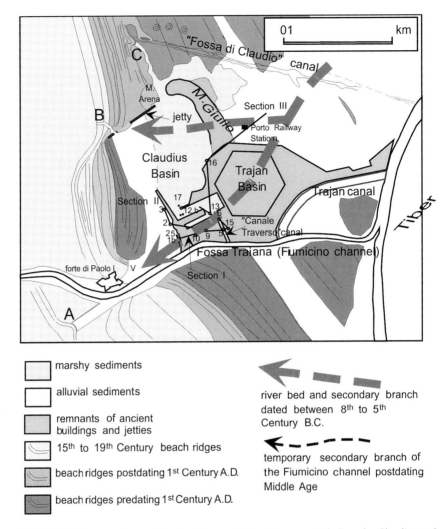

marshy sediments

alluvial sediments

remnants of ancient
buildings and jetties

15th to 19th Century beach ridges

beach ridges postdating 1st Century A.D.

beach ridges predating 1st Century A.D.

river bed and secondary branch
dated between 8th to 5th
Century B.C.

temporary secondary branch of
the Fiumicino channel postdating
Middle Age

3.14. The harbour at Portus. Geological map of the study area, including the Claudius and Trajan harbour. (A) Fiumicino branch dammed by beach ridges; (B) mouth of the secondary branch of the Fiumicino; (C) northern entrance of the Claudius harbour dammed by beach ridges. (By permission of John Wiley and Sons, Giraudi, C. et al. (2009), Late Holocene evolution of Tiber river delta and geoarchaeology of Claudius and Trajan harbour, Rome, *Geoarchaeology* 24(3), fig. 2.

At Castelporziano, Lazio, Italy, an important vicus site has revealed a series of substantial buildings, including a fish farm (Claridge 2007). The coast as an attractive leisure or residential area was not a recent innovation. The Laurentine Shore was Rome's coastal zone, and comprised luxurious villas and the vicus mentioned above. This area was situated in front of an existing dune ridge. Coastal progradation took place during the Roman occupation phase on the Laurentine Shore, and

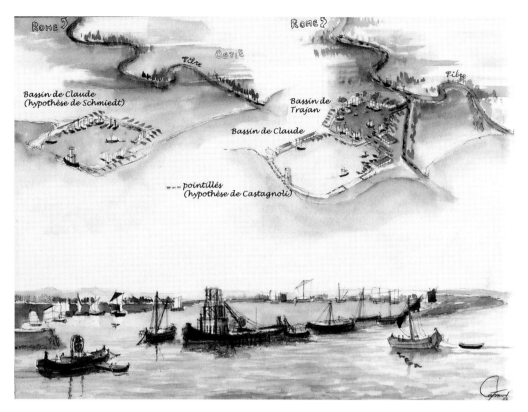

3.15. Watercolour reconstruction of the Claudian and Trajan ports. Note the different hypothesised reconstructions from Schmiedt and Castagnoli (by permission of J.-M. Gassend).

subsequent settlements were established on this new land. However, it seems unlikely that the dunes were reactivated before the end of the Roman Period (Bicket et al. 2010). Situated between the ports of Ostia and Portus, these buildings and the associated dune environment corroborate the argument that this shoreline was relatively stable during the Roman period. The sea level was relatively constant, and new sand source areas were probably not exposed. Consequently, it is likely that dune development was insignificant (Rendell et al. 2007). However, we should not forget that dunes can move suddenly if the holding vegetation is reduced and storms whip up the newly exposed sand.

This Roman coastline was structured via the intersection of several complex environmental, economic, political, and cultural processes, all which combined in the development of this thalassocracy (Purcell 1998: 7). Despite the fact that this coastal area was defined (by some) as a wilderness, it emerged as a domain of *otium* (a concept of leisure that was an alternative to the world of political and military power) (ibid.: 1). However, this domain was also defined via its relationship to the sea and the ever-changing coastline. Seaside retreats, as described by Pliny in his letter to Gallus (Epistles 2.17) (Goalen & Fortenberry 2002), could only exist once economic profits had been extracted via the successful management or mitigation of littoral processes.

Controlling Permeability

All environmental processes operate across a range of temporal and spatial scales. Relative sea-level rise might have been perceptible at a generational level; the results of tectonic uplift or downwarping were often perceptible immediately. These natural processes would have had different consequences for people, and their influence on the structuring of everyday lifeways diverse. As well as emphasising the study of ports and harbours as gateways facilitating connections and economic opportunities, we should put equal emphasis on the assessment of the complex technological engagements, and related environmental knowledge, associated with these places (Horden & Purcell 2000: 391–5). These engagements reveal the underlying environmental constraints that act upon certain forms of coastal activity. The development of ports and harbours would have emerged as a new part of humanity's relationship with the coast and the sea, with people endeavouring to control specific coastal locales – locales that would have been subject to the natural changes highlighted above.

At Atlit-Yam, we saw how the rising sea level not only inundated the village (probably long after its abandonment) but initially spoilt access to fresh water from the wells. Moving to a new site may have been unproblematic, although the rediscovery of a freshwater source might have been the most challenging task facing these people. The mooring or beaching of boats during the Neolithic would have probably taken place on suitable beaches, or against natural geological shelves (wharfs) or in embayments (as natural harbours). Moving into the Bronze Age, the development of early ports and harbours required the development of mitigation schemes to protect these places from environmentally initiated redundancy. As noted at the outset, the Mediterranean Sea influenced the nature of relationships between the various subregions along its coastlines. Changes in relative sea level, whether eustatic, crustal, or changes in coastal configuration because of sedimentary deposition and consequent progradation, would have had an impact on coastal societies as well as those in the hinterlands. Moreover, the activities of those in the hinterlands would have influenced the nature of environmental change along the coast, with eroded sediments eventually making their way to the littoral, resulting in the steady seawards march of deltas in some areas, or contributing to the silting up of ports and harbours. The Mediterranean, more than most regions around the world, is defined by this complex interplay of environmental, economic, and cultural processes that lie between the mountains and the sea. Whilst tectonic activity could not be mitigated, some silting could. The infilling of harbours was managed via dredging or controlled water flow. However, in some cases, no amount of dredging could save harbours from the unrelenting advance of the coastline. Sedimentation was so serious in certain areas that some harbours have never been found by archaeologists, including that at Luna (north-west Italy) (Bini et al. 2012). Lechaion (the western harbour of ancient Corinth) was unfortunately exposed to tectonic uplift and silting, with evidence for mounds of dredged silts still apparent today (Morhange et al. 2012).

Small harbours were often constructed in hazardous areas, such as capes, where unpredictable winds and currents forced boats and ships to take shelter. In some instances, sanctuaries developed close by (Blackman 1982b: 188), representing a particular intersection of cultural and environmental processes, where the ever-present risks associated with the maritime environment were articulated via religious as well as technological engagements with the landscape.

One criterion for the location of ports and harbours is their situation vis-à-vis sea currents and predominant winds; not all places along a coast will be subject to the same currents and winds, thus proffering access to the natural maritime 'highways'. Direct access to certain currents and winds would have been critical prior to the development of the ability to tack and sail against the wind. The wind was even referred to as the Devil until recently in some parts of the Aegean (Powell 1996: 10). Specific proxies that allow us to identify changes in wind regimes are rare. We need to consider to what extent the environment, in the form of climate (wind levels, wind directions, etc.) and sea level (with its direct effects on coastal configuration), would have been different.

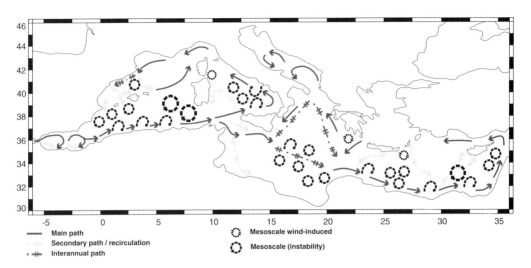

3.16. Surface circulation of waters in the Mediterranean (after credits CLS/Pujol/2006: http://www.aviso.oceanobs.com/ – permission granted).

Morton (2001: 6) considers that sea conditions in the Mediterranean have not changed significantly since antiquity (Fig. 3.16). However, there is no doubt that shifting weather systems (a corollary of climate changes) would have resulted in variations in wind and current patterns, at the very least altering the seasonality and timing of certain winds. We can infer changes in wind direction based on variations in the movement and position of seasonal pressure systems, although much modern research covers the more recent past (Barriendos 1997; Barriendos & Llasat 2003). In the extreme Western Mediterranean, anticyclonic conditions facilitate the flow of superficial Atlantic water into the Mediterranean and littoral drift increases, which enhance progradation, whilst cyclonic conditions create the opposite conditions (Zazo et al. 1994). One argument that involves a claim for a change in the direction of trade winds around the Near East c. 7,000 years ago relates to the evidence for increased humidity during this period, which could have been caused by a reversal in the relationship between the anticyclones in north-east Europe and the Azores (Issar et al. 1992). The Mediterranean comprises a transitional climate. During the summer, it is usually influenced by the Azores anticyclone, and in the winter, southward-moving depressions from Europe create instability and regular north-westerly winds. Research into Little Ice Age climatic changes implies that winter wind speeds in the Mediterranean would have increased during such periods of climatic deterioration (Raible et al.

2007). In fact, some routes might have been easier to navigate during the winter months (Morton 2001: 233), although the summer would have been the time of intense maritime activity with the *etesians* (ancient strong and unpredictable winds) blowing from May to October. The nature of sea currents was so influential that they contributed to the definition of boundaries on dry land. Some regions, although close to one another geographically, were 'separated' because different sea lanes had to be used. For example, the North African regions of Maghrib and the Maghrib al-Aqsa were treated as two distinct zones (B. D. Shaw 2006: 9).

The complexity of maritime and littoral processes resulted in the development of complex forms of environmental knowledge, ranging from navigation through to harbour construction and maintenance. The agency of currents, winds, tectonic activity, and erosion have influenced the very structure of Mediterranean regions, economies, and relationships with the sea and coast. The combination of these environmental and socio-economic processes constitute a core group of traits that characterise the very essence of Mediterraneanism.

The growth and development of technologies and environmental knowledge that would facilitate movement of people, materials, goods, and ideas was of course a process that underpinned the emergence of a connected Mediterranean. These connections (Horden & Purcell 2000: ch. 5) demanded a change from passive to active engagements with the environment. This process of technological intervention was probably more intense across these coastal environments than in the other landscape types dealt with in the following chapters.

4

Rivers and Wetlands

Floods are a fairly common occurrence and cause serious damage across large areas of land. Severe loss of life in Mediterranean floods does occur today, and even when no lives are lost, the economic cost and distress for thousands of ordinary people is beyond doubt. The 2002 flood on the Gardon in the south of France claimed the lives of 21 people and caused extensive damage. Although this flood was higher than those recorded in written records, it was not the highest vis-à-vis floods recorded in the sedimentary records. Deposits from caves 17–19 m above the normal river (base) level, which is 3 m above the 2002 flood height, show how extreme events have taken place in the past (Sheffer et al. 2008). The impact of short-cycle events (that often last between 24 and 48 hours) is something that geoarchaeologists can rarely identify with confidence. However, these events influence humanity's relationship with the environment.

This chapter presents a description of the main types of hydrological systems present in the Mediterranean. Issues of climatic variation and precipitation regimes are considered, as well as the instability and unreliability of water supplies in some parts of the region. A more detailed analysis of erosion histories and human relationships with the soil system appears in Chapters 5 and 6. The examples presented here range from small-scale, individual site-based studies, through to large-scale examples that assess the archaeology of human settlement on or adjacent to important Mediterranean rivers and wetlands.

Studying Mediterranean Rivers and Wetlands: Research Questions and Approaches

Rather than rehearse methodologies and approaches that are covered in a number of books, in particular A.G. Brown's (1997) comprehensive assessment of alluvial geoarchaeology, this section will consider the nature of the dominant research questions that comprise modern alluvial geoarchaeology (see also Howard & Macklin 1999). However, two essential definitions are required: 'fluvial' and 'alluvial'. The first corresponds to processes directly associated with a body of water (usually a river) and its channel; the second, the sediments transported by that body of water and then deposited, producing a terrace or flood plain for example.

A relatively early exposition of research questions that are still current in Mediterranean alluvial geoarchaeology was presented by Judson in 1963. He stated that we needed to know whether changes in the landscape were caused by people or 'by some non-human cause', and that such changes may have had an impact on human exploitation of a given landscape (ibid.: 287). His dating of the river terraces along the Gornalunga Valley in central Sicily suggested a post-325 BC date for the 8–10 m terraces based on the identification of a burial within the terrace deposits. Judson demonstrated that prior to the Greek burial, the valley was 10 m deeper than it is today. Then, subsequent to that burial, the stream would have flowed some 10 m higher than its modern level. Questions of alluvial 'stability' and 'instability', and the probable influence of changes in topographic form along river systems, are the dominant research questions half a century on from Judson's work. Our methods are more refined, but the fundamental research questions regarding people's relationships with the landscape have not altered a great deal. An example of a valuable study that adopts this approach is the work carried out around Basilicata, Southern Italy (Piccarreta et al. 2011). Here, we see that periods were characterised by extensive flood (slackwater) deposits: 5200–4800 BC, 2800–2550 BC, 2300–2100 BC, 1400–1100 BC, 350 BC–150 AD, and 300–680 AD. These sediments imply the movement of water beyond the banks of the river, and that these events occurred during colder, wetter climatic phases, whilst incision of the water body further into its bed took place during warmer periods. The phases of aggradation appear to have been more intense during the last two millennia – possibly a consequence of increased human activity. This *geomorphological* study legitimately presents human activity as a process (Fig. 4.1). However, *archaeologists* need to move beyond narratives where environmental reconstruction divorces people from their environment, where people constitute another forcing mechanism or emerge as an amorphous physical process, implicitly or explicitly characterised as energy inputs and outputs.

The majority of alluvial geoarchaeological/geomorphological work tends to present the alluvial system as a sedimentary record which serves as a proxy indicator for climatic or anthropogenic impact on a landscape (see Bintliff 2002 for a review of such approaches). Some studies also consider human responses to changes in river characteristics, position, and/or form. One example, which moves beyond these research questions, is the work carried out at Fiume di Sotto di Troina River Valley, north-central Sicily (see Fig. 4.2 for a map with sites referred to in this chapter). One aim of this project has been the assessment of the possible impact of past agricultural systems on the Sicilian landscape. In particular, the erosion history of the valley was investigated. The lack of Neolithic material in this study area is possibly a result of destruction or burial of Neolithic sites by colluvial and alluvial sediments, as these early farming sites were located on the flood plain (Ayala & French 2003; Leighton 1999). The models of human impact and erosion suggest that the opening up of the landscape for intensive pastoralism resulted in a greater potential for soil movement and that this '…would have left a landscape more resistant to regeneration after abandonment' (Ayala & French 2005: 164–5). The issues of regeneration or more specifically resilience are notions that are addressed throughout this volume.

CHARACTERISTICS OF MEDITERRANEAN RIVERS
One notable characteristic of Mediterranean rivers is their steep gradients across tectonic landforms, in particular, mountain ranges that embrace the sources of many rivers (Mather 2009: 17). Watercourses are often constrained by topography, and the distances between the source and the coast can be quite short, thus producing the potential for fast-flowing rivers with concomitant sedimentary loads comprised of coarse materials

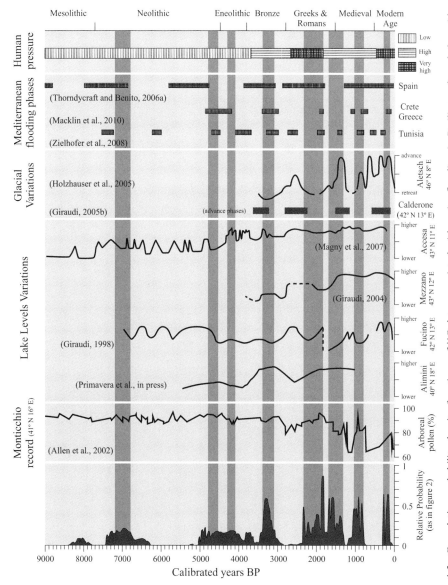

4.1. Cumulative probability density functions of ^{14}C dates associated with major flooding in Basilicata plotted alongside human and several palaeoenvironmental information: pollen records of vegetation change (Allen et al., 2002); hydrological records from central-southern Italy lakes (Giraudi, 1998, 2004; Magny et al., 2007; Primavera et al., 2011; Alps and Apennine glacier variations (Giraudi, 2005; Holzhauser et al., 2005); and Mediterranean Holocene fluvial activity (Thorndycraft & Benito 2006; Zielhofer & Faust 2008; Macklin et al. 2010). (By permission of Elsevier, Piccarreta, M., Caldara, M., Capolongo, D., and Boenzi, F. (2011) Holocene geomorphic activity related to climatic change and human impact in Basilicata, southern Italy, *Geomorphology* 128(3–4), fig. 5, p. 143.)

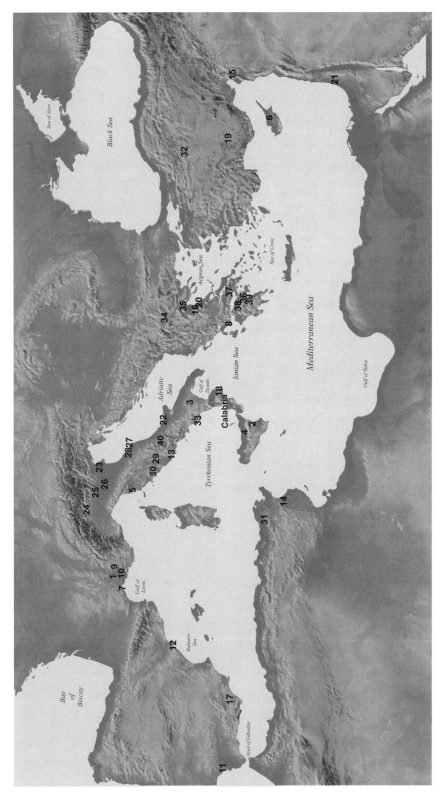

4.2. Rivers, wetlands, and sites referred to in the chapter. 1: Gardon, 2: Gornalunga Valley, 3: Basilicata, 4: Fiume di Sotto di Troina River Valley, 5: Cecina River, 6: Lefkosia, 7: Lez delta, upon which the city of Lattara, 8: The Acheloös Delta, 9: Fontaine du Vaucluse, 10: Camargue/Vallée des Baux/Glanum/Le Carrelet, 11: Coto Doñana, 12: Ebro Delta (Spain), 13: Pontine Marshes, 14: Sebkhet Kelbia, 15: Amuq Valley, 16: Piera, 17: River Aguas and Guadalentín depression, 18: Cacchiavia Valley, 19: Konya plain/Çatalhöyük, 20: Penios River, Thessaly – Platia Magoula Zarkou, 21: Erani Terrace, 22: Biferno Valley, 23: The Po-Venetian plain, 24: Lagozza di Besnate, 25: Campo Ceresole, 26: Villaggio Grande, 27: Ancona, 28: Suasa, Ostra, 29: Narce, 30: Fiora, Marta, and Treia rivers, 31: mid-Medjerda floodplain/*Simitthus*, 32: Gordion, 33: Velia, 34: Stobi, 35: Klidhi bridge, 36: River Xerias/Inachos River valley, 37: Copais, 38: Stymphalos, 39: Marshes at Lerna, 40: Lake Fucino.

4.3. Large boulders and stones are easily transported down many Mediterranean river courses with relatively steep gradients over short distances. The River Golo, Corsica (photo: author).

(Fig. 4.3). Moreover, past tectonic events could also have led to significant changes in hydrological regimes (Caputo, Bravard, & Helly 1994). Tectonic processes are fundamentally important in structuring drainage basins (Mather 2009: 23).

The lower Cecina River (Tuscany, central Italy) is an example of a tectonically controlled river system, where channel instability and migration may have discouraged permanent, extensive human settlement in parts of the valley prior to the late medieval period (Benvenuti et al. 2008). There is some evidence for Roman activity in the middle Cecina Valley (Camin & McCall 2002), and the absence of sites in parts of this valley may well be a function of geomorphological processes that have either destroyed or masked archaeological remains (Terrenato & Ammerman 1996). There is little doubt that settlement during the Etruscan and Roman periods in the wider Volaterrae region was relatively stable, and there is little suggestion that the environment constrained agricultural activity (Terrenato 1998). In addition, much activity would have been centred on the coast (Pasquinucci & Menchelli 1999). It is possible that some of the settlement patterns in this area can be explained by either avoidance of certain parts of the valley or differential survival and destruction of sites. In either case, an assessment of the alluvial regime is a necessity.

Sudden tectonic events may have literally turned water supplies on and off in some places. At Lefkosia, Nicosia, Cyprus, the flood plain is characterised by an extensive series of flood deposits, with palaeosols representing hiatuses between flooding events/phases. Moreover, the change from an aggrading river system to an entrenched or down-cut system is especially interesting, as such a regime change could have been quite sudden – the product of tectonic activity. This situation demonstrates the need for precise dating through the sequence if we are to calculate dates of flooding and sediment accumulation rates. However, dating on such sequences is never straightforward, and demands sensible inferences regarding the development of such a flood plain and the nature of human interaction with that area (Newell, Stone, & Harrison 2004: 75).

Generally, river flows arriving on the Northern Mediterranean coastline tend to be perennial, although many smaller, inland rivers will often run dry during the summer months. Moreover, Northern Mediterranean rivers tend to have extensive catchments and drainage networks, whilst Southern Mediterranean rivers have less extensive networks, and are sometimes supplied by sources beyond the Mediterranean area, such as the Nile (Allen 2001: 65). As the Mediterranean climate is characterised by strong seasonal variation – dry summers with wet/stormy autumns – this has obvious ramifications for river systems. Many rivers are quite 'flashy', in that they will flood during autumn storms. A number of Mediterranean rivers have their sources in mountainous areas, and consequently their flow rates increase during the spring snowmelt period. One problem that archaeologists must address is the extent to which we can identify human responses to these 'normal' annual cycles. Much geoarchaeological work is quite understandably concerned with the identification and analysis of phases that are extra-normal, that is, decennial or secular variations from supposedly normal flow rates and flooding regimes.

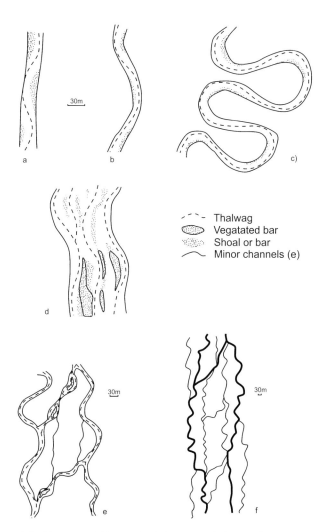

4.4. River types (A) straight, (B) sinuous, (C) meandering, (D) braided, (E) anastomosing, and (F) anabranching. (By permission of Cambridge University Press, Brown, A.G. (1997), *Alluvial Geoarchaeology*, fig. 3.3.)

Mediterranean rivers can be placed into two basic categories: single channel (sometimes, meandering) or braided (Fig. 4.4). There are of course variations within these simplified categories. However, one reason for this simplification is to introduce the notion that rivers, and particularly Mediterranean rivers, can undergo quite profound transformations, evolving from single-channelled rivers to braided (often straight rivers with several small channels separated by bars that may be flooded from time to time) and anastomosing (channelled rivers with bars that are normally stable) (Fig. 4.5). Such changes would not only have had

(a)

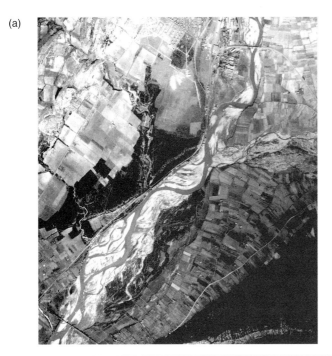

(b)

4.5. Typical braided rivers – (Top) The Durance flows from the Southern French Alps into Provence (aerial photo, by permission of Centre Camille Julian); (Bottom) The River Andarax view from Los Millares (SE Spain) (photo: author).

an important impact on the physical nature of the alluvial landscape, but they would also have had serious repercussions for people living on or near the river. For example, the Lez delta in southern France, upon which the city of Lattara (near Montpellier) was established during the sixth century BC, started to develop from the Neolithic period onwards (Blanchemanche et al. 2004: 159). As the Lez plain expanded, this provided Neolithic populations with new land. Therefore, one of the most notable aspects of fluvial and alluvial environments is their capacity to evolve as landscape forms. River channels can migrate and change their breadth and depth, whilst terraces can form and radically change the relationship of a river to its surrounding landscape. In the same area, we also see how a river channel can also influence the structure of field systems. Here, the digging of early Iron Age ditches and then the location of Roman rural settlement probably represent responses to changes in the alluvial environment (ibid.: 171).

River channels not only contribute to the configuration of activities in the landscape, but they also act as communication routes and boundaries, and are often imbued with deep religious or mythological meanings (Frisone, 2012). One of the mythical twelve labours associated with the hero Heracles includes the diversion of a river to clean the Augeian Stables. The silting up of the river Acheloös caused a border dispute between Acarnania and Aetolia (western Greece). The construction of embankments and channels remedying this dispute was considered one of Heracles' acts (Salowey 1994: 77–8). The changes that can occur in a river system can thus have an effect on any one of these aspects, and therefore the role of rivers and wetlands is primordial within any landscape.

The migration of river channels has serious taphonomic consequences (Fig. 4.6), given that the position of a river course will obviously have influenced the location of settlement sites and had repercussions for the position of any adjacent flood plain. We should note that geoarchaeology is not just concerned with 'reconstructing' past environments, it also has a key role to play in understanding landscape taphonomy, that is, assessing areas of site survival and destruction (Clevis et al. 2006). The destruction of archaeological sites by meandering rivers stands as an important example of direct impact upon society that should then allow us to consider human awareness (or lack of awareness) of environmental dynamics and hazard – a subject dealt with later in this chapter.

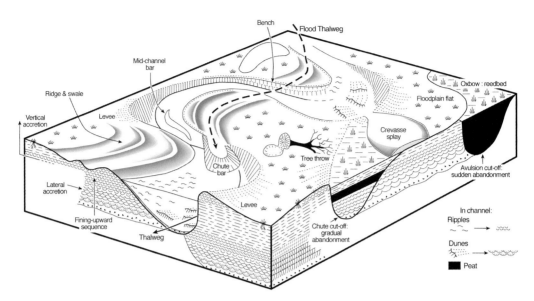

4.6. Block diagram of a typical flood plain with its associated fluvial and alluvial features. (By permission of Cambridge University Press, Brown, A.G. (1997), *Alluvial Geoarchaeology*, fig. 1.1.)

SPRINGS AND KARST

Although this chapter explicitly emphasises the study of rivers and wetlands, there are other noteworthy hydrological elements, in particular, springs/thermal springs, and smaller streams, which are of fundamental importance in Mediterranean landscapes, feeding rivers and wetlands.

Even though karstification is predominantly found on limestone areas, it can also occur on other geologies (Fig. 4.7). It comprises the chemical dissolution of rock by water, thus creating fissures, sinkholes, caves, and underground streams. Phreatic (subterranean multidirectional) streams create passages, and where water still flows in these passages, it can re-emerge into the open landscape. Where these springs emerge from depth under great pressure, they are referred to as Vauclusian springs (resurgences), after the southern French Fontaine du Vaucluse (Lewin & Woodward 2009: 296). Tufa (cold water) and travertine (often hot water) are carbonate precipitates, the analysis of which can contribute to the production of environmental histories. For example, some research has revealed high tufa growth rates during the sixth and fifth millennia BC in the south of France (Vaudour 1994), with certain areas seeing high levels of tufa growth during the climatic optimum, but declining after c. 2000 BC (Pedley 2009: 240). Recent work has presented a more

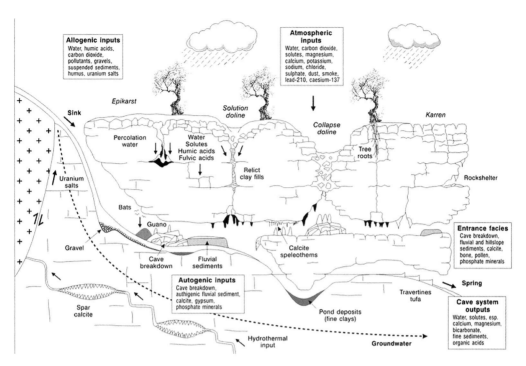

4.7. A typical Mediterranean karst system region showing material inputs, stores, and outputs and associated processes in the vadose phreatic zones (modified from Ford and Williams and Gillieson 1996). The phreatic zone lies below the water table (dashed line). Active tectonics in the Mediterranean can produce hydrothermal inputs into karst systems (By permission of Oxford University Press, Lewin, J., and Woodward, J. (2009), Karst geomorphology and environmental change, in J. C. Woodward (ed.), *The Physical Geography of the Mediterranean*, fig. 10.8, p. 297.)

complex picture of travertine development, with production continuing in some landscapes until the Middle Ages, although the Neolithic saw substantial changes in the travertine production regime (Ollivier et al. 2006).

Most importantly, karst landscapes comprise hydrological systems that are hidden from the eye, with water moving underground and emerging in unexpected places – thus, the set of myths associated with these landscapes and their water sources. These cultural aspects are considered in more detail in the latter parts of the chapter.

WETLANDS

Some of the most important wetlands in the Mediterranean include the Camargue in the south of France, and abutting areas such as the Vallée des Baux, the Coto Doñana and Ebro Delta (Spain), the Pontine Marshes (Italy), and Sebkhet Kelbia (Tunisia).

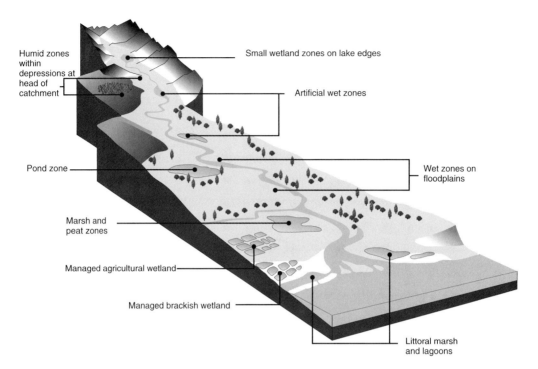

Humid zones
within
depressions at
head of
catchment

Small wetland zones on lake edges

Artificial wet zones

Pond zone

Wet zones on
floodplains

Marsh and
peat zones

Managed agricultural wetland

Managed brackish wetland

Littoral marsh
and lagoons

4.8. A transect of different wetland environment types.

As with any environment type, the characteristics of wetlands vary.
We can divide wetlands into categories founded on different develop-
mental stages: marshes comprise shallow water (fresh through to saline)
and contain grasses, rushes, reeds, and sedges; fenlands comprise developing peat areas and associated vegetation (Mitsch & Gosselink 1993).
These characteristics depend on the levels and cycles of water supply,
how close the wetland is to the coast, and the sedimentary inputs from
the fluvial systems feeding the wetland (Fig. 4.8). Some wetlands are
flooded for the entire year, whilst others may only flood seasonally.
Wetland systems are dynamic, not only over the long durée but also
on the annual scale. As with any environmental system, we need to ask
to what extent changes in the system are the results of climate change
and/or human manipulation. More intriguing from our perspective is
the debate regarding the utility of wetlands versus the potential dangers or risks, especially that of disease (see Horden & Purcell 2000, ch.
VI.5). Some see wetlands as niches that are environmentally marginal
and dangerous due to the presence of malaria. A number of everyday

terms characterise wetlands in a pejorative manner: one can be *swamped* with work, or one can be *bogged* down (Mitsch & Gosselink 1993: 12). However, many wetland zones are incredibly rich in resources (especially in terms of fish, fowl, and flora), and malaria has not always been present. Moreover, some wetlands, especially their edges, have been used for agriculture (Morelli et al. 2008), and some societies have endeavoured to drain wetlands in order to gain permanent agricultural lands.

Alluvial Geoarchaeology: People and Climate

Much research into alluvial histories has considered the long durée (Quaternary and Pleistocene) with a view to assessing riverine responses to changes in climate (I. C. Fuller et al. 1998; Macklin et al. 2002; Macklin & Woodward 2009). As with many environmental processes, the frequency of flooding events is related to climatic cycles. Many models from across the Mediterranean articulate correlations between changes in climate and river regimes. This section presents some brief examples of issues addressed by recent alluvial research around the Mediterranean, before moving on to more detailed regional summaries.

In the Southern Mediterranean (Tunisia and Morocco), rivers appear to be more dynamic during drier periods than during cooler, wetter periods, which is the case in the Northern Mediterranean. A phase of relative aridity at about 4500–4000 BC interrupted an otherwise continuous Neolithic presence in the Moroccan dry lands in the south-west and north-east areas of the country (Zielhofer & Linstädter 2006). By the end of the Neolithic (c. 2800 BC), there was an increase in fluvial activity in Tunisia. However, the relative dearth of archaeological material for the post-Neolithic periods makes correlations between environmental changes and human activities difficult (Zielhofer, Faust, & Linstädter 2008).

Changes in flood-plain dynamics and, in particular, the course of the river will have had important consequences for past peoples and their engagements with and movement around that landscape (Fig. 4.9). In the Amuq Valley, situated between the Tigris-Euphrates and the Mediterranean, late Chalcolithic sites were situated on a low-energy

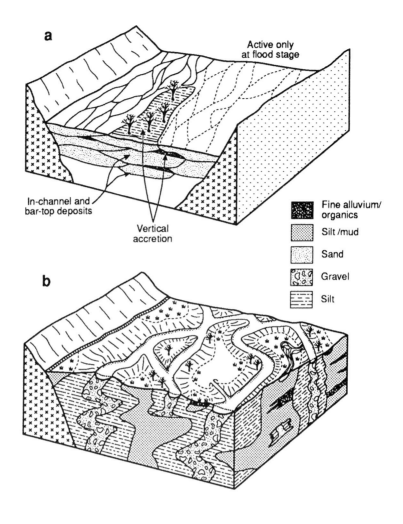

Active only
at flood stage

In-channel and
bar-top deposits

Vertical
accretion

Fine alluvium/
organics

Silt /mud

Sand

Gravel

Silt

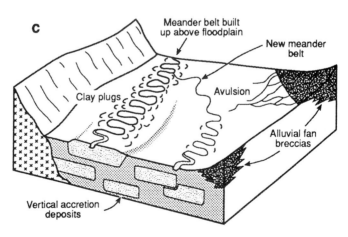

Meander belt built
up above floodplain

New meander
belt

Clay plugs

Avulsion

Alluvial fan
breccias

Vertical accretion
deposits

4.9. Idealised and simplified flood plain sedimentary systems: (a) a low-sinuosity sandy-braided flood plain, (b) an intermediate sinuosity anastomosing flood plain, and (c) a sinuous avulsion-dominated flood plain These complex variations can occur across space but also evolve in the same space over time, thus influencing the ways in which people engage with that landscape. (By permission of Cambridge University Press, Brown, A.G. (1997), *Alluvial Geoarchaeology*, fig. 1.2, p. 22.)

flood plain. This environment appears to have remained stable until the late first millennium BC. A change to more powerful sedimentation could imply an increase in flooding (and the strength of these flows), or a migration of the river channel towards the area where the geoarchaeological work was undertaken. Either way, this part of the landscape clearly changed come the classical period. Increased settlement activity in the surrounding hills could have been responsible for the contraction of the lake and change in the alluvial system during the late first millennium BC or early first millennium AD (Yener et al. 2000).

On reading most alluvial geoarchaeological reports from the Mediterranean, we often see a narrative which (quite understandably) places greater emphasis on human impact on alluvial systems and sedimentation from the Neolithic onwards. Typically, this is when landscape degradation is considered to have increased substantially. In northern Piera (Macedonia, Greece), the study of two streams (the Gerakaris and Agios Dimitrios) revealed long periods of relative stability and soil formation, with infrequent but intense aggradation (the build-up of sediment), incision (the down-cutting into the bed of the river), and lateral migration (movement across the flood plain). An alluvial unit in the Gerakaris Valley was deposited during the final Neolithic, followed by 'at least 1350 years of landscape stability' (Krahtopoulou 2000: 22–3). The next alluvial unit is dated to the period 2464–799 BC, followed by 'stability' for at least 1,100 years. Between the third and sixth centuries AD (Late Roman period), a fill was deposited in the valley, and the stream migrated to the north-east. A similar process was also identified in the Agios Dimitrios stream, although channel migration does not appear to have occurred here. Krahtopoulou (2000: 25) argues that Early and Late Holocene alluvial activity was most likely controlled by climatic factors, whilst Neolithic through to proto-historic changes in these alluvial systems may have been influenced by both climate and cultural factors. What we do see here are relatively long periods of stability and probable landscape resilience, with processes such as channel migration possibly forcing some changes in the location of human activity.

In the Vera basin in south-east Spain, braided rivers, which existed during the Pleistocene, developed into meandering river systems with associated terraces during the Holocene. The development of the river terrace sequence on the River Aguas (which feeds into the Vera basin) is dated using both radiometric methods and archaeological material. Evidence for Chalcolithic and Roman activity was found in one terrace, with erosion phases following in both cases. The fact that terrace deposition in this area is mirrored elsewhere in Spain led Schulte to suggest that climate or sea-level control were probably the dominant factors, rather than anthropogenic influences. Evidence for Neolithic land use – and thereby impact – is considered insignificant. However, during the Chalcolithic (4000–2300 BC), it appears that erosion may have been caused by human activity (Schulte 2002: 96–7), whilst post-Roman deposition may have been caused by climatic factors (Chapman et al. 1998 cited in Schulte 2002).

As stated earlier, the characteristics of rivers are directly affected by tectonic movements. For example, during the last few thousand years, 8–10 m of subsidence in the Calabria region (Italy) has prevented modern streams from incising (the streams have not down-cut, finding the quickest route to the sea) (Abbott & Valastro 1995: 200). Agricultural practices, and the consequent input of fine-grained sediment into the fluvial system, may also explain this lack of incision. Here, the complex interplay of natural and anthropic influences has combined to change the nature of environments within this area over time. Moreover, the fact that this pattern was not repeated in all of the valleys in the region means that each community will have adapted and developed environmental knowledge specific to their valley and river system. In the Cacchiavia Valley, there have been periods of slow, fine-grained sedimentation but with some short periods of incision (ibid.: 201). At c. 3500 BC, a phase of rapid aggradation comprised of silty-clays occurred, followed by incision from about 3000 BC. Depending on the rapidity of the changes, people may well have had to adapt to this changing environment; for example, an incised river might be more difficult to traverse, thus affecting movement around the valley. Another phase of aggradation took place up to 2700 BC, and then slow sedimentation continued for about another millennium. By 800 BC, an incision phase had taken place. River sedimentation has different consequences along the length of a valley, and understanding the links between what happens high up in a catchment vis-à-vis consequences for the lower end of the river is a vital form of environmental knowledge, as aggradation in valleys, such as in Calabria, will result in progradation of the coastline. When combined with poor drainage, this results in the formation of marshes and swamps. Such a development may have had serious consequences for the local population as agricultural land decreased and the potential for disease increased (ibid.: 202–3).

These few brief examples exhibit the dominant narratives in alluvial geoarchaeology/geomorphology. More often than not, we are obliged to identify the causes of erosion or 'instability' within alluvial systems. Prior to the development of agriculture, climate is often identified as the cause, with people emerging as the key drivers of erosion after this. The 'negative' impact of farming on vegetation and the pedosphere undoubtedly did result in erosion in many instances, and this subject will be dealt with in Chapters 5 and 6. We should, however, note here that we sometimes lose sight of the fact that environmental stability and resilience would have characterised long periods in many Mediterranean landscapes, with areas witnessing phases of stability after the Neolithic. Consequently, alluvial geoarchaeology can help elucidate the conditions within in which certain activities and societies developed. For example, the landscape conditions associated with the development of farming.

ALLUVIAL LANDSCAPES AND FARMING IN ANATOLIA AND GREECE

The importance of alluvial landscapes for the development of early agriculture cannot be understated. 'Intensive but localised cultivation of cereal crops on alluvial wetlands is thought to have provided the ecological basis for the primary Neolithic settlement that spread across southwest Asia and southeast Europe' (Roberts & Rosen 2009: 393). In many areas, the introduction of farming occurred on flood plains due to the intrinsic fertility of these zones. However, activity on many flood plains carries with it an inherent risk – that of flooding.

Çatalhöyük was located next to a branch of the Çarşamba River with zones of marshy flood basins and marl hummocks (ibid.: 396). The site developed as an artificial hill in order to avoid flooding on a poorly drained flood plain (Roberts, Boyer, & Parish 1996) (Fig. 4.10). The presence of 'silica-skeletons' or phytoliths (produced within the cells of crops) in large quantities is considered an indicator of irrigated farming or of farming in wet conditions. Despite the fact that the Konya plain (where Çatalhöyük is situated) would have been wetter during the Neolithic,

4.10. Reconstruction of the Çatalhöyük landscape (reconstruction by Jon Swogger; by permission of Çatalhöyük Research Project).

an initial study showed that there were surprisingly few silica skeletons, suggesting that wheat was grown on better-drained soils away from the site itself (Rosen 2005: 211). However, a more recent study of phytoliths indicates that wet farming of wheat was indeed undertaken (Shillito 2011). We should still consider the possibility that the area around the site could have been flooded for parts of the year, and whilst this niche offered a series of wetland resources, arable agriculture and pastoralism might not have been pursued in all zones around Çatalhöyük.

Neolithic mobility, where people responded to changes in specific environmental processes, was the norm. In fact, from a human ecological perspective, mobility is a basic strategy in the maintenance of environmental resilience, even amongst agriculturalists. The flexible application of environmental knowledge across different niches was part of an environmental culture inherited from a time when mobility was a way of life. The landscape around Çatalhöyük did change with time, with alluvial deposition stopping between the Neolithic and the Chalcolithic. Archaeological survey demonstrates that there were increases in population in the Near East from the Early Bronze Age, and the Konya Basin was no exception, with increases in the number and sizes of sites on the Konya plain (Boyer, Roberts, & Baird 2006: 683–9). It appears that people in this area successfully managed a complex hydrological landscape with its changes in river regime and variation in soil salinity.

In Thessaly (northern Greece), Neolithic settlement first occurred on the flood plain of the Penios River during an aggradation phase, possibly caused by soil erosion, although it seems likely that this erosion was not caused by early farmers (Bintliff 2002). People were probably attracted to the annually deposited silts (van Andel, Gallis, & Toufexis 1992: 131). Subsequent to this early phase, occupation mounds developed as 'human accumulation' overtook the natural rate of sedimentation; that is, even though the deposition of alluvial sediments continued, the settlement sites on the plain maintained levels above the accumulating plain.

During the Early and Middle Neolithic, the development of the Platia Magoula Zarkou site (situated on a mound some 5 m high and 200 m across) was contemporary with the deposition of several metres of alluvial sands that represent flooding events (ibid.: 138). Early farmers exploited the moist silts deposited by floods. Despite the risks associated with working in an active flood plain, which included poor yields on wet areas (van Andel, Gallis, & Toufexis 1995: 140), wetland edges and flood plains would have been more suitable for pre-plough cultivation (Bintliff et al. 2006). Consequently, permanent, year-round settlement may not have been possible (Whittle 2002: 17). A void in the site distribution pattern might represent the agricultural land exploited by the sites closest to the lake (Perlès 2001: 130). A similar process has been identified in the Near East, where alluviation increased during the Middle Holocene. However, the sediments deposited by these streams, such as those around the Erani Terrace (the Shephela foothills on the central coastal plain of Israel), were fine, silty units that were characteristic of a flood-water farming system (Rosen 2007: 86–8). In both of these areas, we can see how locating on the edge of a zone susceptible to flooding was important. During the Early Bronze Age, flood-water farming here became impossible as the wadi started to incise. Individual subsistence farmers could probably recover after one or two years of low rainfall. However, more complex societies with a high number of 'non-producers' may have been less resilient (Rosen 1995: 32–3). As the streams cut down over time and water supply to the land was reduced, the 'buffer provided by floodwater farming' diminished (ibid.: 39).

In some instances, Thessalian sites were located some 8–10 km from rivers and streams (Perlès 2001: 135). Certain environmental characteristics in this region may thus have had a 'repulsive role' during the Neolithic (Perlès 1999, 2001); some areas may have been too wet. Statistical analyses assessing the nature of the settlement pattern imply that each village would have had a roughly 450 ha territory. As settlement density on the poor-quality soils (Ayia Sofia soil) was lower, this suggests that these people were aware of variations of soil quality. However, Perlès (2001: 143) does not feel that soil quality influenced settlement choice; it is possible that seasonally flooded zones, along with marshes and arid zones were avoided. The highest density of sites occurred in areas that were never flooded and in environments that Perlès considers 'homogenous'. However, homogeneity is a problematic notion, as people undoubtedly created ecological patches, thus rendering these landscapes heterogeneous. The fact that sites in this area appear to have been close to one another implies a common notion of what environment type was the most productive, and collective or shared resources would have been a cultural characteristic within these landscapes. In central Greece, the settlement distribution was different, with dispersed farms prevalent. Although a common environment type appears to have been chosen, with Early to Middle Neolithic sites also situated adjacent to wetland fields (Bintliff et al. 2006: 671–2), it is possible that in drier climates, areas of high water tables with their associated soils formed discrete zones – quite different to the plains of Thessaly and areas further north (Bintliff 2012: 60). These environmental characteristics had a direct influence on settlement density and distribution.

ASPECTS OF ALLUVIAL ARCHAEOLOGY IN ITALY

A great deal of alluvial geoarchaeological research has been carried out in Italy, and some of this has been combined with landscape survey. The Biferno Valley (central Italy) landscape survey comprised a geoarchaeological element. Here, seven sedimentary units were identified, the first being Neolithic/Bronze Age, then classical, medieval, early post-medieval, nineteenth century, early twentieth century, and then, finally, the late twentieth century. During the Early Holocene, the Biferno developed from a single meandering channel system to an aggraded one (Hunt 1995: 73–4). Most of the settlement sites with later Neolithic pottery were situated in the lower valley, whilst sites with later Neolithic blades tended to be close to the river. Most of the Bronze Age sites were found in the middle valley (ibid.: 138). Therefore, it seems likely that certain activities took place in specific locations along the course of the river. Unsurprisingly, activities directly intersect with the environment. Whilst the identification of specific activities might not be possible, we can assess a range of potential relationships with natural environmental processes. For example, those sites with pottery would have been situated on a part of the river that was slower moving, and thereby represent activities in zones where river behaviour was more predictable. We should not forget that many riverside activities would have been temporary, and one response to a change in the alluvial system would have been quite simply to move somewhere else. During the Iron Age, there appears to have been a trend towards settlement in the lower part of the valley (ibid.: 162), then during the classical period, an intensive aggrading regime developed, centred on the Samnite and Early Roman periods. An increase in activity during the Roman period (between the third century BC and the first to second centuries AD) seems to be contemporary with a phase of aggradation (Barker & Hunt 2003: 187). This landscape process, lacking detailed chronological resolution, may have taken place over a period of time that had no relevance for the communities living and working in this area. At best, such a process may represent periodic soil erosion. Despite these chronological issues, it should be apparent that changing fluvial and alluvial regimes would have engendered changes in activities that took place along the river.

The biggest alluvial basin in Italy is the Po-Venetian Plain. It comprises 71% of the plain zones in that country (Pellegrini 1979 quoted in Marchetti 2002: 361). The development of the Po plain, with its network of meanders, is best appreciated from aerial photographs or satellite imagery (Tozzi 1993) (Fig. 4.11). Even a cursory examination of these documents should convince anyone that this landscape has witnessed a complicated alluvial history that has influenced the distribution of settlements, the structure of field systems, and the day-to-day lives of ordinary people for millennia.

The Po is navigable up to 257 km inland from the sea, plus it is linked with a series of major lakes (Como, Lago Maggiore, and Garda)

4.11. The Po plain with its complex fluvial network – LANDSATT image (courtesy of the U.S. Geological Survey).

(Mikhailova 2002: 370). Perhaps the most noteworthy characteristic of the Po delta is its progradation. Between the Etruscan period (sixth century BC) and 1600 AD, the delta advance rate was 450 m/100 years, but after AD 1600 (during the Little Ice Age), it was 7 km/100 years (ibid.: 375). As already noted, such rates of environmental change may not have been constant, although some transformations would have been perceptible on a generational scale, and we would expect to see the influence on the chronological spread of sites in some areas, with a leading edge trend of more recent sites following the prograding delta outwards.

A number of surveys in Italy have demonstrated how Early to Middle Neolithic settlements were situated above important rivers (Malone 2003: 258). The Vhò culture (5340–3990 BC) settled on terraces and hill slopes on the northern Po plain. The Lagozza culture (4000–3300 BC) was dominant across much of the eastern Po plain with the development of wooden platforms on lake and riverside areas, such as that at

Lagozza di Besnate (Malone 2003: 263–4), articulating a specific form of environmental knowledge and response to the character of this landscape. During the Early Neolithic, people on the Po plain maintained so-called Mesolithic food-gathering strategies (hunting and fishing), but they also developed agriculture. Freshwater fish, molluscs, deer, boar, chamois, beaver, wolf, and turtle were present on sites such as Campo Ceresole (ibid.: 271). Areas such as the Po plain might not have witnessed a swift or complete transition to farming partly due to the richness of the naturally occurring food resources in these areas. Farming in more marginal and arid zones to the south would have made sense as part of a new risk-buffering mechanism that comprised greater specialisation than in the north. We can see how this region, despite what seem to be quite impressive landscape changes across the Po plain in terms of meanders and evidence for progradation on the coast, was a rich and stable source of food resources.

By the Middle to Late Bronze Age (1650–1200 BC), settlements of the Terramare culture (the villages are referred to as 'Terramaras' in the cental Po valley) developed a landscape dominated by cereal fields, pastures, and meadows that appear to have been suddenly abandoned at c. 1150 BC. The possibility of flooding may have encouraged the building of houses on wooden piles between 1600 and 1400 BC. Later, the houses were built directly on the ground, without piles (Mercuri et al. 2006: 56). Many of these sites are associated with a palaeochannel that was active whilst the site was occupied. A series of 45 wells that showed signs of having been regularly re-excavated after collapse was found on the Villaggio Grande site. These wells followed the local water table, which in turn was linked directly to the Po River. Towards the end of the Bronze Age, an arid phase developed, and the flow rate of the Po was reduced. This phase is recorded over much of Europe, with lake levels falling and alpine glaciers retreating (Cremaschi, Pizzi, & Valsecchi 2006: 95). The development of a drier environment is inferred from the presence of *Cichorioideae* (a plant that usually inhabits dry areas), which fits with a picture of increased human pressure on the landscape (Mercuri et al. 2012). The loss of a reliable water supply may have led to the abandonment of this area, or at the very least led to changes in the way in which the landscape was used. Here, we see how certain sets of practices (including elements of the settlement and economic system) are not persistent. We do not know if environmental changes were directly responsible for these changes, as the identification of *correlation* (i.e. climate change coinciding with changes in settlement and economy) is not *explanation*.

LATE PROTO-HISTORIC AND CLASSICAL ALLUVIAL AND
HYDROLOGICAL LANDSCAPES

As complex (urbanised) societies developed, settlements obviously took on greater permanency, and therefore responses to changes in river regimes demanded technological intervention in one form or another. However, evidence is often elusive, such as in the Nemea Valley (Peloponnese), where it seems that after the phases of abandonment or settlement reduction, some form of drainage system might have been required at certain times in order for agriculture to flourish in this area. This was probably the case during the Early Christian and Byzantine periods (Wright et al. 1990: 644–5).

One example that provides archaeological evidence of responses to Iron Age flooding comes from Campania (Italy). The alluvial 'crisis' during the sixth to fifth centuries BC took the form of rising river and stream levels on several sites. At the Piano di Sorrento site (Naples), the first phase comprises Chalcolithic tombs adjacent to a watercourse. A sixth- to fourth-century BC site was then subject to severe erosion from the stream. The size of some of the architectural blocks moved downstream attests to the force of the major flooding events at this time. A second (fourth century BC) structure was built above the stream, and appears to have been regularly covered with flood deposits. An artisan zone on this site was abandoned during the second century BC due to flooding. Then, as a consequence of the AD 79 eruption of Vesuvius, surrounding hillsides became unstable and a layer of up to 3 m was deposited on the site (Albore Livadie 2003: 360). Here, there appear to be three 'events' that probably had immediate consequences for people. However, these events took place over a relatively long period, and our scale of analysis dictates how we assess resilience in such an area. Whilst there is no doubt that people were affected by specific events, as possibly indicated by the abandonment of the artisan zone, over the longer durée, activity appears resilient.

Changes in the form and characteristics of a river channel will have greater repercussions for large, stable, fixed settlements. The change from a meandering to a braided river is a common feature of Mediterranean fluvial systems. Such a change will not necessarily have caused problems for nearby settlements (although navigability might become difficult).

The causes of such a change can be many and varied. In the Marche region, such a transformation may not have been caused by climate but rather by a change in sediment supply. Variations in sediment supply can result not only from quite spatially specific variance in geology, but also human interference in the geomorphic system. Deforestation by Neolithic communities (Malone et al. 1992) is one possible cause (Coltorti 1993: 321–2). The Roman towns of Suasa (along the middle Cesano) and Ostra (along the middle Misa) were partly constructed over Holocene flood-plain deposits, with some buildings at Ostra built on terraces produced by the meandering system, thus implying that this system could have existed up until the Roman period and perhaps even later (ibid.: 317). Moreover, the terrace upon which the Romans built was probably stable and not subject to flooding.

At Narce (Lazio), there are two alluvial terraces, the largest of which is about 4 m above the present river, whilst the lower terrace stands at about 1.5 m (Cherkauer 1976: 108). Just prior to the Roman period, two alluvial units were deposited, and then during the Roman period itself, the stream migrated towards the eastern side of the valley, followed by renewed migration to the west. Therefore, it is clear that channel migration occurred during the Faliscan settlement at Narce (ibid.: 115–7). Brown and Ellis (1996) argue that whilst climate variation had some impact on the Fiora, Marta, and Treia rivers, it seems more likely that changes in the density and nature of human activity had a greater impact on these rivers' regimes and caused higher rates of overbank deposition, especially as settlement density increased during the Early Roman period. Though the dating of alluvial sediments has always posed a fundamental problem, the use of palaeomagnetic and optically stimulated luminescence (OSL) perhaps offers greater accuracy.

During the long period over which the Roman Empire existed, there were obviously substantial changes in some rivers, and people would have had to adapt to those changes. We know that alluvial terraces formed in a number of Mediterranean landscapes during the Roman period, especially in south-east Italy and parts of Sicily (Neboit-Guilhot & Lespez 2006: 340). There is no doubt that flood mitigation strategies existed (a more detailed discussion of urban flooding is presented below), and one specific response comprised the planting of alder trees along riverbanks as a flood-protection measure (Meiggs 1982: 376). Purcell (2005) considers the dynamic relationship between the periods of urban stasis, characterised by architecture and social practices that constitute social memory, and the dynamic changing environment, in particular, that beyond the city walls over which societies have little control. There are numerous instances of towns and cities that have been damaged, destroyed, or gradually eroded by natural processes.

North African alluvial systems are fundamentally different to their southern European counterparts. Rivers will often run dry or, at best, have a minimal flow. Therefore, they rely on seasonal rainfall patterns that vary from year to year. Moreover, some rainfall events might be so extreme that severe flash flooding will not only cause damage, but also result in too much water arriving at once, with water actually being lost from the system and not being stored or exploited by people. As with the examples above, the question of phases of stability and instability also underpins studies of river systems in the Southern Mediterranean. For example, the study of the mid-Medjerda flood plain (northern Tunisia) demonstrated geomorphic stability via a period of soil formation that occurred between 6,000 and 4,700 years ago. This was followed by what the authors refer to a 'Mid-Holocene climatic collapse' (Zielhofer et al. 2004: 859) when alluvial activity increased due to an aridification of the climate (a situation where surface run-off increased due to sparse vegetation). During the Roman period, the area around the flood plain appears to have been stable, even though agricultural activity was intense. During the Roman occupation, settlement was concentrated on the flood plains and the hills of the Medjerda River catchment. Zielhofer and Faust (2003: 210) tell us that 'Archaeological evidence suggests that Roman farming techniques in North Africa were adjusted to the natural conditions'. Whilst it is unsurprising that farming settlements should be located along a fertile river catchment in an otherwise arid region, we should be wary of assertions that imply a 'natural' adjustment, when responses to and engagements with any environment are heterogeneous. There is little doubt that Roman North Africa was an extremely productive part of the Empire and that the management of the flood plain was in many ways a macro-economic success.

Urban Alluvial Geoarchaeology: Glanum, Rome, and Gordion

GLANUM

Whilst the vast majority of this book deals with rural landscapes, more often than not, floods and human responses to fluvial systems are

4.12. Glanum in Provence located within a small limestone valley that is subject to periodic flooding (photo: Lisa Rayar-Bregou).

registered in urban environments. Understandably, the probability of loss of life and damage to property is higher within urban environments than rural ones.

In the south of France, the topographical situation of Glanum proffers an interesting example. The town is located at the opening of two valleys within a complex karstic zone with plentiful water (Fig. 4.12), and has therefore always been exposed to intensive alluvial processes. These valleys were particularly susceptible to flooding from the end of the Neolithic to the end of the Iron Age (Jorda & Provansal 1989). This Iron Age town comprised features designed to mitigate flooding and conserve water for the dry periods. Basins were constructed in the Vallon Saint-Clerg during the second half of the second century BC (Agusta-Boularot & Gazenbeek 2003: 105). The construction of drainage systems was a common occurrence on many late proto-historic sites in the region. The collection and storage of water on the site was so important that the water cisterns, known as the 'nymphée', were monumental in design (Agusta-Boularot et al. 2004: 31). Another hydrological structure was the dam (built during the Roman phase of occupation) that stored water during the summer. Geomorphologists initially suggested that it did not seem logical to settle in this area, as the presence of a 'flashy' stream regime posed an obvious threat, whilst archaeologists consider that such a situation, with available water in an otherwise relatively dry landscape, was an obvious choice for a settlement (Provansal 2006). As much as any other site, Glanum emphasises the risks that people will take in order to ensure an adequate water supply, being a resource so often unpredictable across the Mediterranean.

ROME

Undoubtedly, one of the most culturally significant rivers in the Mediterranean is the Tiber. The river was fundamental for the development of Rome as an artery that facilitated links between the different parts of the city, and then beyond as the key communication route. Settlements manifestly developed along the river, beyond the walls of the city (Patterson et al. 2000) and would have been subject to flooding. However, whilst we should not underplay the impact of floods on rural communities, urban groups do not have the same flexibility of response to major floods in that they are constrained by urban space and architecture. In certain situations, rural communities can move and settle new ground, whilst city dwellers must rely on fixed technologies, planning, and rules of ownership that may or may not successfully mitigate flooding. Moreover, urban dwellers need to consider and manage processes that affect the catchment of their river, in some cases processes well beyond their control, especially if the town is within the catchment of a mountainous area, as is often the case in the Mediterranean. For example, changes in the alluvial regimes of the Central Apennines would have been important for alluvial processes downstream around Rome. Such changes have been correlated with Tiber flooding events around Rome. At Campo Imperatore, in the Central Apennines, the first terrace overlies a soil that is dated to 2830–2410 BC, and the second is dated to 190 BC–AD 10. The second terrace perhaps corresponds with the high number of historical accounts for extensive flooding from the second century BC through the second century AD. This was then followed by another phase of increased flooding from the fifth to ninth centuries AD. There is little documentary evidence for floods during the fourth and third centuries BC, nor for the third and fifth centuries AD.

It appears that the most significant floods were those that occurred during the second and first centuries BC (Giraudi 2005: 771). The location of Roman residential areas above the flood plain suggests that floods must have threatened property on a number of occasions. Moreover, certain public buildings, such as theatres and athletic centres, were situated *on* the flood plain (Heiken, Funiciello, & De Rita 2005: 63). To some extent, these were expendable, in the sense that they were not permanently occupied by large numbers of people or they were easier to protect. Over time, starting in the third century BC, the Romans constructed a major drainage system, the *Cloaca Maxima*, which took flood waters away from the city. Underground drainage systems (*Cuniculi*) were in fact initially developed by the Etruscans (Judson & Kahane 1963).

The central zone of the Tiber delta prograded between the first century BC and the first century AD, and phases of flooding here correspond with the majority of the erosion phases identified in the Tiber catchment in the Central Apennines. Consequently, environmental changes in the mountainous area were having an effect on the flood plain around Rome. As ever, the question is what caused these changes in the alluvial regime? The first candidate for any such change is an evolving glacier system that fed the catchment source. We know that the medieval glacial advances did correspond with the alluvial phases identified at Campo Imperatore and flooding of the Tiber (Giraudi 2005: 772).

Le Gall (1953) produced the first comprehensive list of floods that affected Rome. He detailed 25 floods for a 500-year period (the last 300 years of the Republic and the first two centuries of the Empire), a period which broadly corresponds with Giraudi's (2005) second century BC to second century AD alluvial phase, and activity that was probably caused by changes in the precipitation regime. Contemporary written accounts spanning 800 years describe 33 years in which floods occurred (Aldrete 2007: 14). The peak in the number of recorded floods falls between 200 BC and AD 200 (ibid.: 74). The Campus Martius (which would have included temple of Apollo and the altar of Mars) is one area that was frequently flooded. Extreme floods (20 m above sea level) would have covered many of the important parts of the city, including major political, public, and entertainment structures (Figs. 4.13 and 4.14). Most floods take place from November through to February. Frequent low-level floods (e.g. 10 m above sea level) would have a greater impact

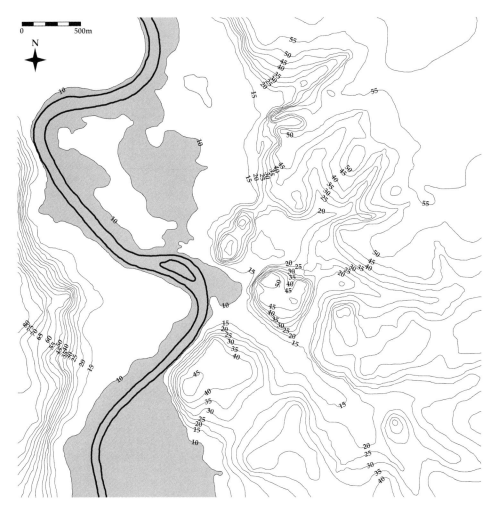

4.13. Rome with 10 m flood height indicated (by permission of G. S. Aldrete).

on the construction of environmental knowledge and concomitant mitigation strategies, not just for city dwellers, but also for those whose farmland around Rome was damaged.

The fact that the peak of settlement activity in the Tiber Valley (Patterson, di Giuseppe, & Witcher 2004) does coincide with peaks in recorded and inferred flood activity raises a number of issues. First, does the increased number of floods reflect increased reporting of such events due to high population levels and concomitant economic concerns with the impact of floods? Alternatively, if the increase in flooding was real (Giraudi 2005; Giraudi et al. 2009), then resilient forms of environmental knowledge and mitigation must have developed in the Tiber catchment

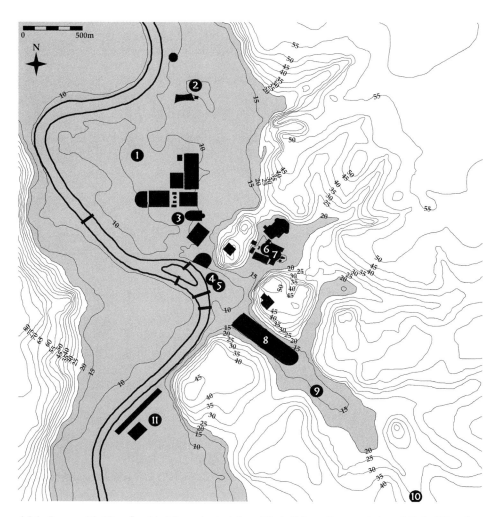

4.14. Rome with 20 m flood height and principle public buildings (by permission of G. S. Aldrete).

that permitted the maintenance of successful agricultural regimes here. Moreover, flood silts could have enhanced the agricultural potential of certain areas, rendering them more attractive.

Rome undoubtedly made the link between rainfall in the mountains and consequent flooding in Rome. Moreover, we know that a number of lakes were altered/managed as part of mitigation strategies. Ateius Capito and L. Arruntius were charged with the development of projects designed to modify the course of the Tiber and its tributaries (Leveau 2008b). Therefore, to what extent were any works concerned with the entire fluvial system? Remote sensing has shown that a Roman drainage system may have been established in the mid-Tiber Valley (De Meo et al.

2003). If the aim of river-channel and drainage-system management was to protect Rome, and thus concentrated on upstream modifications, what happened downstream? We could also consider whether settlements to the east of Rome, and towards the coast, were left to suffer the consequences of upstream mitigation strategies if the protection of Rome was the priority. One obvious outcome for the coastal zones, in particular for ports, was the coastal advancement of sediments, resulting in the silting up of these areas – a topic dealt with in the previous chapter.

Obviously, other important towns were subject to flooding. There is evidence of serious floods around Pisa during the period from the second century BC through to the fifth century AD, in particular, of levee crevassing, where high-energy events and their sediments break levees deposited on the outside of a bank. Such an event could be classed as a high-magnitude, low-frequency event, with instantaneous repercussions for people in the immediate vicinity. In this instance, the moorings in the Etruscan and then Roman harbour would have been at risk. However, despite these problems, the harbour was reused each time (Benvenuti et al. 2006). Whilst the Pisan example above gives us an insight into a Roman response to a threat posed by flooding within a fluvial setting, the response to alluvial risk across settlements is best answered through the study of archaeological sites that have obviously been affected by river systems.

GORDION

The Anatolian Iron Age city of Gordion, situated in the Sakarya Valley to the south-west of Ankara, was covered with alluvial sediments during its occupation. After its abandonment, the site was partly destroyed and buried by these alluvial processes. Situated on a flat-topped mound, there were precursors and successors to the Phrygian city, although it is the Iron Age settlement that constitutes the most significant archaeological evidence (Marsh 1999: 164). Five phases of alluvial activity that affected the site have been identified. The Iron Age city was built on a silt layer, interpreted as a palaeosol, which at that time constituted the flood plain. This may have been a rich agricultural soil, with the city expanding onto an area that had been used for agriculture. After the early Phrygian period, the river aggraded with 5 m of sediment deposited in some areas. A dated stump from the base of this unit produced a ^{14}C estimate of the seventh to sixth centuries BC (ibid.: 167). Sedimentation continued until the present day; 5 m over c. 2,500 years is not substantial, and in situations such as this, we have to ask if the sedimentation actually comprised rapid, catastrophic floods. If so, were there periods when this unit was truncated, and parts of it redeposited? Direct evidence for a response to sediment deposition takes the form of a stone 'walkway' built during the Roman period on top of a 1-m thick deposit covering a Phrygian structure, linking the site to the river. One of the most intriguing geoarchaeological elements on this site is the evidence for 'an Iron Age earth-moving project'. Here, 10 ha of artificially dumped sediment was moved from the river's edge or the river itself. Marsh interprets this as evidence of a channel-widening project. This earth could also have helped raise the next phase of construction above the flood plain (ibid.: 168). The lowest parts of the site were abandoned when this phase of aggradation was taking place. There is also evidence for floods that actually destroyed structures along the river's edge.

The examples above give some notion of the direct engagements that people have had with Mediterranean alluvial and fluvial processes. The subsequent sections deal with specific examples of how past environmental knowledge has developed vis-à-vis wetlands and associated alluvial processes.

Environmental Knowledge in Dynamic Alluvial and Wetland Zones

The Mediterranean comprises zones of plentiful or even excess water, as well as the other extreme: parched, semi-arid landscapes. Mediterranean societies have often found ways to manage and alleviate problems within these zones. In those areas where water is present in excessive quantities, such as wetlands, or where the supply of water is unreliable, settlement activity has often waxed and waned. At times, certain societies have literally moved water from one place to another – Roman aqueducts being the most prominent form of water-supply technology (Hodge 1995).

Water, in terms of its supply and movement, is perhaps the most mutable characteristic of any landscape. Rainfall patterns vary, springs can be unreliable, and rivers can flood, run still, or dry up totally. Moreover, with time, the very course of a river, or the extent and nature of a wetland can change. Here, we will consider some of the themes broached in the previous sections via assessments of environmental knowledge that

4.15. Mycenaean Bridge spanning a dried out streambed (photo: author).

have produced hybrids – technological and cultural mechanisms that
promote successful lifeways in these landscapes.

Occasionally in the Mediterranean, we come across ancient bridges
that are seemingly incongruous, as they do not span running water
(Fig. 4.15). There are three principal explanations: (1) the bridge is tra-
versing a gulley obstacle that has rarely seen running water; (2) water
flow is seasonal, largely occurring during the autumn through to spring;
(3) the watercourse has dried up. Consequently, we need to consider the
nature of the landscape at the time of construction. For example, today,
a remnant arch of Klidhi Bridge sits on the Thessaloniki Plain, Greece,
with water not having run under this bridge for some time (Ghilardi et al.
2010). The relationship of the ruins of the Roman bridge at *Simitthus*
(mid-Medjerda flood plain in northern Tunisia) with the ancient courses
of the river and the sediments deposited by these courses allows us to
consider how and when the river changed course (Zielhofer & Faust
2003: 212). The bridge appears to have been in a useable state between
AD 112 and the third century AD. As the Medjerda River meandered

during this period, it damaged the bridge, which had to be repaired on several occasions. Associated roads had to be re-routed as a consequence of changes in the river. Therefore, whilst the river clearly changed course during the period, the surrounding flood plain appears to have been stable up until the post-Roman period (ibid.).

The River Xerias ('xeros' denoting to 'dry' in Greek) on the Argos plain is an excellent example of the relationship between the physical (fluvial regime) characteristics of a watercourse and its etymology. The Xerias is a torrential river, which is often dry but has produced brutal and devastating floods in the past. Floods were of such amplitude that a series of substantial flood defence walls were established during the fifth to fourth centuries BC. The presence of a second-to-third-century AD pottery kiln near the piles of one Roman bridge indicates that this bridge must not have functioned while the kiln was in use. The presence of two first-century BC Hellenistic tombs just to the north of another 'fossilised' Roman bridge indicates the presence of an ancient arm of the Xerias (Fouache 1999: 176–7). Bridge redundancy is a function of not only a change in channel position, but also changes in climate that comprise a reduction in rainfall as well as changes to spring outflows. Redundancy might only be seasonal in many Mediterranean landscapes, with some watercourses traversable on foot during the summer months, and some bridges serving during periods of water flow, normally between the autumn and spring. The seasonal variation of hydrologic processes is a fundamental agency in the development of human–environment interactions and the cyclical nature of cultural and economic activity.

There is substantial spatial and temporal variability in flooding (and the consequences of floods), especially in areas such as south-east Spain (Hooke 2006: 313). As with all environmental processes, temporal cycles of varying length are crucial to the human experience of these. One fundamental problem that all palaeoenvironmental scientists and archaeologists must confront is that of teasing out weather events from climate (average temperatures and rainfall). The intra-annual temporal spread of rainfall will influence the probability of flooding and erosion events. If, within two separate years, the same annual rainfall is measured, but in one of those years, that rainfall is concentrated within a small number of high-magnitude events, then these events will result in much higher levels of flooding and erosion (Wittenberg et al. 2007).

We need to consider the notion that riverside sites were a corollary of so-called Holocene climatic stability (Burroughs 2005: 245). Whilst proxy records may indicate the possibility or even probability of relative stability, we cannot be sure to what extent the weather was stable and predictable. The evidence for flooding on many sites needs to be considered within the context of how hazards (and risks) were assessed in the past. The greater cycles of alluvial time are comprised of shorter, annual cycles which include seasonal, low-level floods associated with autumn storms, then summer drying of seasonal watercourses and the spring melt waters and rains refilling the rivers. However, we must ask to what extent were people aware of high-magnitude event cycles and possessed a notion that was in any way similar to the modern assessment of cyclical events as falling within a defined cycle (such as so-called 50- or 500-year events).

In central Spain, there were periods with 'clusters' of floods on the Tagus River. The fact that floods tend to cluster is of profound importance for any attempt to understand cycles of human response. It is apparent that there were periods when the probability of a flood occurring was relatively high. Therefore, we might expect to be able to identify phases of human responsiveness to the clustered flood regimes (Benito et al. 2003). It is unclear as to whether flood frequency increases during periods of a colder, wetter climate or during periods of climatic warming. There is no doubt that floods occur under both of these regimes. One climatically driven scenario is founded on the correlation between Atlantic-influenced and Mediterranean-influenced river systems across Spain. Here, the Middle to Late Holocene periods, centred on 2820–2440 BC and 865–350 BC, are characterised by increased flooding. Despite the difference in the flood-producing weather conditions characteristic of the Atlantic and Mediterranean hydro-climatic regions, the radiocarbon date clusters do coincide over the last 3,000 years (Benito et al. 2008: 75). The 2820–2440 BC phase is characterised as a 'warming-dry period' when flooding appears to have been common. As far as past people were concerned, it may well have been sudden, high-magnitude events that were more of a threat. This type of event is not necessarily identified within slackwater deposits (ibid.).

HUMAN ENGAGEMENTS WITH MEDITERRANEAN WETLANDS
Archaeological research in Mediterranean wetlands reveals the development of certain forms of environmental knowledge and historical

ecologies. The evidence from some wetlands allows us to assess responses to environmental processes, thus showing that we cannot necessarily identify a homogenous wetland cultural ecology for any period in the past.

We have to assess the hierarchy or ordering of these ecologies, and how ideological and political processes directly influence this layering. This form of characterisation is referred to as 'Panarchy' by resilience theorists, where Panarchy describes cross-scale interactions, wherein 'the resilience of a system at a particular focal scale will depend on the influences from states and dynamics at different spatial and temporal scales. For example, external oppressive politics, invasions, market shifts, or global climate...' (Walker et al. 2004: 5). In addition, social elites may have one view of how an environment operates and should be managed, whilst those who actually live and work in that environment have different, spatially specific forms of environmental knowledge. These notions inform the assessments of wetland landscapes presented below.

Some of the most ancient evidence for human management of hydrologic processes comes from the Peloponnese and central Greece. These areas comprise the full range of characteristics discussed so far in this chapter: rivers, springs (on karst topography), wetlands, and semi-arid areas. Possibly the oldest (functioning) piece of hydraulic engineering in Europe is that associated with the Bronze Age city of Tiryns on the Argive Plain. Here, a large dam was constructed in order to divert a watercourse, and protect the city from flooding. This system also comprised an artificial canal which was about 1.5 km long (Zangger 2001: 127). A very different problem characterised the area around Copais in central Greece. This riverless zone once had lakes and a wetland that covered an area of 150 km². Here, the Myceneans constructed a drainage system designed to reclaim land and perhaps reduce the risk of disease. During the fourteenth and thirteenth centuries BC, they constructed a canal on the northern edge of the plain. This canal was some 25 km long, 40 m wide, and 2–3 m deep. It transported water from several different watercourses away from this zone (ibid.: 130). Looking at specific areas around the lake, it seems that places, such as the Kephissos Valley, were drained naturally or via human intervention (Farinetti 2009: 105), leaving behind some areas of good-quality agricultural land. According to Strabo, the waters of Lake Copais threatened the town of Copai. The natural sinkholes around this, and other lakes, were often blocked by sediment, thus resulting in the raising of water levels. The area around the lake was occupied since at least the Neolithic, followed by a substantial increase in activity during the Late Helladic period. Recent work suggests successful and extensive drainage of the area centred on the Mycenaean fortress of Gla. Two key elements constituted by the north and south canals diverted the course of the river along the extreme north and southern edges of the lake, the aim being to force these waters to run into the katavothrai (sinkholes) (Iakovidis 2001: 155). The structures associated with the management of the lake (Cyclopean-style dykes) tend to be dated to the fourteenth and thirteenth centuries BC (Knauss 1985). The aim of the management scheme was not only to limit the extent of flood waters, but also to create new agricultural land. A catastrophic event might have taken place at the end of the Late Helladic period. Some have argued that the lake may well have suddenly emptied via the katavothres during the Hellenistic period, in particular at around 338 BC. This could have left behind a disease-ridden marsh (Châtelain 2007: 212). However, extensive research employing GIS analyses of site distributions and reconstructions of the past lake extent do not really support this (Farinetti 2009).

One Greek lake and wetland that has seen important transformations over time is Stymphalos. Modern Stymphalos is situated in the Arcadian Mountains. Best known as the site of Heracles' sixth labour of killing the Stymphalian birds, the remains of the mountain city of Stymphalos are situated on the edge of the lake. However, the location of the first early city (c. 700–375 BC) (Gourley & Williams 2005) is unknown. The lake at Stymphalos is a dynamic and hybrid water system – enigmatic as both a natural and cultural feature. The waxing and waning of the lake has been controlled by a complex series of natural processes as well as technological interventions, including management of the sinkhole on the southern edge of the lake. The lake is largely fed by a series of springs along its northern edge, the ancient town having been built around some of these springs (Fig. 4.16). Other springs are situated along a line higher up the south-facing slopes of the mountains that define the northern edge of the Stymphalos area. The precise nature of the links between the Stymphalos, Scotini, and Alea poljes has interested archaeologists and geologists alike. The subterranean routes followed by these channels emerge at the Kephalovryso and Douka Vryssi springs and in the Inachos River valley (Crouch 2004: 115; Morfis et al. 1985) (Fig. 4.17).

4.16. The ancient city (top) and spring (bottom) at Lake Stymphalos (Peloponnese, Greece). Whilst wetlands might harbour disease, the benefits provided by a guaranteed water-supply are obvious. Moreover, the ritual/cultural importance of water and springs contributes to settlement persistence in many areas such as this (photos: author).

The flow of water is considered intermittent. However, these processes are poorly understood. Today's wetland is an artefact of centuries of human manipulation and management. Moreover, its modern character-istics might lead us to believe that water has been incessantly bountiful,

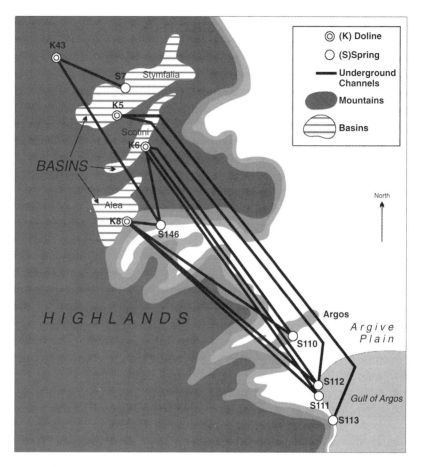

4.17. The karst-spring subterranean network of the north-west Peloponnese –
Underground connections between Tripoli Plain and Argolis coast springs. (By permission
of Oxford University Press, Crouch, D. P. (2004), *Geology and Settlement: Greco-Roman
Patterns*, fig. 4.2.)

accessible, and easy to manage, and that agriculture in this landscape has
always been a relatively straightforward endeavour.

Whereas pre-Roman management of the lake and springs probably
did take place, the first incontrovertible evidence for intervention in the
system dates to the second century AD, when the lake level was controlled through the construction of an aqueduct that provided water to
the major city of Corinth 45 km to the north-east. There is no doubt that
large fluctuations in the water level occurred before this date, as coring
undertaken in the area presents a history of changes in lake level going
back through the Holocene (Brown & Walsh, forthcoming; Unkel et al.
2011).

The hydrological importance of Stymphalos would have been transformed during the Roman period when the Hadrianic aqueduct to supply water for Corinth was built. The manipulation of this plentiful water supply (more specifically, the spring at Driza, just to the north of Lake Stymphalos; Lolos 1997: 276) by Roman technology altered the very nature and meaning of water at Stymphalos. Local people's engagement with the lake and surrounding springs and their associations with sanctuaries and deities would have changed. The capture of this source must have regulated inputs into the lake and certain components of the hydrological system around Stymphalos. Such a structure not only created a physical link between the source and consumers of the water (in this instance Corinth), but it may well have also changed the nature of cultural and ideological links between the source area and the consuming city. This change in a community's or society's relationship with water would have been true in any landscape where such a feat of hydraulic engineering had been undertaken. In Greece alone, there were about 25 aqueducts, plus a dozen across the Greek islands (ibid.: 303–12).

HYDROMYTHOLOGY

Perhaps more than any other cultural feature, the sanctuary articulates a hybrid or intersection of economic, religious, and environmental processes within a landscape. As Jost (1996: 217) argues for Arcadia, '... certain places seem destined to be considered sacred, and certain types of landscape attract cults of one divinity rather than another'. Springs are of particular importance, and there is no denying the influence that the distribution (across both time and space) of water has on all aspects of life. In addition, the deities associated with flooding are another vital component in many classical landscapes. The plains of eastern Arcadia comprise a calcareous soil covered with clay and alluvium that does not drain well, and it is the limestone fissures (the katavothra) that provide a natural drainage system. Thus, these natural features are managed, and were often associated with Artemis (a goddess associated with dampness) as well as Poseidon. Artemis was celebrated as the goddess of the marshland at Stymphalos (ibid.: 220).

There is no doubt that hydrological processes and their associated landscapes were understood via forms of environmental knowledge that were different to our own. However, one characteristic that is as true in the past as it is today is the fact that environmental knowledge varies depending on one's role within society. For Herodotus, a marshland was a veritable ecosystem, characterised by its flora and fauna. A marshland could be seen as a contact zone between two opposite types of water (saline and fresh), or a wetland could be the product of a river having retreated. Herodotus also noted the 'calmness of waters, where there is an absence of activity; a sleeping body of water' (Châtelain 2007: 30–1). Human engagement with any environment is constructed via different forms of environmental knowledge, and these vary not only across the different layers of society but also across time. Moreover, environmental knowledge of rivers and wetlands would have been partly constituted by mythological characterisations of these features and associated characters from the myths. There are some 30 important 'mythological' rivers in Greece. 'The mountains formed an important part of the mythological landscape but they remained inanimate, whereas the rivers were characters in the myths, often their protagonists, as well as essential features of the scenery' (Brewster 1997: 2–3).

Knowledge of environmental potential is partly influenced by the cultural and cosmological ideas associated with a given landscape type. In the ancient world, these were mediated via mythical-religious processes and manifestations (deities, shrines, temples, and stories) (Clendenon 2009; Retallack 2008). There are a number of mythological references to Mediterranean wetlands that imply that these areas were considered repulsive or problematic. The depictions of Heracles slaying the multi-headed serpent of Hydra on Corinthian pottery dating to the period c. 630–570 BC may well be a reference to attempts to drain Marshes at Lerna in the Argolid (Grmek & Gourevitch 1998). Also, the slaying of the birds at the lake at Stymphalos (Heracles' sixth labour) can be interpreted as a metaphor for the dangers associated with wetlands. The possibility that Heracles was (or represents) an infamous hydrological/agricultural engineer of sorts is another intriguing perspective (Châtelain 2007). There is little doubt that drainage was a problem at Stymphalos, rendering use of the land difficult. One myth refers to the blocking of the lake's sinkhole – considered to have been the result of Artemis's actions. She had been angered by the Stymphalians who had stopped worshipping her, and also because their use of the land had damaged the preferred environment of the animals dear to Artemis (Burford 1993: 165). This intersection of mythological narratives – archaeological and environmental proxy data – allows us to address how environmental knowledge may have varied across time and space. This in turn informs our (pre)historical ecological assessment, as myths, albeit unverifiable or even unlikely as actual historic events, do articulate understanding, and therefore possible engagements between peoples and wetlands that have resulted in their modern-day characteristics.

The Pontine Marshes: Roman 'Relationships' with a Wetland

One of the most famous Mediterranean wetlands is the Pontine Marshes, an area that probably did witness a waxing and waning of human activity for much of the Holocene. Roman interventions in this landscape have been much discussed, and a brief overview is presented here.

The Mezzaluna core (from the north-eastern part of the Pontine plain) gives us an indication of how this landscape developed prior to the Roman period. The palaeoecological evidence points towards the development of macchia-type vegetation from c. 4,500 years ago, with alder carr and willow implying the presence of a relatively humid area at the start of the first millennium BC. Other palynological evidence implies the development of cereal growth from the Late Bronze Age (Attema, Burgers, & van Leusen 2010: 35–6). The core from the Lago di Fogliano suggests some agricultural activities around this lake from the Early Bronze Age, and the gradual drying of the lake starting at the end of the Bronze Age or the start of the Iron Age. The Roman period saw the emergence of a drier agricultural zone, with some evidence for olive cultivation on the Mont Lepini slopes (ibid.: 154). During the fifth and fourth centuries BC, Roman colonies were established along the hilltops of the Lepine scarp on the north-east edge of the Pontine. Roman colonisation changed the Pontine region from a sparsely settled and unmanaged environment into a landscape that saw dense settlement in some areas (Attema & Delvigne 2000). The lower graben zone is only about 1 m above sea level, and constitutes the core zone of the Pontine Marshes. Despite this inherent environmental disadvantage, the area was settled at the end of the fourth century BC. Although the chronology for centuriation is not entirely clear, it would probably have post-dated this fourth-century settlement (de Haas 2011). Attema and Delvigne (2000) argue that the alluvial plain was given to the Setia colonists to cultivate in the early fourth century BC, a period when parts of the Pontine landscape appear to have been organised, with the construction of the Via Appia and possibly the digging of the Decennovium Canal. This zone could have furnished agricultural plots for up to 46,000 colonists, suggesting the development of intensive cultivation. During the early Republican period, the Pontine area was identified as a potentially productive landscape, and settlement was encouraged. As with most ecologically heterogeneous landscapes, certain areas were recognised as being useful for specific activities. The central part of this zone, where there is a dearth of evidence for settlement activity, probably functioned as common grazing (de Haas 2011: 167).

A dramatic decline in settlement on the wetland area took place at some point during the Imperial period with 50% of sites having disappeared by the first century AD, earlier than the decline seen along the adjacent coastal zone (Attema, de Haas, & Gol 2011). The contraction of activity on the Pontine Marshes might in part have been the consequence of wider changes in economic and concomitant settlement patterns. The possibility that changes in tax regimes and the economic costs associated with 'marginal' landscapes rendered certain areas economically unattractive is something that we should consider as part of the assessment of interaction with any environment. There is, however, little doubt that the Pontine area did witness environmental problems. It has been argued that the attempt at draining the area by M. Cornelius Cethegus in 160 BC was not successful in ridding the area of malaria (or other diseases) (Sallares 2002: 185). After the widespread settlement activity across the Pontine Marshes during the Republican period, it appears that settlement was subsequently concentrated along the via Appia and on the higher grounds. Drainage was clearly an unrelenting problem, and the area was described as unhealthy by Vitruvius in the late first century, and the term Pomptinae Paludes was used for the first time in the mid-first century by Lucanus (de Haas 2011: 207). After the first century AD, only the higher areas to the south-west were settled. This appears to support the notion that deteriorating environmental conditions were a serious influence on settlement activity. On one site in the south-western area, there is evidence that soil brought in from elsewhere was added before construction (ibid.: 10). Therefore, even on higher zones, there may have been difficulties in draining the land.

One important management technique that may have been applied by the Romans is that of colmatage (the controlled flow of water containing sediment which would fill and render a wetland exploitable). It has been assumed that colmatage was understood by Roman engineers, but there is no clear evidence of its employment on the Pontine wetlands (de Haas 2011: 214). Accepting that there were periods when the Pontine Marshes, or parts of them, were successfully managed, settled, and exploited, we should not forget that life in such an environment can be rendered difficult by disease. Even if malaria is not present, the continual discomfort caused by insects, especially mosquitoes, is something that we should not make light of.

WETLANDS AND DISEASE

There is little doubt that if there is one characteristic of Mediterranean wetlands that constituted a foundation for the construction of environmental knowledge, then it must be the potential for disease in these areas. The integration of landscape ecology and epidemiology recognises that human activity has often been associated with the development of diseases (Balée 2006: 87). Societies develop responses to disease at the local level as well as at the macro-political level. Sometimes these responses actually help generate or propagate the disease.

Mosquito infestation and the possibility of malaria are of course considered the most repellent characteristic of wetlands. A virulent form of malaria may well have been present in Greece by the eighth century BC (Sallares 2002: 22). Whilst Sallares (2002: 33) considers that the three species of malaria that pose a real threat to humans could have been brought into Europe by Neolithic farmers, there is no incontrovertible proof of this, and Packard (2007: 35) considers that its arrival in southern Europe may not have occurred before the first millennium BC. The paucity of direct evidence for malaria in ancient populations is problematic, although David Soren (2003) has argued for the impact of malaria on a population at the site of Lugnano in Teverina, Umbria. There are a number of diseases, such as leptospirosis, that are difficult to distinguish, and malaria per se might not have been the principal threat.

Despite the problems differentiating between different diseases common in wetlands, we should accept that any such illnesses would have radically altered the nature of human lifeways in and perceptions of these environments, with direct consequences for the development of environmental knowledge in these landscapes. Pliny the Elder recommended that farms should not be located close to marshes nor rivers

(Plin. Nat. 18.7, Pliny the Elder 2009). Relatively minor changes in climate or even in interannual weather patterns will have altered the potential for malaria or other diseases such as leptospirosis, where the frequency of infected bodies of water increases. The warm period during the first centuries BC and AD (along with the evidence for flooding in a number of Mediterranean wetland zones) does suggest that conditions for disease vectors would have been ideal. Research on contemporary risks as they relate to changes in climate demonstrates how an increase in temperature along with presence of standing water increases the season for mosquito activity and thereby the transmission of the malaria parasite (Sainz-Elipe et al. 2010). Deforestation does of course increase a landscape's exposure to insolation, and thereby overall ground temperature will increase, thus enhancing the vectors for these diseases. Moreover, deforestation can change hydrological systems, even increasing the presence of run-off and resultant zones of standing water. Consequently, these changes in the environment caused by deforestation may well have provided new niches for mosquitoes and bacteria (YaSuouka & Levins 2007). The palynological evidence for the Tiber delta implies that such processes were common in the wider region, with specific evidence from Stagno di Maccarese suggesting that the lake level here was lower during the Iron Age to Roman period, and a marshland environment developed (Di Rita, Celant, & Magri 2009).

Whereas archaeologists tend to identify cultural processes that relate to settlement and economic trajectories in landscapes, and concomitant management practices associated with these activities, we should also consider how environmental knowledge relating to disease mitigation developed over time. For example, most adaptations to malaria appear to have been biological and genetic (Sabbatani, Manfredi, & Fiorino 2010: 78). Changes in diet, which could have included the increased consumption of broad beans, may also have helped. In addition, increased consumption of milk and milk-based products may have been beneficial. There may even have been some understanding of the difference between the two principal forms of malaria present during the Roman period. Celsus (a physician who lived during the first half of the first century AD) may even have diagnosed the different clinical courses of *Plasmodium falciparum*-related fever and the *Plasmodium vivax*-related disease, which is less threatening (ibid.: 70).

Discussion: Responses to Hydrological Variability

The response of different societies to fluvial risk allows us to consider the fundamental issue of instrumental versus intrinsic values in that society's attitude towards nature. Unsurprisingly, Roman urban planning and rural engineering often managed fluvial risk through the location of buildings away from hazardous areas, or the protection of these areas with banks and dykes, or the management of wetlands via drainage programmes. However, there were periods (especially towards the end of the Roman period) when these management systems either failed or were not maintained. For example, the sewers in Arles (south of France) appear not to have been cleared out from the third century AD onwards, a time when the city fell into political decline (Bruneton et al. 2001). Recent excavations in this city have revealed arches parallel with Rhône, built on the bank of the river that had not been settled prior to Rome's arrival in the region (Isoardi 2010a, 2010b). These arches increase in size towards the interior of the town. The river flowed through the arches from the river towards the town, and the arches thus reduced the velocity and strength of flood waters. There is a possibility that flood waters damaged arches during one flood event. What is more interesting is the fact that the different flood deposits do not seem to have been cleared away after each event, thus gradually reducing the efficiency of the arch system (Fig. 4.18). We have to ask why these deposits were not cleared away. In some ways, this lack of maintenance and mitigation is uncharacteristic of Roman engineers and managers.

Evidence from rural wetland sites also reveals histories of flooding or even destruction. The remedial construction of flood defences is not just a spontaneous response to an environmental event, but demonstrates awareness that an event will/can repeat itself. For example, at Le Carrelet (a vicus on the Camargue, south of France), there is evidence for the placement of boulders along the riverbank which should be seen as part of a response to the threat of flooding (Arnaud-Fassetta & Landuré 2003). This may not have been enough to protect the site, as the presence of silt layers attest to frequent flooding across the settlement (Excoffon et al. 2004: 218). This site did, however, experience a serious flood at some point during the second half of the first century BC, and was then abandoned up until the first century AD. Such actions represent forms of environmental prediction that ultimately contribute

4.18. Excavation of riverbank arches on the Rhône in the City of Arles (south of France) (excavation: D. Isoardi). Note the build-up of sedimentary units comprising Roman archaeological material. The flooding events are dated by archaeological material from the latter half of the first century AD onwards. N.B. This site is now situated within the cellars of a riverside building in the modern centre of Arles (photo: author).

to socio-environmental resilience (Westley et al. 2002). Whilst we might assume that the responses and application of environmental knowledge in the urban milieu would have been quite different to those developed in rural areas, there is evidence for flood defences being constructed in the rural landscape, perhaps mirroring a 'Roman' way of doing things. The transfer of urban environmental knowledge to rural areas, and vice versa, is a characteristic of certain complex societies, and perhaps nowhere more so than in the Roman world. However, such responses may well be maladaptive, and there are certain environments where technological solutions are doomed to failure.

The application of environmental knowledge to a landscape problem is in part constituted by the assessment of risk, that is, the likelihood of a project's success. Such an assessment is not purely instrumental, but also comprises intrinsic cultural, religious, and ideological notions. The transformation of a wetland may render it more meaningful. This may be true if we are merely concerned with the productive value of a place. However, landscapes, especially wetlands, can be meaningful and be characterised by a form of environmental knowledge that is constituted by mythological and ideological notions (Baylis-Smith & Golson 2004). Whilst the draining of an area or the construction of flood defences clearly have an instrumentally rational aspect, the manner in which they were conceived of and enacted would have undoubtedly included pleadings and offerings to the relevant deities. For example, one Roman rite comprised pre-construction auguring that included the examination of livestock livers for discolouration (i.e. liver fluke). If such discolouration was present, this indicated poor-quality wet pasture, and therefore building should not take place (Polio 2005). As such, this constitutes the combination of pertinent environmental knowledge and ritual with a view to making a judgement vis-à-vis economic potential and quality of life within a specific landscape type.

The investigation of fluvial and alluvial systems, and an understanding of humanity's engagement with those systems, has to consider the complexity of tectonic processes, local geomorphology, climate change (and weather cycles), and then the range of human uses and management of these varied environments. Moreover, the cultural and mythological dimensions associated with water cannot be forgotten, as these constitute part of the environmental knowledge that underpins human understanding of and engagements with bodies of water, whether these be the mysterious vanishing and re-emerging of springs or wetlands characterised by their almost incongruous mix of bountiful resources and dormant disease.

The mutability of alluvial and fluvial systems in terms of their changing courses and extent is an ever-present characteristic that Mediterranean peoples have always had to deal with, with such changes engendering variations in human movement and mobility, activities, practices, and cultic rites.

Although much alluvial geoarchaeology does present human activity as a process that contributes to changes in alluvial systems, some have developed specifically archaeological approaches, where archaeological and geoarchaeological evidence are combined in an assessment of human engagements with the landscape. Zangger's (2001: ch. 6) study of technological solutions to alluvial sedimentation problems on the

Argive plain contributes to the discussion of people/landscape dynamics. Even though such research addresses human responses to environmental change within a framework of means-ends rationale, where the success of an economic system is the paramount aim, it does allow us to move away from the traditional geoarchaeological analysis of cause and effect within the sedimentary system. We should also consider how changes in river regime would have affected other resources. Something that is rarely considered is the importance of freshwater fish. As Sternberg demonstrates, this lack of interest in freshwater fish is also reflected in the classical texts. It is only really from the fourth century onwards that freshwater fish are regularly mentioned in economic records as commercialised foodstuffs (Sternberg 2004: 185). Whilst fish were kept in artificial fishponds (Higginbotham 1997), it is also interesting to consider how variations in fluvial action, water flow, oxygenation, temperature, and so on have a profound influence on the potential range of species found in a river. The hydrological regime at the river mouth (salinity levels) also have a profound influence on the species present. These changes in hydrological regime and their influence on fish in the past is clearly another area of study that could develop in the future.

As archaeologists, we must explicitly adopt a nested temporal and spatial framework in the assessment of human interaction with alluvial and fluvial environments. Long-term, landscape-wide alluvial histories clearly have their place, but at the same time, we should strategically adopt methodologies that allow the identification of alluvial units on or abutting archaeological sites. This then facilitates the identification of any possible human response to these environmental events and thus enhances our ability to discuss the range of possible relationships between society and alluvial processes through time.

5

Environmental Change: Degradation and Resilience

One abiding theme running through Mediterranean landscape research is that of environmental degradation (Conacher & Sala 1998). This and the following chapter consider a range of data from across the region in an assessment of evidence for landscape change, degradation, and resilience. This chapter presents some syntheses of vegetation and erosional histories within a perspective that questions the notion of landscape deterioration, but at the same time considers the nature of human engagements with the landscape (see Fig. 5.1 for sites referred to in this chapter).

The examples and case studies take us across the Mediterranean in a broadly east to west direction, with the final case study from Spain presenting a more detailed analysis of human–environmental interactions in that area.

Approaches and Research Questions

As we have seen already, a fundamental debate concerns the evidence for climate versus human impact on Mediterranean landscapes. The variability of climate change across space and time is the only constant; phases of stability exist but are often interrupted or punctuated. Perhaps most importantly, we cannot easily tease apart the relative importance of anthropogenic impact upon the landscape versus that caused by climate (Allen 2001: 39–40).

For a number of decades, palaeoenvironmental research has emphasised the identification of periods of environmental stability and instability that take place within an underlying trend of environmental deterioration, with the term 'environmental crisis' liberally employed. Whilst

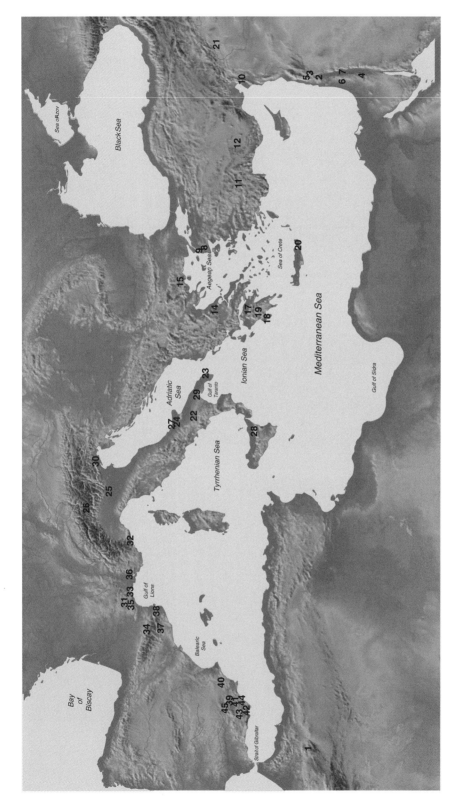

5.1. Map of sites referred to in this chapter. 1: Middle Atlas Mountains, 2: Sea of Galilee, 3: Golan Heights, 4: Negev, 5: Hula Valley and at Tel Yosef in the Harod Valley, 6: Southern Shefela/Tell es-Safi/Gathin in Israel, 7: Dead Sea, 8: The Troad, 9: Kumptepe/Troy, 10: Amuq plain, 11: Gravgaz/Çanakh Lake, 12: Çatalhöyük, 13: Franchthi Cave, 14: Larissa basin/Sesklo, 15: Phlippi plain, 16: Argolid, 17: Phlious basin/Nemea, 18: Pylos/Palace of Nestor, 19: Lousios gorge at Górtys (about 40 km to the south-east of Olympia, on the Peloponnese), 20: Siteia mountains/Karphi/Kavousi, 21: Gobekli Tepe, 22: Laghi di Monticchio, 23: Lago Almini Piccolo, Apulia, 24: Tavoliere plain, 25: Terramare, on the Po plain, 26: Lago Lucone, 27: Biferno Valley, 28: Troina, 29: Basilicata, 30: Palù di Livenza, 31: Languedoc, 32: Etoile, 33: Lattes/Marsillargues, 34: Balma Margineda, 35: Grotte Camprafaud, 36: Glanum, 37: Llobregat River, 38: Banyoles, 39: Segura Mountains, 40: Alicante Province/Polop Alto Valley, 41: Rambla Guadalentín River/Campico De Labor and La Bastida/El Culantrillo, 42: Almería/Los Millares, 43: Alpujarra, 44: Gatas, 45: Castellon Alto.

this approach no longer underpins modern ecological thinking, many archaeologists and some palaeoenvironmental scientists have perpetuated a discourse that emphasises notions of degradation and marginality. Despite this, notions of 'resilience' and 'persistence' have come to the fore in recent years (e.g. Redman 2005), and some archaeologists have developed narratives that move beyond the archetypal scientific assessment of human interaction with landscapes and their sediments (e.g. Jusseret 2010).

THE PHYTOLOGICAL CONTEXT

Sclerophyllous vegetation (plants with tough, leathery leaves on evergreen trees/plants) is dominant across the Mediterranean (Blondel et al. 2010: ch. 6). Whilst the distribution and characteristics of this vegetation today are a product of Holocene climate change and human impact (partly a consequence of early farmers clearing the existing forest) (Pons & Quézel 1998), sclerophyllous vegetation has existed in parts of the Mediterranean throughout the Pleistocene. These plants are considered to have adapted to the long (arid) summers that characterise the Mediterranean, their leaves possessing low surface-to-volume ratios, thus conserving water (Blondel et al. 2010: ch. 8). Many of the sclerophyllous species occupy thermo-Mediterranean zones, that is, areas that are below 700 m and generally towards the Southern Mediterranean. These areas are characterised by hot summers and clement winters. Vegetation histories obviously vary across the region and are the product of changes in climate and human activity, as well as underlying geological and topographical contexts. Figure 5.2 gives one example of such geographical variation, comparing Spain and the south of France (de Beaulieu et al. 2005).

Vegetation degradation is not a linear process but is characterised by fluctuations, with vegetation cover waxing and waning as part of managed ecosystems that are occasionally pushed into disequilibrium (Blumler 2007). In a similar vein, a focus on the identification of the start of severe erosion is in some ways problematic, as many badlands existed well before the development of agriculture in the Mediterranean (Mather 2009: 18), though the contribution of people in the initiation of erosion in places around the Mediterranean is undeniable, albeit historically contingent.

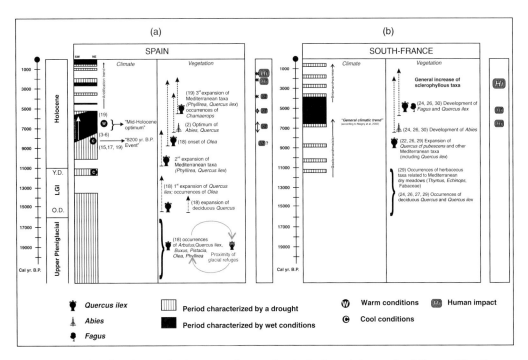

5.2. The glacial and Holocene development of vegetation in Spain and the south of France. The diagram represents the variations in influence of climate and human activity upon the vegetation of these two regions. (By permission of Taylor & Francis: Alpes méridonales françaises, Université Aix-Marseille III: de Beaulieu, J. L., Y. Miras, V. Andrieu-Ponel, & F. Guiter (2005), Vegetation dynamics in north-western Mediterranean regions: Instability of the Mediterranean bioclimate. Plant Biosystems – An International Journal Dealing with all Aspects of Plant Biology, 139(2), 114–26. Figure 2. Instability of the Mediterranean bioclimate: overview proposed for Spain and France (a) and Italy (b). p. 117.)

The Fall from Eden

The evolution of Mediterranean forests is characterised by continual change, even without the presence of sustained and profound human impact. For this reason, the first part of this chapter considers evidence for both vegetation change and periods of geomorphic stability (soil development or absence of evidence for erosion) and instability (phases of erosion). This is followed by an assessment of how people and climate have influenced these developments.

LANDSCAPE CHANGE AROUND THE MEDITERRANEAN

Landscape degradation normally comprises two key stages: vegetation loss and then concomitant exposure of soil to potential erosion via the impact of people, rainfall, and gravity. The importance of vegetation cover in controlling erosion cannot be understated, and has been the

5.3. An eroded zone where vegetation loss has exposed soil and sediment to rainfall and resulted in colluviation (the movement of a soil and sediment due to gravity and the movement of water across a land surface) (photo: author).

subject of much research (Kosmas et al. 2002) (Fig. 5.3). Vegetation, including stem density and leaf litter, protects the soil in a number ways: it prevents rain splash and shade from vegetation reduces evapotranspiration, and it contributes to organic matter (Thornes 1987: 43). It is important to note that the presence of high levels of tree pollen in a pollen diagram necessarily represents extensive tree cover and thereby protection for the underlying soil. Many Mediterranean landscapes will comprise patches of shrubby trees within areas of relatively exposed soil. Grassland or dense growth of weeds and shrubs offer more protection to the soil than sclerophyllous woodland.

Grove and Rackham (2001: 8–9) argued that the contemporary view of a degraded Mediterranean was in essence an eighteenth-century myth, based on a romantic view of pristine ancient landscapes. Forbes (2000: 98–9) demonstrates how, in modern times, some northern and western observers have tended to criticise the purportedly ill-considered landscape-management strategies developed by supposedly unthinking, exploitative Mediterranean peasants. There have, in fact, been successful management strategies during the recent historical period, and '...over-exploitation and degradation of grazing resources have simply not been an option' (ibid.: 107). Soil erosion and related environmental stresses can limit the economic potential of certain landscapes (or parts of them), but any limitations are dependent on the level of technology that a society can employ in the improvement of land or mitigation of environmental problems.

The first key stage in the development of what we consider today as typical Mediterranean landscapes, and thus a precursor to extensive erosion, was the development of shrublands. These are essentially scrub formations and possess different names across the region, such as *maquis* in France (and Israel), *mattoral* and *tomillares* in Spain, and *macchia* in Italy (Di Castri 1981: 3). The emergence of such areas of 'degraded' vegetation is an important part of the story of Mediterranean vegetation, as is the nature of human impact on plants and, in particular, how people have exploited these zones once the pre-existing woodland was replaced by scrub formations or shrublands (Blondel et al. 2010: 122–3).

Shrublands are a testament to human use of the Mediterranean landscape more than any other element in the region, although some types of high maquis might be considered as climax vegetation (Tomaselli 1981: 119). However, the fact that similar vegetation communities are found in other Mediterranean climate areas (*Chaparral* in California and *Fynbos* in South Africa) where there is less human impact suggests that some of these communities represent deflected climax vegetation. Sclerophyllous vegetation developed along the Mediterranean coast about 6,000 years ago, but the presence of xeric vegetation is not necessarily a direct result of human-induced degradation (Collins, Davis, & Kaplan 2012). Moreover, the arrival of this vegetation is not a precursor to irreversible degradation. In fact, there is a case for the strong influence of human-management strategies actually contributing to vegetation resilience – a relationship that built up during the Holocene. In similar Mediterranean-type landscapes, such as California, this resilience is not apparent, as strong human–ecological relations did not develop (Naveh 2004).

The basic evolution of Holocene Mediterranean vegetation starts with certain plants spreading from local refugia in response to warmer and

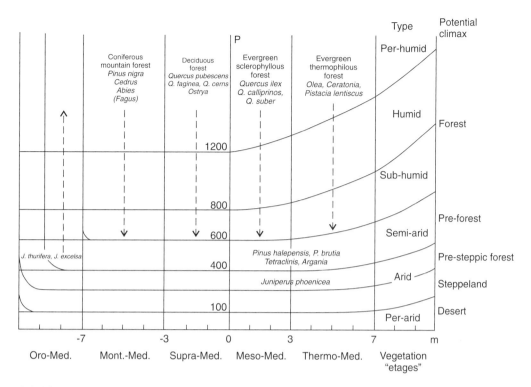

5.4. The distribution of vegetation communities across different Mediterranean topographies (By permission of J. Wiley, Quézel, P. (2005), Large-scale post-glacial distribution of vegetation structures in the Mediterranean region, in *Recent Dynamics of the Mediterranean Vegetation and Landscape*, fig. 1.1.)

more humid conditions right from the start of the late glacial interstadial (Bølling) about 14,000 years ago. Evidence from fossil records, DNA, and ecological modelling suggest that all the southern peninsulas were refuge areas for temperate trees during the last glacial period (López de Heredia et al. 2007; Tzedakis 2009). From about 9,000 years ago, communities that spread from the south-east of the Mediterranean across the region then complemented these initial vegetation structures. These new vegetation structures varied across the region and changed with altitude within relatively small subregions.

We should not forget that the Mediterranean is bounded by mountains and that vegetation characteristics change radically with altitude (discussed in more detail in Chapter 8) (Fig. 5.4). Three main types of Mediterranean forest can be identified: sclerophyllous, broadleaved, and coniferous (largely present in mountainous areas) (see Table 5.1 for the chronology of some of these developments). In the Western Mediterranean, these forests tend to comprise *Quercus ilex* (holm oak),

Table 5.1. Key climatic and vegetation phases from around the Mediterranean.

Broad chronological phase	c. 6200 BC ('Rapid Climate Change Event')	4500–3000 BC	c. 2000 BC	c. 1500 BC	c. 0 AD
North Africa	Middle Atlas Mountains dominated by *Quercus canariensis* (Early Holocene). General aridification of North Africa and Middle East c. 6000 BC (Dusar et al. 2011). Libyan Sahara: wet conditions 4900–4400 BC (Cremaschi & Di Lernia 1999).	Decline in Quercus, increase in Poaceae. Appearance of *Cedrus*. Evidence for human impact from c. 3000 BC. Relative aridity between 4500–4000 (parts of Morocco). Libyan Sahara aridity from c. 3000 BC.	Relative aridity.	Possible arid conditions 1200–700 BC (Linstädter & Zielhofer 2010).	
Eastern Med lake levels (after Roberts, Brayshaw, et al. 2011; (Dusar et al. 2011))	Early Holocene until c. 5000 BC generally wetter.	c. 3200 BC: aridity. Phases of aridity contemporary with Chalcolithic to Early Bronze Age periods (Roberts, Eastwood, et al. 2011).	c. 2300 BC aridity.	Relatively wet.	

Region					
Levant	PPN: relatively wet conditions (Goldberg 1994).	c. 4500 BC – Golan Heights: some evidence for human impact on vegetation (Schwab et al. 2004) Soreq: 3500–2800 BC: wet–dry oscillations.	Relative aridity.	1500–1000 BC, humid phase, followed by aridity.	
Wider Mediterranean		Rapid climate change event.			
Eastern Anatolia Lake Van (1,648 m), Eski Acigöl	Climate moister from about 6200 BC: oak forest expansion.	*Pistacia*, deciduous *Quercus*, max. *Quercus, Corylus* c. 3300 BC.	Human impact on the vegetation important from about 1800 BC. Onset of arid conditions (increase in the oxygen 18 curve, plus an increase in charcoal).	*Pinus* dominant.	Establishment of *Juglans* cultivation.
Central/western Anatolia/Greece	Aridity: abandonment of Catalhöyük-East, movement to western site due to irregular water supply. *Acer, Ulmus, Quercus* all present.	From 4500 BC decline in mesic species. *Fagus* increase. Lower lake levels.	Decline in oak (poss. caused by people).	Drier phase indicated in parts of Anatolia and Greece (Roberts, Eastwood, et al. 2011).	Increased moisture and temperature in some areas. *Olea* above 1,400 m in certain places.

(continued)

Table 5.1 (continued)

Broad chronological phase	c. 6200 BC ('Rapid Climate Change Event')	4500–3000 BC	c. 2000 BC	c. 1500 BC	c. 0 AD
	Oak-terebinth juniper-grass parkland dominant in some areas.	In Greece, diversity of mountain species was reduced due to a warming up of the climate. Peloponnese – between 5200 and 3600 BC, oak woodland became denser. Peloponnese maquis expansion and economic species such as *Cistus salvifolius* and *Olea*. (Jahns 1993). *c.* 3200 BC rapid opening up of forest in northern Greece. 5000–3200 BC declining lake levels.	Northern Turkey, certain indicator species such as *Planatgo lanceolata*, *Rumex* and *Polygonum aviculare*-type appear or increase at *c.* 2200 BC. Isotopes from Gölhisar Gölü generally drier conditions than during the period prior to 3100 BC. Overall reduction of forest in parts of Greece. 2500–2000 BC Konya plain – reduction in swampy conditions & development of topsoil (Boyer et al. 2006). Southern Argolid erosion from *c.* 2500 BC (van Andel et al. 1986). Greek soil erosion identified at third millennium BC in places (van Andel & Zangger 1990).	"Sediment pulse" first half of first millennium BC in settled areas such as Berket basin and Gravgaz (Vermoere et al. 2000; Kaniewski et al. 2007).	Economic species such as *Olea* and *Juglans* appeared from *c.* 500 BC.

Crete	Cretan lowland was quite open with relatively few trees. After c. 6500 BC, oak forest spread to the area around the Delphinos River, probably due to an increase in rainfall.	*Ericaceae* expansion in the mountains at about 4600 BC (poss. burning).	After the Santorini eruption (c. 1600 BC) the Kournas diagram shows low Cerealia-type, plus reduction in olive.	
Italy	Expansion of deciduous oak. *Quercus* forest and *Ulmus*. Northern, coastal zones: vegetation on this coastal area comprised of woodlands – *Abies* was abundant, together with *Pinus*, deciduous *Quercus, Ulmus, Tilia, Alnus* (Mariotti Lippi et al. 2007). Sicily: aridification at around 5000 BC (Sadori & Narcisi 2001).	Forest becoming more open. Decreasing summer humidity from c. 4000 BC (Magny et al. 2011). Between 3500 and 1500 BC the maximum levels of arboreal with the distributions of *Ulmus* and *Fagus*. Cereals appear.	*Abies, Carpinus betulus* (hornbeam) and *Taxus* appearing. *Juglans* and *Castanea* in some places. *Alnus* expanded just prior to this period – indicative of an increase in rainfall or increase in Laghi di Monticchio. Apulia – sudden decrease in tree species, poss. drier climate. 'Climate reversal' Increased variation in precipitation levels from c. 2000 BC (Magny et al. 2011).	*Abies* and *Taxus* became extinct in some areas. Many areas saw the development of complex agricultural landscapes with the usual economic trees such as olive and walnut.

(*continued*)

Table 5.1 (*continued*)

Broad chronological phase	c. 6200 BC ('Rapid Climate Change Event')	4500–3000 BC	c. 2000 BC	c. 1500 BC	c. 0 AD
Southern France	Anthracalogical work: *Pinus sylvestris*, *Juniperus* sp., *Prunus amygdalus* and some deciduous oak. 5400 to 5200 BC evidence for high levels of erosion in some areas (Rhône Valley) (Berger 2005).	Nice: Deciduous *Quercus*. Decline in lake levels at c. 3800–2200 BC. Anthracalogical: decrease in juniper and an increase in deciduous oak along with sclerophyllous oak. Cooler, wetter summers in some parts of the Northern Mediterranean implied by charcoal evidence.	Nice: *Pinus*. Montpellier: deciduous peak at 2200 BC with *Quercus ilex* increasing between 2000 and 400 BC. Anthracological evidence for 5000–3000 BC indicates anthropogenic impact on the vegetation; increase of *Buxus sempervirens* and sclerophyllous oak. *Erica* important in some places, implying the spread of meso-Mediterranean vegetation. Replacement of *Quercus ilex* by *Quercus suber*. Cooler, wetter summers in some parts of the Northern Mediterranean implied by charcoal evidence.		Montpellier: 'Climate becomes Mediterranean at c. 300 BC' (Jalut et al. 2000).

Iberia (high altitude)	Early Holocene: *Quercus* peak continues for almost two millennia. In another diagram, *Quercus* peak continued until c. 5000 BC.	*Corylus* and *Betula* became important.	Evergreen species dominate & juniper and sclerophylous species later on.	Grassland, heath land and shrublands developed.
Northern Iberia	*Abies* colonisation in places.	Decrease in *Corylus* and *Abies*; maximum of *Erica* at Banyoles. Mid-Holocene cooler summers and winters. Coastal zone: *Q. suber*, *Fagus*, *Alnus* and *Q. ilex-coccifera*.		
Eastern Iberia	From 5000 BC evergreen *Quercus*. C. 5400 BC important climatic change.	Thermophilous maquis. 4400 BC: minimum arboreal pollen = climatic deterioration. Then, increase in xeric species, e.g. *Erica*	Expansion of *Buxus* due to human activity.	In some areas *Corylus*, *Alnus*, *Fraxinus* disappeared c. 2000 BC.	1000–500 BC: decrease in deciduous *Quercus*.

(continued)

Table 5.1 (*continued*)

Broad chronological phase	c. 6200 BC ('Rapid Climate Change Event')	4500–3000 BC	c. 2000 BC	c. 1500 BC	c. 0 AD
Southern-central Spain	Towards end of humid phase. *Pinus* & *Juniperus cf. thurifera.*	Aridification phase. *Pinus* and evergreen *Quercus.* Fourth millennium BC – oak, with some hazel, birch, ash and alder. Then, evergreen oak (including *Quercus rotundifolia.*	Evergreen forest maximum.		From c. 600 AD: *Olea, Pistacia, Cistus, Juglans, Prunus* type, *Vitis.*
Semi-arid zone of Almeria	Decrease in pine, increase in evergreen trees.	*Pistacia*, deciduous oak. From 5000 BC, expansion of *Olea.*	Steppe: aridification from 2500 BC. Drier summers in Southern Mediterranean.		
Balearic Islands	*Buxus*/corylus (no longer present) & *Juniperus/Quercus* dominant.	Disappearance of *Buxus* & *Corylus* – maquis dominated by *Olea.*			

Q. rotundifolia (subspecies, holm oak), and *Q. suber* (cork oak) whilst in the east *Q. calliprinos* (Palestine oak) is common. Broadleaved forests often comprise oaks, such as *Q. pubescens* (pubescent oak) and *Q. cerris* (turkey oak), whilst true mountainous forests will include species such as *Cedrus* (cedar), *Abies* sp. (fir), and *Pinus nigra* (European black pine) (Quézel 2004: 8–9).

In the Western Mediterranean, maquis, garrigue, and steppe can individually constitute extensive areas, whilst in the east, the situation is often different, with patches of mixed maquis, phrygana, and steppe. One question is whether these plant communities represent degraded forest. Maquis is normally considered to be degraded forest, and phrygana degraded maquis and steppe (Grove & Rackham 2001: 57). These phases of degradation were supposedly caused by retrodictable stepped phases of overexploitation and/or changes in climate.

Anthropogenic and Climatic Impact: Views from Around the Mediterranean

The Mediterranean climate has changed continuously over time: Jalut et al. (2000) identified six dry phases during the Holocene. The arid phases seem to be contemporary with positive ^{14}C anomalies (where changes in solar activity affect ^{14}C production). The changes in species composition and the ratios of deciduous to sclerophyllous trees allow us to track the evolution and migration of the Mediterranean climate across Spain up in to southern France. The six changes in climate inferred from pollen sequences across the Western Mediterranean are dated to the following broad chronological phases: 8900–7700 BC, 6400–5600 BC, 3300–2200 BC, 2300–1400 BC, 850 BC–AD 270, and AD 700–1250. The late fourth through the third millennia BC aridification is partly supported by Magny, Miramont, and Sivan's identification of a general decline in lake levels at c. 3000–2000 BC. Concurrently, the Eastern Mediterranean saw a mid-Holocene wet phase, followed by a transition during the period 3500–2500 BC to drier conditions (Magny et al. 2002: 49–53; Roberts, Eastwood, et al. 2011). Recent work has also demonstrated north–south contrasts developing at c. 2500–2000 BC, with wetter conditions above 40°S and drier conditions to the south (Magny et al. 2012). The broader trend of a transition to a drier climate

5.5. Mosaic landforms and concomitant variations in vegetation characterise many Mediterranean landscapes –
Landscape around Sikyon (Peloponnese, Greece) (photo: author).

during the Middle Holocene led to the replacement of deciduous trees
by sclerophyllous evergreen trees (Magny et al. 2002: 54).

Palynology and anthracology (the identification of carbonised wood
macrofossils) permit the identification of the presence and absence of
different plant and tree species, and the relative intensity of human activity can be inferred from these data as well as from more conventional
archaeological evidence. Moreover, the definition of possible boundaries
and patches within a mosaic can be postulated. In particular, this can be
done where topographical variation (i.e. a break in slope) could plausi-
bly have influenced the potential for the growth of different species and
could also have influenced the nature of economic activity within the
landscape (Fig. 5.5).

The fact that some fundamental changes, in particular the emergence
of sclerophyllous vegetation, is seemingly synchronous across large parts
of the Mediterranean, at least at the subregional scale, implies that such

changes were caused by climate change (see Table 5.1 for an overview of climatic and vegetation phases). The same can be argued for erosion in that phases of erosion that appear to be contemporaneous across large parts of the Mediterranean could be considered a product of climate change. Localised events that do not fit with a pattern of regional synchronicity can be considered the product of specifically local, possibly anthropogenic, processes. However, if we accept that certain cultural and economic changes took place relatively quickly across a number of regions, and that the chronological resolution of many pollen diagrams and sedimentary records is such that climate-controlled synchronicity is not always easy to identify, then the role of people in certain landscape changes could have been significant and 'synchronous'. It is only once we move into the Little Ice Age (beyond the chronological scope of this volume) where we can identify well-dated and geographically dispersed, correlated erosion events (often referred to as the 'Younger Fill'; Vita-Finzi 1969) that climatically induced erosion might be inferred (Grove 2001).

SOUTHERN MEDITERRANEAN

Some landscapes are characterised as degraded due to the consequences of aridification (climate change) and resultant desertification – the process whereby land degrades in arid zones due to the loss of vegetation, whether this is caused by climate change and/or human activity. Areas where this process is considered to be marked include southern Spain, the Near East, and parts of Mediterranean Africa.

Despite the evidence for soil depletion and landscape degradation, there have been periods when stable soils have developed. For example, studies of Holocene soil development in Libya have contributed important evidence for the existence of relatively humid conditions ideal for pedogenesis (and vegetation growth) during the Early and Middle Holocene (Cremaschi & Trombino 1998). However, much of the Southern Mediterranean has been more susceptible to the consequences of climate change than northern areas, since even subtle changes can mean the difference between vegetation growth and the development of desert. Under an arid, warm climate, these areas can develop pre-desert or desert-like characteristics without passing through a degraded landscape phase. Adequate precipitation, vegetation cover, and ground moisture are crucial for soil development. During arid phases, soils do not develop so readily or, if they do, they will probably have low nutrient levels, and will be susceptible to depletion.

A pollen core from the Middle Atlas Mountains (1700 m) provides a rare example of a North African vegetation history. Here, the Early Holocene vegetation was dominated by *Q. canariensis* (a deciduous to semi-evergreen oak that would have been present on the moist valley floor) with *Q. rotundifolia* (technically the subspecies of the Mediterranean evergreen oak, *Q. ilex*, which is characteristic of the Western Mediterranean) present on the drier slopes. From the Middle Holocene (about 4500 BC), these oaks declined, with more open, grass-dominated areas developing. *Cedrus* (cedar) then appeared for the first time (Lamb, Damblon, & Maxted 1991: 404; Lamb & Van der Kaars 1995: 404). In some areas, there is evidence for human impact on vegetation from c. 3000 BC (Lamb et al. 1991), with a new expansion of *Q. canariensis* coming slightly later.

Relative environmental stability during the Neolithic is also seen in the Moroccan drylands (the south-west and north-east areas of the country). A phase of aridity at c. 4500–4000 BC interrupted an otherwise relatively humid Neolithic (Zielhofer & Linstädter 2006). In Eastern Morocco, the Late Neolithic saw the decline of *Tetraclinis* (Sictus tree) forest, replaced to some extent by *Stipa tenacissima* (halfah or esparto grass) – a sign of probable human activity (Wengler & Vernet 1992). In the Ghardimaou Basin, three phases of soil development have been identified, amongst them a phase of Neolithic soil development that probably occurred before 3500 BC (Zielhofer et al. 2002: 121).

During a period of increased precipitation, a fluvial system in an arid or semi-arid landscape might be expected to provoke extreme erosion. This does not appear to have been the case during the Roman period, where management techniques seemingly mitigated erosion problems (Faust et al. 2004: 1771). Forest clearance occurred during the fourth century AD, with the impact of pastoralism becoming more marked from this period onwards, ultimately creating an open scrub landscape (Lamb et al. 1991). Towards the end of the Roman period, climate and human impact enhanced geomorphic activity (ibid.). At the end of the Roman period, alluvial sediments covered a Roman settlement zone that had never been flooded before (Zielhofer et al. 2002: 122).

In the Libyan Sahara, wet conditions prevailed from 4900–4400 BC, then 'severe' dry conditions developed from c. 3000 BC (Cremaschi &

Di Lernia 1999: 216). Unsurprisingly, the mountainous areas probably received most of the rainfall, and the inner mountainous zones appear to have been the preferred landscape for human habitation, with relatively high levels of pastoral activity recorded. One Algerian study has yielded evidence for soil development on the dunes at 4350 BC. This Neolithic landscape was quite different to that of the present day, with the possibility of a wooded steppe covering this early soil, thus protecting the land surface from aeolian erosion (Ballais 1994: 184). Despite the possibility of a viable environment, Neolithic through to Roman archaeological sites are rare, and transhumant pastoralism may well have been the dominant activity. During the Roman period, *limes* (a system of roads, towns, fortifications at the 'edge' of the Empire) was established. This also included the development of irrigated agriculture. It appears that 'The post-Roman, linear, incision of the wadis has, at the regional level, been linked to the hydrological effects that resulted from the extension of farming' (Ballais 1994: 191).

THE NEAR EAST

The analysis of pollen from a series of marine (sapropel) and land cores from the central and Eastern Mediterranean supports the widely accepted notion of a climatic optimum (with enhanced humidity) during the Early Holocene. However, the suggestion that this environment provided the ideal context for the transition to farming (Rossignol-Strick 1999: 528) should not be considered an explanation for the transition to farming, as such. Rather, environmental instability during the Younger Dryas resulted in vegetation change that probably tested environmental knowledge due to the unpredictability of certain resources. These processes might have prompted the initial steps towards agriculture (Moore & Hillman 1992). The later spread of farming outwards from the Near East might also, in part, have been initiated by climatic instability (Weninger et al. 2006; Weninger et al. 2009). There is little doubt that the period centred on 6200 BC saw shifts in climate across the Mediterranean; for example, a transition from wet winters and dry summers, to wet winters and summers in parts of the Central Mediterranean (Peyron et al. 2011), and a sudden increase in *Quercus* due to climatic deterioration in the Aegean (Kotthoff et al. 2008; Pross et al. 2009). However, some have argued that the 6200 BC 'event' should be seen as part of a broader chronological trend of hemispheric cooling (Robinson et al. 2006).

In parts of the Near East, some settlements could have been situated within areas of dense vegetation or woodland. Stands of wheat and other domesticated plants would therefore have been limited in extent. During this period, the vegetation mosaic would have been the inverse of today's relatively open landscape. Epipalaeolithic and Early Neolithic openings within woodland would have constituted the minor patches. These groups of people could have been more reliant on forest food such as the acorn. However, it is clear that in the Southern Levant, Pre-Pottery Neolithic groups involved in pre-domestication agriculture exploited diverse ranges of plants, applying local environmental knowledge to local niches (Asouti & Fuller 2012). Whatever scenario characterised these food-procurement strategies, we should remember that in some regions, many early farmers would have engaged with relatively dense vegetation or wooded landscapes. Neolithic 'impact' on these milieus would have taken time and would have been patchy (Olszewski 1993). The use of fire to burn vegetation and create patches of exploitable land might have been quite common (Turner et al. 2010).

Evidence from certain areas, including part of northern Israel, suggests low levels of deforestation even by the Early Bronze Age (Rosen 2007: 132). The expansion of evergreen oak during the latter half of the Holocene probably does attest to the increase in human impact across many parts of the region. Deciduous oak forests were 'destroyed' over much of the Mediterranean zone of the Southern Levant (Baruch 1999: 22), whilst anthropogenic indicator species, such as *Plantago lagopus* (hare's-foot plantain) and *Sarcopoterium spinosum* (thorny burnet) expanded. An 'intact' forest comprising *Quercus* species was present around the Sea of Galilee until the end of the third millennium BC. Human impact then led to the demise of forest cover as olive (*Olea*) production developed. As human activity declined after AD 550, 'natural' forest re-established itself (Baruch 1986: 45). In other parts of the Southern Levant, the Early Bronze Age saw the development of olive, vine, and cereal production, activities that extended cultural and managed landscapes (Rosen 2007: 138). Whilst the gradual evolution of managed agricultural landscapes characterised some areas, there are others where there is clear evidence for fluctuations in activity, and a concomitant waxing and waning of forest. For example, at Birkat Ram in the Golan Heights, a core covering the last 6,500 years suggests that human impact occurred at c. 4500 BC, when there was a decrease in deciduous oak (*Q. ithaburensis* type, Tabor oak) as well as heliophilous species, with *Olea* cultivation developing during the Chalcolithic. This is supported by local archaeological evidence for olive use. During the Middle/Late Bronze Age, and through the Iron Age, there was regeneration of deciduous oak forest, probably a result of a decline in settlement activity in the region. An increase in settlement and lead mining during the Hellenistic period unsurprisingly led to a new reduction in forest cover (Schwab et al. 2004: 1730). Running up to the Roman and Byzantine periods, a relatively open environment, with areas of cultivated (arboreal) trees/shrubs comprising *Olea*, *Vitis* (vine), and *Juglans* (walnut) developed.

The Evidence for Soil Erosion

With changes in vegetation, phases of soil erosion are to be expected. However, the earliest erosion, contemporary with the Pre-Pottery Neolithic, correlates with a period of relatively wet conditions (Goldberg 1994), and there is little to suggest that this erosion was caused by farming practices. In the Negev region, there is evidence for erosion after the Pre-Pottery Neolithic B period (Goldberg & Bar-Yosef 1990: 73). Despite this, there is regional evidence for a phase of stability and soil development between 8000 and 4000 BC, a period when lakes in North Africa and Arabia expanded. This relatively humid period also saw the development of the so-called Hamra soils on the coastal zone of Israel, dated to between 8000 and 5000 BC (Gvirtzman & Wieder 2001), whilst in the Hula Valley and at Tel Yosef in the Harod Valley, soil horizons within wetland deposits have been dated to c. 6600–6250 BC. These units were overlain by Pottery Neolithic colluvial sediments at c. 5800 BC (Rosen 2007: 77–8). Erosion did take place here during the Chalcolithic period, while in the Southern Shefela area, a Middle Bronze Age to Late Bronze Age phase of erosion has been interpreted as the consequence of a drier climate and consequently a lower water table (Goldberg & Bar-Yosef 1990: 76). A subfossil of a *Tamarix* (tamarisk) tree near the Dead Sea offers a tantalisingly well-dated glimpse of an arid phase that took place during the Intermediate Bronze Age, the tree having died in 1930 BC (Frumkin 2009). However, despite (overall) drier conditions during the Bronze Age through to the end of the Roman period, it is difficult to argue for a direct relationship between climate change and societal stress. The most effective approach to assessing human–landscape engagements is via local, specific studies (Finné et al. 2011).

One example of a site-based assessment is the geoarchaeological work at Tell es-Safi/Gathin in Israel. Here, we see how erosion processes are often local and caused by specific forms of human activity. Here, a 2 km long, 8 m wide, 5–6 m deep ancient, human-dug trench was studied. Two phases of filling were identified, separated by a so-called phase of landscape stability. The first filling is dated to the Iron Age IIA (late ninth century BC) whilst the second is post-Byzantine (Ackermann, Bruins, & Maeir 2005: 323). Most importantly, the erosion phase (as represented by the ditch fills) does not appear to correlate with climatic events such as increased rainfall but rather with phases of human activity. On the other hand, phases of aridity (rather than wetness) and consequent reduced vegetation may have provided the conditions for erosion (ibid.). Whatever the causes, there is no reason to suggest that such erosion had an impact on human activity at the site.

In certain situations, we see how human activity can contribute to erosion, whilst in others, specific farming practices can conserve soil. Such a process has been demonstrated in the Negev Highlands, where a valley with no evidence of human impact had clearly suffered erosion through the Holocene, whilst in another valley, where farming has a long history, including the Roman and Islamic periods, it was revealed that run-off-harvesting agriculture had prevented desertification (Avni et al. 2006).

It is apparent that the evidence for land degradation, or more specifically, erosion, in the Levant is patchy. Whilst we have seen some areas where Late Neolithic and Bronze Age groups might have contributed to erosional processes, there are other areas, such as the Jebel al-Aqra region of the Northern Levant where erosion does not seem to have started before the second century AD (Casana 2008).

ANATOLIA AND GREECE

Some Anatolian Trends
As Early Neolithic (c. 6500 BC) peoples moved out from the Near East, they would have continued to apply the environmental knowledge associated with the exploitation of forest resources and the development of small arable zones either within or on the edges of such woodlands. Logically, as Neolithic populations expanded and grew in size, vegetation manipulation intensified. Research in the Troad area (Western Anatolia) shows how the composition of woodland did change, with deciduous

oak replaced by evergreen oak from about 3300 BC. In some places, in particular the site of Kumptepe, a break in settlement (c. 4600–3500 BC) saw the development of a soil horizon and open vegetation, with woodland then recovering, thus demonstrating environmental resilience. This phase of woodland recovery probably took place quite quickly. In many locations, Mediterranean landscapes do not take longer than a generation to recover. Once the new phase of activity was underway, from 3500 BC, maquis and shrub vegetation developed. Whilst, to the east, at Troy, intensive human impact on the vegetation was not apparent before c. 1300 BC (Riehl & Marinova 2008).

During the third millennium BC (the Early Bronze Age) in northern Syria and southern Turkey, settlement nucleation and population growth occurred as the environment appears to have become drier, with concomitant reductions in vegetation cover and soil erosion. The fluvial regime on the Amuq Plain (southern Turkey) was probably stable during this period, with a change towards an unstable regime taking place during the late first millennium BC (Wilkinson 2005: 182). The manner in which societies 'manage' the stresses caused by aridity is obviously a key area of discussion. For example, between c. 3500 and 2800 BC there is evidence from Soreq for three wet–dry oscillations that lasted between one-and-a-half and two-and-a-half centuries each (Bar-Matthews & Ayalon 2011). The Bronze Age in parts of the Eastern Mediterranean saw the development of complex, urbanised societies that had to engage with these phases of climatic instability (Roberts, Eastwood, et al. 2011). The evidence for deforestation and erosion attest to some of the environmental problems. The early second millennium BC saw an increase in humidity, followed by an arid phase. This latter period corresponds with a dramatic change in the archaeological record where we see evidence for the collapse of the existing cultural structures. In situations such as this, we have to ask if the emergent social structures facilitated mitigation of these problems or whether they were in fact the root of new rigid systems of environmental management that suffocated local forms of environmental knowledge.

A number of palynological projects in south-west Turkey have identified what is commonly referred to as the Beysehir Occupation Phase, named after the place where human impact on the environment was first identified (Bottema, Woldring, & Aytug 1986; van Zeist, Woldring, & Stapert 1975). The Gravgaz study, some 100 km north of the

Mediterranean coastline, investigated two pollen cores: one at 1,215 m, and the other from the Çanakh Lake at 1,030 m. In this area, deforestation started between 800 and 510 BC and the arboriculture phase, in which *Olea europaea* (olive), *Juglans regia* (walnut), *Fraxinus ornus* (manna ash), *Castanea sativa* (sweet chestnut), and *Vitis vinifera* (vine) were grown, between 400 and 210 BC (Vermoere et al. 2002: 581). Once again, this is an area that did not witness intensive impact on the vegetation until quite late.

In some parts of the Eastern Mediterranean, the day-to-day experiences of many people would have involved movement between relatively small zones of patches of different types of woodland and open spaces (Forman 1995). For example, some of the work at Çatalhöyük demonstrates how the landscape around that site might have been organised and exploited in response to the very particular environmental context within which it sat (Shillito 2011). The archaeobotanical evidence clearly supports the image of heterogeneous patterns of vegetation (Asouti & Hather 2001). *Quercus* and juniper would probably have been collected in 'park woodland' areas, at least 1–12 km from the site, whilst the *Salicaceae* (willows and poplars) and *Ulmus* spp. (elms) would have come from the nearby alluvial zones (Fairbairn et al. 2002).

The image of a complex mosaic of vegetation is also supported further south at Pınarbaşı, south-central Anatolia. The study of charcoal here suggests that the most common taxa were *Pistacia* and *Amygdalus*, with *Celtis* also common in most assemblages, whilst *Quercus* and *Juniperus* were rare in all deposits. This implies a local woodland-steppe environment with widely spaced trees of species that were resistant to drought. Other species are indicative of marshes and riparian woodland (Asouti 2005). Lakeside species were not chosen, implying that people were making choices: almond and terebinth wood burn well, and almond produces a pleasant smell (Asouti 2003b: 1200). A mosaic landscape, with people making niche-specific choices regarding environmental exploitation and management, was probably typical of many sites across the Mediterranean.

Variability Across Greek Neolithic, Bronze Age,
and Classical Landscapes
Bellwood (2005: 73–4) argues for a precocious Neolithic impact on the Greek landscape that may have acted as motivation for population

dispersal. There is a possibility that some Neolithic peoples did discover, after a relatively short period, that they needed to move, as their environmental knowledge was not adapted to a specific locale, and agricultural production became unviable at quite an early stage. However, there is little evidence to support widespread Neolithic degradation. It is once we move into the Bronze Age that the evidence implies more extensive manipulation of the landscape.

Despite a great deal of archaeological evidence for early agriculture in Greece, few data allow us to suggest that the first farmers had a profound impact on the vegetation (van Andel et al. 1995: 131). However, our knowledge of Greek vegetation is often founded on pollen diagrams from relatively high altitudes, and these demonstrate that during the earlier part of the Holocene, land at around 400–800 m on the Greek mainland was covered with an open deciduous oak forest (Bottema 1994b: 53), with more diverse vegetation developing with the appearance of *Pistacia* from about 7000 BC (Ntinou 2002). It is possible that there was an early, if limited, impact of early farmers from about 6000 BC (Bottema 1994b: 55).

Thessalian vegetation remained relatively stable until c. 4500 BC, with the spread of the hop hornbeam (*Ostrya*). From 2000 BC, beech expanded in some of the mountain zones. At the key site of Franchthi Cave, it is difficult to discern any obvious Neolithic impact on the open deciduous oak woodland (Bottema 1994b: 59). Results from many palynological sites in Greece suggest that there was a reduction in the diversity of tree taxa between 4000 and 2000 BC. Such a reduction may have been a result of 'selective felling' or non-regeneration after clearance by early farming communities (Willis 1992: 152). Human impact on vegetation was apparent in many areas by the third millennium BC, although some zones, such as northern Greece, saw the survival of relatively dense vegetation. Nevertheless, there was an early phase of Neolithic erosion recorded at the Thessalian site of Sesklo. Such a phase of erosion is perhaps unsurprising adjacent to a major site. Whether the site's inhabitants caused or responded to the erosion is another question.

On the Philippi Plain area of Macedonia, where there are a number of Tell sites and, one might assume, an area where there would have been relatively high levels of human activity, there is little evidence for erosion (Neboit-Guilhot & Lespez 2006: 336). Important changes in the vegetation started at c. 3000 BC, and from c. 2000 BC, human impact in some parts of Greece led to an overall reduction of forest cover and the emergence of herbaceous vegetation. However, in parts of Greece (in this instance, the north-west), there is evidence for a small re-expansion in woodland species between 1500 and 1000 BC, possibly a consequence of population decline (Willis 1992). We once again see how resilient vegetation does recover during periods of population decline, as was probably the case during this period.

As with other areas of the Mediterranean, the Greek story of Middle Holocene environmental change is one of emerging mosaic vegetation, with many low-lying areas of woodland gradually opened up by farmers, with climate, especially aridification, influencing the species composition in this mosaic. There is no doubt that some areas of the landscape would have comprised zones of exposed sediment and soil, these landscapes being especially susceptible to erosion at the end of long hot summers. We cannot demonstrate that soil loss or sedimentary erosion were catastrophic across large temporal and spatial scales. Studies of contemporary soil–vegetation relationships demonstrate how abandoned cultivated soils soon recover, regaining organic content and becoming stabilised within 10 years (Lopez-Bermudez et al. 1998; Martinez-Fernandez, Lopez-Bermudez, & Romero-Diaz 1995). Many areas are in fact 'metastable', where landscapes are characterised by a series of cycles which might comprise a phase of degradation (loss of vegetation and erosion), followed by stability (woodland regeneration, geomorphological stability) (Fig. 5.6). However, as Roberts (1990: 64) argues for south and south-west Turkey, whilst vegetation may regenerate, soil losses are rarely reversed to the same extent.

In the Argolid, there is little evidence to suggest that erosion coincided with the development of farming. In fact, erosion existed prior to the arrival of the first farmers (Fuchs, Lang, & Wagner 2004: 335) and in many ways is a natural and ever-present phenomenon. However, we should not understate the impact of people, nor the fundamental changes that have taken place in landscapes since the Middle Holocene – changes that have no comparators in previous interglacials. The first clearly identifiable phase occurred during the third millennium BC (van Andel, Runnels, & Pope 1986; van Andel & Zangger 1990: 382) which could well be linked with a phase of hemispheric aridity at c. 2200 BC. Palaeoenvironmental evidence from the Eastern Mediterranean clearly suggests drought and probable physical stress experienced by certain

5.6. The same spot in the Vallée des Baux (south of France) eight years apart. This demonstrates how vegetation can re-establish itself (bottom image) on a poor-quality soil in less than 10 years (photo: author).

populations at the end of the third millennium and start of the second millennium BC (Wossink 2009: 25–6). This contrasts with the history of erosion in the Larissa basin (Thessaly, north-eastern Greece) which is slightly more complex, with the first erosive phases occurring during the Early Neolithic (van Andel & Zangger 1990). Then, even during the period of increased Mycenaean activity, there is little evidence for widespread soil erosion. Studies of alluvial sediments imply that soil conservation schemes may have been in place by this time (see the discussion of terracing in the following chapter). Towards the end of the first millennium BC, a rural 'depression' is correlated with an increase in soil erosion (ibid.: 383). During such periods, farmers may have concentrated efforts on the best-quality soils, thus abandoning any conservation scheme on those soils that were in fact susceptible to erosion.

Around Nemea, there is evidence for at least three phases of post-Early Neolithic erosion on the hill slopes (Wright et al. 1990: 587). In the adjacent Phlious basin, OSL dating of sediments demonstrates a phase of erosion contemporary with the onset of farming in the north-east Peloponnese during the seventh millennium BC (Fuchs et al. 2004). The first phase of erosion in the Nemea area probably occurred during the Middle to Later Neolithic. The presence of early Neolithic material in the sediment and then an Early Bronze Age site on the surface of this sediment act respectively as *termini post quem* and *ante quem*. The fact that the valley seems to have been abandoned during the Middle Neolithic (Wright et al. 1990: 640) implies that Early Neolithic activity may well have had some impact on the geomorphic system. A renewed phase of human activity from the end of the Middle Bronze Age does not appear to have had an impact.

At Pylos (south-west Peloponnese, an area that includes the Palace of Nestor, some 7 km to the north of the Bay of Navarino), the presence of Late Helladic IIIA and IIIB (c. 1400–1200 BC) pottery within a debris flow deposit is clear evidence of an erosion phase that must just postdate this period (Zangger et al. 1997: 566). Erosion did increase from the Late Bronze Age onwards, with the highest rates of sedimentation occurring during the Roman and Early Byzantine periods. The absence of evidence for extensive erosion associated with Neolithic and Early Bronze activity, despite a high settlement density, may well reflect settlement and agricultural exploitation patterns, with little activity having taken place on the slopes of the foothills within the catchment of the streams studied in this research (Lespez 2003).

All of this work demonstrates that the erosion histories appear to follow a broad pattern, in that Bronze Age landscapes appear to have witnessed phases of erosion. However, within this, there is clear variation. The availability of precisely dated units employing OSL dating bodes well for the development of geoarchaeology, although it is always essential that the specific location and process being dated is critically assessed. For example, Fuchs et al. (2004) sampled from a foot slope in the north-east Peloponnese, a context where sedimentation was almost guaranteed. We need to consider how representative such a location is of the human landscape. If we choose situations where we know sedimentation occurred, and moreover in a zone where 'No settlement remnants are directly located' (ibid.: 337), we have to ask to what extent such a study is relevant to the investigation of human experiences of erosion. Sedimentary histories from different cores taken close to one another can vary (as seen in Sagalassos area; Dusar et al. 2012). This does not negate the geoarchaeological interest of such research, especially because people engage with the wider landscape not just the space constituted by the archaeological site. However, archaeologists must consider the nature of sampling situations and the relevance of these to the study of human lifeways.

If we accept that erosion events were not an everyday occurrence but that direct engagement with stable soil surfaces was the normal experience, we should consider phases of stability as represented in the archaeological record by evidence for soil development. The mapping of modern soils can provide information on land/soil quality (Davidson & Theocharopoulos 1992), although we should avoid transposing modern models of soil quality and erosion patterns onto interpretations of past landscape use and landscape change. One interesting and original approach to the investigation of the impact of people on the Cretan landscape is the pedological research carried out by Morris (2002). Studies took place across a number of areas, including the Siteia mountain range in the north-eastern corner of Crete. The research also comprised the analysis of a sediment catchment basin near three Late Minoan IIIc sites and on a Late Minoan IIIc to sub-Minoan site in east-central Crete, and also a final Neolithic to Late Minoan site on eastern Crete. The principal aim of the study was to assess the level of human impact on the soil system (Morris 2002: xvii). The studies of these (and all) soils are informed by models of pedogenesis, where depth and characteristics are dependent on climate, parent material, vegetation relief, and time (Jenny 1994). A phase of Minoan soil stability was inferred from an argillic (clayey) horizon that contained Minoan artefacts. A pedon from an agricultural terrace at the Karphi site revealed the surface of a residual palaeosol also containing Minoan artefacts, thus demonstrating that the terraces were of Minoan origin (Morris 2002: 37–8), a date confirmed by a radiocarbon estimation. This evidence implies a change in climate during the late

Bronze Age, '…with moister conditions prevalent prior to the Minoan occupation around 3000 years ago, followed by drier conditions after the Karphi settlement was abandoned' (ibid.: 43). Terraces then collapsed and were buried by erosion as a result of their abandonment and/or the development of a drier climate. The relatively poor quality of this soil may also imply that terraced hill slopes did not necessarily support good quality soils, and were brought into the agricultural system once all of the prime land had been exploited. At Kavousi, there was a phase of aggradation prior to 1000 BC, with a soil then developing on top of this deposit. It is possible that the erosion phase was triggered by destabilisation upslope, perhaps as the result of Late Minoan IIIC activity. The Minoan soil was also buried (possibly during the Geometric period) (ibid.: 75). Consequently, this and other research from Greece presents us with an image of a landscape characterised by a waxing and waning of erosion and soil stability – products of a complex, undulating topography with people adapting to this mosaic. There is no doubt that there were moments when soils and associated crops were lost, but the identification of specific events is problematic, and we should perhaps balance our quest for the identification of erosion with assessments of soil development, and even the anthropogenic enhancement of soils, as suggested for the Epipalaeolithic (possibly Pre-Pottery Neolithic) site Göbekli Tepe, south-eastern Turkey (Pustovoytov 2006).

The Development of the Anthropic-Climatic Regime

The downturns in settlement and economic activity during the so-called Bronze Age Dark Ages are recorded across much of the Mediterranean (see the following for a range of perspectives: Bachhuber & Roberts 2008; Drews 1993; Mathers & Stoddart 1994) and are considered in a number of places in this volume.

Changes in climate might have tested Late Bronze Age palace economies, although the peak of the arid phase occurred well into the Dark Ages period (L. D. Brandon 2012) when we see the development of new and burgeoning urban-centred economies in many parts of the Mediterranean (Osborne & Cunliffe 2005).

The relationship between changes in the environment and their potential impact upon settlement, economy, political structures, and wider culture requires nuanced approaches that comprise assessments of a wide range of processes that must ultimately consider the ways in which different layers within hierarchical societies develop and modify environmental knowledge. Analyses of environmental, political, or sociocultural resilience provide a framework for such analyses (Butzer 2012). Some would argue that the classical period saw the emergence of an anthropic-climatic regime (as opposed to an earlier climatic-anthropic regime) where a certain threshold is crossed, and human activity becomes the dominant factor in causing erosion (Neboit-Guilhot & Lespez 2006: 344).

The Greek countryside was most densely settled during the classical and Early Hellenistic periods (c. 350–250 BC). Whilst some areas saw an appreciable reduction in activity during the Hellenistic (c. 323–31 BC) and Early Roman periods (c. 31 BC–AD 300) (Alcock 2007: 135–6), other regions witnessed an increase in activity, with a wave of population growth around certain 'peripheral' areas of Greece (such as parts of Macedonia) during the Late Roman period (Bintliff 1997). There is no doubt that erosion during the classical period was common, although we need to consider the specific relationships between our sedimentary facies and the archaeological sites, and the responses that erosion would have engendered. For example, in the Loúsios gorge at Górtys (about 40 km to the south-east of Olympia, on the Peloponnese), the fourth century BC baths had been covered by several metres of sediment. Despite the fact that there is no doubt that substantial erosion has taken place here (sediments had also built up against a Byzantine chapel, indicating a later phase of erosion), the deposition event or events are not precisely dated, and we do not know if erosion actually affected the site whilst it was in use. It is safe to assume that erosion would have been an issue in this steep-sided valley (Fig. 5.7), but it was managed (Dufaure 1976). Here, we should assess the importance of the specific geological characteristics of this area. The eroded material at Górtys is derived from flysch (Fouache 1999: 162). Such material is easily erodible, and we have to consider how an establishment such as a baths would have employed, or forced people to keep the environs clear of, eroded material – an issue that is dealt with in more detail in the final part of this chapter.

PEOPLE AND ENVIRONMENT IN ITALIAN LANDSCAPES

As we move to the Northern Mediterranean, we come to areas that tend to suffer less from long periods of aridity, although the archetypal long, hot Mediterranean summer is still a defining characteristic. Consequently,

5.7. The site at Górtys (Peloponnese) – Fourth century BC baths subject to severe erosion at certain points in the past. Note the build up of sediments against the external walls (photo: author).

the development of vegetation follows slightly different trajectories to the Southern and Eastern Mediterranean regions. Moreover, wetland zones are more common in Italy and the south of France than further south. Whilst there are long-term changes in vegetation (often characterised by woodland reduction), and specific species or groups of species do not demonstrate resilience, human societies in many instances do both cause disturbance and absorb that disturbance (Walker & Salt 2006).

One characteristic central-Italian vegetation history is provided by the pollen diagram from Valle di Castiglione near Rome (Follieri, Magri, & Sadori 1989). Here, we see the expansion of deciduous trees at the start of the Holocene, with the emergence of deciduous oak and *Corylus* (hazel) as dominant species (Magri 1995: 356), a process that is broadly contemporary with those across the Eastern Mediterranean. Although the forest reached its maximum extent at about 3100 BC, the first indications of human activity, in the form of cereal pollen, appeared about 6,000 years ago, with *Juglans* (walnut) and *Castanea* (chestnut) then appearing about 4,200 and 3,300 years ago respectively (Russo Ermolli & di Pasquale 2002: 217). Oak appears to have been important in this area up until about 4,300 years ago. Here, we have to imagine a human-influenced but stable woodland environment that showed little signs of early degradation but rather manipulation and management. By c. 1700 BC, the woodland had contracted, and economically important species such as *Castanea* and *Olea* were present. These species expanded by c. 600 BC, with little change in the other woodland vegetation (Magri & Sadori 1999: 254). Despite a decrease in relative proportions, species such as *Quercus* and *Corylus* may well have been economically valuable, possibly providing fodder but also fuel and building material. Consequently, these species could have been 'curated'.

In southern Italy, at the start of the Holocene, birch and steppe species were replaced by *Quercus* and *Ulmus* (elm). Again, the relatively high altitude of the pollen core sites means that strong evidence for human impact appears quite late in the sequences, with the first significant change at the the Laghi di Monticchio site (656 m) not taking place before c. 2500 BC (Early Bronze Age). *Quercus ilex* (holm oak) also colonised at this time, and may be indicative of warmer winter temperatures. *Abies* spp. (fir) and *Taxus* (yew) disappeared c. 500 BC, with climate change or the impact of agriculture cited as the causes. It is perhaps unusual for *Abies* spp. to disappear entirely, and we might assume that people would usually make some effort to conserve or manage such a valuable resource. It is possible that this tree was killed by disease or a change in climate (Watts et al. 1996: 124). In Apulia, the period between 3900 and 2200 BC saw the presence of mixed oak woodland, followed by a steep decrease in woodland species. The shift towards a drier climate, rather than human impact, might explain this change (Caroli & Caldara 2007). The coastal site at Lago Alimini Piccolo, Apulia, saw a similar pattern, with deciduous oak dominating the landscape between 3200 and 2350 BC, and a reduction in forest cover after this period. However, the presence of extensive Neolithic activity to the west on the Tavoliere plain (Pessina & Tin, 2008: 167–70) would have had some impact on vegetation across the region. Later, during the Bronze Age, an initial, albeit temporary, deforestation phase at around 2000 BC might have been caused by drought. The predictable, anthropogenic woodland mosaic with *Olea* then emerged during the period 1900–100 BC, with the Roman period characterised by the decline in woodland (Di Rita & Magri 2009).

In some parts of Italy, there is relatively little evidence for Early Neolithic activity or impact on the landscape. For example, there is an Early Neolithic 'gap' on the central Adriatic coast (Skeates 1999). During the later Neolithic and into the Bronze Age, arboreal pollen levels were quite high, with *Ulmus* and *Fagus* at their maximum. Other Mediterranean diagrams also fail to demonstrate substantial prehistoric impact on tree taxa. Magri (1995: 357) argues for a 'natural' state where mosaic cycles are dominant, with continuous change characterising forest development.

In the Terramare, on the Po plain, cereal field pastures and meadows characterised the landscape during the Middle–Late Bronze Age (1650–1200 BC). Some consider that climatic deterioration from around 1300 BC may have contributed to the decline of the Terramare di Montale (Mercuri et al. 2006). At 249 m, the Lago Lucone in northern Italy attracted Early–Middle Bronze Age settlers who appear to have cleared the mixed oak forest that had been established during the Early Holocene. From about 1100 BC, the palaeobotanical evidence suggests a reduction in human activity in this area. Here, the decline in activity cannot be explained by climatic deterioration alone (Valsecchi et al. 2006), and may well be part of a broader trend of Late Bronze Age decline.

As in other regions across the Mediterranean, Bronze Age erosion has been identified in a number of areas in Italy, including the Biferno Valley (east-central Italy) (Hunt 1995). Some areas did see earlier erosion, such as the Marche region of central Italy where Neolithic forest clearance might have caused erosion (Coltorti 1993). In Sicily, late fourth-millennium (Sicilian Copper Age) hill-slope erosion in the Troina territory has been identified (Ayala & French 2003), and a similar date range is suggested for erosion at Basilicata in southern Italy. However, this erosive phase has been given two quite different *termini ante quem* through the radiocarbon dating of a buried soil on top of the eroded sediment: one estimation was c. 2100 BC (Neboit 1984), whilst the second estimation gives the buried soil a date of the early to mid-fifth millennium.

Although wetland zones are often considered marginal (a topic considered in Chapter 4), it is possible that malaria was not a threat in the

Neolithic, and the advantage of having access to a constant water supply and aquatic food resources was the fundamental attraction. Palù di
Livenza (30 m above sea level in the Friulian foothills in north-east Italy)
was located within or close to dense forest (Pini 2004: 773), and the
presence of pollen of *Cyperacae* (sedges) and *Sparganium* (bur-reed)
implies the existence of wetland zones in this area. The village comprised pile dwellings, and when the settlement expanded, *Corylus* (hazel)
and *Alnus glutinosa* (European alder) were still present, and species such
as *Hedera* (ivy) appeared, the latter possibly employed as winter fodder
for cattle (ibid.: 774). Wetland species actually decreased, and the forest contracted – a major impact on the woodland would have been the
use of timber for the pile-dwelling structures that covered an area of
about 60,000 m². Three phases of construction have been identified: the
first 4325–4715 BC, the second 3910–4170 BC, and the third phase
3305–3840 BC (ibid.: 771). Although the earliest dates for the settlement indicate a human presence in the area at c. 4495 BC, the pollen
diagram does not indicate any agricultural activity prior to 3960 BC.
Therefore, it is possible that the earliest occupants on the site were not
involved in agriculture or, more likely, that woodland density and concomitant pollen production may have masked the agricultural pollen
signal. The pollen and other archaeobotanical evidence (charcoal, fossil
fruits, and seeds) suggest that the wood used for construction and for
burning came from around the mire, with cereal cultivation taking place
close to the pile dwellings. This emphasises the importance of forest or
woodland agriculture, where vegetation management is dominated by
woodland-management strategies. The same was true to the west in the
Languedoc (south of France) where the first evidence for forest transformation is dated to the Middle Neolithic, with increases in *Buxus* (box)
and *Quercus ilex* (holm oak). Chabal (1998: 77) is quite clear in her definition of the differences between deforestation and clearing, essentially
arguing that, during the Neolithic, clearance – the preparation of land
for agricultural activity rather than the complete suppression of trees –
would have been the norm.

PEOPLE AND ENVIRONMENT IN SOUTHERN FRENCH
LANDSCAPES

A strong case for Early Neolithic erosion is made for the lower Rhône
Valley where we see an increase in the flooding of low-lying levels as

part of a wetter climatic phase c. 5300–5200 BC. This may well explain the subsequent increase in the number of settlements on higher ground (Berger 2005: 164) (Fig. 5.8). High levels of erosion took place during the period centred on 5400 to 5200 BC. The causes are unclear, as population levels would surely have been quite low. However, if we accept that, in some environments, early farmers may have had a disproportionate impact on the landscape if they initially cleared zones situated on lower valley sides and alluvial terraces, when combined with climatic deterioration, this could have led to increased erosion. A newly cleared land surface devoid of grass or weeds would be quite fragile. This might constitute a form of low resilience at a specific time and place. However, as with other regions discussed above, it is unlikely that erosion per se resulted in economic and cultural stress. Moreover, this period was very much a precursor to the ultimate development of what we accept as the Mediterranean climate in this subregion. Many now agree that the transition to a Mediterranean-type climate in the Western Mediterranean occurred about 4,000 years ago, whilst in south-east Spain, these conditions existed more than 10,000 years ago and gradually moved towards south-eastern France, although the growing evidence for spatial and temporal variations in climate across the Mediterranean throughout the Holocene demonstrates that the identification of a single regional trend is impossible (de Beaulieu et al. 2005). For example, as mentioned above, Jalut et al. (2000) have identified six dry phases during the Holocene contemporary with positive ^{14}C anomalies (when sunspot activity is low, the ^{14}C/^{12}C ratio is high – a positive ^{14}C anomaly). This can result in a cooler climate and aridity in the Eastern Mediterranean. We also know that there was a general decline in lake levels during the third millennium BC, whilst in the Eastern Mediterranean, a Middle Holocene wet phase was followed by a transition to drier conditions during the period 3500–2500 BC (Magny et al. 2002: 49–53).

In terms of vegetation development in the south of France, we see at the Etoile site near Nice (Dubar et al. 1986) a familiar pattern of *Alnus, Corylus,* and deciduous *Quercus* dominating the landscape during the Early to Middle Holocene, then, from c. 2000 BC, *Pinus* becoming more prominent. Further west, in the Languedoc, at Marsillargues near Montpellier (Planchais 1982) and Lattes (or Lattara – the Iron Age and Roman settlement near modern Montpellier) (Planchais, Duzer, & Fontugne 1991), deciduous trees reached their peak at the start of

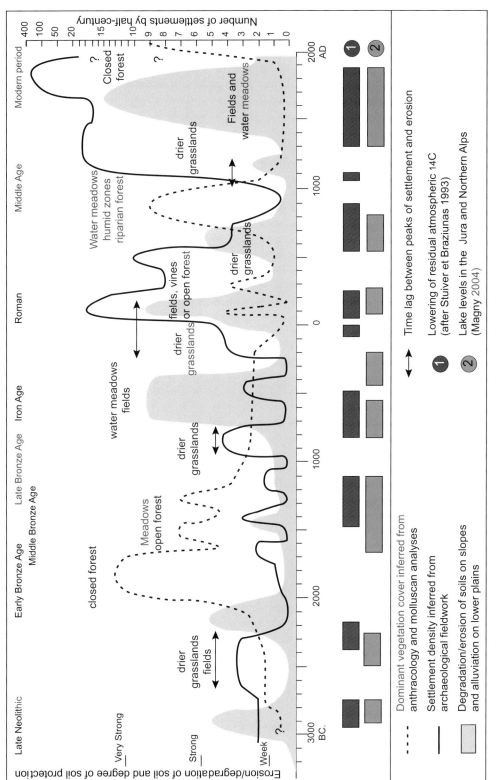

5.8. Erosion and stability in the Rhône Valley. The relationship between settlement activity, certain changes in climate, and erosion. (By permission of Berger, J.-F. (2003), Les étapes de la morphogenèse holocène dans le sud de la France, in *Archéologie et Systèmes Socio-environnementaux: Etudes Multiscalaires sur la Vallée du Rhône dans le Programme ARCHEOMEDES*, fig. 148, pp. 87–167.)

the second millennia BC, after which evergreen *Quercus ilex* (holm oak) increased.

The broader, regional picture of the Neolithic decline in deciduous oak and the creation of open spaces is supported by anthracological research (Thiebault 1997). Anthracology also allows the identification of more nuanced processes. The appearance and structure of oak-dominated vegetation varied enormously, depending on the composition of specific species: *Quercus – pubescens, robur, ilex,* or *suber* (cork oak). Studies of the changes in wood anatomy permit the identification of changes in climate, as certain characteristics are determined by temperature and precipitation (Terral & Mengual 1999). One study suggests that there was an increase of 2–2.5°C in mean annual temperature between the Mesolithic and the Bronze Age, the greatest increase taking place from the Middle Neolithic to the Late Bronze Age (ibid.: 84). The Bronze Age climate could have been quite similar to that of the present day (warm and sub-humid), whilst an increase in rainfall may have characterised the transition from the Bronze Age to the Iron Age (ibid.: 88). From c. 2000 BC onwards, the replacement of deciduous woodland with open, sclerophyllous vegetation was a product of both increased human impact on these landscapes and climate change (Heinz & Thiebault 1998). At the relatively high altitude of 970 m, the Balma Margineda record in Andorra covers the periods from the Azilien (12,000–9000 BC) to the Early Neolithic. By the Early Neolithic, there was forest dominated by *Quercus robur* (pedunculate oak) (Vernet 1997: 93). During this period, we appear to see what Vernet refers to as a balanced exploitation of the vegetation, implying little or no impact from farming (ibid.: 97). However, certain periods do seem to have seen some erosion. A similar situation may well have existed in Lower Provence where the absence of palaeoecological evidence prevents a clear assessment of vegetation change, but geoarchaeological data suggest possible impact on the geomorphic system by Late Neolithic farmers (Jorda & Provansal 1996).

Although Neolithic societies would have experienced – and perhaps even caused – landscape degradation at the local level, there is no evidence to suggest that such environmental changes were insurmountable, causing changes in Neolithic societies or their economic practices.

Moving into the Bronze Age, some have blamed erosion for inducing serious economic and thus cultural problems. For example, a reduction in activity during the Early Bronze Age in the Languedoc might be explained by one of the following: (1) the cultural sequences employed in the definition of the Bronze Age in the Languedoc are imperfect, and sites from earlier or later periods may in fact be Bronze Age; (2) the Early Bronze Age was characterised by economic collapse, and populations were dispersed and/or situated on marginal sites; or (3) Early Bronze Age sites have been removed or masked by certain erosive processes (Wainwright 1994: 287–8). There is little doubt that any such erosion was related to changes in vegetation cover. Here, the development of garrigue would have been important. Garrigue vegetation did develop during this period, but its evolution was not synchronous across the region and was not therefore exclusively caused by a change in climate. Consequently, it is likely that Bronze Age land degradation was caused by overexploitation of environments in upland areas combined with erosion aggravated by extreme storms (ibid.: 300). Gasco (1994: 100) considers that the oak forest in the south of France had already been degraded by the start of the Bronze Age. A wider range of cultural and economic processes, rather than environmental changes, may well have influenced modifications in Early Bronze Age settlement and economy. The possible arrival Beaker (pottery) using peoples could quite easily have led to new forms of engagement with these landscapes that resulted in new influences on vegetation and sediments.

During the Late Bronze Age, deforestation around densely populated areas was marked. However, certain trees such as walnut and hazel may well have been protected, along with oaks, as food sources. At the Grotte Camprafaud (Hérault), wild chestnuts almost disappeared between 2770 and 2115 BC, being replaced by the domesticated variety. Evergreen oak then became dominant from 1990 BC (Gasco 1994: 102). By the end of the Bronze Age, large areas of previously uncultivated land had been cleared. The increase in the area of land under cultivation is a profoundly noteworthy phenomenon when considering how people interacted with the farmed landscape. During the Early Bronze Age, with fields close to the settlement, people did not have to travel any significant distance to work their holdings. By the Late Bronze Age and Early Iron Age, the evidence from storage pits and pollen diagrams suggests extended zones of agricultural activity under the control of individual settlements. Thus, people were engaged with an extensive landscape and experienced a different intensity of engagement with that landscape, as they may have moved through 'corridors', along paths, and so on to go and work patches of land some distance from their settlements. Livestock, especially pigs and cattle, were probably reared in wooded areas, whilst sheep may well have been kept on the edge of the forest, thus degrading it further (ibid.: 103). This pattern of landscape organisation and concomitant impact on vegetation is reflected on the étangs (coastal mixed saline/freshwater bodies) sites in Provence and the Languedoc, where woodland clearance took place from c. 3000 BC onwards. Typical woodland species were replaced by *Juglans*, *Olea*, and cereals, indicating agricultural clearance (Laval, Medus, & Roux 1991: 270). Unsurprisingly, as time moved on, a more extensive range of plants was exploited within an increasingly open landscape. In the Languedoc, *Papaver somniferum* (opium poppy) and flax were grown around the Bronze Age lagoon sites, but wild fruits, including acorns, were still gathered. One interesting feature of the Languedocian settlement pattern is the increase in the number of sites towards the end of the Bronze Age (850–700 BC), with coastal settlements occupied during the summer and hilltop sites providing permanent settlement locations. The two zones share similar sets of archaeobotanical remains, comprising cereals and pulses, implying no profound production differences between the two zones (Bouby, Leroy, & Carozza 1999).

When we visit certain Mediterranean landscapes, we might be surprised by the emphasis placed on discussions of degradation. For example, today, the lower Rhône Valley is quite fertile and green. So to what extent can we demonstrate that degradation was ever a real problem (van der Leeuw, Favory, & Fiches 2003)? The evidence attests to stability from the Late Neolithic through to the Chalcolithic (a period of relative climatic warmth) (Berger 2003: 113), and then erosion phases developed during the Early Bronze Age. To the south-east of this area, at Glanum in the Alpilles (a low, short, limestone mountainous chain in western Provence), quite severe erosion appears to have occurred during the Chalcolithic. It is unclear, however, whether this directly affected people as such (Provansal 1995b). Across the lower Rhône Valley area, the archaeological evidence points to continuous settlement during these periods, such that cycles of stability and erosion did not result in the abandonment of this landscape. Whilst the Early Iron Age landscape appears to have been subject to quite severe environmental degradation (Berger 2003: 121–2), settlement activity, albeit restructured, continued to take place. A newly stable geomorphic milieu provided the context for later Iron Age and Early Roman activity.

PEOPLE AND ENVIRONMENT IN SPANISH LANDSCAPES

Some Iberian research highlights the differences between the Northern and Southern Mediterranean zones in terms of the relationship between climate changes and vegetation development, especially for the Early to Middle Holocene. Most lake and geochemical records indicate that the Early Holocene across much of the Mediterranean was wetter. In the southernmost areas (including southern Iberia) where water is a limiting factor, evergreen taxa flourished during the Early Holocene. Pistacia, for example, is characteristic of the Early Holocene in the Eastern Mediterranean, and evergreen oaks appear to have flourished in southern Iberia and north-west Africa (Fletcher, Boski, & Moura 2007; Fletcher & Sánchez Goñi 2008; Rossignol-Strick 1999). In the northernmost areas where winter temperatures are a limiting factor, evergreen taxa colonised later in the Holocene.

Variations in Vegetation Change Across Spain

One long-term trend in vegetation change across Spain, and indeed most Mediterranean regions, is an ever-decreasing biomass (Pèrez-Obiol et al. 2011). Within Iberia, there are significant variations in vegetation, ranging from the Pyrenees in the north, via the central plains and then central mountains, across to the semi-arid landscapes of south-east Spain. This variation is a consequence of geographical location, topographical position (i.e. altitude), proximity to the sea, wider changes in climate, and, of course, human activity. The variation across Iberia also includes what Carrión et al. (2010) characterise as 'surprises' in the biogeography of Mediterranean vegetation development; that is, Holocene vegetation patterns that seem unusual, in that the species composition is not always what we might expect given the geographical location and concomitant climatic characteristics. This reinforces the need for archaeologists to incorporate local vegetation histories wherever possible, and to avoid making generalising inferences from regional vegetation histories.

As already noted, the Iberian Peninsula covers a range of biogeographical zones. If we can identify one useful geographical boundary from the palaeoecological evidence, it is the Llobregat River (Catalonia) (Fig. 5.1). This serves as a margin between evergreen and deciduous communities (Riera Mora, Léspez, & Argilagés 2004). Close to this boundary, in the Catalan interior areas (Banyoles), deciduous oak forests were dominant until 5500/5000 BC, when pine colonised (Pèrez-Obiol & Julià 1994).

With the Neolithic, a new engagement with woodland emerged, where trees were not only cleared for arable agriculture and the creation of pasture, but wood was also exploited as part of the production process for ceramics and the building of farms and villages. Even if Neolithic populations were comprised of incoming peoples with different attitudes towards the natural world, we should not forget the problems, even dangers, of living and working in a forested landscape, and those early farmers would probably have sought areas that were naturally open or easy to clear. As thermo-Mediterranean vegetation emerged, the opportunistic expansion into zones of open woodland with smaller trees makes perfect sense, especially if incoming agriculturalists brought environmental knowledge from a more arid, Eastern Mediterranean landscape.

In the Segura Mountains (Murcia, south-eastern Spain, about 1,100 m), human impact on the vegetation did not occur until quite late in the Holocene. Pine, deciduous oaks, and other species, including hazel and birch, were dominant during the period 4600–2800 BC, but after this point, there was a 'dramatic' decline in deciduous oak as it was replaced by evergreen oak and other evergreen species. The abrupt shift to an evergreen oak-dominated forest appears to have occurred within a period of 10–30 years (based on interpolated radiocarbon dates) (Carrión et al. 2001). Such a process is too quick to have been a response to climate change. Senescence, nutrient deficiency, or diseases are possible explanations. Whatever the reason, such a change would have been observable within a human generation. After this period, up until c. 2120 BC, evergreen oak – including *Quercus rotundifolia* (holm oak), the acorns of which are used today as fodder – replaced deciduous oak and sclerophyllous (hard-leaved) vegetation, with this woodland achieving its maximum between 2120 and 1630 BC. Survey work in the northern Alicante Province demonstrated how the later Neolithic period saw a concentration of activities within a relatively restricted area (Barton et al. 1999). Based on the isotopic analyses of human remains from sites spanning the Late Neolithic to the Bronze Age in the Alicante region, it seems that there was little change in diet over this period, and, as with other studies in the Mediterranean, there is evidence of nutritional deficiencies (McClure et al. 2011). Such evidence implies a certain level of stability or perhaps inertia in environmental knowledge, as these groups do not appear to have changed their food-production strategies. Neolithic and Bronze Age settlement is sparse in this area, and the palynological evidence corroborates this picture of limited human impact.

In most parts of Spain, there is little evidence of Early Neolithic (5600–4500 BC) influence upon the vegetation, although vegetation patterns may well have changed quite radically prior to this due to the c. 6200 BC rapid climate-change event (González-Sampériz et al. 2009). As we move into the Middle and Later Neolithic (4500–2400 BC), the combination of aridification and probable human impact on vegetation becomes apparent. For example, in the Navarrés region, increased clearance took place between 4000 and 2700 BC. The presence of macro-charcoal (evidence for localised burning events) could represent natural or human-induced fire. An increase in *Plantago* (plantain) pollen just after a decrease in *Quercus* in pollen diagrams certainly supports the case for anthropogenic impact on this landscape (Carrión & Van Geel 1999: 231). Archaeological evidence indicates that the first domesticated cereals (einkorn wheat and barley), legumes (peas, fava beans, and lentils), and animals (cow, sheep, goat, and pig) were present by 5600 BC (Bernabeu et al. 2001; Bernabeu & Bernabeu 1993). Settlements were small and dispersed across the area around Valencia during the Early Neolithic. The settlement pattern appears to shift from dispersed, relatively ephemeral settlements in the Early Neolithic to aggregated villages during the Middle and Late Neolithic (McClure et al. 2006). During the Early Neolithic, it is possible that the rotation of cereals and legumes was frequent under the traditional Mediterranean *el huerto* system of garden-plot cultivation (ibid.: 9). If this were the case, then extensive woodland clearance would not have been necessary, and this should be reflected in pollen diagrams, with tree-pollen values remaining relatively stable for much of the Neolithic.

As discussed in the introductory chapter, different forms of cultural and human ecology have been important in the assessment of human–environment interactions around the world, and certain forms of cultural ecology do underpin some of the discursive sections in this book. However, we should be aware of the limitations of Human Behavioural Ecology (HBE), and in particular, one of its foundational tenets, Ideal Free Distribution (IFD) (McClure et al. 2006). Essentially, IFD posits that animals in a landscape will be distributed across a range of resources, and that the number of animals present within an area will be a direct function of the resource level within that area. This model was initially developed to explain habitat distribution in birds (Fretwell & Lucas 1969). Its application to the study of the agricultural and pastoral potential of Neolithic landscape in Spain allows us to assess and characterise the nature of early farming economies within specific landscapes. However, whilst such a model might be applicable to non-human animals, its application to the study of humans (or, more specifically, ancient human awareness of carrying capacity) is problematic. IFD models implicitly deny the probability of environmental knowledge being culturally, ideologically, and religiously structured: all environmental knowledge *is* mediated by cultural processes. Despite these issues, the IFD model for the Neolithic in eastern Spain does articulate some interesting notions. Relatively small changes in population density can result in settlement shift, and population changes do not need to be substantial in order for land-use changes to take place. A small increase in population density on Early Neolithic settlements on the valley floors may have encouraged movement towards the valley edges, where the growing population used ox-drawn ploughs for the first time and may have constructed terraces, thus improving a landscape that might have been initially considered of secondary value. This change would have been increasingly important as people and settlements moved away from the riverine margins (McClure et al. 2006: 25). The expansion into new wooded areas may also have been facilitated by transformations of the vegetation caused by climate change. Such processes could have invited or encouraged the expansion of certain agricultural activities. As the configuration of woodland evolved into 'Mediterranean' vegetation, with evergreen oaks and other, smaller sclerophyllous species, this more open landscape would have facilitated mobility and new intensified agricultural practices during the later Neolithic.

During the later Neolithic, we see the extraction of surplus products from animals – the defining characteristic of the 'secondary products revolution' (Greenfield 2010; Sherratt 1981). Whilst this might have developed initially during the early stages of the Neolithic (Evershed et al. 2008), the intensification of these processes occurred during the later Neolithic (4500–2400 BC) (Bintliff 2012: 51–2) with greater numbers of cows, sheep, and goats reaching maturity, thus increasing grazing/browsing pressure and concomitant impact on vegetation. In some areas, charcoal analyses suggest that forest was restricted to higher elevations. Therefore, it seems likely that animal husbandry around later Neolithic settlements was responsible for much of the local impact on vegetation at this time.

One of the limits to vegetation reconstruction based on palynological work is that, more often than not, the results can only be used to *suggest* variations in the spatial distribution of different types of vegetation within a landscape. Palynology can only hint at the development of vegetation mosaics in the past. This is a problem in any region, and for the Mediterranean, the history of complex vegetation mosaics and the impact of people upon these is a particularly important issue. Here, vegetation mosaics and patches are vital to our understanding of past human–environment interactions. Mosaics and patches are easily observable in the modern landscape, but cannot be reconstructed with accuracy for past landscapes. However, using palynological and anthracological information in conjunction with geological, geomorphological, and hydrological evidence, we can suggest how different mosaic communities may have been distributed across the landscape. We might place the village at the centre of a postulated mosaic, and consider how the inhabitants of Early to Middle Neolithic villages would logically have opened the vegetation closest to them. Moreover, we should not forget that arable agriculture in open plots was just one of many activities that would have taken place around a Neolithic settlement. The possible variations in the combinations of pastoral, arable, and wild-resource areas and the distribution and relative proportions of these different land-use categories can only be estimated and perhaps modelled via geographic information systems (GIS) (Robb & Van Hove 2003). One process is clear – that of an ever-increasing opening of areas close to sites during the Late Neolithic as new farming strategies emerged in certain parts of the Mediterranean. Considered by McClure to be similar to the traditional Mediterranean farming system known as *secano* or dry-land farming (Bernabeu 1995), it comprised a system where crop rotation was longer, and the distances between newly farmed areas and the village increased. These changes also included the use of cave sites as enclosures for sheep and goats (McClure et al. 2006: 23). Consequently, we would expect to see these changes reflected in pollen diagrams.

Late Neolithic–Bronze Age Landscapes in Spain
Parts of Spain saw the development of complex and successful societies during the later prehistoric periods. The combination of

palaeoenvironmental and archaeological research here allows us to assess some of the relationships that developed between people and landscapes during these periods.

Despite evidence for erosion during the Neolithic, in areas such as the Polop Alto Valley (eastern Spain) (Barton et al. 2002: 165), it seems unlikely that erosion posed a serious threat to Iberian Neolithic farmers. It was during the Bronze Age that potential problems developed – not simply environmental problems, but stresses exacerbated by a complex social hierarchy within a landscape that contained patches of degraded land that may well have become unusable at certain times. Such a scenario seems quite likely for the east and south-east areas of Spain, where a period of change saw a large number of settlements abandoned and new ones created. Thus, a series of well-dated sites show that settlements in eastern Iberia had shorter occupation phases and were abandoned earlier than sites in the west, with many abandoned c. 2200 BC. That environmental processes may well have caused this seems plausible, especially as the east is more arid than the west (Lillios 1997: 173). Specific geoarchaeological and archaeological evidence comes from the Librilla rambla, a torrential tributary of the Guadalentín River in south-east Spain, in whose valley are impressive sedimentary units, one sequence of which, dated to 5409–5149 BC to 3070–2711 BC, is 7–8 m thick. Neolithic sites were found within this sequence, whose accumulation represents a low-energy semi-endorheic environment (a basin that is closed in the sense that there is little discharge to external bodies of water) (see Cano Gomariz 1993 cited in Calmel-Avila 2002: 105). The *rambla* then cut into these earlier layers, depositing 8 m of sediment (sand and pebble bars). Chalcolithic shards and traces of a settlement site dated c. 2360 BC were found within this layer. A third layer, some 11 m thick, cuts and covers the previous units. Such sediments indicate that there were moments of powerful water discharge (Calmel-Avila 2002: 106), most likely storm events, dislodging sediment from exposed areas across a catchment. Consequently, it is important to consider the nature of human activity both on and off site, and thus to assess the possible reasons for sediment removal and then its subsequent redeposition. The study of the relationships of sites with their catchments is crucial, as human experience of activity in the landscape and any environmental processes is not fixed to one particular point in space.

Thus far, we have seen similar patterns in the evolution of vegetation during the first part of the Holocene across the Northern Mediterranean. However, there were some zones that were never covered by dense forest. One such region is the semi-arid zone of Almería near the southeastern coast of Spain. Vegetation here has oscillated between steppe and shrub communities. Between 5000 and 2500 BC, the landscape comprised extensive vegetation cover. Shrubs such as *Pistacia* expanded, and deciduous oak was present (Pantaleon-Cano et al. 2003: 115). This was followed by the establishment of steppe, the disappearance of deciduous oak, and the development of a so-called marginal landscape – a landscape which is considered degraded as a consequence of human activity. One of the interesting aspects of some of the work in the Almería area is the presence of *Olea* pollen from the Early Holocene onwards. The expansion of this tree was tied to the development of shrub communities in general, and its history is not exclusively tied to anthropogenic intervention or exploitation. Moreover, the absence of obvious anthropogenic indicators in these pollen diagrams is also important (ibid.: 115–6). Whilst there is no doubt that this area was economically important from the middle of the third millennium BC onwards, with agricultural and metallurgical activities taking place, these activities were not registered in the palynological record. Any species that might be associated with anthropogenic impact may also have existed under natural conditions (ibid.: 117).

One infamous landscape type in this part of the world is the so-called badlands – zones that do not necessarily represent the inevitable product of extreme erosion processes but rather a specific landform type (Grove & Rackham 2001: ch. 15). They tend to exist in areas characterised by relatively fragile, superficial geological deposits (usually soft marls) and where tectonic activity is important. Quite often, eroded material (via gullying and slumping) is removed from the basal areas of these landforms by rivers or streams. Eastern Spain is one of the most arid zones in Europe and the Northern Mediterranean (Fig. 5.9). Today, parts of this area are considered to be 'Euro-Desert' and, with an annual rainfall of less than 300 mm, there is little chance of vegetation taking hold. Almería and the eastern Alpujarra are the most arid zones in Spain today. This part of Spain is where the Los Millares culture developed, and there is little doubt that this zone was not as arid during the Chalcolithic. The changes in vegetation (as seen in pollen diagrams) imply that this area became more arid at a time (between 1300 and 1000 BC) when many

5.9. Badlands topography (south-east Spain) (photo: author).

of the Argaric settlements appear to have been abandoned (Castro et al. 1999).

Site Catchments in Proto-Historic Spain

So far, no reference has been made to site catchment analysis (SCA) (Vita-Finzi & Higgs 1970), partly because this approach has not been explicitly employed in recent years, although much GIS-based work does incorporate some form of SCA. The assessment of catchment areas around sites is important, and is in fact an integral part of modern landscape archaeology, albeit implicit in many approaches. Characterising Mediterranean landscapes as complex mosaics where patchiness increases with time in many parts of the Mediterranean does mean that we need to consider the range of probable patch types across our study areas. The use of GIS and the development of models is one approach that can help in this endeavour (Robb & Van Hove 2003). Traditionally, SCA involves the characterisation of resources available within a given distance that can be walked within a certain time, often between two and four hours. Sometimes, these zones are subdivided into shorter time–distance zones as well. More often than not, the potential of a landscape is based upon modern vegetation, soils, and agricultural use. More recent developments, employing cost–distances analyses, incorporate characteristics of topography and, when possible, what is known about political or cultural districts (e.g. Farinetti 2009), thus facilitating more 'realistic' assessments of how people engaged with landscapes.

Gilman and Thornes's (1985: 33) pioneering use of site catchment analyses in south-east Spain presented direct and indirect evidence for the development of Bronze Age irrigation. The existence of sites in areas that currently receive less than 250 mm rainfall in a year is indirect evidence, whilst the presence of ditches on some sites might be considered direct evidence. The information on land quality and water supply was then used to inform the assessment of site territories and the evidence for land-use preferences associated with specific sites. The relative proportions of the different land-use categories within the 12- and 30-minute zones were compared with the categories in the two-hour zone (the peripheral zone). It is interesting to note that two sites close to one another (the Campico De Labor and La Bastida sites) do not have direct access to good-quality land suitable for irrigation (according to the land-potential characterisation model developed by Gilman and Thornes). This situation raises an important issue. Can these types of territorial analysis work when several sites occupy the same territories, or when their territories overlap? Whilst many of the areas within which archaeological sites were situated appear to have been stable, it is quite probable that other parts of the landscape (off-site zones), such as fields, were subject to erosion. It is likely that settlement sites were purposely located on stable areas. This does not mean to say that people, as part of their working lives across other parts of the landscape, did not have to deal with erosion.

In many parts of the Iberian Peninsula, the Bronze Age witnessed the emergence of a managed and more open landscape, with arable and pastoral agriculture spreading out over much wider areas, along with extensive exploitation of woodland for timber and fuel, and the use of these materials in processes ranging from construction through to mining. However, the story is not one of ever-increasing human expansion and concomitant impact on the landscape and vegetation, but rather a waxing and waning of activity, where archaeologists must carefully assess the intersection of cultural and environmental processes, where vegetation depletion can be a response to climate change, economic changes, or both. Palaeoecological evidence elucidates these processes in a number of ways.

In south-east Spain, the evidence supports the possibility of dry, rain-fed polyculture farming not being practiced until the second millennium BC. If the climate was stable (i.e. arid), it has been argued that any early settlement in the south-east of Spain must have included the development of irrigation technology, otherwise the arid conditions would have impeded activity here (see Gilman 1976: 316). As Ruiz et al. (1992) observe, evidence for climate change often lacks precision when attempting to understand variations between different chrono-cultural periods. The problem when talking about climate is that we can rarely measure what weather was like within a given climatic period. For example, the *overall* levels of precipitation are less important than the *seasonal* variation in rainfall; rain needs to fall at the right time of year for successful farming.

The first 'peak' in population was the Argaric Bronze Age, with the population growing during the third millennium BC (Los Millares Copper Age). It is during this period that we see the development of social inequalities, differences in access to exotic materials, and the development of fortifications around settlements. The landscape around these settlements was increasingly opened up and woodland disappeared. 'The environmental impact of the Argaric political system was clearly felt in the second half of the second millennium BC' (Castro et al. 2000: 155). During the later Argaric period, slow colluviation and possible slope management in the form of small terraces might represent a response to these environmental characteristics (Wainwright 2004). A non-desert landscape normally passes through a phase of 'degradation' before 'desertification', so certain regions may experience several phases of degradation but recover from these. South-eastern Spain may have gone through at least four cycles of degradation (van der Leeuw 2003: 12), and each time a reassessment of the landscape and the identification of new economically viable niches may well have allowed a group of people to remain active within a given area. The landscape around the enigmatic Argaric site of Castellon Alto provides an excellent example of a complex mosaic landscape comprising a river with its terraces, largely suitable for arable agriculture, then small niches within the surrounding undulating topography that would have provided grazing and zones for arboriculture (Fig. 5.10) (Cortés et al. 1997; Rodriguez-Ariza & Ruiz

5.10. The landscape around Castellon Alto (south-east Spain). Note the variation in landform types, with rich vegetation and agricultural activity concentrated along the valley bottom (photo: author).

1996). The Copper and Bronze Age site of Gatas, which is 13 km away from El Argar and 2 km south of the River Aguas, provides an example for discussion. The botanical remains from the site do not permit the inference of local climatic fluctuations (Ruiz et al. 1992: 20), but they do present a clear image of the natural resources exploited at the site. For example, it is apparent that 90% of the plant resources came from the immediate area.

It is possible that under conditions where the environment came under 'stress', elite groups in Argaric society could not incorporate more extensive areas into their production system. Another possibility is that lower-status groups resisted the developing social inequalities (ibid.: 32–3): an increase in Bronze Age violence is attested to by palaeopathological research (Jiménez-Brobeil, du Souich, & Al Oumaoui 2009). During the post-Argaric phase (1500–1300 BC), the range of crop species grown was greater than the preceding phase, coinciding with the appearance of flax, vine, and olive (Castro et al. 1999: 851–2). The charcoal evidence implies further clearance, as well as a reduction in the use or availability of timber. The presence of *Tamarix* implies the development of saline soils. Between 1300 and 1000 BC, many of the settlements that were established during the Argaric period, including that at Gatas, were abandoned. The range of plant species grown on or near the site decreased, whilst the exploitation of domestic and wild animals increased (ibid.: 853). Deciduous trees also disappeared entirely during this period, as environmental conditions in the area became more arid (ibid.).

Many of these landscapes would have comprised a patchwork of heterogeneous farming practices – systems that may have been more akin to the modern concept of 'permaculture' (sustainable agricultural practices that are successfully adapted to the range of niches within a given area), rather than open landscapes dominated by a restricted number of crops and practices, as often implied by crude percentages of woodland, grassland, arable, and pastoral indicators drawn from pollen diagrams. Agricultural regimes developed strategies for the exploitation of specific niches across valleys, with the agricultural potential of each part of the landscape successfully harnessed, and in particular, the river terrace soils used for arable production, especially for legume crops (Chapman 2008: 202). Despite this legitimately optimistic assessment of environmental potential, we now need to consider a range of specific engagements with these environment types and the evidence for human response to environmental potential and environmental problems. The following chapter therefore assesses a range of specific processes and human engagements with vegetation and geomorphic processes within a perspective that considers temporally and spatially specific examples of human interaction with and impact upon these landscape elements.

6

Working and Managing Mediterranean Environments

Lifeways in Mediterranean Environments

As discussed in the preceding chapter, much palaeoenvironmental work has traditionally been concerned with the description of the history of geomorphological and palaeoecological processes – ascribing natural and/or anthropogenic causes to phenomena observed in the environmental record within a framework that emphasises chronological phases of 'stability' and 'instability', but with an overall trend of landscape degradation. The fundamental questions are when did degradation start, and *who* or *what* were responsible (e.g. Delano-Smith 1996)? For example, the vegetation changes that we see across the Mediterranean through the Holocene might be considered as the product of climate change (and therefore 'natural'), whilst the development of agricultural environments, whether for crops or pasture, is clearly an anthropogenic process. However, those large areas of rarely exploited scrubby woodland which cover large parts of the Mediterranean are in some ways a natural response to changes in environmental conditions. One argument is that this secondary succession vegetation (the sclerophyllous scrubby-woodland) is a direct consequence of both Middle Holocene changes in climate and human impact. This is an example of resilience, and we should consider that the degradation narrative is therefore culturally defined, where researchers imply or assert that cultural determinants were more influential than climatic, with climate change creating conditions that predisposed vegetation to degradation. What we have to consider is the extent to which people and/or climate have rendered landscapes unusable or unproductive in the past.

Unsurprisingly, different researchers involved in the study of Mediterranean landscape change have varied approaches to the analysis of these phenomena (e.g. Bintliff 2002; Thornes 1987; van Andel et al. 1986; van Andel & Zangger 1990). Some scholars have criticised the degradationist paradigm (notably Horden & Purcell 2000; Grove & Rackham 2001), and, to some degree, they have questioned the extent and impact of erosional processes within the Mediterranean. At one level, these narratives accentuate the long and medium *durée*, and articulate models that present humans as an anonymous, nebulous group operating within long timescales (Walsh 2004).

In this chapter, we build upon the processes outlined in the preceding chapter through an analysis of possible scenarios where we can talk about direct engagement with certain environmental processes, and consider practices and lifeways that contributed to the construction of new cultural ecologies. The final section presents specific case studies where we can identify various forms of interaction with landscape processes, and in the case of the Sainte Victoire Mountain (south of France), an example where the assessment of diachronic changes in engagements with the same landscape can be inferred.

CLEARANCE, TERRACING, AND THE CREATION OF THE SUSTAINABLE MEDITERRANEAN LANDSCAPE

As we have already seen, Neolithic populations had some impact on parts of the landscape, but it is difficult to argue for intensive and extensive management of the vast areas of the Mediterranean prior to the Bronze Age. One of the important changes to Bronze Age landscapes was the impact on vegetation. For example, a low-altitude pollen diagram from Lake Lerna on the Argive plain makes a valuable contribution to understanding of the vegetation changes close to a number of important Bronze Age sites: Mycenae, Tiryns, and Lerna (Jahns 1993: 187) (Fig. 6.1). From c. 5700 BC, deciduous species including *Quercus* (oak), *Corylus* (hazel), and *Carpinus* (hornbeam) were common, along with evergreen species such as *Phillyrea*, *Pistacia* (cashew family, incl. pistachio), and evergreen oaks. Later, a changing vegetation pattern does point to some human impact on the environment, but such changes could well be part of a 'normal' successional change, and do not suggest profound anthropogenic influences (Jahns 1993). In the Nemea Valley, some 20 km to the north of Argos, *Ostrya* (hophornbeam), *Tilia*

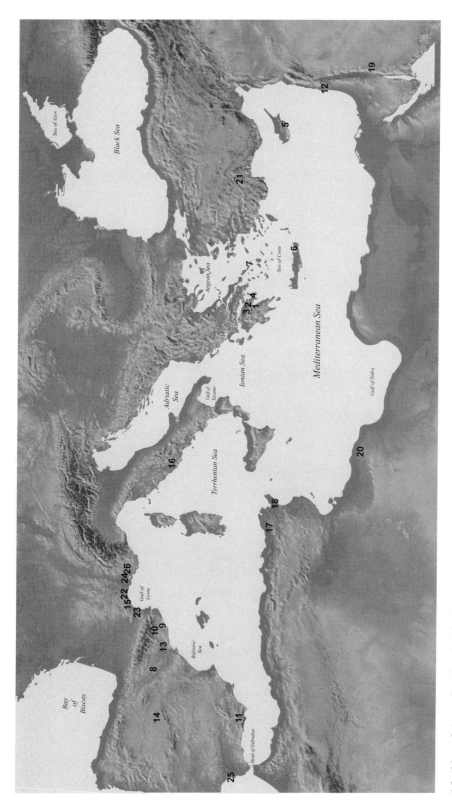

6.1. Map of sites referred to in this chapter. 1: Lake Lerna, 2: Mycenae/Tiryns, 3: Nemea Valley/Kleonai, 4: Methena, 5: Kalavasos Tenta/Mitsinjites, 6: Pseira, 7: Delos, 8: Ebro Valley, 9: Barcelona plain, 10: River Llobregat, 11: Sierra de Gádor, 12: Kfar Samir, 13: Eastern Cossetània, 14: Lozoya Valley, 15: Gasquinoy (Béziers, Hérault), 16: Lago Albao and Lago di Nemi, 17: Medjerda floodplain (northern Tunisia), 18: Segermes valley (north-east Tunisia), 19: At Khirbet Faynan, 20: Tripolitania, 21: Sagalassos, 22: Lattara, 23: Montou, 24: The Crau/Barbegal/Arles, 25: El Acebrón/Las Madres, 26: Sainte Victoire/ Domaine Richeaume/ Bramefan/Roque Vaoutade.

(lime), and *Q. pubescens* (pubescent oak) were present during the Early Neolithic (6300–5100 BC), but it seems unlikely that dense woodland was ever present here. During the Bronze Age, there was an expansion of a maquis vegetation (*Q. coccifera* (kermes oak), *Arbutus* (incl. strawberry tree), *Phillyrea*, and *Pistacia*), with deciduous species such as *Castanea* (chestnut), *Juglans*, and *Platanus* (plane tree), along with *Olea* emerging. From the Late Bronze Age through to the classical/ Hellenistic periods, we see an increase in open-country species, especially *Poaceae* (grasses), taken to imply an increase in agricultural activity. Any 'semi-natural' woodland had disappeared by the Roman period, when an open arable landscape with a dispersed settlement pattern had developed (Atherden, Hall, & Wright 1993: 354–5). Parts of lowland Greece would have comprised open (i.e. unwooded) areas from relatively early on, but there is little evidence for either extensive or intensive woodland clearance.

The creation of relatively open landscape increases the possibility for erosion. However, we cannot escape the fact that many sedimentary sequences will have been truncated, and portions of the erosional record lost (Delano-Smith 1996: 161). For example, Moody's (2000: 58) constructive assessment of the Cretan record contends that certain sediments deposited by intense storms in the past may have been removed by subsequent events. Storms and their associated flash floods and erosion episodes can be localised, especially across landscapes comprised of extreme topography. Therefore, it would require a series of spatially disparate storms at a particular time of year (harvest or sowing time) for such events to have an effect on the economy and society of an island such as Crete (Moody 1997). There is evidence for Minoan flash-flood deposits across Crete, in particular dated to the Middle and Late Minoan periods (broadly the second millennium BC). The fact that there are few flash-flood deposits dated to the Archaic–Hellenistic periods, and that these Minoan deposits are as well preserved as those from the Little Ice Age, suggests that the Late Bronze Age on Crete may have experienced conditions – and, in particular, unpredictable, extreme weather – similar to that of the Little Ice Age (Moody 2000: 58). However, as is argued later, it is quite likely that extreme precipitation events and concomitant erosion are more likely during warmer climates as evapotranspiration and atmospheric instability are enhanced (Diodato et al. 2011), and this Early to Middle Bronze Age phase is characterised by a complex climatic oscillation, with an arid phase bracketed by two wetter periods (Magny, Vanniere, et al. 2009).

Although there is little doubt that deforestation enhances the potential for erosion, it is ploughing followed by heavy rainfall that results in the most serious erosion events (Grove & Rackham 2001: 268). These often-annual events are the most relevant to the study of human engagements with erosion. Modern research into the relationships between ploughing and erosion suggest that once animal-driven ploughs and ards were introduced (during the later proto-historic periods), these may well have led to increased erosion (Wainwright & Thornes 2004: 254). A common response to erosion was terracing (Frederick & Krahtopoulou 2000) or trenching (Foxhall 1996). Despite the fact that ethnographic work has shown that terrace construction is often seen as an aid to tilling rather than a mechanism for controlling erosion (Green & Lemon 1996: 185), there is no doubt that terracing does help mitigate erosion.

Research has been carried out in various regions around the Mediterranean to characterise and date terrace systems. The majority of those apparent today are post-medieval (Blanchemanche 1990). It is possible that terracing was initially developed during the Bronze Age or perhaps earlier. In some areas of the Mediterranean, these systems are, and have been, extremely extensive (Whitelaw 1991: 405). There is convincing evidence for the use of terraces during antiquity (L. Nixon & Price 2005). As Foxhall (1996) suggests, the absence of unambiguous archaeological evidence is problematic, and we have to acknowledge that trenching (which would not be as visible in the archaeological record as terraces) was possibly used on Greek estates. Whatever method was employed, the construction of terraces, or the digging of trenches, is more than an instrumental and economically rational response to hill-slope erosion. The terraces that were constructed around the Aegean during the Bronze Age represent the organisation and control of the landscape by dominant social groups: terraces were as much an articulation of political power in the landscape as they were forms of erosion management designed to enhance food production (Fig. 6.2). Whilst unequivocal evidence for terraced Bronze Age landscapes is rare, there is little doubt that later periods did see extensive and intensive forms of landscape management. Terracing is but one response to erosion. Forbes (2000) demonstrates how place-specific control mechanisms, such as the regulation of the number of grazing animals in a given area, contribute

6.2. Terraces near to Stymphalos. Note Roman tile in section (lower right of section face). Note also the terrace walls visible on the surface that are of course relatively modern. (b) Watercolour reconstruction of the early terraces on Delos (island, top-left; terrace plan, top right) (by permission of J.-M. Gassend).

to the successful management of areas which might otherwise evolve as degraded landscapes.

Archaeological evidence for terraces (in the form of datable lengths of walls that run along slope contours) reveals how erosion and potential instability might have been understood and responded to. Butzer's non-equilibrium model is a useful tool for appreciating the non-linear nature of landscape change, in particular, erosion processes in the Mediterranean. Essentially, non-equilibrium models suggest that repeated disequilibrium (phases of landscape change, such as severe erosion and soil depletion) results in progressively different landscape characteristics that develop over a number of centuries which can lead to complex ecological problems (Butzer 2005: 1784–5). The fact that significant erosion events occurred during the Bronze Age, and that limited erosion appears to characterise the classical period (it is estimated population levels were four times greater during the Roman period than during the Bronze Age) demonstrates that high population levels are not the principal cause of erosion. Whilst one has to agree with Butzer's (2005: 1786) observation that we cannot prove or disprove adaptive responses to prehistoric destructive erosion, it is likely that terraces in some areas did constitute a response.

An attempt to date field terraces in Methena demonstrates how the precise dating of these all-important features is difficult (James, Mee, & Taylor 1994). Links have been posited between the Neolithic site of Kalavasos Tenta and nearby terraces in the Vasilikos Valley, southern-central Cyprus. One notable aspect of this work was the attempt to identify links between terrace formations and property boundaries. Here, many terraces appear to coincide with property boundaries, and they are thus interpreted as possible elements of individual landholdings (Wagstaff 1992: 156–8). An adjacent terrace system at Mitsinjites demonstrates no such relationship with property divisions. As noted before, terrace systems are difficult to date, and the few sherds retrieved from these terraces only allow us to suggest a possible Bronze Age start for their development (ibid.: 160). An early example comes from Pseira, where terraces are dated to 2200–1700 BC (Vogiatzakis & Rackham 2008: 248), and a Bronze Age origin for terraces in Lebanon and Delos is possible (Harfouche 2007: 155, 170), whilst a twelfth to eleventh centuries BC origin for Levantine terraces has been suggested (Gophna 1979). Over time, environmental knowledge and the nature of work in the landscape would have become increasingly socially structured, and the experience of erosion mitigation, via the construction of terraces, would have emerged as an important element in the hierarchical organisation and control of landscape.

As described above, in the Argolid, it was during the middle of the third millennium BC that the first phase of severe soil erosion occurred, whilst the end of the third millennium saw a substantial reduction in the number of sites, probably caused by social and political processes beyond the Argolid (van Andel & Runnels 1987: 93). However, certain parts of the region, and the wider Mediterranean, would have been affected by the c. 2200 BC arid phase, although, as explained earlier, citing this event as a cause of economic and settlement contraction is problematic (L. D. Brandon 2012; Roberts, Eastwood, et al. 2011).

During the Late Bronze Age (in particular, during the Mycenaean period), a structured settlement hierarchy emerged (represented by, for example, the palace sites of Mycenae and Tiryns). The Early Bronze Age erosion phase might be seen as a short-term effect of a change in settlement pattern – an increase in activity on coastal zones and a concomitant increase in the use of surrounding hill slopes (Weiburg et al. 2010). Towards the end of the thirteenth century BC, many sites were destroyed. In the Argolid, there is a gap in the settlement record, with evidence for a markedly reduced human presence until the mid-ninth century BC. As settlement expanded once again, van Andel and Runnels (1987: 102–3) contend (based on a hypothesised soil quality) that the areas of deep soil were chosen, but that poor-quality zones were also exploited – areas that had previously witnessed little activity. Olives will grow on relatively poor-quality land, and will easily grow on hill slopes, especially if the slopes are managed through terracing. Thus, the expansion of cash crop agriculture, with its emphasis on olive production, should be seen as an important thread in a network of processes related to erosion management on terraced hill slopes characterised by poor-quality soils and erosion.

The soil erosion that occurred between 300 and 50 BC took place during a period of settlement/activity decline. This erosion may have been caused by grazing on the areas of poorer-quality land, whilst the good-quality land closer to the settlements was maintained as arable. As van Andel and Runnels (1987: 147–8) note, terracing is an excellent soil conservation mechanism, as long as terraces are maintained, but if

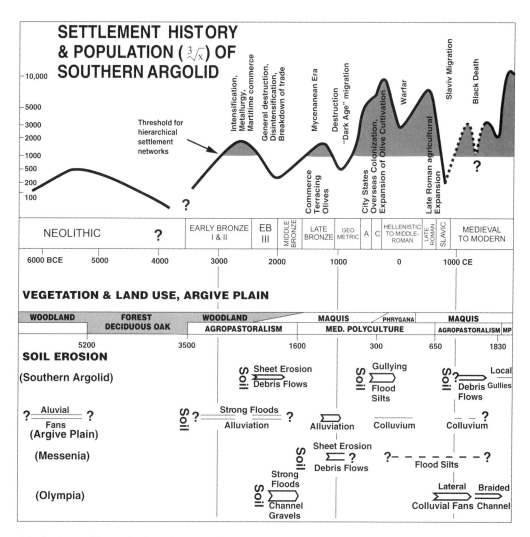

6.3. Settlement history, land-use change, and soil erosion in the Argolid and other locations of the Peloponnese. (By permission of Elsevier, Butzer, K. W. (2005), Environmental history in the Mediterranean world: Cross-disciplinary investigation of cause-and-effect for degradation and soil erosion. *Journal of Archaeological Science* 32(12), fig. 2.)

this does not happen, they may well collapse, and the soil stored behind them will be removed. If an area is depopulated, and terraces are left for some time, it is quite likely that naturally occurring maquis vegetation will colonise and prevent erosion. It is temporary, or partial, abandonment that subjects the soil system to the greatest risk, especially if the terraced slopes are occasionally exploited as pasture. One correlation that is apparent when looking at Figure 6.3 is the evidence for colluviation that occurs after peaks in settlement activity. Therefore, in many instances, environmental resilience in a cultural–ecological system might be the norm until the economic system collapses. As it stands, there is no evidence for erosion having been the cause of an economic downturn. Therefore, mitigation, including terracing along with the management of fields, may well have been quite successful.

The creation of fields is an integral element in the creation of artificial niches for food production. Their management is particularly important within landscapes that are susceptible to relatively minor changes in climate, and leaving fields fallow is an obvious soil conservation technique. If, for some reason, it becomes difficult to maintain adequate periods of fallow (due to increased food requirements, perhaps through crop failure in preceding years), then the probability of erosion occurring may increase. As with terraces, the presence of field systems immediately implies a series of management and political/cultural processes within a landscape.

Whilst we know that Bronze Age field systems and terraces existed in different forms across Europe, research on Iron Age systems across the Mediterranean has suffered to a certain extent because of an emphasis on the study of Roman field systems (centuriation), and the fact that many Iron Age systems were undoubtedly masked by this very process (Buchsenschutz 2004). There is, for example, inconclusive evidence for land division in Provence from the fourth and third centuries BC onwards (Boissinot 2000: 29). Clearly, with time, the evidence for complex field systems and ownership is more abundant.

There is no doubt that the utility of manuring was understood by most Mediterranean societies. There is evidence for knowledge of manuring, crop rotation and tillage in classical Greek societies (Burford 1993: ch. 3). Whereas the management of fields includes rotation systems, manuring, and possibly even the creation of boundary structures that reduce erosion, fields can also contribute to environmental problems, especially when they are applied uniformly to the landscape at the behest of a centralised authority. In classical Greece, many tenancies, both public and sacred (plots 'owned' by the Gods), were subject to strict control regarding farming methods, crops grown, and the exact timing of when certain activities should be undertaken (ibid.: 23). The presence of such systems across parts of the Mediterranean during different periods represents forms of environmental management that might have prevented flexible responses to environmental problems. In the Roman world, as the Late Empire increased state involvement in rural production, there was probably an increase in land division, thus demonstrating the critical link between land demarcation and economic control (Leveau et al. 1993). Some have argued that, at its height, the increased allocation of parcels of land to centuriation during the first to third centuries AD did engender severe soil loss (Marchetti 2002). Despite the importance of centralised land allocation and large *latifundia*, smallholding – or subsistence farming – did exist (Frayn 1979), and there is no doubt that farmers were able to respond to environmental problems in an effective manner.

THE ROLE OF FIRE

Forest and brush fires are a common occurrence across the Mediterranean, and even take place in southern alpine valleys during especially dry summers. Whereas fires have immediate and dramatic consequences for the populations that live in the affected area, we should not see these events as inherently destructive. Rather, they may be part of the normal environmental round or anthropic actions that have a clearly defined and rational purpose vis-à-vis environmental management.

Palynological studies often include the analysis of micro-charcoal, and unsurprisingly, there is often some debate as to whether the charcoal represents natural fires or anthropogenic burning. Fire is, however, the most basic and common management tool in Mediterranean manipulation of the forest (di Pasquale, di Martino, & Mazzoleni 2004: 18). One of the biggest problems in palaeoecology is differentiating natural fires from those started by people as part of a landscape-management strategy (or through accidents and acts of arson).

During the Early Holocene, evidence from the Eastern Mediterranean (in particular, south-west Asia) suggests that (natural) summer fires actually delayed the colonisation of woodland by two or three millennia (Turner et al. 2010). Whilst, during the Neolithic, it is possible that people started to employ fire as part of landscape management and maintenance of agricultural zones (Roberts 2002). However, we should not assume that the control of Mediterranean vegetation was always uncomplicated. Some Mediterranean vegetation is partially resistant to fire. Many species will re-establish themselves quickly after a fire has taken place. These include *Q. coccifera* (prickly or kermes oak), *Q. suber* (cork oak), and *Olea* (wild olive) (Grove & Rackham 2001: 48–9). The deciduous oaks (including *Q. pyrenaica*, *Q. cerris*, *Q. pubescens*, and *Q. brachyphylla*) are also quite resistant to fire (Grove & Rackham 2001: 54).

During the Middle Holocene 'Thermal Maximum' between 5500 and 2500 BC, charcoal records indicate there was an overall increase in fires in the Northern Mediterranean. Between 3500 and 3000 BC, fire activity abruptly changed across the Mediterranean, as fire decreased in northern and eastern regions (because of cooler wetter summers), it progressively increased in southern regions. These southern regions, experiencing drier summers at this time, would not have been affected by increased annual precipitation (Vannière et al. 2011). During the period c. 4500–3000 BC, there was an increase in fire activity in some parts of the Mediterranean (Magny et al. 2011; Vannière et al. 2011). In certain zones, the transition to a more arid environment during the Middle Holocene saw reductions in woodland vegetation and potentially combustible material. In some areas, it seems that more fires occurred during the relatively wet climatic optimum. In certain arid regions of Spain, such as the Ebro Valley or Almeria, the Holocene optimum saw the expansion of scrub and pine forests, thus providing more fuel. Prior to 7500 BC, and after 2500 Cal BC, it has been argued that the amount of biomass was below the required threshold for extensive and regular fires (Riera Mora et al. 2004).

On the Barcelona plain, a number of fires took place near the coast between 6520 and 6400 BC, followed by increases in the pollen record in *Cistus* (rockrose family), *Buxus, Plantago lanceolata* (plantain) type, and *Asteraceae* (daisy/sunflower family). Similar processes also took place to the south of the River Llobregat between 7850 and 6200 BC. Later on, a possible phase with frequent fires occurred on the Castellón coast, where *Plantago* sp. increased between 4850 and 3980 BC. Between 4350 and 3775 BC, *Ericaceae* and *Pistacia lentiscus* increased. Such a sequence, with the development of the vegetation outlined here, strongly suggests that these fires may well have been part of a management system, especially as high percentages of *Cerealia* type and *Vitis* also appear. The radical change in economic strategies that occurred around 3775 BC, when fire use was patchy, can be explained by the development of a more sedentary lifestyle adopted by groups during the Middle Neolithic (Riera Mora et al. 2004). Other fire events during the Middle Holocene had obvious impacts on the forest, and the last of these fires (c. 2000 BC) was followed by a phase of 'instability', and the first clear evidence for anthropogenic impact in the area (Stevenson 2000: 607).

Despite the evidence for biomass availability being the fundamental control on fire occurrence in arid environments and the consequent relatively low frequency of fires during the Later Neolithic and Bronze Age, there are of course exceptions to this trend. The pollen site at Sierra de Gádor in southern Spain (1530 m) is a rare example of a pollen record from a truly Mediterranean arid zone (Carrión et al. 2003: 839). A series of major fires had a significant effect on the vegetation from c. 2200 BC. Bearing in mind the altitude of this site, the increase in fire activity may represent Bronze Age expansion into a new upland zone that had not been cleared prior to the Argaric period.

Each vegetation-burning event has to be studied in context, and a clear assessment of natural or anthropogenic origins has to be made. Fire has always been an essential tool in humankind's suite of environmental management options, and should be studied as the archetypal form of hybrid cultural–ecological practice – one which will be considered again in Chapter 8 as part of the discussion on Mediterranean mountains.

AGRICULTURAL AND PRODUCTIVE VEGETATION

More than most other regions around the world, the Mediterranean agricultural landscape is defined by its arboriculture, in particular the ubiquitous vines and olive trees, with stands of other tree crops such as pistachio, fig, and other fruits that inhabit the terraced landscapes. The range of crops grown across the Mediterranean has varied through time, and is the subject of books on agriculture and archaeobotany (e.g. Zohary & Hopf 2001). We know, for example, that Roman agriculture exploited a wide range of crops and trees well beyond the renowned Mediterranean triad of wheat, olives, and vines (Leveau et al. 1993).

The complexity of knowledge associated with olive propagation, from the use of cuttings and planted ovules to the range of ground preparation techniques, is a research subject in itself, and Foxhall's (2007) definitive analysis of olive cultivation is essential reading. Despite the emphasis on the olive, this tree may well have been grown with other tree crops, such as almonds. The combination of relatively fast-growing crops with olive, a tree that requires longer cultivation, served as a form of risk buffering, with the fast-growing tree crops being removed once the olive trees produced their full potential yield (ibid.: 113). Successful olive production also involves complex soil-management techniques, including trenching and a continuous maintenance of the soil system (ibid.: 124).

The identification of the moment when these species were first domesticated is one of the significant questions in Mediterranean palaeoecology, and some work has seen contributions from genetics (Guillaume et al. 2011), with one study demonstrating that genuinely wild olive varieties still exist in a number of Mediterranean forests (Lumaret & Ouazzani 2001). One way of assessing evidence for human cultivation of olive is the identification of olive pollen values that are higher than 'natural' values, that is, where pollen levels indicate that olive trees constitute a higher than 'natural' proportion of the local vegetation. In the Southern Levant, olive pollen levels fluctuated throughout the Holocene, with peaks achieving levels higher than expected during a number of periods, but in particular during the Hellenistic–Roman–Byzantine periods (Baruch 1999: 20). Prior to this, Neolithic evidence for olive exploitation comes from the now-submerged Kfar Samir site to the south of Haifa, where a date in the fifth millennium BC is given. Here, archaeobotanical evidence implies the large-scale use of olives. Intensive olive use is also implied archaeobotanically for the Bronze Age, although there is no direct archaeological evidence for intensive olive exploitation at this time (ibid.: 21).

Evidence from the Eastern Pyrenees for the selective exploitation and management of olive trees reveals that, from the Late Neolithic to the Late Bronze Age, only younger branches were cut. Such a practice might imply that olive-tree management started during the Late Neolithic. Increases in these thermophilous tree crops such as *Olea europaea* and *Pistacia lentiscus* may have been a result of anthropogenic manipulation rather than an increase in temperature (Heinz et al. 2004: 625). Increases in olive are seen during the proto-historic periods in eastern Cossetània (Spain), this being accompanied by a concomitant decrease in *Quercus* sp. (Burjachs & Schulte 2003).

The combination of botanical remains (seeds and wood) of vine, along with the archaeological evidence for the technological apparatus required for grape pressing and suitable fields for vine growing, allows the unequivocal identification of certain areas as wine-producing zones. Whilst the classical periods witnessed the development of intensive and extensive wine production (Brun 2004), increasingly we see evidence for prehistoric viniculture, with much of the evidence generated by traditional archaeological as well as bioarchaeological research (McGovern 2003; Schlumbaum, Tensen, & Jaenicke-Després 2008). Research into the DNA of *Vitis vinifera* suggests domestication c. 8,000 years ago (Arroyo-García et al. 2006). However, incontrovertible evidence for landscape management associated with wine production has a much later date. For example, vineyards of some description, as represented by vine ditches, existed in the Marseille area from the fourth century BC (Boissinot 2001) (Fig. 6.4), and evidence from the Gallo-Roman site Gasquinoy (Béziers, Hérault) in the south of France comprises vine plantation marks delimited by drainage ditches. Perhaps one of the most interesting aspects of this work is the study of plant macrofossils, and the evidence for a complex mosaic landscape around the actual site. The following environments or vegetation zones were identified: cereal production areas, cultivated trees, forest edges, dry areas, grasslands/meadows, and wetlands (Figueiral et al. 2010: 144).

Other than vine and olive, there are other species that emerged as significant Mediterranean tree crops, in particular nuts such as *Castanea* (sweet chestnut) and *Juglans* (walnut). Whilst *Castanea* makes an early (c. late eighth millennium BC) appearance in some pollen diagrams, such as that from the Kleonai core on the Peloponnese (collected as part of the Nemea Valley Archaeological Project) (Wright et al. 1990: 593), there is no clear evidence for its intensive exploitation until much later. Chestnut trees, which are useful for both their nuts and timber, have quite stringent moisture requirements.

The development of landscapes with patches of managed tree crops occurs across the Mediterranean, with many zones seeing an intensification of arboriculture during the Iron Age and Roman period. Some species, such as *Juglans*, are even considered by palynologists as chronological markers in this instance, marking the impact of Rome on the landscape. At the central Italian pollen sites of Lago Albano and Lago di Nemi, there is evidence for Iron Age *Cannabis* (hemp), followed by increases in *Castanea*, *Juglans*, and *Olea* (Mercuri et al. 2002). The introduction and exploitation of *Castanea sativa* is considered to be a very Roman affair, although it is likely that the intensive propagation of sweet chestnut was not that common (Conedera et al. 2004). *Castanea* was also naturally present in parts of the Mediterranean. Palynological evidence from the Lozoya Valley, Sierra de Guadarrama (1,113 m), central Spain, aimed to answer the question as to whether *Castanea* was introduced by the

6.4. Traces of vine plantations. Top: Saint Jean du désert; bottom: Les Girardes Lapalud (photos: Philippe Boissinot).

Romans or was in fact native (Franco Mugica, Garcia Anton, & Sainz 1998: 70). *Castanea* and *Olea* appear early in the Holocene within a landscape dominated by *Pinus*. It is likely that an opportunistic use was made of chestnut, but intensified exploitation did then develop in this area during the Roman period.

Come the Greek and Roman periods, we have to imagine the development of a complex mosaic of plants, and geomorphic processes, perhaps even more heterogeneous than today. We should not forget how, in recent years, EU quotas and financial support have resulted in the relative homogenisation of certain productive strategies, and this, combined with relatively low rural populations, means that many areas of the modern Mediterranean countryside are once again covered in woodland (Obando 2002).

Olive production, more than any other agricultural activity, gave rise to the creation (albeit relatively temporary) of intensively managed agricultural systems in landscapes that had otherwise seen relatively low levels of agricultural production. The infamous incorporation of North African semi-arid and arid landscapes into the Roman productive zone is perhaps the best example of the successful application of environmental knowledge by a hegemonic political structure. However, it is likely that this knowledge was founded on an adaptation of indigenous practices, which certainly seems to be the case in Tripolitania (Mattingly 1996). There is little doubt that the indigenous Garamantes exploited the hydrological sources along cliff base lines in the area (Leveau 2009). Despite variations in the climate, it is likely that for about 3,000 years, the Libyan pre-desert climate was relatively stable, with some phases of increased precipitation. One of these phases was contemporary with the Roman Empire. At the Wadi Tanezzuft, a period of increased precipitation rendered the area economically viable during the Roman period (Cremaschi 2003). At a broader regional level, evidence from the mid-Medjerda flood plain (northern Tunisia) indicates the stabilisation of forest cover during the Roman occupation, a period preceded by phases of environmental instability (Zielhofer & Faust 2003: 211). The Roman environmental optimum in this area may have been characterised by the development of more humid conditions. This may have supported vegetation persistence, as seen in the Segermes valley (north-east Tunisia), where Roman impact on the vegetation was no more intense than in preceding periods. The most important change was the introduction of olive production (Kolstrup 1994).

Responses to climate change (and day-to-day environmental processes) are influenced by the politics pursued by ruling elites (see McIntosh, Tainter, & McIntosh 2000; Rosen 2007: 2). Classical period exploitation of desert areas occurred during a period of improved climatic conditions, which may have included some phases of greater precipitation (Rosen 2007: 3). Although we cannot generalise and state that this period was noticeably wetter than the preceding periods, some minor changes in rainfall patterns may have been enough to allow movement into arid zones – although it was the political and economic will to exploit those areas that was of paramount importance. Technological innovation (or adaptation of existing practices) appears to have helped render parts of this region profitable. Romano-Libyan farmers practised flood-water farming, building walls to divert surface run-off after seasonal storms (Gilbertson, Hunt, & Smithson 1996). Cereals were grown, including six-row hulled barley, durum or hard wheat, and bread wheat, plus lentils, peas and grass peas, olive, linseed, vine, almonds, and peaches (Van Der Veen 1996). At Khirbet Faynan (southern Jordan), olives and vines did grow in the area, and charcoal from mining areas show how Roman miners had to bring in wood from the plateau – a different experience to that of Nabataean people who were using local wood (Barker 2002; Engel 1993).

During the first to the fifth centuries AD, flood-water farming in certain pre-desert zones was probably established by Rome within a climatic context perceived as being stable, and identified as suitable for agricultural production given the right technological and management structures. Eventually, landscape degradation led to a loss of efficiency in this flood-water farming system, and pollution may have become a serious problem (Barker 2002). One possible effect of intense agriculture and grazing in an arid zone is an increase in dust storms (Gilbertson 1996: 299). Also, after some time, soil exhaustion as a result of short fallow periods may have posed problems for pre-desert farming systems (ibid.: 304–5). Soil erosion in arid environments is potentially disastrous. Gullying, in particular, is a problem on wadi floors, and there is no doubt that periods of soil loss did occur during antiquity. Gilbertson (1996: 314) suggests that neglect and inadequate maintenance of landscape management features, rather than the intensification of agriculture, may well have led to increased erosion. It could be that erosion was restricted because of an emphasis on tree crops, and this may have helped maintain a relatively stable landscape for a certain time (Barker et al. 1996: 278). However, evidence for interbedded aeolian sands and flood-loam deposits do indicate important, perhaps short-lived, changes in the wadi environment during the Romano-Libyan and later periods (Anketell et al. 1995: 239). Consequently, whilst Rome managed the successful optimisation of the environmental potential of these landscapes, there would undoubtedly have been years, even decades, when environmental conditions were difficult. In particular, annual rainfall would have fluctuated and inhibited production. Despite the potential for erosion, and even periods of crop failure or reduced yields, there is no doubt that this arid landscape was productive, and represents the successful application of environmental knowledge and concomitant technologies within such areas. However, we should not lose sight of the potential hardship for those who worked in these landscapes. There is evidence for an awareness of the importance of conservation strategies amongst Romano-Libyan desert farmers in Tripolitania. Sluices were blocked, possibly to restrict flood-water flow into the fields (Barker 2002: 496). Despite the evidence for regional drying towards the end of the Roman period in the Eastern Mediterranean (Orland et al. 2009), and probably the South as well, the demise of this successful agricultural exploitation cannot be put down to environmental change (Gilbertson 1996). The contraction of the Roman Empire and its markets, and the possible loss of pertinent environmental knowledge, may well have contributed to the eventual decline of this productive system.

WOODLAND AND LANDSCAPE MANAGEMENT (DEHESA AND OTHER SYSTEMS)

The 'Fall from Eden' discourse is partly founded on the notion of humanity's removal and mismanagement of Mediterranean vegetation. Whilst there is no doubt that people have cleared vast swathes of woodland and forest, Mediterranean vegetation has often demonstrated natural resilience, secondary woodland recolonising areas with surprising ease. There is a long history of woodland management, with economic needs balanced with specific woodland ecologies. A complex multi-proxy study (using pollen, charcoal, phytolith, and sedimentary analyses) of the Middle Neolithic landscape in the Middle Rhone Valley demonstrates the emergence of a mosaic of agro-sylvo-pastoral management that allowed the emergence of grasslands under relatively open woodland of deciduous oaks. This configuration seems similar to the dehesa system (discussed below), although it appears that this landscape *was* sensitive to either environmental change or cultural change (or a combination of the two), as it had disappeared by the end of the fourth millennium BC (Delhon, Thiébault, & Berger 2008).

There are some parts of the Mediterranean where there is no doubt that woodland never managed to recover from early human impact. For example, in Lebanon, cedar was present during the first part of the Holocene. However, by 5900 BC, these trees were subject to clearance, and by 3700 BC, much of the forest had totally disappeared as olive groves expanded. In the epic of Gilgamesh (written some 4,600 years ago), Lebanese cedar is mentioned, as the King of Uruk required timber from this tree in order to construct his city. However, if the King had come to this area in search of cedar, he would not have found any (Yasuda, Kitagawa, & Nakagawa 2000: 133). Levantine peoples were obliged to trade for timber during the Bronze Age, with societies in this region looking to maritime trade as the only means for economic advancement (Akar 2009). Moving into the Iron Age, we see how Phoenicia, delimited and protected to the east by the Lebanese mountains, lacked access to an extensive range of arable land and woodland resources. The narrow band of land suitable for agriculture between the mountains and the coast meant that Phoenicians looked to the sea for economic expansion and the supply of essential materials (Aubet & Turton 2001).

The notion that early farmers lived in harmony with the environment and cared for the natural world (Hughes 2005: 21) requires careful assessment. We could consider that if human impact does not change the ecology of a certain area to the extent that any reversion to a previous state becomes impossible, then a form of metastability is possible and quite common in many landscapes. As presented in the previous chapter, there is limited evidence for extensive impact on woodland and soils during the Early Neolithic. We can identify some human impact on the vegetation, especially from the Late Neolithic onwards (Reille & Pons 1992; Vernet 1997), and some have suggested that shortages of timber affected societies as far back as the Bronze Age. As Meiggs (1982: 98) notes, Arthur Evans felt that the Minoans suffered a shortage of timber, not being able to fulfil their requirements from within Crete. Evans had considered that one of the causes of the downfall of the Minoans was the destruction of timber resources (Evans quoted in Meiggs 1982: 98). This is unlikely, since there are no signs of timber shortage on some of the palace sites (Meiggs 1982: 99).

Some have argued that human impact on vegetation only becomes apparent during the Roman period, and that all preceding changes can be explained by climate change (e.g. Magri 1995; Yll et al. 1997). The project directed by Frenzel and Reisch (1994) provides one of the most useful contributions to this debate. Arboreal pollen percentages for the Roman period across Greece vary quite substantially. Some have argued that the proportion of open landscape in southern lowland Greece was very high and comparable to recent levels before reafforestation commenced (Bintliff 1993). Others have suggested that the notion that low-altitude sites would have been subject to intense deforestation whilst higher altitudes were relatively untouched cannot be demonstrated: There are low-altitude and high-altitude sites with high arboreal pollen percentages, and some high-altitude sites with low arboreal pollen percentages (Bottema 1994a: 70–1).

Pliny the Elder stated that, during the fourth century BC, the beech tree grew towards sea level along the Tiber. However, during his lifetime (first century AD), the beech was considered to be a mountain tree (Reale & Dirmeyer 2000: 167). This type of documentary evidence, in combination with archaeological site evidence (the presence of large settlements in now semi-arid, arid, or desert-like environments) and vegetation models based on palynological evidence from around the Mediterranean, demonstrates a substantial difference between the density and distribution of modern-day vegetation compared with that from 2,000 years ago (Reale & Dirmeyer 2000; Reale & Shukla 2000). At Sagalassos in the western Taurus mountains in Turkey (situated between 1,490 and 1,600 m), there is little evidence that the Roman forest was depleted. It seems that this area was comprised of woods and open areas (Waelkens et al. 1999: 702). The charcoal evidence shows that most of the wood employed in smelting came from pine and juniper, with some oak also being employed (Schoch 1995 cited in Waelkens et al. 1999). Moreover, the presence of olive wood in these assemblages and stone weights that may well have been parts of olive presses, combined with evidence for slightly warmer winters during the Graeco-Roman period, implies that olive was probably grown in the vicinity, whereas today it cannot grow (Waelkens et al. 1999: 705). The development of today's open landscape did not actually occur until after the Roman period.

The primordial use of wood was for making fire. The use of fire ranged from the obvious functional roles of providing heat for people and for cooking through to warding off wild animals and producing aesthetic experiences that would have had a range of social and ritual functions. Wood for fire would normally have been gathered from the forest floor rather than procured through the wholesale felling or destruction of trees; the gathering of wood was probably a task carried out as part of other agricultural activities, with wood collected from extended geographical areas. This is implied in the charcoal assemblages that often comprise a wide range of species present across a set of varied niches that must have been visited during the collection of wood. This was especially true for the Roman period, when timber and wood exploitation was intensive. In some areas, such as the plain around Lattara (the Iron Age and Roman settlement near modern Montpellier), we see an absence of species from the wider landscape, implying that, by the end of the Iron Age, this area was completely opened up for agriculture (Chabal 1998: 134–5). Charcoal data do not merely confirm or complement palynological histories, but they provide specific information on the species of tree exploited by people in the past. The charcoal evidence from the Middle Neolithic to the Late Bronze Age Montou site (270 m above sea level) shows that firewood was collected from upland areas as well close to the site. It is also possible that this wood, comprising *Pinus sylvestris* type (Scots pine) and *Abies alba* (silver fir), could have floated downriver and thus represents opportunistic exploitation (Heinz et al. 2004: 624).

Flexible forms of environmental knowledge allow people to practice the exploitation of natural resources without causing degradation and instability. Woodland management, and in particular the dehesa system (and regional variations of that system), are one example of such a practice. One of the most important management strategies within woodland would have been the creation of openings for grazing for both wild and domesticated animals. Grazing animals have had to shoulder the blame for the 'degraded' Mediterranean environment (more specifically, vegetation) more than any other agent. In some landscapes, there is evidence for severe Roman impact on local ecologies through livestock pasturing. For example, focussed ecological research on arid grasslands demonstrates the importance of the Roman 'footprint' upon certain types of

6.5. Roman sheep enclosure on the Crau (Provence): The site of Négreiron 6 (photo: Gaëtan Congès). Note the impoverished vegetation.

vegetation. The Crau, an extensive semi-arid plain in the south of France, witnessed intensive pastoral activity during the Roman period (Fig. 6.5). The soil seedbank (the viable stored seeds within a specific soil unit) in the areas exploited during the Roman period show how these grasslands have failed to recover, both in terms of plant species richness and abundance, as well as in terms of soil quality (F. Henry 2009).

Dehesas are perhaps the best example of a persistent landscape type that demonstrates successful management. These areas are open parklands in which the woodland has been managed with a view to providing a whole series of resources: fuel, fruits, cork, wood, and pasture (Fig. 6.6). They are predominantly found in the south and south-west of Portugal and Spain. If these areas are overgrazed, they often develop into scrub. It is argued that such a system of dehesa would have existed

6.6. Dehesas in the distance with pastoral structures in the foreground (photo: Santiago Riera-Mora).

during the second millennium. This is reflected in the palynological evidence. Harrison (1994: 85) considers that Mediterranean Spain did not adopt the 'typical' Mediterranean triad of wheat, olives, and vines due to the threat of drought. Instead, a system which made efficient use of the secondary products from animals provided the foundations for the economy in this part of the Mediterranean. Palynological work from El Acebrón and Las Madres in south-west Spain demonstrates a pattern of vegetation change that is quite different from the so-called natural succession that one would expect in this area, with the first simple dehesas appearing during the Copper and Bronze Ages. The first phase (4000–2500 BC) from the pollen diagrams from Las Madres indicates the presence of large amounts of *Vitis* and low values for trees. Such a signal may represent viticulture or the management of wild vine in order to collect the autumn fruits. At the same time, there were increases in *Quercus* along with *Plantago*, *Anthemis* type (dog fennel chamomile), *Rumex* type (docks), and *Artemisia* (wormwoods). The second phase (2500–1600 BC) saw the re-emergence of oak and pine forest with some high values for ruderal indicators, and this may be the first phase of true oak dehesa

(Stevenson & Harrison 1992: 241–2). This is contemporary with the climax of the Millaran societies. Phase III (1600 BC–AD 500) saw the destruction of the forest cover in the Las Madres area. Despite the fact that this destruction is put down to anthropogenic activities, there is little evidence for settlement before the end of this phase. Olive pollen appears in the Las Madres core for the first time during this phase. During phase IV (500 BC–1200 AD), there is a clear peak in oak values along with pollen from ruderal indicators, a combination typical of a classic dehesa. The dehesa system was 'fully defined' by 500 BC, and is thus considered a Phoenician product (ibid.: 243). Research demonstrates that dehesas actually mimic ecosystems, in that these human-made agro-ecosystems appear stable and have certainly been resilient whilst providing a range of useful resources (Joffre, Rambal, & Ratte 1999). Dehesa-montado systems have existed for many centuries. Humans manage these hybrid systems, enhancing the available ecological characteristics in the production of a particularly successful socio-environmental niche (Pereira & da Fonseca 2003). The essential element in the notion of hybridity is that all manifestations of activity in the landscape, whether terracing or forest management, are the product of a complex intersection of a range of cultural processes, ranging from the economically rational through to ritual (Latour 1997; Whatmore 2002).

Environmental management often manifests itself through forms of proscription. We know that some woodlands were sacred. One such possible sacred 'deciduous-oakery' – Skotitas – was named after Zeus Skotitas. This was situated on the borders of Lakonia, and still exists as a substantial coppice (Rackham 2001: 16). There is little doubt that certain places at certain points in the past have witnessed vegetation exhaustion, but relatively few palaeoecological studies imply long-term, extensive vegetation loss. There are many examples of persistent woodland, and whilst the dehesa system might represent an unusually successful example of sustainable woodland management, it is quite likely that similar forms of environmental knowledge have been successfully applied across other parts of the Mediterranean during the Middle to Late Holocene.

Environmental Change and Social Geoarchaeology

In order to develop some of the notions and themes presented in this and the preceding chapter, two specific examples of landscape archaeological

6.7. The Sainte Victoire landscape with the c. 1,000 m high mountain ridge (running west–east) and the plain in front (to the south of the mountain) (photo: author).

research and environmental reconstruction work are considered below. The aim is to provide an example of how we might make inferences in situations where archaeological and environmental evidence intersect.

THE SAINTE VICTOIRE: CHANGING PATTERNS OF INTERACTION WITH ENVIRONMENT

One example of a notionally 'degraded' (comprised of steep slopes and relatively poor soils) Mediterranean landscape is the Sainte Victoire massif (south-east France). This area was the object of detailed landscape survey and excavations, designed to investigate the Iron Age and Roman settlement and economy of this area, as well as the changing nature of human engagements with landscape processes, including hydrology and erosion (Walsh & Mocci 2003). This landscape comprises a 1,000 m high mountain that dominates a relatively flat plain to the south, and undulating topography to the north, with steep, heavily eroded zones and a more stable, agriculturally 'rich' plain to the south (Fig. 6.7). This landscape witnessed a waxing and waning of activity during the Iron Age and Roman periods.

The Early Iron Age is represented by only six sites over an 8,500 ha area: four oppida and two low-lying sites. It appears that, during the Early Iron Age, the Sainte Victoire was not considered as economically valuable vis-à-vis neighbouring areas. Other areas in eastern Provence appear to have been relatively highly populated, whilst the Sainte Victoire was neglected (Bérato 1995; Trément 1993; Walsh & Mocci 2003). The perception of peoples from beyond the Sainte Victoire may well have been one that saw this micro-region as too risky and difficult to manage, and this might explain the relatively low levels of settlement during this period. The Middle and Late Iron Ages (which correspond to La Tène I, II, and III) saw an important increase in settlement activity. Fifty sites were active across the late third and second centuries BC, and a recognisable settlement hierarchy emerged, with 10 oppida, at least 35 minor sites, as well as 30 indications of other smaller sites (Fig: 6.8).

The Roman period saw no settlement on the mountain itself, with sites now located at the foot of the mountain and across the plain. Many of these low-lying sites were often established on or close to their Late Iron Age precursors. The first villas were located adjacent to low alluvial terraces with direct access to the best agricultural land. During the first and second centuries AD, there was a gradual intensification of settlement on the massif, with a total of 35 sites dated to this period. The third century AD saw a decline in activity, followed by a re-emergence of many settlements during the fourth century. The final decline then took hold during the sixth century, and this situation continued into the early medieval period.

The combination of landscape survey and excavation of specific sites permits the assessment of two spatial scales – that of the wider landscape and changes in engagements with topography and location vis-à-vis resources, and then the scale of the site. Here, we can make inferences relating to specific responses to and engagements with localised environmental processes.

Excavations on the Domaine Richeaume, at the foot of the Cengle (a limestone bar that delimits the southern edge of the Sainte Victoire mountain), provided stratigraphic and geoarchaeological detail for this landscape research. The excavation of one Early Iron Age site (Richeaume III) and a Roman villa (Richeaume I) allowed the comparison of two decidedly different sites, with very different environmental characteristics.

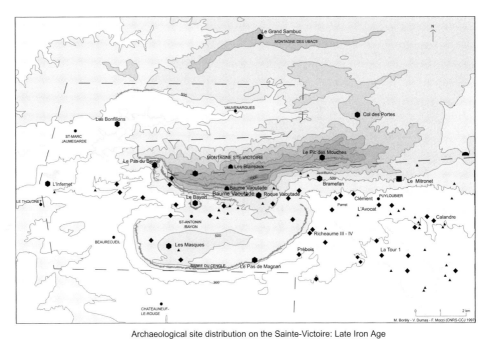

Archaeological site distribution on the Sainte-Victoire: Late Iron Age

⬣ Major settlement   ⬬ Tumulus   ■ Minor upland settlement   ◆ Minor settlement   ▲ Cave site   ▲ Isolated find or indication of site

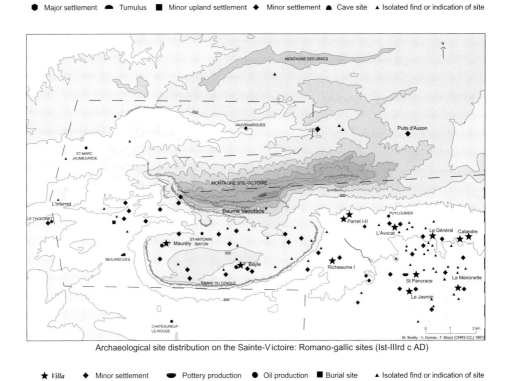

Archaeological site distribution on the Sainte-Victoire: Romano-gallic sites (Ist-IIIrd c AD)

★ *Villa*   ◆ Minor settlement   ⬬ Pottery production   ● Oil production   ■ Burial site   ▲ Isolated find or indication of site

6.8. The Sainte Victoire landscape with sites referred to in the text plotted. Note the changes in settlement density and location across the Iron Age and Roman periods (figure: F. Mocci, V. Dumas, & K. Walsh).

Richeaume III was located on a talus of eroding Pleistocene clays at the foot of the Sainte Victoire. More than 500 sherds of hand-thrown pottery, along with an example of an imported kylix from Marseille, dated this site to the beginning of the sixth century BC. There was no convincing evidence for any kind of structure on the site. An in-filled palaeo-ravine contained sherds of Early Iron Age pottery at the base of the fill. The basal layer of this ravine was the local red clay sub-strate. The cutting and the filling of the ravine must have taken place at the end of the Early Iron Age. This process might have taken place once the site was abandoned, although it is possible that this erosion phase forced people to abandon the site (Fig. 6.9). This provides an example of the interface between human activity and a sedimentary process, where we can demonstrate via (geo)archaeological stratigra-phy that people must have had direct experience of the sedimentary environment. At the regional level, there are a number of other sites across Provence that also demonstrate phases of erosion during this period (Provansal 1995b). The evidence from several sites in Provence for an Early/Middle Iron Age phase of erosion is convincing, although one cannot argue for exact synchronicity. Locally, just 2 km from Richeaume, the Bramefan oppidum also saw a phase of erosion which has been dated to the end of the first occupation phase (sixth century BC) (Jorda & Mocci 1997). This was followed by a second occupation phase dated to the La Tène III period (Bofinger, Schweizer, & Strobel 1996). Here, it seems that the erosion marks a hiatus between the two phases of settlement, but not necessarily the reason for the end of the first settlement.

As there were remarkably few Early Iron Age sites on the Sainte Victoire, we can be quite sure that there was little pressure on land because of a low population density. In such circumstances, even dra-matic erosional events may not have been perceived as a problem. This would be especially true for semi-sedentary populations who had yet to establish permanent substantial settlements, which may well have been the case in parts of Early Iron Age Provence (Garcia 2002: 90–2). In addition, if an agricultural system allows the avoidance of the hazard posed by degradation, that is, through mobility, then people may just move to a new zone where erosion is not a problem. However, degrada-tion does have an impact in stratified societies with rigid land-ownership mechanisms that prevent low-status groups from taking up new land.

6.9. Richeaume III – An Iron Age site comprised of a dense pottery scatter located on an eroding slope. It seems likely that the response to erosion in this landscape was a decision to relocate close by (photo: author).

Consequently, the agency of mundane environmental processes is contingent upon class and proprietorial institutions within a landscape.

The Roman villa (Richeaume I) is situated just 500 m to the south of Richeaume III. However, its topographic and geomorphic situation is quite different, located on a flat area, the eastern extremity of the site abutting a stream terrace. The site comprises a range of typical villa buildings, including the owners' domestic areas, plus an ornamental garden and some agricultural buildings. Here, we are more interested in the zone abutting the stream where hydraulic structures and a palaeochannel were discovered. One aqueduct transported water away from the site – this element runs from north to south, and was built during the first half of the second century AD. The structure turns east and would have emptied into the stream channel (now an in-filled palaeochannel). The agricultural buildings, located just to the west of the aqueduct junction, were subjected to flooding, as alluvial sediments abut all of the buildings in this area. Four distinct phases of channel activity were identified, covering the second through to sixth centuries AD. These phases reflect the principal periods of flood-plain development and management. The first phase of alluviation is dated by ceramic material that provides a *terminus ante quem* of the fifth century AD. However, the date proposed for the construction of the aqueduct demonstrates that the channel was active from the second century AD. On or after this date, overbank deposits were laid down either side of the channel and threatened some of the villa structures. As a consequence, a dyke was constructed, undoubtedly as a response to the flooding. The dyke is dated by a second-century, upturned, votive, sealed jar containing burnt grain. The next phase comprised the cutting of the flood-plain silts by a new channel with almost vertical sides. Coarse colluvial material entered this channel, probably during the sixth or seventh centuries. These sediments were washed down from the surrounding hill-slopes – areas that had undoubtedly been managed (possibly terraced) during the Roman period. There is other evidence for a late/post-Roman phase of erosion in the area. At Roque Vaoutade, 2 km upstream from Richeaume, results from geo-archaeological work also suggest a Late or post-Roman phase of sedimentation; one radiocarbon-dated sequence yielded a date centred on AD 566 (Ballais & Crambes 1993: 472). At this Roman site, erosion contemporary with the villa's use was managed via technological intervention, seen in the construction of protective walls and the maintenance of the aqueduct.

THE ROMAN WATERMILL AT BARBEGAL

Another example of how we might directly assess the interaction between archaeological sites (more specifically, the people associated with the site) and the geomorphic system comes from the Roman watermill at Barbegal (in the Vallée des Baux, 7 km east of the city of Arles in western Provence) (Fig. 6.10). This mill is one of the most impressive pieces of hydrological engineering in the Roman world. It was supplied with water by an extensive aqueduct system that also supplied Arles. This type of site undeniably represents a very different form of interaction

6.10. Barbegal in its landscape setting. Left – Aerial view of Barbegal situated on a limestone bar (photo: by permission of Centre Camille Jullian). Right – View of the Barbegal mill from the south (photo: author).

with the landscape and natural process, as its function is almost entirely economic.

The mill is located on the south-facing slope of a limestone bar (part of the Alpilles) (Leveau 1995; Leveau et al. 2000). The wetland in front of the mill was relatively dry during the Roman period (Bruneton 1999, 2000), probably managed and drained by Roman engineers. Palynological research reveals the development of a typical Middle Holocene, Mediterranean, mixed-oak forest in this area. Moving into the Iron Age and Roman period, there was a notable increase in arable farming, especially during the Roman period when we also see the presence of *Juglans* in the pollen diagram (Andrieu-Ponel et al. 2000).

Geoarchaeological work at the mill identified a series of 11 colluvial units, the earliest of which were hydromorphic clays and the limestone slope on which the Roman activities took place. The subsequent units directly lain upon these clays were coarse and stony, and contained Roman archaeological material (Walsh 2004). The inception of hill-slope erosion is therefore dated to the post-Roman period. However, the hill slope would have witnessed earlier phases of colluvial activity throughout the Holocene. Consequently, the construction of the mill undoubtedly included the removal of pre-existing sediments in order to facilitate construction. This removal of sediments extended down as far as the hydromorphic clays that define the northern edge of the wetland, and the limestone slope that dips down under these clays. Immediately to the east of the mill, four Late Roman burials were discovered (the pottery directly associated with one of these burials is dated between the end of the third and the start of the fourth century AD). The trenches for these burials were dug into the hydromorphic clays. The different events represented by the construction of the mill and by the burials demonstrate that the area around the mill was managed, and any colluvial deposits present around the site were removed, or the slope was managed to such an extent that the potential for colluviation was obviated during the Roman Period, with colluviation starting again, and no longer subject to clearance, once the mill went out of use. A similar sequence was also recorded at the Pont Simian Roman Bridge, less than 2 km from Barbegal (Ballais & Bellamy 2000). At these sites, the geoarchaeological work demonstrated that sediments were removed as part of construction and maintenance practices.

DISCUSSION: THE HUMAN SCALE OF INTERACTION WITH PAST
ENVIRONMENTAL PROCESSES

At both Barbegal and Richeaume I, anthropogenic manipulation of
environmental features and processes is a critical issue. Anthropogenic
truncation of sedimentary records should not be seen as a problem but
rather a phenomenon with a cultural aspect that archaeologists should
attempt to understand and interpret. The colluvial facies at Barbegal
(and the nearby Pont Simian) reveal periods of direct intervention in
the landscape. Such endeavours were designed to facilitate engineering projects that would contribute to agricultural production, as well
as the supply of water to the city of Arles. This intervention in the
geomorphic system may seem banal, but it should be studied in the
same way as the architecture and statuary that represent economic and
political power within urban and rural imperial landscapes. The manipulation of the environment is very much associated with a certain attitude towards nature, and an appreciation of what can and cannot be
controlled within the natural world. We know that in Pliny the Elder's
Natural History, '…man was at the centre of the story: nature had
made all things for him, and Pliny's book was partly a survey of what
was available' (R. French 1994: 207). Economically valuable landscapes
were controlled and managed. Barbegal and Richeaume I represent two
decidedly different types of site, but the geoarchaeological work in both
places reveals evidence for direct management of the landscape. When
considered in conjunction with other types of evidence for landscape
management (in particular, centuriation), this type of geoarchaeological sequence is unsurprising. Such sequences, which often represent
phases of human truncation of the geoarchaeological record, may mean
that strata representing earlier erosional events were in fact removed
by Roman intervention and land-management practices. We need to
ask if these landscapes were characterised by geomorphological stability, or whether the Roman management of the geosystem disguised or
masked some phases of erosional activity. Stability is often assigned to
periods where facies are either absent or comprised of fine sedimentary material. This relative dearth of evidence for Roman erosion in
this region does not necessarily imply that erosion was not a problem.
As Beagon (1996: 293) demonstrates, Pliny observed the destructive
effect of certain types of activity on the landscape. Whilst one would
have to disagree with the general tone of Hughes's (1994b) pessimistic

account of the impact of Greek and Roman civilisations on the natural environment, his assessment of attitudes to the environment is nevertheless useful. It is apparent that classical philosophers questioned the notion that the gods were active in every facet of environmental, and in particular, agricultural processes. Consequently, we see the development of an ethical system that allowed more pragmatic approaches to the management of the environment and that involved direct, and sometimes significant, intervention.

At Richeaume, we certainly see the intersection of pragmatic and spiritual engagements with the landscape. As well as the votive jar beneath the dyke (designed to protect the site from flooding), the anthracological evidence from recent excavations at the Richeaume Necropolis, 200 m to the east of the villa, suggests quite specific choices of wood for cremation rites (Cenzon-Salvayre & Durand 2011). The anthracological assemblages comprise *Pinus halepensis* (Aleppo pine) along with the *Q. coccifera* and *Q. ilex* (evergreen oaks), as well as examples of vitis and beech. It would seem that the Roman vegetation mosaic in this area was not that different to that present today. Whilst it is unsurprising that the wood for cremation pyres was gathered from around the immediate area, specific choices were made regarding the employment of different species in the staged construction of the pyre. In one cremation, two different layers of carbonised wood have been identified, the bottom layer comprised almost entirely *Q. coccifera-ilex*, and the upper layer, *Pinus halepensis-pinea*. When we look at the combined archaeological, palaeoenvironmental data and assess topographical characteristics on specific sites, we can start to evaluate the full range of instrumental (technological) engagements with the landscape, as well as more spiritual relationships with nature. This complex intersection of technological (pragmatic) responses to landscape processes with spiritual notions reiterates the point that the range of societies that occupied that space over time will have perceived the same landscape with its associated natural processes differently.

One way to assess how perceptions of the geomorphic system have evolved over time is to consider how notions of risk and hazard change with specific spatial and chronological contexts, ideally through the diachronic study of particular micro-regions. On the Sainte Victoire, the change in settlement organisation (density and location of sites; Fig. 6.8) between the Late Iron Age and Roman period would have comprised

substantial changes in the ways in which people engaged with the landscape (in terms of movement and work) across this incredibly varied
topography. Changes in settlement patterns and associated economic
practices expose sites and people to different environmental processes –
a site on a hill slope (or mountain side) would be subject to colluvial
processes (soil erosion through to rock slides); a site on the plain would
probably have increased interaction with alluvial processes (from the
deposition of useful silty sediments through to the dangers posed by
flooding). The possible flexibility of the Early Iron Age settlement system on the Sainte Victoire demonstrates how mobility may well have
been the answer to erosional events. As we move into the Roman period,
we see how a society attempts to control the same landscape through
engineering and complex landscape management.

The apparent success of the Roman system in controlling erosion
belies the probability that small, independent peasant farmers and slaves
working on the villas or on processing-sites such as Barbegal would have
been obliged to deal directly with any hazards on behalf of the villa or
mill owners. Storm erosion and flood damage would have been repaired
by these workers, and even the mundane, annual, small-scale hazards
would have had a direct impact on their lives. Erosion is a process, an
agency that people have to engage with, and in the case of Barbegal, it
was not merely an inconvenience that had to be removed, but a phenomenon that impinged upon the workers who had to remove the sediments.
Erosion, and thereby soil quality, are therefore culturally transformative
in that their characteristics affect people. It is the relationship between
the human and non-human agents that is absent from the macro-scale
discourses promoted by many archaeologists and ancient historians. If
we accept this, then archaeological sites (human technologies) constitute 'hybrids', phenomena that develop in a network where distinctions
between the social and the natural might not exist. Sustainability of
any activity is the product of human management of natural processes,
whereby successful forms of environmental knowledge contribute to the
maintenance of resilience. The watermill at Barbegal was the product
of a very specific socio-economic system – the Roman Empire, with its
desire to manipulate and control nature through complex forms of engineering. The decline of the mill was the product of changes in wider
economic and political processes, whilst the associated re-emergence of
the unmanaged wetland at the foot of the watermill was not necessarily

caused by environmental change, but was another consequence of the demise of the Empire.

As discussed in Chapter 5, we have to consider how forms of environmental knowledge varied across time, space, culture, and class. Greek, Roman, and perhaps even earlier urban groups and elites possessed different attitudes to environmental processes. Roman managers and elite classes may have developed an asymmetric view of the world, in which humans could control and manage the environment as part of endeavours to maximise economic output. In *Critias*, Plato describes the environment of Athens, and in particular, he comments on the excellent quality of the soil. Plato's discussion of deforestation and soil erosion thus implies that he was aware that humanity depended on a certain awareness of the impact that different actions could have on the environment (Goldin 1997). However, we can only postulate the extent to which this form of environmental understanding was shared across society, and if understood, how this knowledge was then applied in the landscape.

The issue of temporal scale is also important, along with the notion of the palimpsest (G. Bailey 2007). Erosional events occurred over periods that we cannot precisely date. The seven phases of sedimentation identified in the Argolid '…were brief, lasting from a few thousand to as little as a few hundred years, whereas the intervals when erosion was negligible…' were longer (van Andel & Runnels 1987: 138). This notion of 'briefness' is problematic if we reconsider the relevance of these phases and their chronologies at a resolution that correlates with that of human experience. The sediments examined in the field may well cumulatively represent processes that took place over the 'long term', but can we be sure that the processes responsible for the deposition of these sediments were experienced by people who lived and worked on or near these sites? It is their direct relationships with these non-human agents that are relevant. As with many environmental processes, there would also have been a temporal aspect to the relationship between people and erosion. Colluviation in a Mediterranean environment is invariably cyclical, often associated with late summer and autumn storms. Thus, the sedimentation and its removal may well have acted as a temporal marker within the annual round of tasks. As societies become more complex, the decisions regarding how such environmental processes should be understood and responded to may be made by people who do not actually work the land. Thus, the perceived temporality and transformative characteristics of the environmental processes are contingent upon how the process is experienced: the landowner may associate erosion with a fall in production and a loss of profit, while the peasant or slave would see a purely physical task – sediment that had to be removed. As such, sedimentation is transformative but heterogeneous in its influences on different actors within and beyond the actual environmental niche. The heterogeneity of different peoples' engagements with the landscape would also have been class and gender-based. Actions and being within any landscape become more heterogeneous as social hierarchies become more complex. Labour is increasingly divided and subdivided between different groups, and is often controlled/influenced/manipulated by social elites, who in turn influence the understandings and perceptions that workers would have had of non-human agents, including erosion.

Most societies demonstrate resilience in the face of menacing environmental processes. High-frequency events, such as soil erosion induced by annual storms, are often 'shifted' to occur at a lower frequency (Redman & Kinzig 2003). This 'shifting' transpires through technological and cultural management practices that are specific to each society; for example, terraces built to control erosion, or defensive walls and drainage channels to protect sites from flooding. Essentially, we should be asking for whom were these processes relevant in the past? It is perhaps useful to think of sediments as an integral agent within the cultural world. People would have possessed the environmental knowledge vis-à-vis the local causes of erosion. The removal of vegetation upslope of a site followed by storms is in some ways an uncomplicated set of events that anyone living in such a locale would understand. People do often contribute to the causes of erosion. In some instances, erosion can be beneficial, as much re-deposition is comprised of sediments that have been removed from unusable mountain slopes down to readily exploitable flood plains. We know that some Nepalese farmers actually cause landslides themselves in order to bring down more fertile soil from the upper slopes (Forsyth 1998: 109).

In Mycenaean landscapes, palace-based elites commissioned terrace building as part of a wider socio-economic-ideological strategy – an example of where erosion mitigation possibly constituted the imposition of forms of environmental knowledge upon low-ranking groups. At the same time, local farmers might have applied their own forms of environmental knowledge and developed specifically local forms of terrace construction, choosing specific points on a hill slope, repairing terraces at specific times of the year, and so on. For the workers at Barbegal and other landscapes around the Mediterranean, the sediment would have created a task that had to be completed under coercion from land owners or managers, or possibly even 'the gods'. Soil quality (and problems with the soil) is a phenomenon that would have been understood via discourses that are quite different to today's post-enlightenment scientific descriptions of the physical world. The intersection with other worlds, those of the gods, would have been an integral part of the environmental knowledge of soils and sediments (Retallack 2008). It is interesting to consider the forms of environmental knowledge that relate to human engagements with erosion. In particular, we should aim to assess not only evidence for erosion caused by past societies, but also their responses to erosion. Do periods of erosion that follow on from the collapse of mitigation strategies, such as terracing, represent a loss of environmental knowledge, or inability to maintain a sustainable landscape and/or incongruent forms of environmental knowledge where there is a mismatch of environmental management strategies promoted by social elites and local environmental knowledge held by those who work the land (Redman 1999: 212)? Or are we looking at phases when erosion was an irrelevance, as eroding areas were not economically valuable? It is more useful from an archaeological perspective to assess the human–environment dynamic as one characterised by transformation rather than destruction (Butzer 2005: 1773), although there have been and still are moments when people have created environmental domains that could or cannot support economic activity.

7

Islands: Biogeography, Settlement, and Interaction

All Mediterranean Islands resemble each other; each island is different in its own way. (Vogiatzakis, Pungetti, & Mannion 2008: 3)

Introduction

There are about 5,000 islands and islets across the Mediterranean, although the number of larger, inhabited islands is closer to 100. This statistic in itself demonstrates the extent to which many islands have not supported long-term human activity. Sicily, Sardinia, Cyprus, Corsica, and Crete are the largest Mediterranean islands, with Mallorca, Minorca, and Malta falling into the medium-sized category. This chapter will only consider one of the larger islands, Corsica, with some material from Cyprus, Crete, and Sicily considered in other chapters. As the environments on these larger islands possess a potential similar to that of continental zones, the island biogeographical notions considered in this chapter do not apply in the same way. There are several groups of small islands: the Aeolian Islands, the Ionian Islands, the Sporades, the north Aegean Islands, the Dodecanese Islands, and the Cycladic Islands (Fig. 7.1). Many of the islands possess historical significance that is disproportionately greater than their physical size. This chapter will start with an assessment of island biogeography and its application in Mediterranean archaeology. Then, an overview of how the study of island environments has been employed by archaeologists will provide the core of this chapter.

Environmental characteristics across the various groups of islands in the Mediterranean are of course largely influenced by their respective positions across the various biogeographic zones outlined in Chapter 2. Two of the larger islands in the northern-central Mediterranean – Corsica

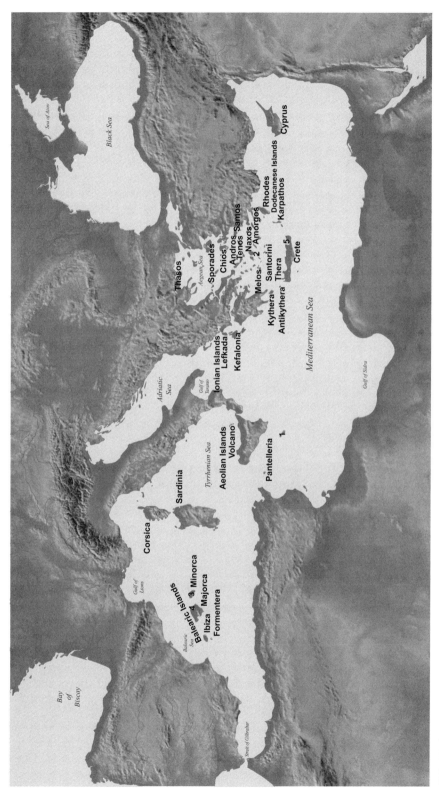

7.1. Mediterranean island groups and islands mentioned in the text. Islands named on map: Sicily, Sardinia, Cyprus, Corsica, Crete, Mallorca, Minorca, Malta, Sporades, Aeolian Islands (Vulcano), Dodecanese Islands (Rhodes, Karpathos), Cycladic Islands (Thasos, Andros, Naxos, Tenos, Santorini/Thera, Melos, Amorgos, Chios, Samos), Pantelleria, Kythera, Antikythera, Ionian Islands (Kefalonia and Lefkada), Ibiza, Formentera, Karpathos. 1: Skorba, 2: Daskaleio-Kavos on Keros/ Heracleia (Irakleia), 3: Cova des Moro/Cova des Mussol (Minorca), 4: Alcudia (Majorca), 5: Pseira.

and Sardinia – share similar geologies and environmental characteristics, whilst at the western end of the Mediterranean, the Balearics are situated within a biogeographical zone which shares traits with Spain and North Africa. Moreover, this archipelago is unusual in that only 4 of the 151 islands and islets are settled today (Vogiatzakis et al. 2008: 12). Whilst island size is obviously important, the presence of island groups, or archipelagos such as in the Aegean, has significant biological economic and cultural ramifications. Even though UNESCO defines 'small' as 10,000 km^2 or less (ibid.), within the context of this chapter, where the assessment of small islands is prioritised, 'small' is taken to be islands of about 5,000 km^2 or less (the Balearics as group constituting 5,014 km^2, and Malta 316 km^2).

If there is one aspect of Mediterranean archaeology that has been dominated, or at least heavily influenced, by environmental models, it is the study of islands (see Van Dommelen 1999: 247). Due to the bounded nature of islands (especially small islands), they offer a unique perspective on environmental processes and their history. In some ways, human settlement on islands is concerned with managing the fragility and restrictions of island resources (soils, vegetation) that in some instances degrade more quickly than they might do on continental zones. The fact that some researchers do group mammals and people when assessing the settlement of Mediterranean islands has led to some biogeographic models ignoring the importance of cultural processes in influencing human decisions to explore and settle. The discourses employed by some are unsubtle, and refer to the invasion of islands by people and the consequent 'extermination' of fauna by these people (Schuele 1993). Therefore, an assessment of island biogeography and its application in Mediterranean archaeology is one of the themes running through this chapter. However, the relative dearth of palaeoenvironmental landscape reconstruction work on many of these islands is problematic. Obviously, those environmental processes that have been dealt with in the preceding chapters are all pertinent to the study of islands. The difference, however, is that islands, especially the smaller ones, might show less resilience, and could therefore have been subject to precocious and irreversible environmental degradation.

The Mediterranean is in many ways defined by its islands and mountains. These zones constitute the quintessential domain for the intersection of local, specific environmental knowledge and imposed structures of environmental knowledge. These environmentally complex zones have always demanded local, specific forms of environmental understanding and management. When systemised forms of environmental knowledge, imposed by social elites, and local understanding of the environment diverge, these zones may well witness periods of socio-economic and environmental volatility – forms of environmental instability that are not controlled by changes in climate, but rather by changes in the relationships between local and elite forms of knowledge. The success or failure of many islands, especially the smaller ones, is in part related to their position within wider economic and cultural networks (Knappett, Evans, & Rivers 2011). During the Bronze Age in particular, one might argue that the environmental, economic, and cultural trajectories of islands were linked to the development of networks of storage and exchange managed by social elites, this being particularly true in Eastern Mediterranean, where maritime economies were a defining characteristic of complex societies (S. W. Manning 2008).

An overview of the great variety of island types and their physical characteristics forms the introduction to this chapter. Whilst there has been much discussion of the idea that insularity leads to the development of cultural characteristics that are peculiar to islands (Patton 1996), this chapter also focuses on the environmental trajectories that some Mediterranean islands have taken, and the nature of human interaction with these particular environment types. Where possible, archaeological and environmental data are employed in an analysis of how island populations responded to environmental and landscape changes, and are used to consider whether these responses are specific to island environments. As with all of the chapters, a diachronic approach (from the Neolithic to the Late Roman period) employs archaeological evidence in an assessment of how different societies responded to similar sets of environmental problems.

Mediterranean Islands and Island Biogeography

Without a doubt, MacArthur and Wilson's (1967) *The Theory of Island Biogeography* has been of fundamental importance in the development of ecologically informed island archaeological projects. Then, Evans's (1973) early paper on the topic established the archaeological adaptation of these ideas. The most significant variables that affect the development of island ecologies are the distance of an island from a continental landmass, and the size of the island. Therefore, a small island should only be able to support a reduced number of plant and animal species, and the greater the distance of an island from a continental land mass, the more difficult it will be for species to colonise and recolonise that island (MacArthur & Wilson 1967). One consequence is that many islands possess a limited range of floral and faunal resources (Patton 1996: 2). The island laboratory supposedly presents archaeologists with an opportunity to study a (partially) closed environment, and therefore assess the manner in which a given island community interacts with a bounded environment. Of course, such definitions are spurious, as the sea, despite its own set of risks, is not necessarily a barrier to communication and the transfer of people, ideas, plants, and animals. Island trajectories may be different to those on the continent, but then so is the development of a continental mountainous landscape, or even a wetland. They are all the product of an infinite network of influences that are both 'natural' and cultural.

According to Simmons (1998: 232), human impacts on Mediterranean island environments '…have been especially harsh from Neolithic times up to the present'. There is no doubt that, in some instances, the effects of human activity on an island ecosystem can be disastrous, the most infamous example being Easter Island (Rainbird 2002). As Patton (1996: 7) observes, Mediterranean islands tend to be less isolated than their Pacific counterparts. Consequently, if we wish to test the notion that the cultural and environmental trajectories followed by island societies are in some way different to those followed in continental zones, we have to demonstrate first that there are environmental processes or outcomes of these processes that are peculiar to islands, and that, in turn, there are cultural responses to these environments which are also quite original: are there facets of past island cultures (including landscapes) which are a consequence of insularity?

In order to identify changes in island environments and the nature of the relationships that people had with the natural aspects of their landscape, we need to consider some of the evidence for settlement, economy, and cultural aspects of island life during the past. As noted above, one aim is to identify processes that are peculiar to islands that did not develop on the continental Mediterranean zones.

Islands do possess environmental characteristics that differ from continental zones. The relatively low number of plant and animal species, along with a high number of endemic species, are the defining ecological characteristics of many islands. Though a plant or animal species is more likely to arrive on a large island close to a continental zone, we also need to consider the 'stepping stone' effect: animals and plants may move across a sea from one island to another. Such a process would certainly have been common in the Aegean. Such island biogeographical models cannot be applied to the study of human colonisation of islands: people do not behave like animals and plants. Decisions to explore and colonise are cultural decisions, although movement across the sea is constrained by maritime technology, and the awareness of currents and weather cycles (ibid.: 24). In some ways, one might argue that the very idea of applying biogeographical principles to human behaviour is problematic and results in studies of humanity that are not particularly enlightening. At the same time, we must accept that the availability of island resources and carrying capacity are a matter of biogeography. What interests us here is the story of how island environments develop over time, and how people interact with these environments. We then need to consider if the characteristics of human/landscape dynamics on islands are in any way different from those that occur in continental zones. Islands might be considered as 'habitats surrounded by radical shifts in habitat', or even as places where the task of controlling one's fate is rendered more difficult than on a continental area (Terrell 1999: 2040–2).

COLONISATION OF MEDITERRANEAN ISLANDS

Whilst the chronological remit of this book does not include the Mesolithic, a brief overview of the evidence for the earliest human arrivals on the Mediterranean islands is useful. Whereas people were present on the Mediterranean continental zones from the Lower Palaeolithic onwards, and there is growing evidence for pre-Neolithic activity on a number of Mediterranean islands (Broodbank 2006; Cherry 1990), it appears that many islands, especially the smaller ones, were not settled until the Mesolithic or later. Moreover, the biogeographical characteristics of many islands would have been quite different prior to and at the start of the Holocene. Some islands would have been connected or closer to the continental zones (van Andel & Shackleton 1982). Biogeographical variables are still pertinent, and the most recent research still suggests that it was the Neolithic period that saw the settlement of many islands across the Mediterranean (Dawson 2011), whilst initial visits, such as those to the Cyclades, took place during the

Upper Palaeolithic (Phoca-Cosmetatou 2011b). In fact, many islands are not suited to hunting and gathering. Smaller islands would probably not have possessed the wide range of resources required by hunter-gatherers, and this might explain the dearth of Mesolithic evidence on most Mediterranean islands. However, herders and farmers with focussed food-production strategies could successfully explore without colonising these islands (Patton 1996: 139). Some islands, such as Melos, may have been discovered at quite an early stage, as access would have largely been across dry land (van Andel & Shackleton 1982). Whereas resource availability would have influenced cultural processes in the Adriatic during the Early Neolithic, it is quite likely that distances between the continent and islands were not considered significant (Bass 1998: 183). A Late Epipalaeolithic occupation of Cyprus has been recognised for some time (Peltenburg 2003; Peltenburg et al. 2000; Simmons 1991), along with the early development of Early Aceramic Neolithic communities (Knapp 2010). This is an example of early exploitation. Moreover, it is possible that the transition to farming on Cyprus was forager led, with peoples who had been present on Cyprus from the Early Holocene developing new food-production strategies (S. Manning et al. 2010). This does of course mean that domesticates would have been brought in subsequently by other people. Alternatively, some fisher-foragers continued to exploit coastal resources for a few thousand years more at least (see Ammerman 2010; Knapp 2010), and these groups developed strategies that were different to the typical 'Neolithic' farming communities. Recent research has demonstrated that many of the larger islands did see Palaeolithic and Mesolithic activity, for example Lower Palaeolithic and Mesolithic activity on Crete (Strasser et al. 2010, 2011). Mesolithic occupation is also known on Sardinia (Sondaar et al. 1984), Corsica (Costa 2004; Lanfranchi & Weiss 1973; Lanfranchi & Weiss 1997), and Mallorca (Ramis et al. 2002). It is possible that migrant farmers were the first to colonise Malta fully, with the earliest settlement dating to the transition of the sixth and fifth millennia based on the dates from Skorba, perhaps colonised by groups from Sicily (Guilaine 2003: 231).

Patton notes that the chronology of colonisation does not fit the visibility-based predictive models. A number of medium-sized, less visible islands were discovered or colonised at a relatively early date (Patton 1996: 55). Although the biogeographic ranking models provide a

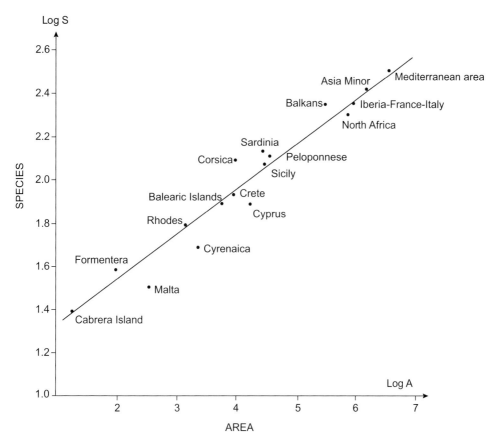

7.2. Double-logarithmic, species/area relationship of birds in some islands and mainland regions of the Mediterranean (Blondel, J. (2010), *The Mediterranean Region Biological Diversity in Space and Time*, p. 142, fig. 7.3; originally published in Blondel, J. (1986), *Biogeographie Evolutive*, Paris: Masson.)

reasonable prediction of island colonisation, it should be noted (as per Fig. 7.2) that biogeographic ranking models work particularly well for non-human animals.

It is possible that dry-shod colonisation of some islands took place where people settled prior to sea-level rise (Broodbank 1999: 22–3). The Aegean islands of Thasos and Chios were probably examples of islands where dry-shod colonisation occurred, followed by insularity (ibid.: 30). In such cases, farmers would have had to make decisions as to whether it was 'worth' remaining in an area where rising sea levels possibly contributed to an enhanced feeling of insularity – island life imposed by the natural world. From the perspective of this book, we can take this to imply that at the time of insularisation, these island environments were perfectly capable of supporting their farming communities, and there was clearly no need to abandon these zones. Moreover, the process of insularisation would have been a slow one, allowing time for people progressively to adapt their lifeways.

SETTLEMENT, ECONOMY, AND INSULARITY

With the right maritime technology, the sea is not a barrier and, in certain cases, may actually prove to be a more effective medium for movement and communication than dry land. Consequently, the notion of insular carrying capacity might be considered increasingly irrelevant, as trading and communication networks became reliable and complex. However, if a region enters a period of reduced economic activity, islands might be the first to suffer, especially if their productive environment is already fragile. Our task as archaeologists is to assess how the natural environment was exploited, and of particular relevance to island archaeology, we have to consider if carrying capacity for *people* was reduced by human impact. People can reduce the carrying capacity of an island to sustain certain species, in particular, domesticates, thus enhancing the capacity to sustain people. Perhaps more intriguing is the issue of whether the unique cultural trajectories often found on islands reflect the development of cultural ecologies that coped with the exigencies of island environments. For example, it seems that Later Neolithic peoples on certain Cycladic islands emphasised sheep and goat rearing, as opposed to cattle, suggesting that there was an adaption of strategies to the ecological exigencies of the island environments (Phoca-Cosmetatou 2011b: 89).

In many ways, islands are far from being the ideal 'laboratories' for the investigation of well-defined relationships between people and their environments. They are in fact nodes in the most complex web of historical ecological processes. At one level, they provide an insurmountable set of fascinating questions rather than answers. Even without considering cultural processes, biologists have noted the almost infinite variability that characterises Mediterranean islands. The variation in ecology and environments across Mediterranean islands is such that it led Greuter (quoted in Vogiatzakis & Griffiths 2008: 66) to state, 'In the Mediterranean the choice is yours: there are about 5000 of them … Just define your problem and choose the island or islet tailored to your needs'.

Aspects of Insular Environmental and Cultural Change

In the following section, a discussion of the principal environmental and cultural developments on a series of Mediterranean islands is considered. Where available, evidence for the impact of climate change along with evidence for vegetation change and so-called phases of sedimentary instability are considered in conjunction with pertinent archaeological evidence.

MALTA

Malta is a relatively small island (300 km²) situated between Sicily and Tunisia. One notable and potentially challenging environmental characteristic is that it is largely dependent on meteoric water. There are no lakes or permanent rivers on the island. Today, Malta is heavily reliant on desalinised water. In recent years, palaeoenvironmental research has developed on the island (Caroll 2004; Carroll et al. 2012; Hunt 1997; Marriner et al. 2012; Schembri 2009), and some key results are presented below.

Early colonisation on Malta probably started c. 5000 BC. Evidence for Neolithic impact on the landscape comes from molluscan analysis and palynology which implies that the areas around the Neolithic monuments on Malta were cleared quite quickly, and this could have produced 'the potential for serious ecological stress, provided population levels were sufficiently high' (Bonanno et al. 1990: 195). The sedimentological and malacological analyses imply increased aridity, and the consequential reduction in plant cover is broadly contemporary with the first colonisation of Malta (Fenech 2007: 106). Furthermore, a significant erosive event is contemporary with the construction of the first megalithic sites. Of course, the relationship between possible environmental destabilisation and temple building is almost impossible to articulate, but this is a process and relationship that we should consider. As there is nothing to suggest that the Maltese population grew beyond the carrying capacity of the island, Evans (1977) argued that some kind of mechanism must have been developed in order to limit population growth. Evans thus developed a model for small island development that tried to draw a link between island biogeographical characteristics and cultural development. There is no denying that the evidence for prehistoric 'difference' on Malta vis-à-vis other areas and islands. However, this type of difference is in many ways similar to that seen in other well-known or enigmatic prehistoric landscapes such as the Stonehenge environs or Val Camonica (Robb 2001). The building of Maltese temples started c. 3600 BC. There are 30 temples (plus numerous other ruins) on Malta and Gozo. Some argue that the temples on Malta developed during the fourth to third millennia as an ideological response to the stresses produced by biogeographical isolation (Stoddart et al. 1993). Recent environmental research clearly suggests early clearance of vegetation and later soil erosion that was a product of human activity and also climatic aridification at c. 2300 BC (Carroll et al. 2012). One important change to the island's environment was the loss of the Burmarrad Ria (a coastal embayment/floodplain zone) which proffered a range of useful resources. Sedimentary inputs (probably a consequence of environmental degradation referred to above) in-filled much of the bay (Marriner et al. 2012). We must accept that it is highly probable that all small to medium-sized island environments are susceptible to quite rapid environmental deterioration, with changes across certain small niches having had important consequences for an entire island.

Islands like Malta had strong links with other parts of the Mediterranean – in Malta's case, Sicily. However, this does not have to mean that the island's natural environment did not have an active role to play in constituting insular culture. In fact, the possible 'fragile' nature of the island environment and its limits on certain types of economic production would have encouraged, even necessitated, contact with the outside world. One consequence of such regular contact with other groups might have been the emergence of a perceived need to articulate an original and overt identity vis-à-vis this world. It is possible that the temples and the art within them represented components of the islanders' cosmology – the land and the sea. Therefore, these temples might be seen as metaphors for the island (Grima 2008). Robb (2001: 177) considers that 'islands did not fashion Maltese temple society but that, Maltese temple society created cultural islands in the process of forming a local identity'. Whilst this is an appealing idea, it denies agency for the island itself, as constituted by all of its environmental and geographical characteristics. Another important characteristic of any place is the manner in which the strength and extent of contact with the wider world varies over time. Therefore, levels of insularity on the same island must also vary. After a possible period of reduced contact with wider networks,

Stoddart (1999: 141) considers that during the later third millennium BC, Malta was reincorporated into the Mediterranean system (see also Malone et al. 2009).

As noted above, one of Malta's environmental weaknesses is the relative dearth of water. On parts of the island, there would have been an adequate water supply, with aquifers supplying natural reservoirs (Fig. 7.3). However, part of the distribution of temples covers an area where there may not have been adequate water for farming. Yet, Bonanno (2005) argues that the situation would have been quite different during the temple-building period, and it is quite likely that water capture and storage mechanisms guaranteed the maintenance of a flourishing culture. However, the only dated evidence for water storage is constituted by later Bronze Age cisterns. It is only in recent centuries that human activity, and perhaps climate change, have contributed to the development of a dry Maltese landscape. Moreover, research from eastern Spain suggests that the all-important levels of summer rainfall may have been higher in parts of the Western Mediterranean at certain points during the Holocene (Aguilera et al. 2012). The famous, ubiquitous Maltese 'cart ruts' may have been field boundaries and/or irrigation channels. It is also feasible that this system of ruts was related to the development of ridges and furrows and the creation of artificial soils (Fig. 7.4). The fact that some of the areas that comprise these ruts are now barren implies that the system ultimately failed. Sagona (2004: 54–6) argues that despite the difficulty of dating these ruts, it would be reasonable to assume that a Temple Period date (c. 4000–2500 BC) could be possible, as this period saw a high level of landscape management and 'social cohesion'. Moreover, this complex culture would have probably tried to expand its agricultural basis to the absolute limits, exploiting land that may once have been considered marginal. It is of course possible that the sudden end of the Temple Period at c. 2500 BC was a result of environmental mismanagement and the inability of a small island with a limited biodiversity to recover from such a process (Sagona 2004). However, this is difficult to demonstrate without well-dated palaeoenvironmental evidence (which could take the form of well-dated pollen diagrams, as well as OSL-dated sedimentary sequences that demonstrate soil depletion or exhaustion). As we have seen above, some new evidence does seem to support the notion that climatic and anthropogenic processes did combine, with some areas experiencing degradation.

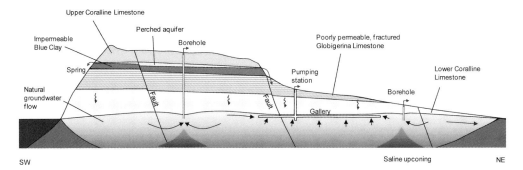

7.3. Malta's hydrological characteristics – schematic cross-section of Malta. It is important to note that supply from a perched aquifer is limited and that ground water on an island like Malta can be affected by saline inputs from the sea. (By permission of Marianne Stuart, BGS/NERC – http://www.bgs.ac.uk/research/groundwater/quality/Malta.html.)

7.4. Maltese cart ruts (photo: Shirley Cefai).

Tilley (2004) notes the main differences in the two limestone types – the (harder) Coralline limestone and the Globigerina limestone – that exist on Malta and Gozo. He argues that the very different characteristics (hardness, colour, surface appearance, tactility) result in the monuments made from these two different rocks being perceived/experienced in different ways. It is argued that the relationship of the temples to the landscape was mimetic (ibid.: 97). Temples, such as Ggantija supposedly mirror features of the surrounding landscape (ibid.: 109). Whilst we are unable to present a clear image of the nature of the landscape within which these temples were situated, it is fair to assume that unlike northern Europe, these temples were probably situated within a relatively open environment. At the very most, woodland would have comprised low-maquis or mattoral formations, probably not affecting temple-landscape inter-visibility. Despite these shortcomings in our data, it seems plausible that these temple complexes are one articulation of a form of social storage that relates to human–environment relationships. As Broodbank (2000) observes in his discussions of the Cyclades, communities in more favoured environments would not need to involve themselves in networks of social storage. It might therefore be interesting to consider the impact of climatic variability between different islands and attempt to identify if the relative intensity and extension of social storage networks was greater in more marginal zones; that is, small islands at relatively great distances from their nearest neighbours (ibid.: 176). In addition, we have to ask if these temple complexes developed as more strain was placed on natural resources.

As it stands, there is limited evidence for Phoenician and Punic rural settlement sites, whilst Roman rural activity is clearly attested to (Spanò Giammellaro, Spatafora, & Van Dommelen 2008: 153). Pollen analysis of a Punic ash pit implied a mosaic of grassland with areas of cereals and olives plus small trees and scrubland. The number of Roman villas (Fenech 2007: 17), and inferences made by reference to Ceres (goddess of abundance), might suggest that Malta was a relatively fertile island during this period. Ovid states that compared with sterile Pantelleria, Malta was a fertile island (ibid.: 55–6). The pollen evidence for the Phoenician and Punic periods implies relatively intensive arable agriculture. Arable activity was also high during the period between the second century BC and first century AD. This was followed by a relatively slow recovery of the vegetation roughly between the first and second centuries AD. Cereal pollen was at its lowest during the period between the third and fifth centuries AD before recovering during the sixth century AD. Whilst the island or the area around Marsa where these cores were obtained appears quite resilient, it is interesting to note that *Juglans'* (walnut) success was short-lived, only appearing briefly during the Phoenician/Punic phase (ibid.: 111–14). Here, we see how a possible attempt to introduce a certain species fails, as environmental knowledge did not encompass a full understanding of the environmental limits of the island.

Malta offers one of the most enigmatic examples of the evolution of an insular culture that may represent the evolutions of different populations' relationships with their island and its natural environment. We should never lose site of the fact that, for most pre-industrial people, culture was in many ways an articulation of relationships and understandings with the natural world. Environmental stress or restrictions would have made profound contributions to these cultural configurations.

SMALLER ISLANDS

If biogeographical models were to have any value, it would be in their application to the study of smaller islands – taken in this section to be smaller than 500 km^2 and including islands such as Antikythera (20.8 km^2) (Bevan & Conolly 2013). There are a number of islands that clearly have seen levels of environmental degradation greater than those seen on most continental zones. It is on these smaller islands that we see the development of the most enigmatic manifestations of cultural activity. These cultures, which include the temple builders of Malta, are not the product of insular environments per se, but as with any culture, they are without a doubt the product of the complex interplay of socio-economic processes and environmental agents, where the perception of the environment has a role to play in the construction of the day-to-day lives of all people.

As stated above, there are a number of small Mediterranean islands whose cultural/historical importance belies their diminutive size. These 'successful' islands tended to have important but relatively short-lived roles (within the context of the Holocene), and exploited a specific resource and/or occupied a fortuitous geographical position within the Mediterranean, having access to important maritime routeways. Clearly, if small islands were exploited for traditional arable and pastoral agriculture, then in many instances their inherent environmental fragility would eventually have curtailed this. However, small islands do have some important environmental advantages. They present the inhabitants with easy access to marine resources, even if they live towards the interior. However, as Broodbank (2000: 85) argues, marine resources in the

Mediterranean are less abundant and predictable than in other oceans. Activity on small islands will be influenced by environmental characteristics that are localised and specific to that island. An essential resource is water, and there are important inter-annual variations in rainfall over relatively small groups of islands such as the Cyclades. For example, the geological structure of Naxos (one of the 'large' small islands) means that there are plenty of natural springs across the island (Dalongeville & Rénault-Miskovsky 1993); not all small islands will possess natural springs. There is also plentiful groundwater on Andros and Tenos (Broodbank 2000: 78). Islands like Santorini, with little topographic variation and that are quite low, tend to be drier than continental areas, although they will experience more fog (Rackham 2008: 37).

Although identified as possessing poor environments (Broodbank 2008: 47), life on the Cyclades was certainly not one characterised by a struggle for survival. Many Saliagos culture sites do demonstrate a preference for 'environmentally clement niches' (Broodbank 2000: 147). This seems to mean that people made seemingly logical choices regarding easy access to water and topographical situations with access to flat valley lands. Moreover, Saliagos settlement seems to have taken place only on the medium and large islands. Therefore, there may have been some notion or understanding of how large an island should be in order to minimise risk, possibly a 'list' of attributes including fresh water, arable land, and a safe landing for boats. Homer refers to these very characteristics in Book 9 of the Odyssey where he describes the land of the Cyclopes (Butler 2006).

Whilst agriculture was practised on many smaller islands, some of these places were exploited for specific resources from at least the Neolithic onwards, the most famous example being obsidian extraction on Melos (Renfrew & Wagstaff 2005; Tykot 1997, 2004) where the earliest obsidian exploitation is now dated to the period between 13,000 and 10,000 years ago (Laskaris et al. 2011). During the late fourth to third millennium BC, the dispersed settlement pattern of Melos characterised an island which at this point was probably relatively independent from the rest of the world (Wagstaff & Cherry 1982b: 251). Throughout its history, the waxing and waning of the island's prosperity was more influenced by its economic and political relationships with the wider world than any 'constraints' placed upon it by the environment. Despite economic specialisation, at the very least, subsistence farming would have been necessary in order to support the population. As it stands, the only dated evidence for landscape degradation is derived from alluvial units that contain pottery sherds with dates between c. 600 BC and c. 500 AD. In landscapes such as those on Melos, it is difficult for soils to redevelop once the bare bedrock is exposed, and there is little hope of vegetation colonisation from abutting zones. On a small island, the possibility of movement to new 'soil-rich' areas is reduced (Davidson & Tasker 1982). This erosion may have been caused by demographic growth during the late eighth century BC (Wagstaff & Cherry 1982a). Despite these environmental problems, Melos continued and continues to produce a wide range of agricultural products successfully, and in recent centuries has managed to respond to changes in external economic demands (Wagstaff & Augustson 1982: 131). The vegetation history of Melos is one characterised by gradual degradation, although sudden degradation due to long-term drought or human impact has to be considered a possibility. Away from Melos, Herodotus referred to a seven-year drought on Thera (fifth century BC) during which nearly all of the trees withered (Wagstaff & Gamble 1982: 96).

The transition towards a drier climate during the Neolithic and Bronze Age is perhaps one process that needs to be assessed more carefully. On the Cyclades, it is clear that there was a move towards dairying subsistence economies and an emphasis on small farmstead-size settlements. This is taken to represent a more flexible economic pattern. The 'Saliagos settlements represent, in effect, a small number of precious eggs placed in large baskets chosen for their safety, whilst Grotta-Pelos settlements represent a great number of individually expendable eggs distributed in small baskets of variable quality' (Broodbank 2000: 155). The emergence of the late Neolithic and early Bronze Age Grotta-Pelos culture represents a move into the smaller islands and also the adoption of niches that had hitherto been unsettled (ibid.: 151). Whilst this macro-economic perspective is interesting, and undoubtedly provides a useful resume of two different situations, it does not explain how human–landscape interaction actually operated on the smaller scale.

Broodbank (2008: 53) considers that the plough, in comparison with continental areas, would have had less impact on the broken terrain that characterised these islands. In explaining the changes in the late-third millennium Cycladic society, Broodbank (2000: 338) suggests that overexploitation through farming practices may have led to some desertion episodes, and as a result some settlements may have moved towards lowland areas that 'benefited from hill slope soil loss'. Such a process may be represented in the soil profiles at Markiani on Amorgos. However, it is unlikely that such a process would have been uniform throughout the Cyclades. It is difficult to demonstrate that sudden climate change could have been responsible for these late third millennium changes. A new arid phase should have registered settlement shift towards areas with a reliable water supply.

As the economies of small islands developed, their integration into wider Bronze Age economic networks clearly influenced the manner in which their landscapes evolved. For example, it is argued that changes in the settlement patterns on Naxos were linked to the island's integration into the Minoan and Mycenaen exchange systems. One might argue that for a relatively small island such as Naxos, the development of links with other islands and continental zones was necessary. During the period of close integration (LH IIIA1–IIIA2), the settlement pattern became nucleated, and small settlements were abandoned. After this period, and the reduction in levels of Mycenaean trade, the settlement pattern takes on a dispersed structure once again (Cosmopoulos 1998).

The Ionian island of Kythera is just under 300 km² and was clearly large enough to support a relatively dense settlement pattern. For example, Bevan (2002: 225) refers to the Neopalatial (c. 1700–1440 BC) as '…a brief pulse of settlement activity and an example of pioneer efforts at colonizing new terrain'. Holdings may have been quite small and concentrated around the farm building. In the Kytheran environment, it has been suggested that ecological risk was probably managed in different ways, via a diversification of crops and animals within intensely farmed plots rather than over a dispersed set of plots. Alternatively, there may have been a form of social storage, with neighbouring farms assisting one another in times of need (ibid.: 237–8). What is interesting from a human and island-landscape dynamics perspective is that this level of dispersed settlement was quite short-lived on Kythera. It is possible that an island such as this could only support such a system for a relatively short period, and even then, the success of the system was due to a high level of mutual support amongst the peoples of Kythera during the Neopalatial period. Small islands such as Antikythera (about 40 km to the southeast of Kythera) may well have witnessed quite dramatic changes in population (Bevan et al. 2007) as economic networks, and possibly even forms of environmental knowledge fluctuated. In some islands, including Kythera, a number of farmsteads with 'a Minoanising material culture' spread into zones that had seen relatively little activity prior to the Neopalatial period (Broodbank 2004: 69).

Antikythera provides an example of a diachronic landscape survey of a small-island where the historical ecology of the landscape was assessed (Bevan & Conolly 2013). As with many small islands, it seems likely that early exploitation comprised short-term hunting and/or gathering trips, which could have included the exploitation of terrestrial fauna such as hare, deer, or goat, as well as migratory birds (ibid.: 139). Even during the later Neolithic to Early Bronze Age, permanent, all-year-round settlement might not have been established. The evidence suggests that these sites did not necessarily prioritise the best agricultural land. Sites were often situated in zones that offered 'good points of departure for hunting and gathering expeditions around the island' (ibid.: 147) – an interpretation supported by the presence of projectile points on these sites. The seasonal (spring–autumn) occupation on the island once again fits with the notion of mobility across groups of islands, with larger neighbouring islands or mainland acting as the core zones. As there are no known obsidian projectile points from Crete, it is possible that the Late–Final Neolithic phase of exploitation was undertaken by Cyclades or Argo-Saronic Gulf communities (Bevan, pers. comm.). However, by the third millennium BC, Cretan communities are responsible for the settlement of the island (the shortest crossing between the two islands is 35 km) (Fig. 7.5). At the latest, the late third and second millennia saw some permanent settlement located in zones more suited to arable agriculture. As with other small islands, it seems unlikely that continuously high levels of population were maintained. The Hellenistic name for the island – 'Aegila' (Goat Island) – possibly signifies the nature and limited extent of activity (or even abandonment) during this period. The Early Roman period was also characterised by low levels of activity (Bevan & Conolly 2013: 164). However, an increase in population characterised the later Roman period.

This waxing and waning of activity is typical of certain landscapes (islands, wetlands, mountains, and arid zones) that receive people for different reasons at different times. In these landscapes in particular, the notion of anthropogenic niche creation (ibid.: 132) is important, as such processes can have long-term benefits (whether purposeful or

7.5. Photo taken from the far south of Antikythera with north-west coast of Crete visible 35 km away. (By permission of Cambridge University Press, Bevan, A., and Conolly, J. (2013), *Mediterranean Islands, Fragile Communities and Persistent Landscapes: Antikythera in Long-term Perspective*, Plate 22. 6.4.)

accidental) for settlers who return to an island in that the legacy of certain forms of landscape management constitute in situ markers of environmental knowledge (Fig. 7.6). Evidence suggests that vegetation would have recolonised agricultural zones quite quickly (possibly within 20–60 years) (Palmer et al. 2010). Therefore, in many instances, periods of abandonment allowed recovery. Phases of abandonment or reduced human pressure and concomitant recovery might be seen as 'natural' historical-ecological cycles, or as changes imposed upon island dwellers by a demanding and marginal landscape.

Another example of a 'small-island adventure' is represented by the site at Daskaleio-Kavos, situated on the 'small and environmentally marginal' island of Keros (Broodbank 2000: 223). With no known earlier or later settlement evidence, this site provides us with an interesting example of how people took risks at certain times in the past in what appear to be environmentally marginal niches.

On some medium-small Ionian Islands, there is evidence of environmental degradation. Parts of Kefalonia (781 km²) and Lefkada

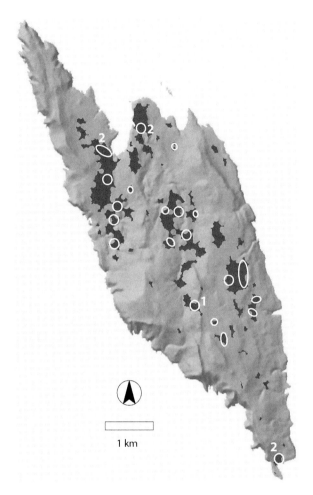

7.6. Antikythera – Zones of more continuous or repeatedly episodic use ('anthropogenic niches'), where relatively stable and resilient systems of landscape exploitation developed. (By permission of Cambridge University Press, Bevan, A., and Conolly, J. (2013), *Mediterranean Islands, Fragile Communities and Persistent Landscapes: Antikythera in Long-term Perspective*, fig. 9.1.)

(336 km²) possess evidence for sheet-wash fans and hill-wash mounds and a number of abandoned terraces on now denuded slopes, all of which indicate an ongoing cycle of erosion/deposition (Souyoudzoglu-Haywood 1999: 5). Even relatively minor tectonic events can have a particular relevance for small islands and their people. On Samos in the Aegean, sudden coastal uplift has been identified from a number of dated wave notches (Stiros et al. 2000). A sudden relative drop in sea level c. 3,900–3,600 years ago and possibly 1,500 years ago could have had implications for coastal installations such as harbours, as well as the water

table, wells, and springs. However, there is no direct evidence for such a problem on Samos. The lack of wells and springs may explain the difficulty of maintaining permanent settlement on the volcanic island of Pantelleria in the Sicilian Channel. Obsidian was exploited during the Neolithic, and the island was abandoned from the Late Bronze Age until the arrival of the Phoenicians when rural activities did take place and continued into the Roman period. Almost 590 cisterns have been found on the island; half these are clearly Punic (Spanò Giammellaro et al. 2008: 150–1).

THE BALEARICS

Constituted by 151 islands and islets, the Balearics provide an interesting case study, largely because research on the principal islands – Mallorca, Minorca, Ibiza, and Formentera (which comprise around 99% of the total land surface; Morey & Ruiz-Perez 2008: 272) – includes palaeoecological work. Biogeographical frameworks have been useful and important in certain aspects of the study of these islands. For example, the extinction of certain fauna has been employed as an indicator of when people may have arrived, based on the notion that people and any fauna that arrived with them contributed to changes in Mallorca's fauna and vegetation. Taking into account the various dates of faunal extinctions and the chronology of the first archaeological sites, it is inferred that people had colonised the island by 2350–2150 BC. The use of extinction dates for the identification of human arrivals is an approach deeply informed by island biogeography, and is implicitly founded on the idea that such environmental impact might be peculiar to islands. However, new populations with new practices might have caused extinctions on the continent as well. Despite this, it is apparent that the various forms of evidence that date the arrival of people on some islands do correlate. Shrews disappeared on the Gymnesic Islands (the eastern Balearics) sometime after 3030 BC, and *Myotragus balearicus*, a dwarf caprine, became extinct. The reasons for its extinction have been debated, and some are now convinced that the chronological pattern of extinction and human colonisation suggests that extinction was caused by people (Bover & Alcover 2003). However, if Ramis and Bover (2001) are correct, the correlation between settlement and extinction is much less obvious.

When archaeologists (and biologists) discuss extinction of a species, they rarely move beyond a discourse that states that the loss of the animal or plant was probably due to human impact or climate change. The discussion of the consequences for local ecologies caused by the extinction is not discussed, let alone the probable change in the wider landscape and the way in which the perception of that landscape may have changed due to the absence of that animal. Such a phenomenon would have been even more important on a small island, where large animals were either rare or absent. Moreover, if *Myotragus* had been domesticated, which seems unlikely (ibid.), the impact for islanders would have been even greater. As we know that the preferred food of *Myotragus* was box (*Buxus balaerica*) (Alcover et al. 1999), there may have been an increase in this tree once the animal died out. Perhaps this is an event that might one day be identifiable in high-resolution pollen diagrams.

The earliest unequivocal archaeological evidence for settlement indicates permanent stable colonisation from 3000 BC for Mallorca and late in the third millennium for Minorca. Between 2600 and 2500 BC, it appears that 'adaptation to the island environment on Mallorca is fully completed' (Guerrero-Ayuso 2001: 148). However, some consider that the archaeological data are at best ambiguous. Ramis et al. (2002) posit that the arrival of humans on Mallorca is registered in the sedimentary record at the site of Cova des Moro where there is a 'sedimentary discontinuity' characterised by an increase in charcoal. This process has been dated to c. 2400 BC (ibid.: 17). The review of the reliability of dates from the Balearics carried out by Ramis et al. suggests that people did not settle on Mallorca prior to the third millennium BC. Whilst colonisation of Minorca may not have occurred prior to 1930 BC, there is some possibility that humans did arrive prior to this period (ibid.: 18). These islands receive irregular amounts of rainfall. Whilst the average on Ibiza is 400 mm per annum, only 50 mm fell between April and September 1971 (Gómez Bellard 1995: 445), and people may well have had to negotiate similar fluctuations in the past. An initial phase of occupation on Ibiza and Formentera, two of the smaller Balearic Islands (570 km² and 83 km² respectively), is dated to c. 2000 BC. Though there is a possible Neolithic site (c. 4500 BC) on Ibiza, this phase is followed by what appears to be a hiatus lasting about 600 years. It seems likely that the limited natural resources, in particular water, may have rendered these islands less attractive to colonisers (Gómez Bellard 1995). Again, the development of an island-specific form of architecture (the navetas) is another manifestation of enigmatic insularity (Ramis 2010).

The availability of pollen diagrams renders the assessment of environmental change on these islands more effective. There is clear evidence for human impact on the vegetation on Mallorca and Minorca from c. 2300 BC. It seems that the initial human impact on some of the Balearics was quite profound. Moreover, deterioration in certain habitats may well have been brought about by introduced rodents that arrived with people (Bover & Alcover 2008). Pollen diagrams from Mallorca and Minorca imply impact on these islands' ecosystems after 4500 BC (Yll et al. 1997). Yll et al. consider that the changes in vegetation that occurred on Mallorca and Minorca could have been caused by a change in climate and/or the impact of people (1997). In Mallorca, there was a clear reduction of boxwood (*Buxus balaerica*) and juniper (*Juniperus*) and a marked increase in wild olive (*Olea europea*). Moreover, evergreen oak increased, replacing deciduous oak (Pèrez-Obiol et al. 2011). The substitution of mesophilous plants by maquis scrub could have been due to the development of a relatively dry climatic phase (Pèrez-Obiol & Sadori 2007). The fact that this same process occurs on Minorca about one millennium later leads Guerrero-Ayusos (2001: 145) to question the hypothesis that climate change was responsible for the evolution of these new vegetation patterns. Whilst the demise of tree cover does not necessarily constitute a 'fragile' environment and concomitant economic problems, it is a fundamental change in the nature of that environment and landscape, and will therefore affect the way in which that landscape is perceived and engaged with. Such a change would have been a constitutive element in the construction of an 'insular' culture. However, the range of cereals present during the Bronze Age was probably the same as that on the mainland (Moffett 1992). Therefore, despite the evidence for an initial impact on the environments of these islands, it seems that a period of relative resilience followed. The finds from the enigmatic Cova des Mussol burial site (situated on a cliff face), perhaps literally defining the edge of life, include wooden carved figures made from *Olea europaea* and *Buxus balearica*. The objects dated to 1393–1295 BC and 1192–1027 BC (Pèrez 2005) were probably carved from local wood – wood that possibly took on more value as scarcity increased. Despite the undoubted changes in the later prehistoric environment, the absence of new technologies with a drastic impact on the environment and the possibility that an insular form of environmental knowledge emerged engendered equilibrium. Consequently, these islands did not really witness any profound changes before the arrival of Rome (Alcover 2008).

An extensive Beaker phase of settlement with concomitant agricultural and other economic activities is attested to on the islands (Waldren 1997). Ramis (2010) argues convincingly for a late third-millennium colonisation with evidence for cultural (Beaker) links with the south of France.

It is interesting to note that people on a relatively small island did not appear overly reliant on marine food sources, despite the obvious benefits of replacing terrestrial-based proteins with marine proteins as part of curation of the terrestrial environment. There is little evidence for consumption of marine resources by prehistoric communities on the Balearic Islands (Van Strydonck et al. 2009). Even in the Roman period, marine proteins appear to have been minimal. The low biotic productivity, touched upon in Chapter 3, might go some way in explaining this. However, there was also the notion that a marine diet was considered to be a sign of poverty (Purcell 1995), although the upper classes did consume garum (B. T. Fuller Márquez-Grant, & Richards 2010).

The proto-historic and Roman periods are not always covered in the Balearic pollen diagrams. However, the diagram from Alcudia in Mallorca does demonstrate that woodland vegetation did not recover (Burjachs et al. 1994). Important changes in the culture of the Balearic Islands occurred during the ninth century BC, including the development of the Talayotic culture with its enigmatic stone-built towers. This period saw the demise of the navetas on Minorca and a change in burial rite also appearing on Mallorca. The absence of evidence for new arrivals on the Balearic Islands between 1500 BC and the Roman period might imply that people were aware that emigration from the continent was not viable (Van Strydonck 2004). One interesting Late Holocene process is the evidence for the probable impact of alien rodents (which may well have arrived during the Roman period) on the islands' ecosystems (Traveset et al. 2009). The potential impact of rodents on island environments should not be underestimated (Drake & Hunt 2009).

Unsurprisingly, the trajectories of small islands are often different to their continental neighbours. There is evidence that small islands are more susceptible to environmental degradation. However, such processes do not necessarily lead to abandonment, as islands emerge as important nodes in trade networks and often possess raw materials that are valued elsewhere. Some small islands were settled quite late on, and may have witnessed periods of abandonment. For example, Ibiza and Formentera were probably not settled until the end of the third millennium BC, and were then abandoned between the thirteenth and seventh centuries BC. The Phoenicians then settled these islands – probably the only islands settled by the Phoenicians not to have an indigenous population (Gómez Bellard 2008: 46). Once settled, some small islands developed intensive forms of production concentrating on the export of a limited range of goods or materials. Rural activity on parts of Ibiza and Formentera was quite intensive, with evidence for olive oil and wine production, especially from the third century BC onwards (ibid.: 67). This specialised agriculture undoubtedly suited the relatively poor-quality soils on these islands.

Discussion: Are Islands Different?

There is no doubt that the environmental development (including the waxing and waning of flora and faunal diversity and species numbers) of islands is often different to that on continental areas. Whilst islands and continental landscapes share common niche types, the issue is that the same habitat on an island may not recover from degradation in the same way as that on the continent. Islands do possess a series of environmental characteristics that differentiate them from continents, and these characteristics will have influenced the development of insular cultures. Species richness and diversity are often such that recovery from a phase of environmental degradation is more problematic. Mediterranean island vegetation is especially important, and plant communities can be quite different to their continental counterparts. For example, Crete possesses about 200 endemic species and subspecies (Rackham 2008: 37), thus demonstrating difference vis-à-vis continental landscapes but not necessarily environmental resilience. Environmental change on islands might accelerate at greater rates than on continental areas. For example, on Minorca, box-juniper was quickly replaced by olive, phrygana, and steppe (ibid.: 49) – a development that is not always mirrored in continental landscapes.

From an environmental perspective, one key question in the study of people and islands is the issue of human impact on endemic species (both plants and animals) and the importation of alien species. Whereas most plants and animals on continental Mediterranean areas migrate naturally (there are of course exceptions), some species are either purposefully or accidentally brought onto islands. In some instances, certain domesticated animals may have been brought onto islands but for some reason became feral (Groves 1990). The impact of such animals on the environment can be quite devastating, as was the case with certain rodents. Moreover, on islands, certain unusual processes can occur. For example, in the absence of a competitor, some animals on islands (that also exist on the neighbouring continent) may extend to their full fundamental niche, rather than the realised niche occupied in the presence of that competitor or other constraint (Blondel 2008). Such changes not only have ecological repercussions, but also demand the development of new forms of environmental knowledge. This intersection of cultural and environmental processes once again articulates a historical ecology where the boundaries between culture and nature are necessarily blurred. The very act of environmental manipulation is an ecological-cultural process. Successful colonisation demands processes of 'landscape learning' (Phoca-Cosmetatou 2011a: 20; Rockman 2003). As people adapt to the specificities of their environment, environmental knowledge manifests itself via economic and cultural practices. An ethnographic study of crop processing on the Aegean islands of Karpathos and Amorgos demonstrated the 'time-stress' associated with harvesting and crop processing. The level of labour required within a short period places extreme demands on peasant farmers. This research also demonstrated that farmers were flexible in their day-to-day decision making regarding the effects of weather and other commitments (to family and other more economically attractive tasks). The dispersal of fields across the island also appeared as an advantage, as rainfall patterns can vary across an island quite substantially, thus spreading the risk of crop failure should there be low rainfall on one particular part of the island. Variation in the type of crops grown is also an important risk buffer (Halstead & Jones 1989: 50–1). Perhaps the one key environmental characteristic that renders certain small islands marginal is the fact that crop growing on or near exposed windy coasts is extremely difficult (Halstead 2008: 234).

We have also seen how some small islands were exploited for a specific 'niche'-based activity, such as grazing. The potential of some small islands seems surprising. Published in 1910, Seager's (2000: 6) account

7.7. Mochlos – a small island off the north-east of Crete with Minoan house tombs (photo: Berengere Perez).

of his work on the Island of Pseira (2 km off the north-east coast of Crete) starts with the observation that this barren rock of an island could have offered little to even Minoan settlers, other than its harbour. However, despite its small size, the site at Pseira boasted a series of Minoan buildings, including a shrine and a cemetery (Betancourt & Davaras 1988). The cemetery constructs a specific identity for something as environmentally insignificant as an islet, but at the same time, demonstrates that 2 km is not far enough to render an islet insular. We see a similar situation on the small island of Mochlos, also off the north-east coast of Crete (Fig. 7.7) with its rich Minoan house tombs (Soles 1992). Clusters of islands that have easy sea access between them might well be considered as a single entity. This serves as an example of how finely honed environmental knowledge vis-à-vis insular climate, weather, and topography characterises certain stages of island histories. For example, it seems that early metalworkers on eastern Crete chose topographical situations where the wind was funnelled, thus improving the action of furnaces (Betancourt & Farrand 2006: 20). However, with the resilience of an island's environment damaged, life can become more complicated for the island's inhabitants in a relatively short period. For example, small changes in weather patterns, such as those that may have constituted the more arid Bronze Age climate, may have made some agricultural activities more difficult (ibid.). In addition, the impact of sea-level change on island communities may be greater than for those living on the continent, especially on smaller islands, as such changes in coastal configuration have a proportionally greater effect on the landscape available to islanders.

If simple biogeographical models were to work, then we would expect the cultural 'richness' and variety to observe some basic rules. Larger islands close to continents should develop stable, rich cultures (as represented by material culture, settlement evidence, etc.). There should then be a reduction in richness on smaller islands that are further away from core, continental cultures. The development of influential cultures on Crete, then, should not surprise us. In turn, large, 'successful islands' such as Crete should then influence adjacent smaller islands. We do see such trends at certain points during the past. Consequently, some islands are often subservient to an external (continental) power. Rich, albeit temporary, cultures on smaller islands, such as the Cyclades, Melos, or Santorini, do not necessarily observe the rules articulated by biogeographical models. However, the often-temporary nature of the cultural and/or economic influence of these smaller islands is something that we must consider. Moreover, we should assess the influence of the biogeographical/environmental characteristics and changes on such islands. If a small island is exploited for a specific resource, then the environmental impact associated with that exploitation will be intense. For example, some particularly small islands were sometimes used for pasture. Therefore, the impact on vegetation would have been intense, and we know that grazing and burning on some Greek islands have adversely affected woodland conservation (Thornes 2009: 572). Goats were in fact proscribed on some islands. As Constantakopoulou (2007: 210) observes, the decree forbidding the import and feeding of goats on Heracleia must be due to the problems caused by large herds of unsupervised goats destroying crops and threatening agricultural production in a sensitive environment.

A most useful definition of insularity is that employed by Knapp (2008: 18): 'The quality of being isolated as a result of living on islands, or being somewhat detached in outlook and experience. Insularity can result from personal, historical or social contingency'. The limitations posed by insular resources are fundamental attributes of island life. Nevertheless, it is the attitudes of each society to insularity and the sea that truly influence how insular any given society becomes. Important changes in the Chalcolithic economy and society on Cyprus occurred as numbers and the 'stress' on resources increased. One hypothesis that will need continuous testing is the idea that increased competition on islands (with their inherently reduced carrying capacities) led to an increased investment in monuments (Renfrew 1976). At the same time, we should also consider the 'cultural isolation model', where island populations may follow different trajectories to those on continental areas in terms of landscape manipulation and management. Patton (1996: 136) also argues that we should consider the relevance of the sociogeographic model, in particular, the idea that certain ritual practices and the authority associated with such practices is exaggerated on island communities. Patton feels that the sociogeographic model is useful. However, it seems that we should examine how the various threads from each of these models interconnect and have led to specific and original human–landscape relationships on some Mediterranean islands. Costa (2008: 7) implies that insularity itself could explain why there is a certain similarity in megalithic forms across various Mediterranean islands. The southern part of Corsica alone has 25 stone alignments (800 stones in total) (ibid.: 92). In a discussion of the third millennium in France, Lichardus et al. (1985: 557) comment that 'Corsica, as in all periods, presents cultural facies that are different to those found on the continent' (authors' translation). Also, as Guilaine (2003: 308) notes, despite their proximity, Corsica and Sardinia develop quite different cultural trajectories.

The presence of several megalithic tombs on Pantelleria (a small island about 70 km to the east of Tunisian coast and about 200 km to the north-west of Malta) is interesting, as the principal economic activity here seems to have been the mining of obsidian (one of the few sources present in the Western Mediterranean). As with many Bronze Age societies around Europe, what we see across much of the Mediterranean is the removal of the domestic habitats away from agricultural land. The emergence of complex funerary monuments across these landscapes is unsurprising as different groups, now some distance from their land, ensure that their ownership is clearly articulated. These processes should also be understood as part of a wider network of changes in relationships with the natural world, a world which in some places, such as on smaller islands, may have become more ecologically fragile (Costa 2008). It is wrong to claim that the monument building on these islands was a product of complete isolation from the continent. Rather it was a process of island societies remembering links with continental areas, and then moulding and developing new specific monument forms and related cultural practices (Gili et al. 2006).

What we have seen in this chapter is a notable variation in the approaches to the study of human–island interactions across the Mediterranean. Archaeologists do critically assess approaches underpinned by biogeographical notions. Each island has its own set of specific contingent historical and environmental histories (Cherry 2004). The changes that we see on some small islands do demonstrate how insularity can prevent environmental recovery. However, the environmental and landscape histories of many larger islands are not so different from their continental counterparts, although the impact of a small number of alien (floral and faunal) species has had important consequences for some insular landscapes. The study of endemic floras and faunas – such as the work carried on Corsica (Vigne & Valladas 1996) and the Balearic Islands – is one important and productive research strategy. However, many islands lack integrated palaeoecological and geoarchaeological research, and it is often difficult to assess the extent to which human impact on island environments has diverged from that on continental zones. One mechanism for assessing the historical fragility of insular environments vis-à-vis similar continental analogues is to carry out vegetation and soil surveys and compare these with one another, as ultimately island landscapes should be more degraded than their continental counterparts if both have experienced similar histories of human settlement and activity. We cannot equate islands with isolation; the complex set of metaphors associated with insularity has hindered the development of a nissology that avoids the wholesale application of a rigid biogeographical paradigm (Eriksen 1993; Hay 2006). Early islanders did not necessarily live in harmony with their environments, and the notion of endemic equilibrium is clearly unfounded (Broodbank 2000: 7). However, environmental knowledge that was specific to island life did develop. Degraded island environments may well constitute the quintessential example of diverging forms of environmental knowledge. Those people who directly engaged with the natural world would have been influenced by elite socio-economic structures and imposed forms of environmental knowledge. The attraction of certain islands as nodes with a cultural economic network may have increased demographic pressure to the point where the normal carrying capacity of these islands was exceeded, and the now infamous island cultures with their enigmatic monuments and material culture must be seen as being partly the product of island environmental trajectories.

8

Mountain Economies and Environmental Change

Introduction: Vertical Spaces, Cyclical Time

Extreme topographical variation within Mediterranean subregions has led to complex understandings of and engagements with these landscape mosaics, thus engendering intricate forms of environmental knowledge. For these reasons, mountainous landscapes are the focus of the final thematic chapter. Here, we draw together the themes and environmental processes discussed in the preceding chapters. Mountain environments comprise most of the landscape characteristics and processes discussed in the previous chapters. Issues of human engagements with vegetation, fluvial and alluvial systems, and terrestrial (colluvial) processes are considered here within a framework which assesses the chronological and spatial variation of different societies' relationships with the most enigmatic of all landscape types. In some ways, even the question of insularity is relevant. Mountain peoples have often been viewed as 'alien' vis-à-vis their lowland counterparts. The topographical relief (the peaks and ridges) are to mountain peoples what the sea is to islanders. As McNeil (1992: 12) suggested, the Mediterranean is not so much the sea between the lands, but rather the sea amongst the mountains. The changes in the patterns of exploitation of these different horizontal zones are the fascinating phenomena here. It is rare for any permanent settlement to exist above 2,000 m. In the Alps, the highest parish or communes are Trepalle (Italy) at 2,209 m and Saint Verran (France) at 2,040 m – places at the very edge of the Mediterranean world (Fig. 8.1 – map of places referred to in this chapter). Mountains protect the Mediterranean lowlands from almost guaranteed desertification and insurmountable aridity. The 'relief' proffered by mountains traps passing air masses, and ensures orographic

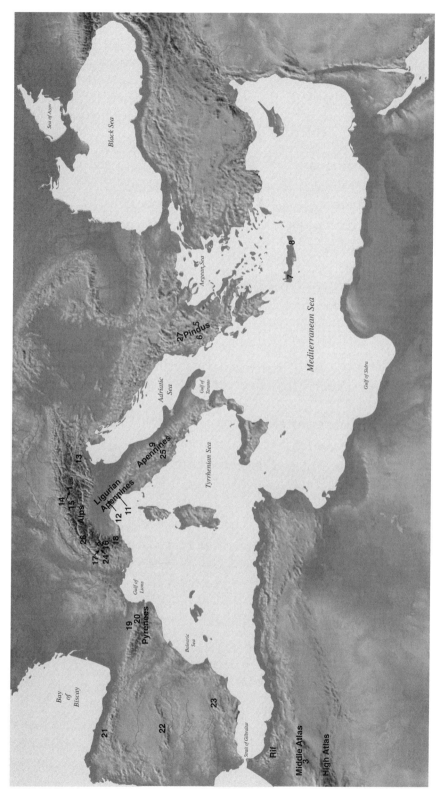

8.1. Mountain ranges of the Mediterranean, and places referred to in the chapter. 1: Trepalle, 2: Saint Verran, 3: Tigalmamine, 4: Samarinia, 5: Grevena highland zones, 6: Rezina Marsh, 7: Sphakia/Cretan White Mountains, 8: Lasithi plain Dikataian Mountain range, 9: Calderone Glacier, 10: Prato Mollo, 11: Pian del Lago, 12: Prato Spilla (Emilia-Romagna), 13: Palughetto basin, 14: Forcellin-Foscagno glacier/Val Febbraro, upper Valle di Spluga, 15: Lago Basso/Val Vidröla/Borghetto Sotto/Lago Grande west, 16: Ubaye Valley/Col de Roburent, 17: Puy-St-Vincent/Rama/Fangeas, 18: Mercantour/Mont Bego, 19: Vicdessos, 20: Cerdagne/ Donezan/Enveig Mountain – Madriu valley (Andorra), 21: Asturia, 22: Sierra de Gredos, 23: Segura Mountains, 24: Lac des Lauzons, 25: Aniene Valley/Simbruni Mountains, 26: Petit Col Saint Bernard, 27: Lake Ohrid.

precipitation that feeds the streams and ultimately the rivers that run into the lowlands. This process is as true on those islands with mountain ranges as it is of the continental areas with the Alps, the Pyrenees, and Atlas Mountains.

This chapter will start with an overview of archaeological and environmental characterisations of Mediterranean mountains, followed by a Mediterranean-wide review of environmental research, and, where possible, associated archaeological work. The final sections comprise a synthesis of recent integrated environmental and landscape archaeological work in the Pyrenees and the Southern French Alps. These latter examples are situated within a historical and cultural ecological framework that once again considers notions of environmental knowledge. The key precept is that, as with small islands, life in the mountains demands varied sets of environmental knowledge. This knowledge is constituted locally, and periods when rigid, hierarchical socio-economic systems (such as empires) attempt to impose incongruous forms of institutionalised environmental knowledge may often see the emergence of environmental problems or even the withdrawal of people from certain landscape types.

DEFINING MOUNTAIN LANDSCAPES

The defining characteristic of mountainous areas is vertical zonation – the relationship between environments (climate, vegetation, soil, etc.) across the vertical zones, the types of activity that can take place therein, and when (in which season) these activities can take place. These notions underpin the framework and models for much research in mountains (Fig. 8.2). The reduction in temperature of 1°C for every 300 m climbed is one of the key defining environmental variables in mountainous areas. Consequently, as with the study of islands, biogeographical models have influenced the ways in which we interrogate and interpret human–environment engagements in mountains. One important observation in mountain ecology is the idea that the high altitudes are 'buffered' by lowland forests, grasslands, or deserts in the same way that islands are buffered by seas. Moreover, the fact that high-altitude zones tend to be cold adds another form of buffer (Billings 1979: 97). As with discussions of island biogeography, we must avoid the uncritical application of such models when assessing human colonisation and life in high-altitude zones. There are, however, simple, unavoidable biogeographical rules: the level of pedogenesis decreases with altitude, and unsurprisingly, the

Alpine
2100–3000 m

Summer pasture
hunting, limit of forest
in many mountain ranges

Subalpine
1600–2100 m

Summer pasture, hay making,
some arable at lower limit,
forestry, mining

Montane
1000–1600 m

Arable, permanent settlement

8.2. Vertical zonation in mountain landscapes: ecological characteristics and principal human activities. Note certain activities such as mining are not constrained by ecological zonation. Also, the vertical zonation heights (montane, subalpine, and alpine) vary across the Mediterranean (figure: F. Mocci and K. Walsh).

number of different species of plants and animals also decreases. These characteristics are directly influenced by the amount of exposure to sunlight, wind, slope, geology, and so on (ibid.: 105). It is the exposure to sunlight – the different orientations of mountain slopes – that is possibly the defining characteristic in many mountainous zones, and thus leads to specific designations for north- and south-facing slopes, such as *ubac* and *adret* in French. The orientation of the slope is a fundamental control on vegetation growth and the upper limit of the forest. The natural limit of the forest is the timberline (the limit of the closed canopy), and the tree line is the limit of tree growth. Those limits both advance and retreat, being influenced by changes in climate and human exploitation of the forest. Whilst the primary productivity of an alpine zone will influence what people do at high altitude in terms of farming and hunting, there are certain resources, especially minerals and ores, that attract people to live and work in these zones no matter what the primary ecological productivity. However, humans are usually absent from high-altitude zones during periods when plants are dormant – a situation that is not true of other environments. Many alpine zones are only productive for 10–25% of the year (ibid.: 113), although longer periods of productivity characterise some Mediterranean high-altitude zones. Using the Andes as an example, Winterhalder (1994: 35) observes that the predictability of monthly precipitation is reduced at higher altitudes, implying a concomitant increase in subsistence risk. However, risk is entirely dependent on environmental knowledge, and the effectiveness of any culture in successfully applying that knowledge in the mitigation of unpredictable events.

One of the fundamental problems in assessing the impact of climate change on mountain communities is the fact that each valley, and even different zones within a valley, will experience differing consequences from any change in climate. Valley weather systems are exceptionally complex, and modelling such processes is difficult. Mountains and uplands are sensitive to environmental stresses and environmental change. We tend to assume that environmental stress is a corollary of increased environmental change, but this depends entirely on the nature of the change. Climatic cooling can actually engender the conservation of certain environment types, whilst warming may lead to an increase in extreme weather events in certain landscape types, particularly in mountainous zones. Therefore, climatic cooling should not necessarily be considered as causing environmental stress in mountainous environments, whilst climatic warming might well lead to new stresses via extreme weather events such as summer storms (Beniston 2000).

Although it is partly true that the dearth of evidence for early human activity in areas above 2,500 m around the world is explained by the relative remoteness and ecological poverty of such zones (Aldenderfer 2006), we should not forget that the difficulties in accessing high-altitude areas varies from region to region, and, moreover, that the levels of ecological productivity vary. Many Mediterranean high-altitude zones are relatively easy to access, and the extreme variation in Mediterranean topography results in landscapes where vertical height can be attained over relatively short horizontal distances; mountains are not impenetrable (Horden & Purcell 2000: 131). One problem in demonstrating that people have always incorporated these zones into their lifeways is the fact that the archaeological signals tend to be ephemeral, as mobile peoples rarely leave substantial built remains (Cribb 1991). Moreover, detailed research in many mountainous areas is limited.

Several questions are paramount in the study of mountainous landscapes. In particular, we need to assess whether human exploitation of mountains is continuous. Can we identify certain periods when there was an expansion into higher altitudes, and conversely, were there periods when mountainous areas were avoided? An important theme in mountain archaeology and history is the idea that mountainous areas act as marginal zones that 'receive' people at times of climatic amelioration. However, the examples cited in the latter part of this chapter question this sentiment, and comprise an assessment of sociocultural reasons for the waxing and waning human activity in mountainous zones.

Human–Landscape Engagements Across Mediterranean Mountains

This section comprises an assessment of some of the work that has taken place across Mediterranean mountains. As ever, emphasis is placed on research that combines palaeoenvironmental data with archaeological evidence. Archaeological survey in high-altitude zones is either rare or demands a great deal of time and effort for low 'archaeological' rewards (i.e. sites and artefacts). One approach to the study of mountainous archaeological landscapes and their environments is the use of palynology and anthracology as proxies for human activity. Whilst some palaeoenvironmental research has been carried out in North African highland areas, such work is still relatively uncommon.

Prehistoric settlement appears to have been sparse in the Rif range (about 350 km in length and 80–100 km wide) in northern Morocco (McNeill 1992: 83). Today, long-distance transhumance does not exist in the Rif, perhaps due to intertribal conflict. However, short-distance movement of flocks does exist (ibid.: 48). The nature of seasonal movement of people and animals obviously structures the nature of the relationships that people have with mountainous landscapes. In the Middle Atlas Mountains (1,700 m), the palynological evidence does not suggest an early anthropogenic influence on the vegetation, although there is some evidence for Neolithic impact, and tentative evidence for browsing during the first millennia BC and AD. Pastoral activity was certainly taking place from the fourth century AD onwards (Lamb et al. 1991; Lamb & Van der Kaars 1995). Pine was also cleared periodically about 2,000 years ago, and then about 500 AD, as pastoralism was replaced by arable agriculture (Lamb et al. 1991). It seems likely that pre- and proto-historic peoples were active in North African mountain ranges, but the archaeological and palaeoecological evidence rarely implies high levels of activity, or these were forms of activity that left ephemeral traces in both the archaeological and palaeoecological records. However, as we move into the Roman period, the nature of society's relationships with some of these areas did change. Palynological work from Tigalmamine (1,626 m) in the Middle Atlas reveals human impact in this area from the third century BC when there was a decline in *Fraxinus* (ash) (Lamb et al. 1989: 72).

One important advantage of settlement in some North African mountain ranges is the relatively large quantities of water present therein. In the Libyan Sahara, where wet conditions prevailed from 4900–4400 BC, the inner mountainous areas appear to have been the preferred landscape, where relatively high levels of pastoral activity took place. Then, 'severe' dry conditions developed from c. 3000 BC, and this appears to be correlated with a reduction of activity in the mountains (Cremaschi & Di Lernia 1999: 216). During the Roman period, the capture and control of waters emanating from the mountains was essential for the successful development of economies in lower-lying areas (Trousset 1986).

The impact of Imperial Rome on mountainous zones across the Mediterranean is of fundamental interest, as such zones, which are often on the edges of empires, may have developed characteristics that are quite different to the Romanised lowlands. In some instances, they maintained a level of cultural and economic independence, with environmental trajectories that were in many ways a continuation of Iron Age processes. In other areas, mountainous zones emerged as fully incorporated landscapes. As Roman agriculture and landscape organisation was imbued with many different systems of technological and ideological control (the two being inherently intertwined), we need to consider the extent to which these systems (initially developed in the more hospitable landscapes of Italy) were successfully transposed onto these decidedly different mountainous zones across the Empire. For some time, ancient historians and archaeologists considered mountain societies as detached from those on the plains. This notion was particularly prevalent amongst French geographers and historians in the French North African colonies, an attitude which in many ways merely reflected the reality of a French colonial economy that itself avoided the mountainous zones, considering them marginal (Leveau 1977, 1986). In this view, Roman civilisation spread like water; it invaded the plains without covering the mountains (Courtois 1955: 121).

In the low mountainous zone, or high steppe (800 m and above) around Kasserine (Tunisia), a large number of Roman sites were established. Based on the palaeobotanical work that has been carried out in this area, it seems that this zone has been best suited to nomadic pastoralism. Even though this landscape may well have been slightly different to the present steppe environment, it certainly appears that pastoralism was the dominant activity prior to the arrival of Rome (Hitchner 1988: 8). Essentially agricultural in function, many of these Roman sites were involved in oleiculture as well cereal and pulse production. The amount of olive oil potentially produced in this area would have exceeded local needs, whilst crop production was probably for local consumption. Animal husbandry was also a significant activity. One important element in the development of this landscape would have been the construction and/or maintenance of terrace systems, essential for enhancing and protecting the soil required for crop production in semi-arid zones (Fig. 8.3) that are highly susceptible to erosion during extreme precipitation events. A number of cemeteries formed part of this Roman

8.3. Djebel Chambi near Kasserine (photo: Bruce Hitchner).

landscape, whilst zones that included earlier burials under cairns appear to have been what Hitchner (1990: 244–5) refers to as 'negative space' – areas that remained 'marginal' to the core Empire. Although research into North African mountainous areas has not been as intensive as other parts of the Mediterranean, what we do see is a heterogeneous pattern of activity during the Holocene, with some evidence for Rome in particular adapting indigenous environmental knowledge and linking core economic and social processes in these areas, but not necessarily integrating them.

GREECE AND ANATOLIA

The Pindus Mountains comprise parallel limestone ridges that extend from Albania down to the Gulf of Corinth. This part of the Mediterranean is characterised by complex, extremely varied topography, from the hinterland right down to the coast (Fig. 8.4). Much of this landscape is seemingly barren, but people have settled in those 'ecological islands'

8.4. The coastal zone before the Pindus Mountains, north-west Greece. In many Mediterranean regions, the mountains are never far from the coast, creating complex topographies and niches that are often difficult to exploit (photo: author).

nestled between the ridges and peaks of the mountains. Whilst geological formations do not dictate behaviour, the topographical characteristics of a mountainous region do considerably influence the ways in which people move across a landscape (Llobera & Sluckin 2007). We have to consider if geological and topographical configurations have any specific cultural ramifications. Whilst the structure of valley systems, passes, and ridges do influence mobility and links that people have with different places (towns, villages, farms, pastures), this spatial organisation of the mountainous zone only becomes relevant if we can truly demonstrate that the day-to-day human experience of life in this zone would have been different had the geological and topographical characteristics been different. There is no doubt that topographical configuration does influence settlement and the ways in which spaces are used and engaged with. Ecological zonation, and therefore the limit for vegetation growth, obviously varies across Mediterranean mountain ranges. The altitude at which good quality pasture will grow also differs. These and other factors affect the maximum height at which village or hamlet settlement occurred. In the Pindus Mountains, the highest village (Samarinia) is situated at 1,650 m. In the Grevena highland zones (the Pindus chain of western Macedonia, Greece), regular use of these upland areas may well have started at the end of the Neolithic, with pastoral activity probably practised during the Middle to Late Bronze Age. This is supported by some now rather dated palynological evidence that suggests a change in vegetation during the Bronze Age (Higgs 1978). However, more recent work from the northern Pindus Mountains (the Rezina Marsh site) indicates human impact from as early as 6,000 years ago, when there was a rapid reduction in tree diversity and density, although *Acer* (maple) and *Carpinus betulus* (common hornbeam) increased (proportionately). A thousand years later, some woodland species did increase. Then from about 4,000 years ago, forest clearance took place, and the increase in *Rumex* (docks) implies that this later phase was one characterised by anthropogenic impact (Willis 1994). Human activity appears to have taken place at a range of altitudes, between 285 m and 1,800 m (and probably above and below these heights, as allocthonous pollen would have been present in these cores). The study of the soils in the area suggests that the weakly developed profiles are a product of human disturbance of vegetation, and consequent churning and soil creep. Despite this, there is no evidence to suggest that this has prevented pastoral activity, although it may well have reduced flock capacity in the area. The constant cycle of activity in this fragile environment is thus deemed to have put pressure on the landscape (Efstratiou et al. 2006: 430). When Rome imposed itself upon the area, the enslavement of a large proportion of the population seems to have led to a long-term decline in activity in the Pindus (McNeill 1992: 78). Despite the fact that there is little archaeological evidence that allows us to test this hypothesis, such a process does correspond with what we see in other mountain ranges.

Other evidence from the northern mountainous zones of Greece shows how deciduous oaks and lime dominated the Middle Holocene woodland. Between c. 2130 and 1320 BC, *Abies* (fir) and *Pinus* gradually replaced these trees, whilst *Fagus* (beech) started to expand. Eventually, from about 800 BC at the lowest sample site, and later in the higher altitude sites, *Abies* became almost extinct and *Fagus* became dominant. *Juglans* (walnut) and *Castanea* (chestnut) also appear during this period (Gerasimidis & Athanasiadis 1995: 113).

On the extreme northern edge of this subregion, the Galičica National park (on the border of Macedonia and Albania), with mountains as high as 2,250 m, includes Lake Ohrid. This lake possesses some of the most important palaeoenvironmental archives in Europe, and they comprise a range of proxy indicators for both climate change and human impact on the surrounding landscape. Whilst specific archaeological evidence for the exact nature of human activity in the mountains around the lake might be absent, or as yet unrecorded, pollen, fungal spores, and sediment chemistry, including lipid biomarkers, provide a broad image of the development in human activity around Lake Ohrid. Coprostanols (a lipid biomarker that is indicative of faecal matter) suggest the presence of people and animals around the lake from more than 8,000 years ago (Holtvoeth et al. 2010). Incontrovertible evidence for the impact of people in this area is attested to (by pollen and fungal spores) from c. 3000 BC, with the landscape undergoing a significant transformation (probable opening up for agro-pastoral activities) from c. 400 BC (Wagner et al. 2009). Whilst it is possible that these signals represent lakeside activity, it may be that they are the consequence of increased human activity in the upland areas of the lake catchment. As discussed later in this chapter, an increase in upland activity is a phenomenon that we see in many mountainous areas around the Mediterranean during the Chalcolithic and Bronze Age.

The Cretan Mountains

Archaeological research is rare in the mountains of the major Mediterranean islands, although research on Crete provides a useful exception. Today, the upper limit of permanent settlement on Crete is 800 m (Rackham & Moody 1996: 93). The Sphakia survey covered a district in south-western Crete, an area which covers a number of different zones from the coast up to the White Mountains. The highest point in the Cretan White Mountains (Lefka Ori) is 2,453 m. What is more striking is that this peak is only 16 km from the coast, and therefore presents people with an incredible variation in topography over a very short distance.

Prehistoric pottery was found over all of Sphakia, suggesting an 'extensive, not intensive, exploitation of the entire area during this period' (L. Nixon et al. 1990). Whilst there are a large number of prehistoric sites comprising artefact scatters and structures such as cisterns, precise dates and the specific function of this upland area are difficult to ascertain without excavation, although the role of herding in the later proto-historic economy appears to have increased in the Cretan mountains (Nowicki 1999). A possible reduction in activity at higher altitudes occurred during the Graeco-Roman phase, a period when settlement was concentrated down towards the coast (Moody & Nixon 2006). Although documentary sources suggest an increase in pastoral and associated upland activities during the Classical and Hellenistic period (Chaniotis 1999), we do not know where and at what altitudes. Despite the archaeological evidence for high-altitude human activity, the palynological evidence that exists implies no significant vegetation change in the White Mountains prior to the second Byzantine period (eleventh to twelfth centuries AD) (Atherden & Hall 1999). The apparent low level of impact on vegetation may be due to the catchment from which the pollen core was taken, or human activities were such that impact was low.

At an average altitude of 840 m, the Lasithi plain (eastern central Crete) in the Dikataian Mountain range is encircled by peaks that reach an altitude of almost 2,150 m. One difference between this area and other mountainous zones discussed in this chapter is that arable agriculture has probably been a key element in the local economy due to the relatively low mean altitude. The earliest sites date to the Late Neolithic or Early Minoan periods, and probably represent seasonal pastoral activity (Watrous 1982: 10). Activity in the plain continued to develop during the Minoan period. However, the evidence for the Late Minoan I period is quite ephemeral, and may be explained by emigration towards the principal Neopalatial sites (ibid.: 15). Population and activity levels seemed to contract throughout the rest of the Late Minoan periods. During the Geometric and Archaic periods, settlements re-emerged around the edge of the plain. However, the plain was largely depopulated during the Classical and Hellenistic periods, perhaps due to a perception that such upland zones were unproductive. There may well have been other political and cultural reasons for this reduction in activity. During the Roman period, the plain was repopulated, with some sites situated on the alluvium rather than on the slopes (ibid.: 24).

In Crete, the work that has been done on mountainous landscapes does reveal patterns that we will see repeated as we move into the Alps and the Iberian mountains. Cretan societies made use of the high-altitude zones during the later prehistoric periods. However, impact on the mountains was not continuous, as there seems to be a withdrawal from the highest altitudes during the Roman period, or a change in the way these zones were exploited.

Italy, France, and Spain (the Apennines, Alps, and Pyrenees)

As we move into the Euro-Mediterranean mountain ranges, the amount of palaeoenvironmental evidence and integrated archaeological research increases. This alone is the rationale for concentrating on projects from this part of the Mediterranean.

There is no doubt that parts of the Northern Mediterranean witnessed a change in climate c. 4,000 years ago. There are variations in the characteristics of this climate change, and ostensibly subtle differences between the Apennines and the Alps to the north. The Calderone Glacier is Europe's southernmost glacier (situated in the Apennines). This re-formed during the latter half of the third millennium BC, and subsequently expanded during the eighth century BC and then again during the seventh century AD (Giraudi et al. 2011: 107). The Bronze Age is when many mountainous zones were incorporated into structured, economically productive, vertical landscapes – a later phase within the Mediterranean secondary products revolution (Greenfield 2010). As recently observed, this phase, which marks the transition between the Middle and Late Holocene, is characterised by a complex pattern of wet/dry oscillations (Magny, Galop, et al. 2009). The key issue for the Apennines, and other mountainous areas, is that different palaeoenvironmental records support the inference of a short cool period (glacial advance and lake-level increase) that was followed by cool and arid conditions (glacial advance and lake-level decrease) (Giraudi et al. 2011: 112). Moreover, the climatic oscillations that characterise this period sometimes took place over relatively short periods of time and would have had significant consequences for high-altitude landscapes and the resource base available to the people who were starting to live and work at these altitudes in greater numbers (Giraudi et al. 2011). These relatively quick changes in climate are important, as they, as much as anything, would have tested the ability of mountain communities to adjust and develop their environmental knowledge vis-à-vis changes in precipitation, the length of growing seasons, and associated environmental hazards.

In the Ligurian Apennines (north-western Italy), a complex series of human–environment relationships developed during the fourth and third millennia BC, with the establishment of the earliest western European copper mines in this area. Here, we see evidence for a practice that became widely used across mountain ranges – the use of fire in order to clear woodland for pastures, plus the use of wood in the mining process. These initial clearances of woodland, where there was little or no grass or understory to protect the soil, could have resulted in substantial erosion. Such early phases of woodland clearance may well have created some of the most unstable or sensitive environmental conditions during the entire Holocene. Extensive pastoralism developed throughout the Copper and Bronze Ages. At Prato Mollo (1,480 m), tree cover declined as a result of fire between 3079 and 2642 BC, and between 2889 and 2472 BC. Lower down towards the coast, at 830 m, the site of Pian del Lago produced evidence of local cereal production prior to 5000 BC (De Pascale et al. 2006: 116–17). If people were using fire to manage vegetation, were the Copper and Bronze Age uses of fire at higher altitudes the result of differing attitudes towards different altitudes, or due to the application of a more extreme and haphazard measure in the higher altitudes, where the potential risk to settlement and arable lands was minimal (ibid.)?

Palynological work at Prato Spilla (Emilia-Romagna), at an altitude of 1,500 m, indicates that, at the start of the Holocene, this area was covered with an *Abies–Pinus* (fir–pine) woodland that was soon replaced with a *Quercus–Abies* (oak–fir) woodland with some *Corylus* (hazel). Human impact may have started during the late fifth millennium BC, when tree pollen totals start to decrease with reductions of *Ulmus* (elm) and *Fraxinus* (ash). This period may reflect forest clearance that was taking place lower down in the valley towards 700 m. The next 'anthropogenic event', during the early fourth millennium BC, comprised a change in the composition of the woodland, in particular the establishment of *Fagus* (beach); the extreme reduction in *Abies*; the disappearance of *Fraxinus*, *Tilia* (lime), and *Ulmus*; the re-emergence of *Betula* (birch); and the first appearance of *Olea* (Lowe et al. 1994: 157). The end of the Neolithic and the start of the Copper Age saw burning and soil disturbance across Liguria, and it seems plausible that this type of disturbance was taking place at Prato Spilla as well. Moreover, the appearance of some nitrophilous herbs at this time is indicative of human activity. About 4,000 years ago, changes in the composition of the woodland continued apace (Lowe et al. 1994), and may have been related to human activity which is known to have taken place up to altitudes of about 1,500 m from the Neolithic into the Bronze Age in parts of Liguria (Maggi 1999: 30).

THE ALPS

Even though the alpine arc covers countries other than Italy and France, these nations (Switzerland, Austria, and Germany) are not defined as Mediterranean. Therefore, the examples presented here are taken from the two principal Mediterranean Alpine countries: Italy and (southern) France. Ecologically (based on climate and vegetation patterns), some of these French and Italian alpine areas would be defined as Supra- to Oro-Mediterranean (Quézel 2004) (see Fig. 5.4).

As already stated, the interpretation of human activity in mountains has often cited environmental change as a driver of developments in human activities. Although there have been periods of relative cooling and warming, the Holocene has seen a steady overall increase in temperature, but human activity in the high-altitude zones has waxed and waned rather than continuously increased. The analysis of stable isotopes from stalagmites from the south-east Italian Alps demonstrates this increase in temperature, with warmer periods during the Roman and high medieval periods (Frisia et al. 2005). However, the relatively cool early stages of the Holocene in certain valleys did not deter activity. There is now no doubt that people moved into the high-altitude zones for hunting early on during the Holocene. In the Venetian Pre-Alps, a palynological core from the Palughetto basin at about 1,000 m and archaeological sites between 1,900 m and 2,400 m demonstrate that late Early Mesolithic peoples were in this area, with hunting activity occurring in a newly afforested environment. Despite evidence for Palaeolithic and Mesolithic activity, there is no archaeological evidence for a Neolithic presence (Avigliano et al. 2000: 798).

The upper limit of activity in the Alps is not only influenced by the waxing and the waning of the tree line, but the ebb and flow of glaciers is also important. Activity at the edge of a glacier is possible, but an advancing glacier destroys pasture and, as we know from the Little Ice Age, can even destroy villages, although this was less true in the more southern Alpine areas. As far as the Neolithic period is concerned, a phase of glacier advance occurred in the eastern Alps between 3350 and 2700 BC, and readvanced during the Bronze Age, possibly centred on the period 1930 to 1250 BC. This was followed by an Iron Age readvance (which is difficult to date precisely due to the flat zone on the ^{14}C calibration curve for this period) between 980 and 370 BC (Grove & Rackham 2001: 147). Quite early in the Holocene, the Forcellin–Foscagno glacier in the Italian Central Alps (between 2,800 and 2,500 m) completely retreated, with evidence for a glacial advance about 3,000 years ago. The glacier once again retreated during the mid-first millennium BC, and permafrost formed (Guglielmin, Cannone, & Dramis 2001).

In the Val Febbraro, upper Valle di Spluga (Italian central Alps), Neolithic to Roman activity is attested to at altitudes between 1,830 and 2,304 m, inferred from both archaeological and palaeoecological evidence. The upper limit of this activity probably existed at the extreme edge of viable vegetation. The presence of charcoal dated to the early Neolithic at the timberline at Lago Basso may represent human impact on the forest (Wick 1994). Similar evidence is present in neighbouring valleys (Fedele 1992). There was general reduction in forest cover during the Neolithic and into the Bronze Age, along with a lowering of the tree line. Species such as *Rumex acetosa* (common sorel or spinach dock) increased. Whilst archaeological evidence is quite common below 2,000 m, the research in this area has produced four finds between 2,000 and 2,500 m. During the Middle Bronze Age, there were notable changes in the high-altitude vegetation, with the development of grass meadow. There are some archaeological sites, but their precise function is unclear. These later Bronze Age people either collected or burnt wood, and used the area for grazing. Whilst the period before 1000 BC is considered to have been warm and dry, climatic deterioration followed on from this period. Despite this, human activity in the high-altitude zone continued. The Iron Age in particular saw activity at the full range of altitudinal zones within this area. However, the Roman period saw a recovery of the woodland (at Val Vidröla, 2,235 m, and at Borghetto Sotto, 1,897 m). This trend is seen in other areas, such as at Lago Grande west and Val di Starleggia, about 1,830 m (Moe & Fedele 1997; Moe et al. 2007). This seemingly surprising trend of relatively low Roman impact on some high-altitude areas is considered in detail later.

SOUTHERN FRENCH ALPS

The Southern French Alps is one of the few mountainous zones where extensive palaeoecological research – with a pedigree dating back to the 1970s (de Beaulieu 1977) – can now be incorporated with archaeological evidence. Unsurprisingly, the palaeoecological work is dominated by palynology, and provides us with a detailed history of vegetation in these supra-Mediterranean valleys. Palynological reconstructions of changes in the different vegetation belts at different altitudes are problematic, as the wind can easily transport pollen up to mountain lakes from the valley bottom, bringing up pollen from all of the vertical zones (Ortu, Brewer, & Peyron 2006: 622–3). However, when combined with anthracology, an assessment of timberline movement is possible. Moreover, these spatially specific data allow the identification of choices of wood made by people for their fires, and provide evidence of localised burning and management activities.

The composition and vertical extent of the forests and woodlands do not just provide the floral context for human activity, but allow us to characterise one of the key environmental elements with which people have engaged during the Holocene. Trees are not only a valuable economic resource, but they also influence the way in which the landscape is perceived. Woodland affects movement through the mountains and the nature of relationships with other animals, including wolves and bears – animals that pose a threat to humans and their livestock. Miners from the Copper Age onwards would have used wood and timber in a whole range of mining-related practices, including fire setting for the extraction of copper ore (Barge & Talon 2012; Bourgarit et al. 2008). Ultimately, the earliest pastoralists managed the woodland and created openings for pasture. Although open pasture might have been preferred, access to this would have been controlled by the natural limit of the forest – the timberline and the tree line. The limits of the forest are an ecotone, not only beneficial to pastoralists but also to hunters, the edge being the zone where prey becomes clearly visible and easier to kill.

The composition of the Middle Holocene forest in the Southern Alps changed quite dramatically: *Abies alba* (silver fir) suffered two phases of decline, the first at c. 5000 BC and the second at c. 4000 BC. This second phase was succeeded by localised extinctions of fir trees in areas below 1,000 m. The probable primary cause of *Abies* decline was the reduction in moisture supply due to climate change, human impact, and fire, which presumably could have had both natural and anthropogenic causes (Wick & Möhl 2006). However, it is unlikely that Mesolithic hunters created clearances via burning. Early Mesolithic charcoal within travertine deposits at 1,750 m in the southern French pre-Alps is unlikely to be the product of fire setting by hunters (Roiron et al. 2006).

Pinus cembra is one key species that has gradually retreated from its highest altitudes. When it was first present in the Southern French Alps some 9,000 years ago, it attained altitudes 375 m beyond the present-day tree line. In any valley, the tree line is directly influenced by glacier configuration, and in the Ubaye, glaciers may well have totally melted between 8,000 and 6,000 years ago (Assier 1996: 4). Fire events dated to the mid-sixth and late fifth millennia were probably started by lightning, as there is no evidence for human manipulation of the forest at this time (Touflan, Talon, & Walsh 2010). It is assumed that human activity from the Neolithic onwards contributed to the contraction of the forest (Ali, Carcaillet, et al. 2005). However, the possibility that Neolithic hunters and pastoralists had such an impact on the forest in the high-altitude zone is a hypothesis that requires testing. In the Ubaye Valley in the Southern French Alps, the tree line (dominated by *Pinus cembra* (Swiss pine)) was at close to 2,400 m during the Neolithic, descended to 2,200 m during the Bronze Age (the altitude at which the Bronze Age structures, discussed below, are often found), and then returned to 2,400 m during the Iron Age (Ali, Roiron, et al. 2005).

The spatial and chronological heterogeneity of human activity and vegetation change is rarely inferred from single pollen diagrams. Fortunately, research in the Southern French Alps (centred on the Ecrins National Park) demonstrates how the analysis of records from a range of altitudes permits the diachronic assessment of human activity across the full range of altitudinal zones (Court-Picon 2007; Richer 2009). It is apparent that Neolithic populations were actively farming and managing the valley bottoms, and that human impact on the high-altitude (or subalpine and alpine zones; those areas above 2,000 m) landscapes did not develop until the very end of the Neolithic and Chalcolithic. As soon as the glaciers retreated at the start of the Holocene, early hunters followed their prey up into these areas, probably during the summer months. Hunting continued in these areas even after the establishment of agricultural groups at lower altitudes (Walsh & Mocci 2011). The highest find in this area is a flint arrowhead at 2,510 m on the Col de Roburent: located on a large plateau dominated by two lakes, an area

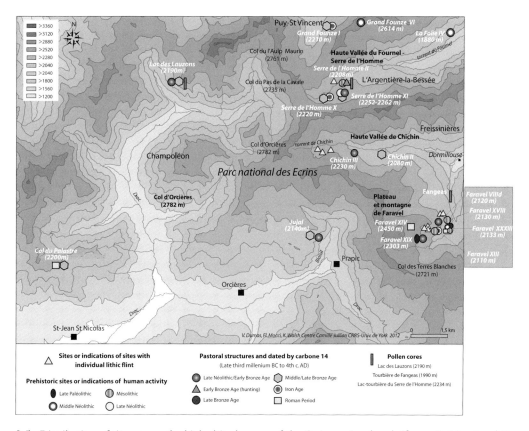

8.5. Distribution of sites across the high altitude zone of the Ecrins national park (figure: F. Mocci and K. Walsh).

that would have been a rich hunting zone, partly as a higher tree line would have provided the ideal niche for game. This situation is quite similar to that at the Grand Founze VII site, Puy-St-Vincent at 2,600 m. In the Ecrins, there are about 10 Neolithic sites that comprise flint scatters; some are quite ephemeral. A Late Neolithic arrowhead at 2,450 m in the Ecrins once again implies the continuation of hunting at high altitudes during this period. The nature of human engagement with the high altitudes changed dramatically during the late third millennium BC. From c. 2500 BC, the first built structures appeared at altitudes between 2,100 and 2,400 m. Most of these sites comprise a similar architectural form, often exploiting the presence of naturally occurring erratics and large boulders. These sites have been interpreted as animal enclosures (Tzortzis et al. 2008; Walsh 2005). There are now 12 well-dated sites of this type, plus at least 30 other typologically similar sites from across the Ecrins National Park (Fig. 8.5). In the Ubaye Valley, 23 prehistoric sites have been found, all above 1,200 m (up to 2,509 m). The majority of the 23 prehistoric sites tend to be located on one of the five axes that lead to and from the Mercantour area which includes Mont Bego. The prehistoric sites tend to be situated on moraine, plateaux, or at the confluence of water sources. Palynological evidence for the third and second millennia BC indicates an intensification of pastoral activities (Court-Picon et al. 2007; Mocci et al. 2009; Walsh et al. 2005). During the Neolithic, such activities were concentrated towards the valley bottoms and lower slopes. Then, during the third millennium, these activities expanded, moving into the high-altitude areas. On certain high-altitude sites, fungal spores and nitrophilous plant pollen indicate Bronze Age pastoral activity in the immediate vicinities of these sites (Walsh & Richer 2006). Moreover, charcoal evidence from the pollen cores, along with charcoal from sediments found within and around the archaeological sites, is indicative of woodland clearance designed to create more suitable pasture. Charcoal and palynological evidence from one series of Bronze Age sites demonstrates how the low-lying area at the foot of a moraine would have seen standing water during extreme rainfall events. All the structures were thus located on the moraine, above this intermittently wet zone (Fig. 8.6). Moving into the Iron Age, there appears to have been a reduction in high-altitude activity. Although some palynological signals imply continued human impact on these landscapes during the first millennium BC and into the Roman period, there is a strange absence of archaeological sites in the high-altitude zone, but a radical reconfiguration of the valley bottoms, with the development of towns and associated communications. Decisions to change the nature of high-altitude pastoral activity may have been influenced by climatic deterioration during the Middle Iron Age, although we must also consider the importance of changing cultural perceptions of the mountains. The sheer range of data types that indicate a relatively warm climate during the Roman period should leave us in no doubt as to the general characteristics of climate at this time (Frisia et al. 2005; Mangini, Spötl, & Verdes 2005; Schmidt, Kamenik, & Roth 2007). It is also quite possible that the Roman period was more moist than other periods, which not only has consequences for vegetation but, more importantly, for weather and in particular the probability of summer storms (Reale & Dirmeyer 2000; Reale & Shukla 2000). The Roman climatic 'amelioration' could have comprised an increase in extreme precipitation events and storms

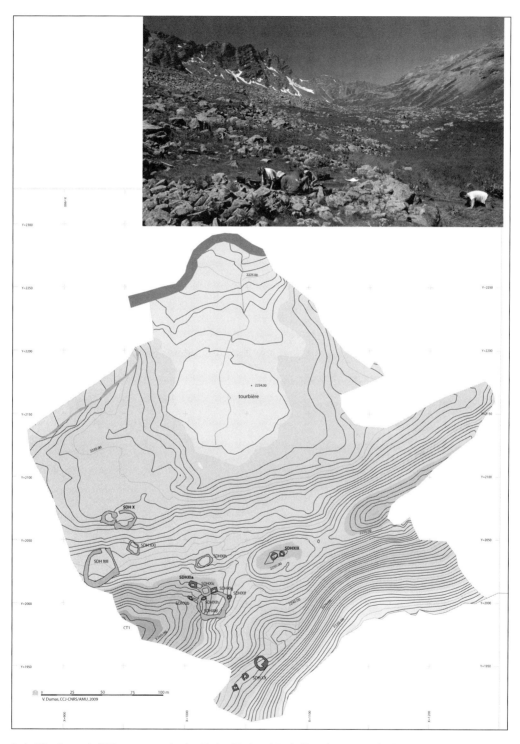

8.6. The Serre de l'Homme area in the Ecrins National Park (Southern French Alps) at about 2,200 m. A complex of Bronze Age enclosures located along the entirety of the moraine. Despite being more exposed to winds, this location avoided the wet zone at the foot of the morraine (figure: V.Dumas, F. Mocci, and K. Walsh; photo: author).

8.7. Altitudinal zonation of sites by period in the Ubaye Valley – alt. 700–2,650 m, Alpes de Haute Provence, France. (Programme collectif de Recherche 2001–2006, dir. D. Garcia and Fl. Mocci, Centre Camille Jullian). Prehistoric includes Mesolithic and Neolithic flint; proto-historic tends to be Iron Age pottery, with some possible Bronze Age pottery along with enclosures which typologically appear to be Bronze Age. Note that the chronology of these sites is usually determined by the nature of the material culture found on the soil surface. At lower altitudes, architectural remains of Roman sites are also present.

at high altitude caused by increases in convective currents – a product of a warmer climate (Giguet-Covex et al. 2012). Such weather patterns may have also conditioned certain responses to life at high altitude, with people avoiding these zones at certain times of the year. The relative absence of Roman archaeological sites at high altitude is repeated further south in the Ubaye Valley (Garcia, Mocci, & Walsh 2007) (Fig. 8.7). Non-Romanised people might have continued to use the higher altitude areas at this time, whilst the main focus of activity shifted to the lower altitudes and urban centres. These changes include the development of towns, communication networks, and 'stations' that provide interme- diate resting places for travellers moving around the Empire. One such station is that at Rama, at the foot of one of the valleys studied as part of research in the Ecrins National Park. The presence of spores associated with soil erosion, dated in a pollen diagram from a lake next to this site, also suggests phases of erosion during the Early Roman period (Farjon 2007; Richer 2009), this erosion probably being caused by one or more extreme precipitation events.

THE PYRENEES

The results of recent research in the Pyrenees mirrors some of the gen- eral processes described above for the Southern French Alps. Research on both the French, Spanish, and Catalan areas of the Pyrenees has incorporated detailed palaeoenvironmental work, combined with archae- ological survey and excavations. As with the Alpine research, understand- ing of environmental change and human activities during the Holocene has dramatically improved during the last 15 years (Ejarque et al. 2010; Mazier et al. 2009; Palet et al. 2007; Rendu 2003).

In the French Pyrenees, the earliest evidence for agro-pastoral activ- ity dates to the end of the Early Neolithic (c. 4900 BC) through to the first half of the Middle Neolithic (4400–3800 BC). During this period, people were exploiting the lower and mid-range altitudes, and whilst impact on the subalpine zone was minimal, it seems that there was some activity taking place there as well. During this period, high-altitude veg- etation would have adjusted to changes in climate. We know that in the eastern Pyrenees, thermomediterranean-type vegetation developed dur- ing the Middle Neolithic and comprised *Olea europaea*, *Pistacia lentiscus*, *Phillyrea* sp., *Cistus* sp., *Rhamnus alaternus* (Mediterranean buckthorn), and *Quercus ilex/coccifera* (Heinz et al. 2004). As with the Southern

French Alps, it was the late third and second millennia that saw the development of human activity at higher altitudes. This is when anthropogenically modified mountainous landscapes started to develop, when forest was cleared through a process of slash and burn (Galop 1998: 254–5). The later Iron Age and the Roman period are interesting phases in the Pyrenees, as there was probably some continuity in the exploitation patterns established during the Bronze Age, but the dramatic changes witnessed in other landscapes across the Roman Empire did not manifest themselves in the Pyrenees. In some areas, such as Vicdessos, Cerdagne, and Donezan, there appears to have been a reduction in human activity during the Iron Age and perhaps at the start of the Roman period. A similar sequence of events has also been identified on the Enveig Mountain. With massifs above 2,500 m, its highest pastures are situated between 2,200 and 2,600 m. The earliest activity here is dated to c. 3000 BC, implied by the appearance of *Plantago lanceolata* (ribwort plantain), as well as evidence for the opening up of the forest by burning as high as 2,100–2,300 m (Davasse, Galop, & Rendu, 1997: 587). Between the fourth century BC and the first century AD, there appears to have been a hiatus or at least a reduction in high-altitude pastoral activity in this area. The anthracological evidence indicates localised opening of the forest between the first and eighth centuries AD. Pastoral activity was probably reoriented towards the low-altitude mountainous zones during the Roman period (ibid.: 591).

On the southern-central (Andorran) area of the Pyrenees, evidence for early high-altitude pastoralism is dated to c. 5000 BC onwards (Ejarque 2010: 241; Ejarque et al. 2009). The Neolithic pastoral hut in the Madriu Valley (2,530 m), dated to the mid-fifth millennium BC, provides supporting archaeological evidence. Slightly later, the relatively cool period c. 5,500 years ago (as seen by Magny & Haas 2004) would have resulted in a more open forest suitable for grazing, and may well have attracted Neolithic pastoralists to this area (Ejarque et al. 2010). Pastoral activity appears to have been taking place between 4300 and 3500 BC at around 2,500 m, as indicated by coprophilous spores and apophytes. Moreover, the earliest stone-built structures in this area are dated to the late fourth to early third millennia BC (Orengo 2010). As in the Ecrins, there is also evidence for burning in some Pyrenean Neolithic landscapes, with consequent erosion caused by this deforestation. A substantial increase in pastoral indicator species at 2350 BC, along with a number of Late Neolithic and Early Bronze Age high-altitude sites in the Vallé de Madriu, suggests a significant increase in pastoral activity (Ejarque 2010: 66). In some areas, the Bronze Age saw lower grazing pressure than during the Middle Neolithic, and this waxing and waning of activity is reflected by woodland recovery. More specifically, we see a reduction in pastoral activity in some areas during the Middle Bronze Age, this having been preceded by the most intensive phase of human activity between 1850 and 1750 BC. This phase was followed by renewed activity in some areas between 1650 and 1050 BC. Here, we see how problematic the traditional 'evolutionary' model is; we cannot assume that human impact on a landscape increases continuously from the Neolithic onwards (Ejarque et al. 2010).

In the French Pyrenees, there is evidence for Chasséen activity at altitudes of between 1,600 and 1,800 m (Rendu 2003: 420), with more intensive activity developing towards the end of the Neolithic and into the Chalcolithic. However, there is relatively little archaeological evidence in the high-altitude zones above 2,000 m. The Bronze Age witnessed the first obvious structuring of some Pyrenean mountainsides (ibid.: 513), with grazing emerging at the end of this period as an important practice between 1050 and 700 BC. Between 700 and 400 BC, an increase in *Pinus* is inferred as evidence for reduction in pastoral activity at high altitudes. In the eastern Pyrenees (the Vallée de Madriu-Perafita-Claror), several pastoral structures in the subalpine zone have been dated to the first and second centuries AD. What we do not appear to have is a continuous record of activity in these areas during the Roman period, nor an intensity of activity that we might associate with the levels of economic activity seen elsewhere in the Empire. However, six pitch-ovens do represent a highly specific and important activity in this area (Leveau & Palet-Martinez 2010: 180–1). The intensification of charcoal burning during the Roman period (especially during the third century AD) is attested to by a number kilns and corroborative palaeoecological evidence across a range of altitudes (Pèlachs et al. 2009). The evidence implies that the Roman period was not that different to the Bronze Age in terms of the relative intensity of pastoral activity, with low grazing pressure attested to on some sites. Here, the Roman period is characterised by the development of a complex mosaic of grazing, burning, and forest management activities, in some ways different to the evidence from the alpine zones in the Southern French Alps (Ejarque et al. 2009).

In particular, the presence of resin ovens dated to the first to second centuries AD is interesting, as this demonstrates the direct use of a forest resource. In Asturia (the north-western Iberian Peninsula), the mountainous zone appears to have been integrated into the Roman economic system. Here, Roman mining activity had a noticeable impact on the vegetation (Ruiz del Árbol et al. 2003). Mining, like any activity, is one element within a network of activities. In Asturia, agricultural terraces and terraces on settlement sites were created, this practice being common on many managed Roman landscapes. When the mines and adjacent zones were abandoned at the end of the second century AD, the forest re-established itself to a certain extent, and eroded soil covered the Roman horizons that had once formed the terraces in this area. Here, we see how this upland area was fully integrated into the Roman economy, and provides a contrast with other mountainous zones, such as the Sierra de Gredos in central Spain. This area does not appear to have been fully incorporated into the Roman system, with little evidence for human activity between c. 15 BC and the fifth century AD (López-Merino & López-Sáez 2009: 48). Low levels of impact also characterise this period in the Segura Mountains (Murcia, south-eastern Spain), where significant human impact on the vegetation did not occur before the seventh century AD (Carrión et al. 2004). Once again, this palaeoenvironmental evidence demonstrates how some areas remained relatively unaffected, although probably not untouched, by people until the historic periods. Even areas that saw precocious Neolithic activity were not necessarily the domain of continuous human impact.

Patchy Porosity: Mediterranean Mountains and Variable Integration

What we see now in the archaeological and palaeoenvironmental data from European, Mediterranean mountains are clear demonstrations of how traditional, environmentally determined hypotheses are untenable. Some researchers argued that cold, wet periods should lead to lower levels of human activity in mountainous areas, and clement periods to an increase in activity (Bocquet 1997). Moreover, the fact that there has *not* been a continuous, steady exploitation of the high-altitude zone during the last 6,000 years implies that knowledge of, and attitudes towards, these landscapes has fluctuated over time. Furthermore, there is little evidence to suggest a diachronic, incremental evolution of such environmental knowledge. At a very basic level, ecological decisions require knowledge of the seasons, weather, hydrology, vegetation, geology, as well as domestic and wild animal behaviour. More specifically, such knowledge also includes an awareness of hazards associated with activity in the subalpine and alpine zones. This environmental knowledge changed with each period; Bronze Age environmental knowledge was probably different to that of the Roman Period. During the Holocene, the manner in which such environmental knowledge was mediated, controlled, and transmitted changed continuously.

If there is one activity that has been continuously linked to life in the mountainous zone, it is pastoralism – more specifically, transhumance (Fig. 8.8). Although there is no doubt that pastoralism has been an important activity in many mountainous areas across the Mediterranean, we must also consider the nature of other engagements with mountainous landscapes. One of the problems with the mountain-pastoralist discourse is its inherent ecological foundations; that is, the notion that transhumance in particular is an economic strategy that best exploits the seasonal and vertical changes that characterise mountainous zones. In some ways, the pastoralist/transhumant discourse is one dominated by a rational instrumental view of humanity's relationship with the landscape, or perhaps more subtly 'transhumance reveals the existence, via animals, a way of living that and the appropriation of space that conditions the ensemble of a social organisation' (Duclos 2006: 17; author's translation). When compared with arable agriculturalists, pastoralists have a decidedly different relationship with the land. Arable farmers rely upon the earth/soil itself, and must invest much of their time safeguarding or improving this essential resource. Pastoralists, however, simply rely upon the seasonal growth of pasture, and rarely invest much time and effort in its maintenance, let alone improvement. Although, as we have seen, there is evidence to suggest that areas of forest were opened/burnt in order to create a clearing for grazing, this may well have been the extent of pastoral land management in the high-altitude zones.

From the middle of the fifth millennium BC, archaeological and palaeoenvironmental evidence suggests the emergence of a pastoral system where individual (or very small numbers) of shepherds worked in the lower-altitude zones in some mountain ranges. These shepherds were probably detached from the larger community (Brochier & Beeching

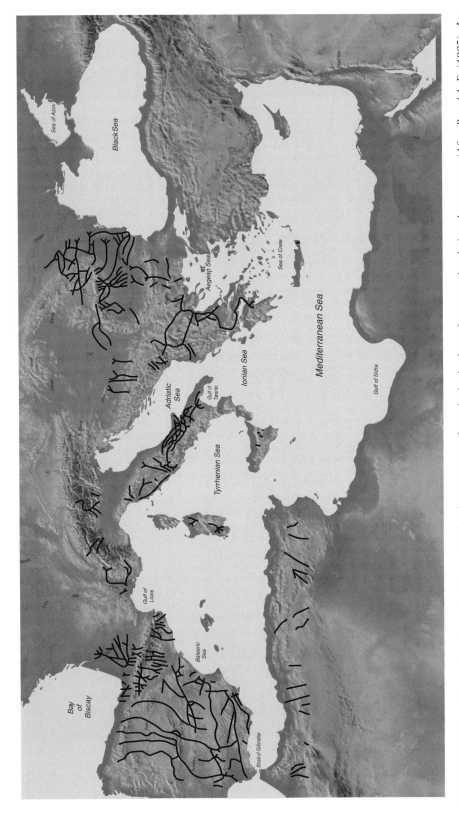

8.8. Principal long-distance transhumant routes – most involve movement from the lowlands to the mountains during the summer. (After Braudel, F. (1985), *La Méditerrannée et Le Monde Méditerrannée*.) One of the key research questions in Mediterranean landscape archaeology is when did this model of transhumance develop.

2006: 151). In fact, prior to the Late Bronze Age, the high-altitude zone might have been perceived as a remote landscape, rarely witnessed by the vast majority of people. The most enigmatic evidence for this 'individu-alistic' landscape comes in the form of 'Otzi', although he, like all moun-tain dwellers, would have been a member of valley-based community. The archaeological and archaeozoological evidence points to small groups of specialised Neolithic pastoralists carrying out specific activities across a range of different sites – activities and sites that would have been exploited at different times of the year as a part of the pastoral round (Bréhard, Beeching, & Vigne 2010). As time progressed, we can see that one char-acteristic shared by both the Alps and the Pyrenees is the evidence for prehistoric burning of the woodland. Possibly this clearance was a form of fire setting, which might be classified as a form of landscape 'manage-ment', implying controlled engagement with the natural world where outcomes are usually predictable. This may well have been the case, but it is an important notion that requires some reflection. Management sug-gests planning and control, which might mean that exploitation of high-altitude landscapes was part of a wider socio-economic strategy, perhaps manipulated by an elite. Were these pioneer shepherds entirely aware of the environmental consequences of their actions? To what extent did the initial impact of woodland clearance induce a phase of relative instability, where soil erosion was in fact quite extreme, and decreased once new agricultural practices were established and grasslands stabilised (Jacob et al. 2009). Whilst a form of fire setting appears to be common to both the Pyrenees and the Southern French Alps, there is a significant differ-ence in terms of evidence for built structures. There appear to be more structures in the Alps than in the Pyrenees, and in turn, fewer sites on the French side of the Pyrenees than on the Catalan/Spanish flanks. Again, this implies variation in the Bronze Age forms of environmental know-ledge and day-to-day ways of life between the two mountain ranges and even within ranges. The construction of animal enclosures represents a specific and innovative engagement with the mountains, and implies a development of a new form of environmental knowledge related to the pastoral round (Walsh & Mocci 2011). Despite the relatively low num-bers of people active in the high-altitude zones, it is likely that the initial impact of this activity on the environment was disproportionately high due to the fragility and low sustainability of certain activities in the alpine zone.

In the Pyrenees, there were two phases of human expansion during the late third and second millennia BC: the first just prior to the start of the second millennium BC, and the second at the start of the first millennium BC. From 2000 BC, the reduction of heliophilous species (birch and hazel) implies a shortening of the forest fallow period (Carozza et al. 2005: 9). The study of lead isotopes implies the development of mining during the Late Bronze Age, and come the end of the Bronze Age, other indicator species emerged in grassland fallow zones, revealing the development of prairies and pasture. This transition from an agro-forest to an agro-pastoral system is a fundamental change in the landscape. In the Basque mountains, pollen cores from three different altitudes (500 m, 910 m, and 1,300 m) spanning the period between 2100 and 1700 BC show how beech expanded as pastoral and arable activity became prominent at most altitudes with little substantial deforestation taking place. Then, from 1700 to 1300 BC, pastoral activity increased at the expense of arable agriculture. During this period, there was still little destruction of overall forest cover. The archaeological evidence (in the form of sites with clear evidence for a pastoral economy) supports the interpretation of the palynological evidence (ibid.: 17). From 1300 to 1000 BC, arable agriculture re-emerged as an important activity, with pastoral activity decreasing in some areas except in the altitudes centred on 1,100 m. Between 1000 and 750 BC, an increase in agro-pastoral activity and deforestation occurred at all altitudes. In both the Pyrenees and the Southern French Alps, the end of the Bronze Age was characterised by an overall reduction in activity at high altitude (around 2,000 m and above). However, some palynological signals do imply continued pastoral activity. Does this combination of evidence (a lack of structures but a continued presence of pastoralism) indicate a new form of engagement with the subalpine zone? Was it perceived and managed in a different way?

There is no doubt that there was a complex relationship between ritual and landscape, along with the associated cycles of seasons, activities, and ritual events. A fundamental part of daily life in the high-altitude zone includes dealing with radical changes in weather, even during the summer. These changes in weather affect both people and animals, and are something that we must take into consideration (Strauss & Orlove 2003). What we can be sure of is that the high altitudes are characterised by geomorphic and meteorological processes that are so much more

dramatic than the lowlands – areas with which mountain peoples supposedly shared cultural traits. Human interaction with the environment is a
constitutive element in the development of culture, and mountain cultures were (and are) different from their lowland counterparts. This is not
to say that mountain peoples were completely isolated from or entirely
different to their lowland counterparts, but that there were undeniable
differences in their everyday experiences of landscape and environment
and therefore in their cultural ecologies. Bronze Age shepherds in the
high-altitude zones were probably influenced by a hegemonic system
and associated ideological-religious actions. Environmental knowledge
via a cosmology can sustain equilibrium within an environment, whereas
imperfect knowledge – where key knowledge-bearers disappear or where
a change in an environment is misread – can lead to environmental and
societal problems. A change in the quality of environmental knowledge
(a cosmological imbalance, if you like) can lead to phases of instability in
the environment. Consequently, we have to ask how unstable or unpredictable the environments were that would have characterised these
landscapes, and to what extent the waning of activity can actually be
explained by instances of poor knowledge and maladjusted responses to
changes in the environment.

The Middle Iron Age did undoubtedly witness a phase of climatic
deterioration that affected both the Alps and the Pyrenees (Van Geel &
Berglund 1997), but this alone cannot explain the apparent reduction in
pastoral activity in the subalpine zone. As well as an obvious reduction in
the number of sites, pollen diagrams such as that from Lac des Lauzons
in the Southern French Alps (Richer 2009) and the eastern Pyrenees
(Ejarque et al. 2010) reveal woodland regeneration. Changes in weather
and climate, along with associated developments in vegetation, would
have engendered developments in environmental knowledge. Whilst the
high and middle altitudes may have held some ritual significance in the
Early Iron Age, most day-to-day activities were at lower altitudes. As
Iron Age societies developed stronger economic ties with the Roman
world, there would have been a concomitant development of new proto-
urban centres in the valley bottoms.

We might expect that the arrival of Rome in the Alps and the Pyrenees
(and the other mountain ranges mentioned in this chapter) to have her-
alded dramatic changes in the cultural ecologies and associated forms
of environmental knowledge that operated in these mountainous

landscapes. There is no doubt that such changes did occur at lower altitudes – the development of urban centres and roads being the obvious developments. During the Roman warm period (centred on the first centuries BC and AD), there is relatively little archaeological evidence for activity in the subalpine and alpine zones of the French Alps, despite the climatic amelioration. This reflects trends in the Italian Alps described earlier (Moe et al. 2007). Meanwhile, in the Pyrenees, there was a radical change in the manner in which (productive) landscapes were organised, but this was not a decisive moment in the history of human impact on the subalpine and alpine milieus. There is little archaeological or palaeo-ecological evidence to suggest dramatic change in the 'natural' environment at this time. Certain areas were heavily exploited, whilst other areas saw the reestablishment of woodland, with the concentration of pastoral activity towards lower altitudes (Davasse et al. 1997). In some places, such as Vicdessos, Cerdagne, and Donezan, there seems to have been a reduction in human activity during the Iron Age, and perhaps even at the start of the Roman period (Galop 1998), with other areas showing a decrease from the third to sixth centuries AD (Mazier et al. 2009). A change in dietary preferences might be one explanation for a change in the pastoral regime, with a new Roman emphasis on forest-based husbandry, where pigs were the principal domesticate. Thus, there may not have been the same requirement for high-altitude pasture. This cannot be the sole explanation for the relative withdrawal from the high-altitude zone, and may have been quite specific to the Pyrenees. We know that Strabo referred to the excellence of the hams from the Kerretani territory. As Rendu (2003) observes, there may well be two (non-contradictory) explanations for this change during the Roman period: a clean break vis-à-vis earlier periods in the use of different parts of the landscape (plains, piedmonts, and slopes), which led to a gradual marginalisation of the higher reliefs; whilst the zones along the plain edges were more integrated as part of an increase in agricultural production. This lowered the 'centre of socio-economic gravity' towards the lower altitudes, and this included pastoral activity that had once exploited the higher zones (ibid.: 520–1).

What we see in the Alps and the Pyrenees is an adaption of the 'traditional' Roman rural economy to these mountainous areas. The appearance of cultivated trees within a mosaic landscape, where some zones are employed for arable agriculture whilst others continued to be used for pasture, is in part a chronological extension of some pre-existing 'Iron Age' activities, with the development of certain Roman elements, perhaps the most noteworthy being the development of mining. Mining activity (with concomitant deforestation) was clearly a core activity during the Roman period (Monna et al. 2004). The fact that there is little evidence for an increase in agricultural activities suggests that mining was the core activity. The Roman period unsurprisingly saw the appearance of certain cultivated trees (walnut, chestnut, and even olive, at some distance from the high altitudes). At Fangeas in the Southern French Alps, the reduction in woodland may well have been related to mining indirectly inferred from a recorded increase in lead isotopes (Segard 2009: 197–200). However, the nature of the subalpine and alpine zones meant that there was also a continuation of the heterogeneous Alpine landscape, with certain zones going in and out of use depending on local cultural and socio-economic factors. In the Pyrenees, incontrovertible archaeological and environmental evidence for specialised activities, such as mining, resin collection, and exploitation, are all indicative of complex suites of environmental knowledge, where the influence of a diversified and multifaceted imperial economy affected the manner in which human ecologies developed in these mountains. The pre-existing forms of environmental knowledge were probably adapted. Awareness of the dangers and the resources present in the mountains continued, but new economic prospects resulted in the opportunistic intensification of certain 'niche' activities, such as charcoal burning and pitch production. It is the combination of a suite of activities and practices that constitute a specific cultural ecology – a way of living and working in the mountains. These forms of environmental knowledge probably existed prior to the arrival of Rome, but their intensity and configurations evolved as different valleys developed economic ties with the imperial network.

If we accept that some evidence does reflect a reduction in activity in the high-altitude zone during the Roman period, we have to explain this. At one level, we might consider the nature of taboo and apprehensions that existed in various societies (and classes) regarding certain types of environment and animals and plants therein. Whilst the start of the Roman Period in the Alps is supposedly characterised by a climatic amelioration, it is unclear to what extent that this had an influence on people's lives in the Alps. Perhaps the most salient characteristic of environmental knowledge is its contingency vis-à-vis social groups, whether these are defined by class or the geographical origins of the group. Research into population mobility should allow us to consider how changes in the forms of environmental knowledge and cultural ecologies are influenced by immigration and emigration. People arrive and leave with environmental knowledge. Mountainous landscapes are certainly not closed landscapes, but there is evidence to suggest that some areas have been relatively isolated for quite long periods of time. Physical geography can have an important influence on genetic diversity (Rosser et al. 2000). Some studies have revealed genetic isolation, with one community from the South Tyrol possessing a higher Palaeolithic genetic component than their neighbours (M. G. Thomas et al. 2007). Even the relatively accessible mountains of central Italy (the Aniene Valley and the Simbruni Mountains not far from Rome) include populations that are genetically isolated (Messina et al. 2010). Consequently, we are forced to revisit well-rehearsed discussions relating to acculturation for the prehistoric periods, and Romanisation for later chronological phases.

The verticality of mountains and understanding of the environmental characteristics of ecological zones are fundamental for any activity in these areas. There has been much discussion of Roman society's attitudes towards mountains and what might be described as a Roman anguish regarding such landscapes. First, we must accept that there is no one, single Roman society, and that environmental knowledge within the Roman Empire would have been socially and culturally contingent. Moreover, the discussion of Roman angst vis-à-vis the high altitudes is misplaced and far more complicated than stating that the presence of Roman activity at high altitude in one place demonstrates that the trepidation that certain parts of Roman society had towards mountains did not exist. For example, an altitude of 2,200 m in one valley might be easily accessible, such as over certain passes (e.g. the Petit Col Saint Bernard), whereas the same altitude in a topographically diverse zone, such as many of the valleys in the Ecrins National Park, is in fact difficult to reach. A simple cost–surface analysis would demonstrate this. We cannot demonstrate that Rome tried to 'manage' all mountainous areas in the same manner. The Pyrenees may well have been perceived a distant frontier, whilst the Alps were possibly considered as a more sensitive, core frontier, defining the edge of the Roman homeland. Moreover, practices specific to these different mountain ranges would have developed as a consequence of regional economic processes, but also because

Rome may have encouraged certain forms of management. For example, as Leveau (2008a) argues, Rome did raise awareness about and respond to hydrological problems, in particular, increases in flooding intensity due to deforestation in the Appenines. Such increases in flood-related problems may also have been a consequence of increased storm intensity during periods of relative climatic warming. Consequently, we see how the nature of human engagements is characterised by a complex interplay of environmental processes, socio-economic patterns, myth, and religion, all intersecting to produce historical ecologies that are specific to each valley and even different zones within that valley due to the radical changes in environmental characteristics which are directly influenced by vertical zonation. The history of human–environment interaction in the mountains is characterised by variations in the emphasis placed on the incorporation and exploitation of each vertical zone. It is this complex vertical ecology that demands an environmental perspective if we are to develop a clear understanding of how these landscapes have changed.

Conclusion

The study of mountainous landscapes has been dominated by ecological models. These have operated at two levels: first, the underlying notion that climate has directly influenced the waxing and waning of human activity in mountainous areas; second, that when people do live and work in mountains, their activities are structured by vertical ecological zonation. Transhumance, with the seasonal movement up through different areas of pasture during the summer, is the most obvious example of such an ecologically driven process. Whilst it is untrue that the presence and absence of people in mountainous zones has been directly influenced by climate, there is a certain amount of truth in the nature of activities being influenced by the ecological potential of a given altitudinal zone. However, in the past, we have placed too much emphasis on two or three essential forms of activity: pastoralism, mining, and sylviculture. There were clearly many other important activities which varied in their extent and intensity, depending on the socio-economic context and forms of environmental knowledge present within each valley or set of valleys. As the transfer of culture, ideas, and environmental knowledge has varied across time, we have to accept that valleys or groups of valleys will have experienced variations in 'permeability'; the strength of links and connections with other places varies with each period. Activities and practices, settlement density, and human impact on mountains vary across time and space. There are no homogenous trends. Not all valleys saw the construction of enclosures during the Bronze Age, not all valleys witnessed a Roman absence or decline in activity. The location of individual sites was influenced by comprehension of potential hazards (flooding, rock slides, and avalanches). Recent ethnoarchaeological research also suggests that shepherds avoid zones where there is a high probability of lightning strikes (Carrer 2012: chs 5 & 6). It is apparent that certain zones within valleys have a higher probability of being hit by lightning, and bearing in mind that storm intensity could increase during periods of climatic warming, we have to consider the importance of probable trends in weather events and the influence of these on settlement, economy, and culture in Mediterranean landscapes. The combined effects of these environmental variables engender enormous variation in the choices made for site location in mountainous zones, as past peoples applied locally specific environmental knowledge when making choices about site location and the patterning of economic activities. The notion that we can develop generalised arguments regarding the nature of human–mountain relationships based on the commonality of environmental characteristics across vertical mountain zones is clearly problematic. This form of cultural ecological approach possesses all the dangers of any normative analysis. So many descriptions of mountain economic systems are founded on fundamental precepts that then lead us unwittingly into an environmentally deterministic discourse. Moving on, some have then argued that success in mountainous zones is based upon the flexible responses of humans to the demanding environmental conditions. The response types defined by R. B. Thomas (1979: 161–7) were rotation, regulation, cooperation, mobility, and storage – indeed, response mechanisms that one might expect to find in any landscape. As Guillet (1983: 562) remarks, 'adaptiveness' can become a tautology for any situation. What we should not forget is that the study of human–environment relationships often overlooks the *people* behind the 'anthropogenic processes'. Human activity in mountains, and, indeed, in any environment, operates on many different scales and is a class-based experience. By their very nature, the vertical stages within mountains may well have reflected the structure of some societies in the past: the urban rich at low altitudes, and the rural poor in the most elevated and harshest areas. This may appear a simplistic and rather crass form of determinism, but such a structure is in fact quite common. These different groups have left different environmental signals and produced different historical ecologies. Mountains, more than any of the landscapes discussed in this book, proffer a myriad of resources, but are at the same time harsh, difficult, and often deadly environments. The environmental processes that constitute these landscapes are a part of everyday life and contribute to the construction of Mediterranean cultures.

9

Conclusions – The Mediterranean Mosaic: Persistent and Incongruent Environmental Knowledge

The preceding chapters have assessed the evidence for changes in human engagements with a range of Mediterranean landscapes – landscapes constituted by dynamic mosaics that shift with time and can only be understood via the analysis of spatially specific palaeoenvironmental and archaeological records. In many instances, the essence of Mediterranean environmental management does not lie with the imposed, macro-economic structures and concomitant networks of trade and commerce, but with the environmental knowledge developed by those who worked the land. Whilst we can never identify specific stories of human engagement and concomitant social relationships, we can imagine scenarios not so dissimilar from those articulated in modern literature. Conflicts over land, and especially water, may well have been common in the pre- and proto-historic pasts. The human experience and the development of social relations are formed via interactions with the natural world. Novels such as *Jean de Florette* (Pagnol 1988) or *Batailles dans la Montagne* (Giono 1979) paint images of human relationships with the environment and the manner in which these contribute to the development of interpersonal interactions within specific landscapes. Such relationships are of course contingent upon a number of specific historical and geographical phenomena, and, as archaeologists, we can only ever propose possible scenarios. An integrated landscape archaeology, which operates within historical and cultural ecological frameworks, does enhance the elucidation of the lifeways of those peoples who engaged with the environmental processes discussed in this volume.

We know that those who worked the land were often influenced or even controlled by macro-economic structures and political hegemonies – structures that would have passively (via ideological and belief systems) and aggressively imposed certain forms of environmental knowledge and concomitant management strategies. The periods of environmental stability and instability that we identify were not necessarily the consequence of natural changes in the environment (Kuniholm 1990), and phases of instability in particular were not the result of unthinking, unfettered anthropic exploitation of these landscapes. Any changes in the environment were the product of intersecting socio-economic, ideological, and environmental processes. This is perhaps best characterised by the notion of 'Panarchy' by resilience theorists (Gunderson & Holling 2002). Panarchy describes cross-scale interactions, and 'the resilience of a system at a particular focal scale will depend on the influences from states and dynamics at scales above and below. For example, external oppressive politics, invasions, market shifts, or global climate...' (Walker et al. 2004: 5).

It is important that we investigate the two dominant paradigms in Mediterranean environmental history. The first is the notion that Mediterranean landscapes can be characterised as ruined, and that their history is one of a downward spiral of degradation, with humans and climate working together to ensure their blight (see Hughes 1994b esp. ch. 11; 2005 esp. ch. 7). The other position in this dichotomised debate is represented by the more recent and fashionable model, which considers that the above process of degradation is overstated, and that people have continuously managed to exploit the various niches across the Mediterranean through adaptive strategies which have guaranteed success and avoided disaster (see Horden & Purcell 2000 esp. ch. 8).

One phenomenon that we cannot directly identify as archaeologists but needs to be considered is the variation in perceptions and understandings of landscapes and their natural processes. During those periods when activity, especially political and economic control, was centred on fixed settlements (from the Neolithic onwards), the agricultural world would have been centred on the village and the abutting areas (Robb 2007). Here, the view of nature might have been one centred on the productive zones close to the settlement, whilst more distant activities, including transhumance, wood, and wild-produce collection, might have been detached experiences for certain people. Consequently, if reconstructions of past environmental processes are inferred from sample locations that were not adjacent to activity zones, then the inferred environmental processes may not have been perceived as important by most people.

Moreover, we have to consider explicitly how the environmental processes that we characterise would have been spread across different scales of time, even if this means making inferences not directly supported by the data. One of the problems with archaeological conceptions of time is that – as with the traditional, Western view of nature – we place ourselves outside of these different realms of time, and consider processes and the associated experiences of time as remote phenomena. The *longue durée* is normally defined as being that category of time associated with environmental processes (Braudel 1985). However, it is the day-to-day (*événementielle*) experience of environmental processes (such as weather and erosion) combined with the annual cycle of seasonal activities that actually define human experience of the natural world. Some have argued for two forms of time in agricultural societies: cyclical, relating to the annual round of tasks in the landscape, and then a longer-term, linear form of time as represented by monuments and important natural places (D. W. Bailey 1993). In fact, there is no need to oppose cyclical time and linear time (Lucas 2005: 93), and the existence of such discrete chronological frameworks should also be questioned (G. Bailey 2007). Landscape features are often hybrids, where natural and cultural characteristics intersect. These imbue landscapes with temporal character, where a defined notion of linear time is replaced by a notion of 'pedigree' or ancestry. People would have discovered traces of the past when working the land. They would also have come across evidence of past environmental processes (Bradley 2002: 13–14), and environmental knowledge of these processes contributed to landscape resilience. In societies where notions of linear time did not exist, an appreciation of long-term landscape degradation was probably absent, and if any temporal notion was noteworthy, it would have been that association with seasonal-cyclical time.

Retrodicting Human Engagement with the Landscape

Each moment of human–landscape interaction is 'perfect' in the sense that the nature and characteristics of cultural environmental processes are peculiar to each moment in time and space (Phillips 2007). We will rarely identify specific moments of human–landscape interaction, sometimes characterised as the 'Pompeii Premise' (Binford 1981; Schiffer 1985). Perhaps we should accept that we can only ever infer 'fuzzy' landscapes, where space is measurable but time is blurred, where we can never have a direct handle on the time at which an environmental event took place. We can know that certain processes took place within a certain time frame, and can assess the extent to which these processes were experienced and the consequences acted upon. This 'fuzzy' process can be identified when palaeoenvironmental evidence and contemporary archaeological evidence intersect with one another in the same landscape (e.g. Pucci et al. 2011). Environmental processes have a past (the event), present (the state of the environment as perceived at a point in time), and future (an appreciation of how and when this process might reoccur and its implications for landscape, economy, etc.). Environmental management, in all its forms, implies not only a comprehension of past events, but also an awareness of the possibility/probability of an event reoccurring. Such management practices can include terracing, woodland management, flood prevention and mitigation systems (such as at Tiryns), or site movement or relocation. The length of time (i.e. the start and end of an event or process) is less important than the frequency of human engagement with that process (or space). It is this frequency that gives environmental processes their level of relative importance.

Horden and Purcell (2000 ch. VII.2) rightly identify the potential for local, community-level manipulation of landscapes, but at the same time question the somewhat romantic notion of cooperation, especially in hydraulic landscapes. Here, their examples tend to be medieval, with some reference to earlier periods. If we are to assess such processes for the proto- and prehistoric pasts, we require well-dated, overlapping palaeoenvironmental and archaeological records. Where sedimentary sequences need to be dated and the waxing and waning of hydrological processes identified, future research may well need to call upon well-dated sequences of OSL dates that have been subject to Bayesian analysis (Blaise & Balasse 2011). Only then can we hope to develop narratives of past, local-scale human–environment engagements. What we might aim for is evidence of predictive or anticipatory (ex ante) actions vis-à-vis the environment, or reactive (ex post) responses to an environmental process. The identification of these two very different actions would allow a clearer characterisation and assessment of environmental knowledge in the past. Once we see the emergence of similar (technological) responses to comparable environmental processes across the Mediterranean, we might be able to consider a Mediterranean-wide cultural ecology. However, this can never be a full human ecology, as responses to any environmental process will include cultural filters and religious attitudes which will have varied across space. For example, it is apparent that from the Bronze Age onwards, different societies across the Mediterranean were adopting similar strategies across certain landscape types: the development of ports, terracing, dams, irrigation, and so on. If we see a homogenisation of technological responses to environmental problems, then this might be due to the presence of an imperial power or a particularly strong political force within a region. However, certain categories of environmental knowledge and associated forms of landscape management would have been transmitted between and across societies via a number of mechanisms, including elite interactions, the movement of traders (Kristiansen & Larsson 2005), and perhaps even people with specialist environmental knowledge.

Revisiting Mediterranean Environmental Problems

One environmental constant across Mediterranean landscapes is the presence of tectonic structures and associated hazards, such as volcanic eruptions and earthquakes. These do not merely provide the physical backdrop for the development of human landscapes across the Mediterranean, but these processes are active agents in the construction of Mediterranean culture, belief systems, and socio-economic processes. Whereas certain catastrophic events clearly have immediate consequences, tectonic activity also contributes to the structuring of more mundane processes, in particular, erosion. The complex mosaic of undulating topography also influences the composition and distribution of vegetation. The cultural importance of the catastrophe narrative is perhaps nowhere more apparent than with the story of the universal flood myth (Wilson 2001), possibly grounded in actual events early on in the Holocene. We should of course be aware of the dangers of placing too much emphasis on catastrophism (Morhange et al. 2013). Catastrophes, such as tsunamis, provide a stark contrast with the more mundane but significant low-magnitude processes, such as sea-level changes and the threats often posed to coastal sites by the salinisation of water and sedimentation leading to coastal advance and the silting-up of harbours. These latter processes tie the coastal zone to the hinterland, with its constant but variable scales of erosion, sediment transport, and (re)deposition. The potential risks posed by sea-level rise today are widely acknowledged. The combination of subsidence (in north-east Italy, for example), thermal seawater expansion, and glacier and ice-sheet melting could result in a relative sea-level rise of between 180 mm and 1,400 mm by AD 2100 (Lambeck et al. 2011). It is this combination of low-magnitude, seemingly mundane processes that pose some of the greatest threats.

Alluvial records are often used in the assessment of erosional histories; that is, sediments removed and transported due to increased precipitation and/or human disturbance. However, it is human engagement with and responses to the floods that are just as interesting. Moreover, we can identify society's responses to floods in the archaeological record. It is the explicit amalgamation of archaeological and palaeoenvironmental data that permit the development of the richest stories of the development of environmental knowledge across different times and spaces. For example, there are times when people appear to have abandoned wetlands, possibly due to disease or simply because inundation became a common occurrence. It is difficult to demonstrate that enhanced flooding or wetland encroachment can be correlated with periods of climatic deterioration (i.e. increased precipitation). It is likely that flooding occurred under warmer climatic conditions, with concomitant concentrated seasonal storminess – an all too common process in the Mediterranean. Just as important are the changes in river-channel configurations – changes in size and depth to the migration of channels across a flood plain. Rivers and their flood plains clearly provide rich opportunities, the most important being the deposition of silts in relatively moist zones that permit the development of arable agriculture. This continual process of sediment removal and transportation means that environmental productivity is in some ways moved from one part of the landscape to another (Bintliff 2002). Eroded material from one (now partially, pedologically impoverished) area, redeposited within a landscape, can provide a new ecological potential. Over the long term, relatively few landscapes have witnessed degradation that has ultimately rendered them permanently unusable, although many places have witnessed phases of environmental instability to which specific populations or groups of people have had to respond.

Responses to environmental features and changes in the landscape were not merely economically rational and instrumental; they were also cultural, ideological, and religious. Some religious systems, such as the Minoan religion, possessed distinctive features, including large quantities of 'religious' material culture, a relative dearth of temples, and a large number of nature sanctuaries that constituted the key component in this society's relationship with nature and landscape. As Herva (2006: 593) suggests for the Minoan religion, the emphasis on a form of animism, rather than an importance of divinities, might be explained by the incredible variation of environments and niches across Crete, which is in turn a product of its tectonic characteristics and its insularity. In the continental Greek context, the presence of so many deities and their sanctuaries across the landscape (Cole 1996; Jost 1996) might imply a level of environmental insecurity. The need to imbue the productive rural world with sanctuaries and offerings suggests that the natural world needed to be coaxed into guaranteeing arable and pastoral success.

The greatest threat to agricultural production and, indeed, all plant and animal life in the Mediterranean is aridity and drought. Whereas the development of the arid, notionally archetypal Mediterranean environment might be seen by some as the friable foundations for subsequent landscape degradation, the stabilisation of eustatic sea level, the emergence of sclerophyllous vegetation, and the other characteristics that define many Mediterranean zones today could be considered as the framework within which relatively stable and complex forms of environmental knowledge could develop. However, continued changes in climate and associated transformations in weather patterns with their concomitant effects on crops, pasture, and soil were never predictable. Long-term climatic stability does not explain the success of civilisations (Crumley 1994a), but unpredictable weather will test socio-economic resilience. The likelihood of environmental degradation may well have increased where local, community-based responses to environmental problems broke down. Therefore, periods of environmental instability may not necessarily correspond with demographic pressure and the zenith of a given civilisation's power, but rather with periods of civilisation collapse or phases of internal conflict. Such phases of internal conflict can of course occur when a civilisation is at its most powerful, and certain environmental initiatives imposed by hegemonic structures may cause environmental stresses due to incongruous hegemonic and local forms of environmental knowledge (as discussed in Chapter 4). A period when aridity might have had a dramatic effect on societies is the Bronze Age (at c. 2200 BC and c. 1000 BC (Finné & Holmgren 2010), when some consider that deterioration in climate might have been responsible for some socio-economic crises (Kaniewski et al. 2010). Rather than continuous aridity, the probability of climatic instability – of a drying trend with shorter phases of humidity, as seen in Central Anatolia (Kuzucuoglu et al. 2011) – could have tested the flexibility of environmental knowledge. Moving on to the Iron Age, climatic variability is underpinned by the emergence of increased aridity in some areas (Roberts, Brayshaw, et al. 2011), whilst some regions were wetter and cooler than the preceding and subsequent periods. It seems likely that the Northern Mediterranean did witness similar changes to those seen across north-west Europe (Provansal 1995a; Van Geel & Berglund 1997). Increased flooding (because of enhanced precipitation) may well have caused problems for some Iron Age settlements (Simeoni & Corbau 2009; Veggiani 1994). The Iron Age site at El Gallo, near Cadiz in south-west Spain, saw the development of an enhanced fresh-water marsh and an increase in riparian vegetation (Saez et al. 2002), whilst changes in the anatomy of olive-wood structure in parts of Spain and the south of France suggest an increase in rainfall during the transition from the Bronze Age to the Iron Age (Terral & Mengual 1999). Despite evidence for increased precipitation during the Iron Age – possibly solar-influenced changes (Biserni & Van Geel 2005; Mauquoy et al. 2002) – we see little evidence in the Mediterranean for such changes in climate having a negative effect on these emerging civilisations. The development of the Greek and Etruscan civilisations, and ultimately the Roman Republic, took place during a period that some geomorphologists would characterise as being one of environmental deterioration – essentially defined by increased precipitation and lower average temperatures. In fact, enhanced rainfall would have rendered many marginal arid zones more productive. The earlier phase of the Iron Age in the Near East may have witnessed slightly more arid conditions, whilst during the Persian, Hellenistic, and the Early Roman periods, rainfall may have been slightly higher than the preceding periods (Rosen 2007: 42–3). What is apparent is the fluctuation in climatic patterns and, in particular, precipitation. Until we have clear evidence for the seasonal (weather) precipitation, assessing the possible role of aridity in causing socio-economic stress will be problematic.

The first centuries BC and AD are documented as being a period of climatic amelioration. Climatic amelioration, of course, means different things in different parts of the Mediterranean. Some areas saw increased average temperatures (Chen, Zonneveld, & Versteegh 2012), which as noted elsewhere in this volume, should not be interpreted as an entirely positive development, as such a change can enhance seasonal evapotrans-piration in the Mediterranean and result in extreme storm events. The opportunities proffered by this period of climatic amelioration varied from one part of the Mediterranean to the other. For example, more alpine passes were open for longer periods during the Roman climatic optimum. The high-altitude pastoral season would have been longer as well, although this was not necessarily taken advantage of by all Roman or Romanised societies. This phase of climatic amelioration might have provided the ideal conditions for intensive arable and pastoral activity if these landscapes were well managed. However, zones which were sub-ject to several seasons of aridity and poor plant growth may well have witnessed seasonal erosion. This is why this volume has included spe-cific landscape and site-based examples, as no general rules or trends can be inferred. Only trajectories can be considered, characterised by the notion that a trajectory comprises a predictable starting condition for a landscape – its geology, hydrology, probable soils – but that its develop-ment will vary depending on a number of external influences (climate, weather, human activities, with all their abundant socio-economic and cultural elements).

Some have argued that Mediterranean societies and, in particular, the Greeks and Romans mistreated the natural environment (Hughes 2005: 197). There is limited evidence for this. As already demonstrated, certain places have witnessed environmental degradation at certain times in the past. However, we can infer management practices that were designed to mitigate degradation, undoubtedly with a view to maintaining agri-cultural production. Some classical thinkers did articulate a philosophy which might be considered 'conservationist'. There is an argument that some of Plato's ideas were akin to modern 'deep ecology' (the belief that humanity should respect the natural world) because Plato rejected ego-ism and anthropocentrism (Mahoney 1997: 48), although some argue that Plato's ethics were essentially egocentric. Moreover, it seems that Plato saw the natural world as a connected organism of which people were an integral part. For the Roman period, some of the writings of the agronomists might also be considered conservationist, although these accounts were blatantly concerned with an economically rational per-spective vis-à-vis productivity. Nevertheless, such institutionalised and systematised forms of environmental knowledge, compounded with an unbalanced market, may well have contributed to certain types of environmental problems.

Horden and Purcell's integrated Mediterranean serves as a useful framework for the assessment of different levels of environmental knowledge. However, their integrated network implies the existence of some forms of universal environmental knowledge. In fact, environmental knowledge is socially structured and specific to each group's form of engagement with the environment. There are undoubtedly certain forms of ancient landscape management that have demonstrated both cultural and ecological resilience. For example, centuriated fields appear to have supported the ecological structure and resilience of some agricultural landscapes (Caravello & Giacomin 1993), whilst there are some niches that appear to have never fully recovered from Roman exploitation, including the Crau in the south of France (F. Henry 2009; F. Henry, Talon, & Dutoit 2010).

Despite the emphasis on correlating culture and environmental change over the long and medium durée (e.g. using climate change to explain culture collapse or settlement abandonment within a given region), our data are actually more suited to the assessment of specific local events (the *événementielle*). The combination of archaeological and palaeoenvironmental evidence do allow the identification of site-based responses to environmental events or specific examples of human manipulation of the environment. Once we have established a series of such studies within a micro-region, we then have the foundations for the analysis of longer-term responses to environmental changes in the past.

Mediterranean Landscapes: Past, Present, and Future...

Whereas the causes and trajectory of twenty-first century climate change are in many ways different to past phases of climate change, there is no doubt that similar conditions were witnessed in parts of the region at different times during the Middle and Late Holocene. Local forms of environmental knowledge that are not driven by homogenising political and hegemonic structures are fundamental to the mitigation of environmental problems across landscapes with multiple niches and economic potentials. Increased aridity and possible desertification are the greatest problems facing some parts of the Mediterranean (de Wrachien, Ragab, & Giordano 2006). Future climate change will probably exacerbate the seasonal characteristics of Mediterranean weather, with longer, hotter summers characterised by extreme orographic precipitation (Diodato et al. 2011). Such events undoubtedly took place in the past, such as the catastrophic flooding event at the end of the fifth century AD at Mahuzah d'Iamnin (associated with Yavneh-Yam) on the coast 15 km south of Jaffa-Tel Aviv (Fischer 2005). Climate change is producing substantial variations in inter- and intra-annual precipitation and thereby freshwater supply across the Mediterranean. Overexploitation of aquifers and the potential for salinisation is another twenty-first century problem that has been with Mediterranean societies for millennia. Today, many of the nations with the highest water footprint (cubic metres per year per capita) globally are Mediterranean, including Portugal, Spain, Greece, Italy, Israel, Tunisia, and Libya (Hoekstra & Mekonnen 2012).

One important change that has taken place over the last 50 years or so is the enormous decline in the rural population, especially on the northern half of the Mediterranean, from 46 million in 1960 to 12 million in 2000. To a certain extent, if we accept that vegetation will protect soils (as it has done in the past), then these depopulated zones may well witness a phase of unprecedented environmental stability, even if there is a swing towards potentially damaging, intense, and concentrated storm-related precipitation. However, falling water tables and increased levels of combustible vegetation will probably lead to more forest fires and consequent erosion. Nevertheless, some Mediterranean rural zones are now witnessing a stabilisation and small growth in populations (Benoit & Comeau 2005: 250–3). This is part of newly diversifying rural economies, and the impact on environmental resources will not be the same as during the nineteenth century (when the rural population was at its highest). There is no doubt that good-quality agricultural land is being lost across the Mediterranean. Perhaps the most dramatic statistic is the 37% loss of good-quality land on Malta in 90 years (ibid.: 267). Bringing us back to the question of insular biodiversity, this statistic alone demonstrates how, up until recent years, Maltese environmental management was in many ways successful. Even with today's models, ex ante or predictive responses to environmental change, especially regarding hydrology, are extremely difficult (Arnold, Walsh, & Hollimon 2004), and there is no doubt that prediction in the past of many environmental processes was even more problematic. Therefore, flexibility and adaptability underpinned successful mitigation. As we have seen, certain societies in the past that were situated within semi-arid, degraded landscapes still successfully exploited specific niches – an obvious example being the Argaric culture in south-east Spain. However, flexibility is often stifled when hegemonic political structures control the use and management of landscapes. In recent decades, Northern Mediterranean agriculture has adopted a 'delocalised' form of production that adapts to large-scale markets rather than adapting to the ecological characteristics of the locales within which production takes place (Benoit & Comeau 2005: 272). Although such homogenisation would never have been as intensive and extensive in the past, there were undoubtedly periods when local landscapes were obliged to respond to regional, hegemonic imperatives. Despite these problems, there are many examples of successful anthropogenic niches. Possibly the best example is the cork oak savannas, where diversity and resilience are only guaranteed by active management (Bugalho, Caldeira, et al. 2011). Here, management practices sustain grazing and augment habitat heterogeneity. More specifically, the diversity of herbaceous plants and invertebrates is promoted (Bugalho, Lecomte, et al. 2011). As with many regions around the world, Mediterranean cultures' inter-actions with the environment in the past have often been influenced by overarching ideological processes. The geological and ecological com-plexity of Mediterranean landscapes has always demanded complex and adaptable forms of environmental knowledge. Environmental problems can include drought, flooding, coastal change, forest fires, and erosion, and because of some (or all) of these, the results may include downturns in agricultural production and even injury and death. Insurmountable problems have rarely been caused by the environment alone, but have rather been the product of intersecting social and environmental issues, where rigid forms of environmental knowledge (often overly structured by hegemonic forces) have prevented individuals or small communities from mitigating these threats.

Bibliography

Abbott, J. T., & S. Valastro, 1995. The Holocene alluvial records of the chorai of Metapontum, Basilicata, and Croton, Calabria, Italy, in *Mediterranean Quaternary River Environments: Refereed Proceedings of an International Conference University of Cambridge/United Kingdom/28–29 september*, eds. J. Lewin, M. G. Macklin, & J. C. Woodward. Rotterdam: AA Balkema, pp. 195–205.

Ackermann, O., H. J. Bruins, & A. M. Maeir, 2005. A unique human-made trench at Tell es-Sâfi/Gath, Israel: Anthropogenic impact and landscape response. *Geoarchaeology*, 20(3), 303–27.

AEMET, Valores climatológicos normales – Agencia Estatal de Meteorología – AEMET. Gobierno de España.

Aguilera, M., J. P. Ferrio, G. Pérez, J. L. Araus, & J. Voltas, 2012. Holocene changes in precipitation seasonality in the Western Mediterranean Basin: A multi-species approach using δ13C of archaeobotanical remains. *Journal of Quaternary Science*, 27(2), 192–202.

Agusta-Boularot, S., M. Christol, M. Gazenbeek, Y. Marcadal, V. Mathieu, J. L. Paillet, A. Rapin, A. Roth-Conges, J. C. Sourisseau, & H. Treziny, 2004. Dix ans de fouilles et recherches à Glanum (Saint-Rémy-de-Provence): 1992–2002. *Journal of Roman Archaeology*, 17, 27–56.

Agusta-Boularot, S., & M. Gazenbeek, 2003. Glanum (Saint-Rémy-de-Provence, Bouches-du-Rhône): les installations hydrauliques du vallon Saint-Clerg de la fin de l'âge du Fer à nos jours. *Revue d'Archéologie Narbonnaise*, 36, 93–132.

Akar, M., 2009. The Role of Harbour Towns in the Re-Urbanization of the Levant in the Middle Bronze Age (1800–1600 BC). Perspectives from Eastern Cilicia and the Amuq Plain of Hatay, PhD. dissertation, Università degli Studi di Firenze, Italy.

Aksu, A. E., R. N. Hiscott, P. J. Mudie, A. Rochon, M. A. Kaminski, T. Abrajano, & D. Yasar, 2002. Persistent Holocene outflow from the Black Sea to the Eastern Mediterranean contradicts Noah's flood hypothesis. *GSA TODAY*, 12(5), 4–9.

Albore Livadie, C., 2003. Piano di Sorrento (Naples): évidence d'une modification du réseau hydrique sur le site archéologique de la Trinité, in *Variazioni Climatico-Ambientali e Impatto sull'uomo nell'area circum-Mediterranean durante l'Olocene*, eds. C. A. Livadie & F. Ortolani. Bari: Edipuglia, pp. 359–64.

Alcock, S. E., 2007. The essential countryside: The Greek world, in *Classical Archaeology*, eds. S. E. Alcock & R. Osborne. Oxford: Wiley Blackwell, pp. 120–38.

Alcover, J. A., 2008. The first Mallorcans: Prehistoric colonization in the Western Mediterranean. *Journal of World Prehistory*, 21(1), 19–84.

Alcover, J. A., R. A. M. O. Perez-Obiol, E. I. Yll, & P. E. R. E. Bover, 1999. The diet of Myotragus balearicus Bate 1909 (Artiodactyla: Caprinae), an extinct bovid from the Balearic Islands: Evidence from coprolites. *Biological Journal of the Linnean Society*, 66(1), 57–74.

Aldenderfer, M., 2006. Modelling plateau peoples: The early human use of the world's high plateaux. *World Archaeology*, 38(3), 357–70.

Aldrete, G. S., 2007. *Floods of the Tiber in Ancient Rome*. Baltimore: Johns Hopkins University Press.

Ali, A. A., C. Carcaillet, B. Talon, P. Roiron, & J. F. Terral, 2005. Pinus cembra L. (arolla pine), a common tree in the inner French Alps since the Early Holocene and above the present tree line: A synthesis based on charcoal data from soils and travertines. *Journal of Biogeography*, 32(9), 1659–69.

Ali, A. A., P. Roiron, J. L. Guendon, P. Poirier, & J. F. Terral, 2005. Holocene vegetation responses to fire events in the inner French Alps (Queyras Massif): Data from charcoal and geomorphological analysis of travertine sequences. *The Holocene*, 15(1), 149–55.

Allen, H. D., 2001. *Mediterranean Ecogeography*. Harlow: Prentice Hall/ Pearson Education.

Allen, J. R., W. A. Watts, E. McGee, & B. Huntley, 2002. Holocene environmental variability – The record from Lago Grande di Monticchio, Italy. *Quaternary International*, 88(1), 69–80.

Altunel, E., I. S. Stewart, A. Barka, & L. Piccardi, 2003. Earthquake faulting at ancient Cnidus, SW Turkey. *Turkish Journal of Earth Sciences*, 12, 137–51.

Ambraseys, N., 2009. *Earthquakes in the Mediterranean and Middle East: A Multidisciplinary Study of Seismicity Upto 1900*. Cambridge: Cambridge University Press.

Ammerman, A. J., 2010. The first argonauts: Towards the study of the earliest seafaring in the Mediterranean, in *The Global Origins (and Development) of Seafaring*, eds. A. Anderson, J. Barrett, & K. Boyle. Cambridge: McDonald Institute For Archaeological Research, pp. 81–92.

Ammerman, A. J., N. Efstratiou, M. Ntinou, K. Pavlopoulos, R. Gabrielli, K. D. Thomas, & M. A. Mannino, 2008. Finding the Early Neolithic in Aegean Thrace: The use of cores. *Antiquity*, 82(315), 139–50.

Andreou, S., M. Fotiadis, & K. Kotsakis, 1996. Review of Aegean prehistory V: The Neolithic and the Bronze Age of northern Greece. *American Journal of Archaeology*, 100(3), 537–97.

Andrieu-Ponel, V., P. Ponel, A. J. T. Jull, J. L. Beaulieu, H. Bruneton, & P. Leveau, 2000. Towards the reconstruction of the Holocene vegetation history of Lower Provence: Two new pollen profiles from Marais des Baux. *Vegetation History and Archaeobotany*, 9(2), 71–84.

Anketell, J. M., S. M. Ghellali, D. Gilbertson, & C. O. Hunt, 1995. Quaternary wadi and floodplain sequences of Tripolitania, northwest Libya: A synthesis of their stratigraphic relationships, and their implications in landscape evolution, in *Mediterranean Quaternary River Environments: Refereed Proceedings of an International Conference University of Cambridge, United Kingdom, 28–29 September*, eds. J. Lewin, M. G. Macklin, & J. C. Woodward. Rotterdam: AA Balkema, pp. 231–45.

Ånstöm, P., & K. Demakopoulou, 1996. Signs of an earthquake at Midea?, in *Archaeoseismology*, eds. S. C. Stiros & R. E. Jones. Athens: Institute of Geology and Mineral Exploration & The British School at Athens, pp. 37–40.

Antonioli, F., M. Anzidei, K. Lambeck, R. Auriemma, D. Gaddi, S. Furlani, P. Orrù, E. Solinas, A. Gaspari, S. Karinja, V. Kovačić, & L. Surace, 2007. Sea-level change during the Holocene in Sardinia and in the northeastern Adriatic (central Mediterranean Sea) from archaeological and geomorphological data. *Quaternary Science Reviews*, 26(19–21), 2463–86.

Anzidei, M., F. Antonioli, K. Lambeck, A. Benini, M. Soussi, & R. Lakhdar, 2011. New insights on the relative sea level change during Holocene along the coasts of Tunisia and western Libya from archaeological and geomorphological markers. *Quaternary International*, 232(1–2), 5–12.

Armijo, R., H. Lyon-Caen, & D. Papanastassiou, 1991. A possible normal-fault rupture for the 464 BC Sparta earthquake. *Nature*, 351(6322), 137–9.

Arnaud-Fassetta, G., & C. Landuré, 2003. Hydroclimatic hazards, vulnerability of societies and fluvial risk in the Rhone delta (Mediterranean France) from the Greek period to the Early Medieval Ages, in *The Mediterranean World Environment and History*, ed. E. Fouache. Paris: Elsevier, pp. 51–76.

Arnold, J. E., M. R. Walsh, & S. E. Hollimon, 2004. The archaeology of California. *Journal of Archaeological Research*, 12, 1–73.

Arroyo-García, R., L. Ruiz-García, L. Bolling, R. Ocete, M. A. López, C. Arnold, A. Ergul, G. Söylemezoğlu, H. I. Uzun, F. Cabello, J. Ibáñez, M. K. Aradhya, A. Atanassov, I. Atanassov, S. Balint, J. L. Cenis, L. Costantini, S. Gorislavets, M. S. Grando, B. Y. Klein, P. E. McGovern, D. Merdinoglu, I. Pejic, F. Pelsy, N. Primikirios, V. Risovannaya, K. A. Roubelakis-Angelakis, H. Snoussi, P. Sotiri, S. Tamhankar, P. This, L. Troshin, J. M. Malpica, F. Lefort, & J. M. Martinez-Zapater, 2006. Multiple origins of cultivated grapevine (Vitis vinifera L. ssp. sativa) based on chloroplast DNA polymorphisms. *Molecular Ecology*, 15(12), 3707–14.

Asouti, E., 2003a. Wood charcoal from Santorini (Thera): New evidence for climate, vegetation and timber imports in the Aegean Bronze Age. *Antiquity*,
77(297), 471–84.

Asouti, E., 2003b. Woodland vegetation and fuel exploitation at the prehistoric
campsite of Pınarbaşı, south-central Anatolia, Turkey: The evidence from
the wood charcoal macro-remains. *Journal of Archaeological Science*, 30(9),
1185–201.

2005. Woodland vegetation and the exploitation of fuel and timber at
Neolithic Çatalhöyük: Report on wood-charcoal macro-remains, in
*Inhabiting Çatalhöyük: Reports from the 1995–99 Seasons (Çatalhöyük
Research Project)*, ed. I. Hodder. Cambridge: MacDonald Institute for
Archaeological Research.

Asouti, E., & D. Fuller, 2012. From foraging to farming in the Southern Levant:
The development of Epipalaeolithic and Pre-pottery Neolithic plant management strategies. *Vegetation History and Archaeobotany*, 21(2), 149–62.

Asouti, E., & J. Hather, 2001. Charcoal analysis and the reconstruction of ancient
woodland vegetation in the Konya Basin, south-central Anatolia, Turkey:
Results from the Neolithic site of Çatalhöyük East. *Vegetation History and
Archaeobotany*, 10(1), 23–32.

Assier, A., 1996. *Glaciers et Glaciers Rocheux de l'Ubaye*, Barcelonnette: Sabenca
de la Valeia.

Atherden, M. A., & J. A. Hall, 1999. Human impact on vegetation in the White
Mountains of Crete since AD 500. *The Holocene*, 9(2), 183–94.

Atherden, M. A., J. Hall, & J. C. Wright, 1993. A pollen diagram from the
northeast Peloponnese, Greece: Implications for vegetation history and
archaeology. *The Holocene*, 3(4), 351–6.

Attema, P., T. de Haas, & G. W. Gol, 2011. Between Satricum and Antium:
Settlement dynamics in a coastal landscape in Latium Vetus. Leuven:
Peeters.

Attema, P., & J. Delvigne, 2000. Settlement dynamics and alluvial sedimen-
tation in the Pontine region, central Italy: A complex relationship, in
Geoarchaeology of the Landscapes of Classical Antiquity, eds. F. Vermeulen &
M. De Dapper. Leiden: Stichting Babesch, pp. 35–47.

Attema, P., G.-J. Burgers, & P. M. van Leusen, 2010. *Regional Pathways to
Complexity: Settlement and Land-Use Dynamics in Early Italy from the
Bronze Age to the Republican Period*. Amsterdam: Amsterdam University
Press.

Aubet, M. E., & M. Turton, 2001. *The Phoenicians and the West: Politics, Colonies
and Trade*. Cambridge: Cambridge University Press.

Auriemma, R., & E. Solinas, 2009. Archaeological remains as sea level change
markers: A review. *Quaternary International*, 206(1–2), 134–46.

Avigliano, R., G. Di Anastasio, S. Improta, M. Peresani, & C. Ravazzi, 2000.
A new late glacial to Early Holocene palaeobotanical and archaeological

record in the Eastern Pre-Alps: The Palughetto basin (Cansiglio Plateau, Italy). *Journal of Quaternary Science*, 15(8), 789–804.

Avni, Y., N. Porat, J. Plakht, & G. Avni, 2006. Geomorphic changes leading to natural desertification versus anthropogenic land conservation in an arid environment, the Negev Highlands, Israel. *Geomorphology*, 82(3–4), 177–200.

Ayala, G., & C. French, 2003. Holocene landscape dynamics in a Sicilian upland river valley, in *Alluvial Archaeology in Europe*, eds. A. J. Howard, M. G. Macklin, & D. G. Passmore. Lisse: Swets & Zeitlinger, pp. 229–35.

Ayala, G., & C. French, 2005. Erosion modeling of past land-use practices in the Fiume di Sotto di Troina river valley, north-central Sicily. *Geoarchaeology*, 20(2), 149–68.

Bachhuber, C., & R. G. Roberts, 2008. *Forces of Transformation: The End of the Bronze Age in the Mediterranean*. Oxford: Oxbow Books.

Bailey, D. W., 1993. Chronotypic tension in Bulgarian prehistory: 6500–3500 BC. *World Archaeology*, 25(2), 204–22.

Bailey, G., 2007. Time perspectives, palimpsests and the archaeology of time. *Journal of Anthropological Archaeology*, 26(2), 198–223.

Balée, W., 2006. The research program of historical ecology. *Annual Review of Anthropology*, 35(1), 75–98.

Ballais, J. L., 1994. Aeolian activity, desertification and the 'green dam' in the Ziban range, Algeria, in *Environmental Change in Drylands: Biogeographical and Geomorphological Perspectives*, eds. A. C. Millington & K. Pye. London: Wiley, pp. 177–98.

Ballais, J. L., & A. Crambes, 1993. Morphogenèse Holocène et anthropisation sur la Montagne Sainte Victoire, in *Archéologie et Environnement de la Sainte-Victoire aux Alpilles*, eds. P. Leveau & M. Provansal. Aix-en-Provence: Publications Université de Provence, pp. 467–83.

Ballais, J. L., & P. Bellamy, 2000. Le pont Simian à Fontvieille: Étude géo-archéologique d'un pont-aqueduc, in *Milieux et Sociétés dans la Vallée des Baux*, eds. P. Leveau & J. P. Saquet. Montpellier: Revue archéologique de Narbonnaise, pp. 25–38.

Balmuth, M. S., D. K. Chester, & P. A. Johnston, 2003. *Cultural Responses to the Volcanic Landscape: The Mediterranean and Beyond* (AIA Colloquia and Conference Papers). Boston: Archaeological Institute of America.

Bar-Matthews, M., & A. Ayalon, 2011. Mid-Holocene climate variations revealed by high-resolution speleothem records from Soreq Cave, Israel and their correlation with cultural changes. *The Holocene*, 21(1), 163–71.

Barge, H., & B. Talon, 2012. Attaque au feu au Bronzeancien sur le gîte de cuivre de Saint-Véran (Hautes-Alpes). *Bulletin de la Société Préhistorique Française*, 109(1), 145–54.

Barker, G., 2002. A tale of two deserts: Contrasting desertification histories on Rome's desert frontiers. *World Archaeology*, 33(3), 488–507.

Barker, G., & C. Hunt, 2003. The role of climate and human settlement in the evolution of the Biferno Valley (Molise, Central-Southern Italy), in *Variazioni Climatico-Ambientali e Impatto sull'uomo nell'area circum-Mediterranean durante l'Olocene*, eds. C. A. Livadie & F. Ortolani. Bari: Edipuglia, pp. 183–91.

Barker, G., D. Gilbertson, C. O. Hunt, & D. Mattingly, 1996. Roman-Libyan agriculture: Integrated models, in *Farming the Desert: The UNESCO Libyan Valleys Archaeological Survey*, ed. G. Barker. London: Society for Libyan Studies, pp. 265–90.

Barriendos, M., 1997. Climatic variations in the Iberian Peninsula during the late Maunder Minimum (AD 1675–1715): An analysis of data from rogation ceremonies. *The Holocene*, 7(1), 105–12.

Barriendos, M., & M. C. Llasat, 2003. The case of the 'Malda' anomaly in the Western Mediterranean Basin (AD 1760–1800): An example of a strong climatic variability. *Climatic Change*, 61(1/2), 191–216.

Barton, C. M., J. Bernabeu, J. E. Aura, & O. Garcia, 1999. Land-use dynamics and socioeconomic change: An example from the Polop Alto Valley. *American Antiquity*, 64(4), 609–34.

Barton, C. M., J. Bernabeu, J. E. Aura, O. Garcia, & N. La Roca, 2002. Dynamic landscapes, artifact taphonomy, and landuse modeling in the Western Mediterranean. *Geoarchaeology*, 17(2), 155–90.

Baruch, U., 1986. The Late Holocene vegetational history of Lake Kinneret (Sea of Galilee), Israel. *Paléorient*, 12(2), 37–48.

  1999. *The Contribution of Palynology and Anthracology to Archaeological Research in the Southern Levant*, eds. S. Pike & S. Gitin. London: Archetype, pp. 17–28.

Bass, B., 1998. Early Neolithic offshore accounts: Remote islands, maritime exploitations, and the trans-Adriatic cultural network. *Journal of Mediterranean Archaeology*, 11(2), 165–90.

Baylis-Smith, T., & J. Golson, 1999. The meaning of ditches: Deconstructing the social landscapes of New Guinea, Kuk, phase, in *The Prehistory of Food: Appetites for Change*, ed. J. G. Hather. London: Routledge, pp. 199–231.

Beagon, M., 1996. Nature and views of her landscapes in Pliny the Elder, in *Human Landscapes in Classical Antiquity: Environment and Culture*, eds. G. Shipley & J. Salmon. London: Routledge, pp. 284–309.

Bellotti, P., F. L. Chiocci, S. Milli, & P. Tortora, 1994. Sequence stratigraphy and depositional setting of the Tiber delta: Integration of high-resolution seismics, well logs, and archeological data. *Journal of Sedimentary Research Section B*, 64(3), 416.

Benedetti, L., R. Finkel, D. Papanastassiou, G. King, R. Armijo, F. Ryerson, D. Farber, & F. Flerit, 2002. Post-glacial slip history of the Sparta fault (Greece) determined by 36 cl cosmogenic dating: Evidence for non-periodic earthquakes. *Geophysical Research Letters*, 29(8), 1–87.

Beniston, M., 2000. *Environmental Change in Mountains and Uplands*. London: Arnold.

Benito, G., A. Sopena, Y. Sanchez-Moya, M. J. Machado, & A. Perez-Gonzalez, 2003. Palaeoflood record of the Tagus River (central Spain) during the Late Pleistocene and Holocene. *Quaternary Science Reviews*, 22(15–17), 1737–56.

Benito, G., V. R. Thorndycraft, M. Rico, Y. Sánchez-Moya, & A. Sopeña, 2008. Palaeoflood and floodplain records from Spain: Evidence for long-term climate variability and environmental changes. *Geomorphology*, 101(1–2), 68–77.

Benoit, G. & A. Comeau, 2005. *Méditerranée: Les Perspectives du Plan Bleu sur l'Environnement et le Développement*. Sophia Antipolis: Éditions de l'Aube.

Benoit, G., A. Comeau, L. Chabason, 2005. *Méditerranée: Les Perspectives du Plan Bleu sur l'Environnement et le Développement*. Valbonne: Éditions de l'Aube.

Benouar, D., 2004. Materials for the investigation of historical seismicity in Algeria from the records of past earthquakes. *Annals of Geophysics*, 47(2/3), 555–60.

Benvenuti, M., M. Bonini, G. Moratti, M. Ricci, & C. Tanini, 2008. Tectonic and climatic controls on historical landscape modifications: The avulsion of the lower Cecina River (Tuscany, central Italy). *Geomorphology*, 100(3–4), 269–84.

Benvenuti, M., M. Mariotti-Lippi, P. Pallecchi, & M. Sagri, 2006. Late-Holocene catastrophic floods in the terminal Arno River (Pisa, central Italy) from the story of a Roman riverine harbour. *The Holocene*, 16(6), 863–76.

Bérato, J., 1995. L'Âge du Fer dans la dépression permienne, et dans les massifs des Maures et de l'Esétrel (Var). *Documents d'Archéologie Méridionale*, 18, 45–77.

Berger, J. F., 2003. Les étapes de la morphogenèse Holocène dans le sud de la France, in *Archéologie et Systèmes Socio-environnementaux: Études Multiscalaires sur la Vallée du Rhône dans le Programme ARCHEOMEDES*, eds. S. van der Leeuw, F. Favory, & J. L. Fiches. Paris: CNRS, pp. 87–167.
    2005. Sédiments, dynamique du peuplement et climat au Néolithique ancien, in *Populations Néolithiques et Environnements*, eds. J. Guilaine, P. Chambon, J. Zammit, J. D. Vigne, & Collectif. Paris: Éditions Errance, pp. 155–212.

Bernabeu, J., 1995. Origen y consolidación de las sociedades agrícolas. El País Valenciano entre el Neolítico y la Edad del Bronce. *Actes de les Segones Jornades d'Arqueologia*, 37–60.

Bernabeu, J., C. M. Barton, & M. Perez Ripoll, 2001. A taphonomic perspective on Neolithic beginnings: Theory, interpretation, and empirical data in the Western Mediterranean. *Journal of Archaeological Science*, 28, 597–612.

Bernabeu, J., & J. Bernabeu, 1993. *Al Oeste del Eden*. Valencia: Sintesis Editorial.

Betancourt, P. P., & K. Davaras, 1988. Excavations at Pseira, 1985 and 1986. *Hesperia*, 57, 207–25.

Betancourt, P. P., & W. R. Farrand, 2006. The natural environment. *Hesperia Supplements*, 36, 19–44.

Bettinger, R., P. Richerson, & R. Boyd, 2009. Constraints on the development of agriculture. *Current Anthropology*, 50(5), 627–31.

Bettinger, R., 1991. *Hunter-Gatherers: Archaeological and Evolutionary Theory*. New York: Plenum Press.

Bevan, A., 2002. The rural landscape of neopalatial Kythera: A GIS perspective. *Journal of Mediterranean Archaeology*, 15(2), 217–55.

Bevan, A., J. Conolly & A. Tsaravopoulos, 2007. The fragile communities of Antikythera. *Archaeology International*, 10, 32–6

Bevan, A., & J. Conolly, 2013. *Mediterranean Islands, Fragile Communities and Persistent Landscapes: Antikythera in Long-term Perspective*. Cambridge: Cambridge University Press.

Bevan, A., J. Conolly, & A. Tsaravopoulos, 2007. The fragile communities of Antikythera. *Archaeology International*, 10, 32–6.

Bicket, A. R., H. M. Rendell, A. Claridge, P. Rose, J. Andrews, & F. S. J. Brown, 2010. A multiscale geoarchaeological approach from the Laurentine Shore (Castelporziano, Lazio, Italy). *Géomorphologie: Relief, Processus, Environnement*, 4(2009), 241–56.

Bicknell, P., 2000. Late Minoan IB ware, the marine environment of the Aegean, and the Bronze Age eruption of the Thera volcano, in *The Archaeology of Geological Catastrophes (Geological Society Special Publication)*, eds. D. McGuire, D. Griffiths, P. L. Hancock, & I. Stewart. London: Geological Society Publishing House, pp. 95–103.

Billings, W. D., 1979. High mountain ecosystems, in *High-altitude Geoecology*, ed. P. J. Webber. Boulder: Westview Press, pp. 97–125.

Binford, L. R., 1981. Behavioral archaeology and the 'Pompeii Premise'. *Journal of Anthropological Research*, 37(3), 195–208.

Bini, M., H. Brückner, A. Chelli, M. Pappalardo, S. Da Prato, & L. Gervasini, 2012. Palaeogeographies of the Magra Valley coastal plain to constrain the location of the Roman harbour of Luna (NW Italy). *Palaeogeography, Palaeoclimatology, Palaeoecology*, 37–51, 337–8.

Bintliff, J., 1993. Forest cover, agricultural intensity and population density in Roman imperial Boeotia, central Greece, in *Evaluation of Land Surfaces Cleared from Forests in the Mediterranean Region During the Time of the Roman Empire*. Stuttgart: Fischer Verlag, pp. 133–43.

1997. Regional survey, demography, and the rise of complex societies in the ancient Aegean: Core-periphery, meo-Malthusian, and other interpretive models. *Journal of Field Archaeology*, 24(1), 1–38.

2002. Time, process and catastrophism in the study of Mediterranean alluvial history: A review. *World Archaeology*, 33(3), 417–35.

2009. The implications of a phenomenology of landscape, in *Die Landschaft und die Religion. Stuttgarter Kolloquium zur Historischen Geographie des Altertums 9, 2005*, ed. E. Olshausen & V. Saue. Stuttgart: Franz Steiner Verlag, pp. 27–45.

2012. *The Complete Archaeology of Greece*. New York: John Wiley.

Bintliff, J., E. Farinetti, K. Sarri, & R. Sebastiani, 2006. Landscape and early farming settlement dynamics in central Greece. *Geoarchaeology*, 21(7), 665–74.

Biserni, G., & B. Van Geel, 2005. Reconstruction of Holocene palaeoenvironment and sedimentation history of the Ombrone alluvial plain (South Tuscany, Italy). *Review of Palaeobotany and Palynology*, 136 (1–2), 16–28.

Blackman, D., 1982a. Ancient harbours in the Mediterranean, Part 1. *International Journal of Nautical Archaeology and Underwater Archaeology*, 11(2), 79–104.

1982b. Ancient harbours in the Mediterranean, Part 2. *International Journal of Nautical Archaeology and Underwater Archaeology*, 11(3), 185–211.

Blaise, E., & M. Balasse, 2011. Seasonality and season of birth of modern and late Neolithic sheep from south-eastern France using tooth enamel $\delta18O$ analysis. *Journal of Archaeological Science*, 38(11), 3085–93.

Blanchemanche, P., 1990. *Bâtisseurs de Paysages: Terrassement, Pierrement et Petite Hydraulique Agricoles en Europe (XVIIe–XIXe Siècles)*. Paris: Maison des Sciences de l'Homme.

Blanchemanche, P., L. Chabal, C. Jorda, & C. Jung, 2004. Le Delta du Lez dans tous ses états: quels langages pour quel dialogue?, in *Fleuves et Marais, Une Histoire au Croisement de la Nature et la Culture*, eds. J. Burnouf & P. Leveau. Paris: CTHS, pp. 157–74.

Blondel, J., 1986. *Biogéographie Évolutive*. Paris: Masson.

2008. On humans and wildlife in Mediterranean islands. *Journal of Biogeography*, 35(3), 509–18.

Blondel, J., & J. Aronson, 1999. *Biology and Wildlife of the Mediterranean Region*. Oxford: Oxford University Press.

Blondel, J., J. Aronson, J. Y. Bodiou, & G. Boeuf, 2010. *The Mediterranean Region: Biological Diversity in Space and Time*. Oxford: Oxford University Press.

Blumler, M. A., 2007. Near Eastern pollen diagrams and 'deforestation'. *Middle States Geographer*, 40, 150–7.

Bocquet, A., 1997. Archéologie et peuplement des Alpes françaises du Nord au Néolithique et aux âges des Métaux. *L'Anthropologie*, 101(2), 291–393.

Bofinger, J. P., P. Schweizer, & M. Strobel, 1996. Das Oppidum Bramefan (com. Puyloubier, dép. Bouches-du-Rhône) und die südfranzösiche Eisenzeit: Ein Beitrag zum Stand de Forschung (Seminar Marburg, Sonderban 10, 1996), in *Europe Celtique, Untersuchungen zur Hallstatt-und Latsnekultur*, ed. T. Stillner. Marburg: Verlag Marie Leidorf, pp. 55–84.

Boissinot, P., 2000. L'environnement at la construction des paysages, in *Les Temps des Gaulois en Provence*, ed. J. Chausserie-Laprée. Martigues: Musée Ziem, pp. 26–30.

2001. Archéologie des vignobles antiques du sud de la Gaule. *Gallia*, 45–68.

Bonanno, A., 2005. L'acqua presso le comunità preistoriche di Malta, in *Il Culto Mediterraneo delle Acque*, Sito archeologico di S. Cristina, 26–28 settembre 2003.

Bonanno, A., T. Gouder, C. Malone, & S. Stoddart, 1990. Monuments in an island society: The Maltese context. *World Archaeology*, 22(2), 190–205.

Bottari, C., M. D'Amico, M. Maugeri, A. Bottari, G. D'Addezio, B. Privitera, & G. Tigano, 2009. Location of the ancient Tindari harbour from geoarchaeological investigations (NE Sicily). *Environmental Archaeology*, 14(1), 37–49.

Bottari, C., & P. Carveni, 2009. Archaeological and historiographical implications of recent uplift of the Peloro Peninsula, NE Sicily. *Quaternary Research*, 72(1), 38–46.

Bottema, S., 1994a. Forest, forest clearance and open land at the time of the Roman Empire in Greece: The palynological record, in *Evaluation of Land Surfaces Cleared from Forests in the Mediterranean Region During the Time of the Roman Empire*, eds. B. Frenzel & L. Reisch. Stuttgart: Gustav Fischer Verlag GmbH, pp. 59–72.

1994b. The prehistoric environment of Greece: A review of the palynological record, in *Beyond the Site – Regional Studies in the Aegean Area*, ed. P. N. Kardulias. New York: University Press of America, pp. 45–68.

Bottema, S., & A. Sarpaki. 2003. Environmental change in Crete: A 9,000-year record of Holocene vegetation history and the effect of the Santorini eruption. *The Holocene*, 13(5), 733–50.

Bottema, S., H. Woldring, & B. Aytug, 1986. Palynological investigations on the relation between prehistoric man and vegetation in Turkey: The Beysehir occupation phase, in *5th OPTIMA Meeting*, Istanbul, pp. 315–28.

Bouby, L., F. Leroy, & L. Carozza, 1999. Food plants from late Bronze Age lagoon sites in Languedoc, southern France: Reconstruction of farming economy and environment. *Vegetation History and Archaeobotany*, 8(1/2), 53–70.

Bourgarit, D., P. Rostan, E. Burger, L. Carozza, & G. Artioli, 2008. The beginning of copper mass production in the western Alps: The Saint Véran mining area reconsidered. *Historical Metallurgy*, 42(1), 1–11.

Bover, P., & J. A. Alcover, 2003. Understanding Late Quaternary extinctions: The case of Myotragus balearicus (Bate, 1909). *Journal of Biogeography*, 30(5), 771–81.

Bover, P., & J. A. Alcover, 2008. Extinction of the autochthonous small mammals of Mallorca (Gymnesic Islands, Western Mediterranean) and its ecological consequences. *Journal of Biogeography*, 35(6), 1112–22.

Boyer, P., N. Roberts, & D. Baird, 2006. Holocene environment and settlement on the Carsamba alluvial fan, south-central Turkey: Integrating geoarchaeology and archaeological field survey. *Geoarchaeology*, 21(7), 675–98.

Bradley, R., 2002. *The Past in Prehistoric Societies*. London: Routledge.

Brandon, C. J., L. H. Robert, & P. O. John, 2008. The concrete construction of the Roman harbours of Baiae and Portus Iulius, Italy: The ROMACONS 2006 field season. *International Journal of Nautical Archaeology*, 37(2), 374–9.

Brandon, L. D., 2012. The influence of climatic change on the Late Bronze Age Collapse and the Greek Dark Ages. *Journal of Archaeological Science*, 39(6), 1862–70.

Braudel, F., 1985. *La Méditerranée et le Monde Méditerrannéen à l'Époque de Philippe II*. Paris: Arnaud Colin.

Brayshaw, D. J., C. M. C. Rambeau, & S. J. Smith, 2011. Changes in Mediterranean climate during the Holocene: Insights from global and regional climate modelling. *The Holocene*, 21(1), 15–31.

Bréhard, S., A. Beeching, & J. D. Vigne, 2010. Shepherds, cowherds and site function on middle Neolithic sites of the Rhône valley: An archaeozoological approach to the organization of territories and societies. *Journal of Anthropological Archaeology*, 29(2), 179–88.

Bresson, A., 2005. Ecology and beyond: The Mediterranean paradigm, in *Rethinking the Mediterranean*, ed. W. V. Harris. Oxford: Oxford University Press, pp. 94–114.

Brewster, H., 1997. *The River Gods of Greece: Myths and Mountain Waters in the Hellenic World*. London: I. B. Tauris.

Brochier, J. L., & A. Beeching, 2006. Grottes bergeries, pastoralisme et mobilit, dans les Alpes au Néolithique, in *Aux Origines de la Transhumance: Les Alpes et la Vie Pastorale d'Hier à Aujourd'hui*, eds. C. Jourdain-Annequin & J. C. Duclos. Paris: Picard, pp. 131–57.

Broodbank, C., 1999. Colonization and configuration in the insular Neolithic of the Aegean, in *Neolithic Society in Greece*, ed. P. Halstead. Sheffield: Sheffield Academic Press, pp. 15–41.

2000. *An Island Archaeology of the Early Cyclades*. New York: Cambridge University Press.

2004. Minoanisation. *Proceedings of the Cambridge Philological Society*, 50, 46–91.

2006. The origins and early development of Mediterranean maritime activity. *Journal of Mediterranean Archaeology*, 19(2), 199–230.

2008. The Early Bronze Age in Cyclades, in *The Aegean Bronze Age*, ed. C. W. Shelmerdine. Cambridge: Cambridge University Press, pp. 47–76.

Brown, A. G., 1997. *Alluvial Geoarchaeology*. Cambridge: Cambridge University Press.

Brown, A. G., & C. Ellis, 1996. People, climate and alluviation: Theory, research design and new sedimentological and stratigraphic data from Etruria. *Papers of the British School at Rome*, 63, 45–73.

Brown, A.G., & K. Walsh, forthcoming. Archaeology and hydro-environment in the Stymphalos Valley from the prehistoric to classical periods. *Geoarchaeology.*

Brückner, H., 1997. Coastal changes in western Turkey: Rapid delta progradation in historical times. *Bulletin de l'Institut oc, Anographique (Monaco)*, 18, 63–74.

Brückner, H., 2001. *Delta Evolution and Culture – Aspects of Geoarchaeological Research in Miletos and Priene*, eds. G. A. Wagner, E. Pernicka, & H. P. Uerpmann. Berlin: Springer, pp. 121–42.

Bruins, H. J., J. A. MacGillivray, C. Synolakis, C. Benjamini, J. Keller, H. J. Kisch, A. Klugel, & J. van der Plicht, 2008. Geoarchaeological tsunami deposits at Palaikastro (Crete) and the Late Minoan IA eruption of Santorini. *Journal of Archaeological Science*, 35(1), 191–212.

Brun, J. P., 2004. *Archéologie du Vin et de l'Huile, de la Préhistoire à l'Époque Hellenistique.* Paris: Éditions Errance.

Bruneton, H., 1999. *Evolution Holocène d'un hydrosystème nord méditerranéen et son environnement géomorphologique. Les plaines d'Arles à l'interface entre le massif des Alpilles et le Rhône.* Unpublished PhD thesis.

2000. La dynamique Holocène des paysages du Marais des Baux: Une première approche morpho-sédimentaire, in *Milieux et Sociétés dans la Vallée des Baux*, eds. P. Leveau & J. P. Saquet. Montpellier: Éditions de l'Association de la Revue archéologique de Narbonnaise, pp. 15–24.

Bruneton, H., G. Arnaud-Fassetta, M. Provansal, & D. Sistach, 2001. Geomorphological evidence for fluvial change during the Roman period in the lower Rhone valley (southern France). *Catena*, 45 (4), 287–312.

Bruni, S., & M. Cosci, 2003. 'Alpheae veterem contemptlor originis urbem quam cingunt geminis Arnus et Ausur aquis'. Il paesaggio di Pisa etrusca e romana: materiali e problemi, in *Il Porto Urbano Di Pisa Antica: La Fase Etrusca il Contesto e il Relitto Ellenostico*, ed. S. Bruni. Milan: Silvana Editoriale, pp. 29–43.

Buchsenschutz, O., 2004. Réflexion sur les parcellaires de L'âge du Fer en France septentrionale, in *La Dynamique des Paysages Protohistoriques, Antiques, Médiévaux et Modernes*, eds. J. Burnouff, J. P. Bravard, & G. Chouquer. Sophia Antipolis: Éditions APDCA, pp. 13–20.

Bugalho, M. N., M. C. Caldeira, J. S. Pereira, J. Aronson, & J. G. Pausas, 2011. Mediterranean cork oak savannas require human use to sustain biodiversity and ecosystem services. *Frontiers in Ecology and the Environment*, 9(5) 278–86.

Bugalho, M. N., X. Lecomte, M. Gonçalves, M. C. Caldeira, & M. Branco, 2011. Establishing grazing and grazing-excluded patches increases plant and invertebrate diversity in a Mediterranean oak woodland. *Forest Ecology and Management*, 261(11), 2133–9.

Burford, A. 1993. *Land and Labor in the Greek World.* Baltimore: Johns Hopkins University Press.

Burjachs, F., R. Perez-Obiol, J. M. Roure, & R. Julia, 1994. Dinaïmica de la vegetacioïn durante el Holoceno en la isla de Mallorca, in *Trabajos de palinología Básica y Aplicada*, eds. I. Mateu, M. Dupré, J. Güemes, & M. E. Burgaz. Valencia: Universitat de València, pp. 199–210.

Burjachs, F., & L. Schulte, 2003. El paisatge vegetal del Penedès entre la prehistoria i el mon antic, in *Territoris antics a la Mediterrània i a la Cossetània oriental: actes del Simposi internacional d'arqueologia del Baix Penedès, El Vendrell, del 8 al 10 de novembre de 2001*, eds. J. Guitart, J. M. Palet, & M. Prevosti. Barcelona: Generalitat de Catalunya Departament de Cultura, pp. 249–54.

Burroughs, W. J., 2005. *Climate Change in Prehistory: The End of the Reign of Chaos.* Cambridge: Cambridge University Press.

Butler, S., 2006. *The Odyssey: Rendered Into English Prose for the Use of Those Who Cannot Read the Original.* Whitefish: Kessinger.

Butzer, K. W., 2005. Environmental history in the Mediterranean world: Crossdisciplinary investigation of cause-and-effect for degradation and soil erosion. *Journal of Archaeological Science*, 32(12), 1773–800.

  2012. Collapse, environment, and society. *Proceedings of the National Academy of Sciences*, 109(10), 3632–9.

Buxton, R., 1994. *Imaginary Greece: The Contexts of Mythology.* Cambridge: Cambridge University Press.

Cagatay, M. N., N. Gorur, O. Algan, C. Eastoe, A. Tchapalyga, D. Ongan, T. Kuhn, & I. Kuscu, 2000. Late Glacial-Holocene palaeoceanography of the Sea of Marmara: Timing of connections with the Mediterranean and the Black Seas. *Marine Geology*, 167(3–4), 191–206.

Calmel-Avila, M., 2002. The Librilla 'rambla', an example of morphogenetic crisis in the Holocene (Murcia, Spain). *Quaternary International*, 93–94, 101–8.

Camin, L., & W. McCall, 2002. Settlement patterns and rural habitation in the middle Cecina Valley between the Hellenistic to Roman age: The case of Podere Cosciano. *Etruscan Studies*, 9(1), 19–27.

Caputo, R., J. P. Bravard, & B. Helly, 1994. The Pliocene-Quaternary tectosedimentary evolution of the Larissa Plain (Eastern Thessaly, Greece). *Geodinamica Acta*, 7(4), 219–31.

Caravello, G. U., & F. Giacomin, 1993. Landscape ecology aspects in a territory centuriated in Roman times. *Landscape and Urban Planning*, 24(1–4), 77–85.

Carayon, N., 2005. Le cothon ou port artificiel creusé. Essai de définition. *Méditerranée*, 104(1.2), 5–13.

Carmona, P., & J. M. Ruiz, 2008. Geoarchaeological study of the Phoenician cemetery of Tyre-Al Bass (Lebanon) and geomorphological evolution of a tombolo. *Geoarchaeology*, 23(3), 334–50.

Caroli, I., & M. Caldara, 2007. Vegetation history of Lago Battaglia (eastern Gargano coast, Apulia, Italy) during the Middle–Late Holocene. *Vegetation History and Archaeobotany*, 16(4), 317–27.

Carozza, L., D. Galop, F. Marembert, & F. Monna, 2005. Quel statut pour les espaces de montagne durant l'âge du Bronze? Regards croisés sur les approches société-environnement dans les Pyrénées occidentales. *Documents d'Archéologie Méridionale*, 28, 7–23.

Carrer, F., 2012. *Etnoarcheologia dei Paesaggi Pastorali nelle Alpi Strategie Insediative Stagionali d'Alta Quota in Trentino, Università degli Studi di Trento*. Unpublished PhD thesis.

Carrión, J. S., A. Andrade, K. D. Bennett, C. Navarro, & M. Munuera, 2001. Crossing forest thresholds: Inertia and collapse in a Holocene sequence from south-central Spain. *The Holocene*, 11(6), 635–54.

Carrión, J. S., & B. Van Geel, 1999. Fine-resolution Upper Weichselian and Holocene palynological record from Navarrés (Valencia, Spain) and a discussion about factors of Mediterranean forest succession. *Review of Palaeobotany and Palynology*, 106(3–4), 209–36.

Carrión, J. S., E. I. Yll, K. J. Willis, & P. Sánchez, 2004. Holocene forest history of the eastern plateaux in the Segura Mountains (Murcia, southeastern Spain). *Review of Palaeobotany and Palynology*, 132(3–4), 219–36.

Carrión, J. S., P. Sánchez-Gomez, J. F. Mota, R. Yll, & C. Chain, 2003. Holocene vegetation dynamics, fire and grazing in the Sierra de Gador, southern Spain. *The Holocene*, 13(6), 839–50.

Carrión, J. S., S. Fernández, P. González-Sampériz, G. Gil-Romera, E. Badal, Y. Carrión-Marco, L. López-Merino, J. A. López-Sáez, E. Fierro, & F. Burjachs, 2010. Expected trends and surprises in the Lateglacial and Holocene vegetation history of the Iberian Peninsula and Balearic Islands. *Review of Palaeobotany and Palynology*, 162(3), 458–75.

Casana, J., 2008. Mediterranean valleys revisited: Linking soil erosion, land use and climate variability in the Northern Levant. *Geomorphology*, 101(3), 429–42.

Castro, P., S. Gili, R. W. Chapman, E. I. Yll, V. Lull, R. Mico & R. Risch, 2000. Archaeology and desertification in the Vera basin (Almería, southeast Spain). *European Journal of Archaeology*, 3(2), 147–66.

Castro, P., R. W. Chapman, S. Gili, V. Lull, R. Mico, C. Rihuete, R. Risch, & M. E. Sanahuja, 1999. Agricultural production and social change in the Bronze Age of southeast Spain: The Gatas Project. *Antiquity*, 73(282), 846–56.

Cenzon-Salvayre, C., & A. Durand, 2011. The cremation structures of the Roman Empire: Anthracological data versus historical sources, in 5th International Meeting of Charcoal Analysis: Charcoal as Cultural and Biological Heritage, *Saguntum*, 11, pp. 191–2.

Chabal, L., 1998. *Forêts et Sociétés en Languedoc (Néolithique Final, Antiquité Tardive)*. Paris: Documents d'Archéologie Française.

Chaniotis, A., 1999. Milking the mountains: Economic activities on the Cretan Uplands in the classical and Hellenistic period, in *From Minoan Farmers to Roman Traders: Sidelights on the Economy of Ancient Crete*, ed. E. Chaniotis. Stuttgart: Franz Steiner Verlag, pp. 181–219.

Chapman, R., 2008. Producing inequalities: Regional sequences in later prehistoric southern Spain. *Journal of World Prehistory*, 21(3–4), 195–260.

Châtelain, T., 2007. *La Grèce antique et ses marais: Perception des milieux palustres chez les Anciens.* Unpublished PhD thesis, Université de Neuchâtel and Université de Paris IV – Sorbonne.

Chen, L., K. A. F. Zonneveld, & G. J. M. Versteegh, 2012. Short term climate variability during 'Roman Classical Period' in the eastern Mediterranean. *Quaternary Science Reviews*, 30(27–8), 3880–91.

Cherkauer, D. S., 1976. The stratigraphy and chronology of the River Treia alluvial deposits, in *A Faliscan Town in South Etruria. Excavations at Narce 1966–71*, ed. T. W. Potter. London: British School at Rome, pp. 106–20.

Cherry, J. F., 1990. The first colonisation of the Mediterranean Islands: A review of recent research. *Journal of Mediterranean Archaeology*, 3(2), 145–221.

2004. Mediterranean island prehistory: What's different and what's new?, in *Voyages of Discovery: The Archaeology of Islands*, ed. S. M. Fitzpatrick. Westport: Greenwood, pp. 234–48.

Cita, M. B., & G. Aloisi, 2000. Deep-sea tsunami deposits triggered by the explosion of Santorini (3,500y BP), eastern Mediterranean. *Sedimentary Geology*, 135(1–4), 181–203.

Cita, M. B., A. Camerlenghi, & B. Rimoldi, 1996. Deep-sea tsunami deposits in the Eastern Mediterranean: New evidence and depositional models. *Sedimentary Geology*, 104(1/4), 155–74.

Claridge, A. J., 2007. Interim report on archaeological fieldwork at Castelporziano April–May 2007. Unpublished report. Accessed online (10 April 2013) from http://www.rhul.ac.uk/classics/laurentineshore/ASSETS/PDF-files/Excavation%20report%20April%202008%20website%20version.pdf

Clark, G., 1968. *Prehistoric Europe: The Economic Basis.* London: Taylor & Francis.

Clendenon, C., 2009. *Hydromythology and the Ancient Greek World: An Earth Science Perspective Emphasizing Karst Hydrology.* Michigan: Fineline Science Press.

Clevis, Q., G. E. Tucker, G. Lock, S. T. Lancaster, N. Gasparini, A. Desitter, & R. L. Bras, 2006. Geoarchaeological simulation of meandering river deposits and settlement distributions: A three-dimensional approach. *Geoarchaeology*, 21(8), 843–74.

Cole, S. G., 1996. Demeter in the ancient Greek city and its countryside, in *Placing the Gods: Sanctuaries and Sacred Space in Ancient Greece*, eds. S. Alcock & R. Osborne. Oxford: Clarendon Press, pp. 199–216.

Collins, P. M., B. A. S. Davis, & J. O. Kaplan, 2012. The mid-Holocene vegetation of the Mediterranean region and southern Europe, and comparison with the present day. *Journal of Biogeography*, 39(10), 1848–61.

Collombier, A. M., 1988. Harbour or harbours of Kition on southeastern coastal Cyprus, in *Archeology of Coastal Changes.* Proceedings of the First International Symposium 'Cities on the Sea. Past and Present', ed. A. Raban. Oxford: British Archaeological Reports, pp. 35–46.

Coltorti, M., 1993. Human impact in the Holocene fluvial and coastal evolution of the Marche region, Central Italy. *Catena*, 30(4), 311–36.

Conacher, A. J., & M. Sala, 1998. *Land Degradation in the Mediterranean Environments of the World: Nature and Extent, Causes and Solutions.* Chichester: John Wiley.

Conedera, M., P. Krebs, W. Tinner, M. Pradella, & D. Torriani, 2004. The cultivation of Castanea sativa (Mill.) in Europe, from its origin to its diffusion on a continental scale. *Vegetation History and Archaeobotany*, 13(3), 161–80.

Constantakopoulou, C., 2007. *The Dance of the Islands: Insularity, Networks, the Athenian Empire, and the Aegean World.* Oxford: Oxford University Press.

Cortés, F. C., O. R. Ariza, J. A. C. Serrano, & A. M. Onorato, 1997. *Hace 4000 Años ... Vida y Muerte en dos Poblados de la Alta Andalucía.* Grenada: Junta de Andalucia.

Cosmopoulos, M. B., 1998. Reconstructing Cycladic prehistory: Naxos in the Early and Middle Late Bronze Age. *Oxford Journal of Archaeology*, 17(2), 127–48.

Costa, L. J., 2004. *Corse Préhistorique: Peuplement d'une Île et Modes de Vie des Sociétés Insulaires (IXe–IIe Millénaires av. J.-C.).* Paris: Éditions Errance.
2008. *Mégalithismes Insulaires en Méditerranée.* Paris: Éditions Errance.

Court-Picon, M., 2007. *Mise en place du paysage dans un milieu de moyenne et haute montagne du tardiglaciaire à l'époque actuelle, L'U.F.R. des Sciences et Techniques de l'Université de Franche Comté.* Unpublished PhD thesis.

Court-Picon, M., K. Walsh, F. Mocci, M. Segard, & J. M. Palet-Martinez, 2007. Occupation de la montagne et transformation des milieux dans les Alpes méridionales au cours de l'âge du Bronze: Approche croisée des données palynologiques et archéologiques en Champsaur et Argentiérois (Hautes-Alpes, France), in *Environnements et Cultures à l'Âge du Bronze en Europe Occidentale*, eds. C. Mordant, H. Richard, & M. Magny. Aris: CTHS, pp. 89–106.

Courtois, C., 1955. *Les Vandales et l'Afrique.* Paris: Arts et Métiers Graphiques.

Cremaschi, M., 2003. Steps and timing of the desertification during Late Antiquity. The case study of the Tanezzuft Oasis (Libyan Shara), in *Arid Lands in Roman Times*, ed. M. Liverani. Florence: All'Insegna del Giglio, pp. 1–14.

Cremaschi, M., & L. Trombino, 1998. The palaeoclimatic significance of paleosols in Southern Fezzan (Libyan Sahara): Morphological and micromorphological aspects. *Catena*, 34(1/2), 131–56.

Cremaschi, M., & S. Di Lernia, 1999. Holocene climatic changes and cultural dynamics in the Libyan Sahara. *African Archaeological Review*, 16(4), 211–38.

Cremaschi, M., C. Pizzi & V. Valsecchi, 2006. Water management and land use in the terramare and a possible climatic co-factor in their abandonment: The case study of the terramara of Poviglio Santa Rosa (northern Italy). *Quaternary International*, 151(1), 87–98.

Cribb, R., 1991. *Nomads in Archaeology*. Cambridge: Cambridge University Press.

Crouch, D. P., 2004. *Geology and Settlement: Greco-Roman Patterns*. New York: Oxford University Press.

Crumley, C. L., 1994a. The ecology of conquest: Contrasting agropastoral and agricultural societies' adaptation to climatic change, in *Historical Ecology: Cultural Knowledge and Changing Landscapes*, ed. C. L. Crumley. Santa Fe: School for Advanced Research Press, pp. 183–201.

    1994b. *Historical Ecology: Cultural Knowledge and Changing Landscapes*. Santa Fe: School for Advanced Research Press.

Dakoronia, P., 1996. Earthquakes of the Late Helladic III period (12th century BC) at Kynos (Livantates, Central Greece), in *Archaeoseismology*, eds. S. C. Stiros & R. E. Jones. Athens: Institute of Geology and Mineral Exploration & The British School at Athens, pp. 41–4.

Dalongeville, R., & J. Rénault-Miskovsky, 1993. Paysages de l'île de Naxos, in *Recherches dans les Cycaldes, Résultats des Travaux de la RCP 583*, eds. R. Dalongeville & G. Rougemont. Lyon: Maison de l'Orient Méditerranéen, pp. 21–32.

Davasse, B., D. Galop, & C. Rendu, 1997. Paysages du Néolithique à nos jours dans les Pyrénées de l'Est d'après l'écologie historique et l'archéologie pastorale, in *La Dynamique des Paysages Protohistoriques, Antiques, Médiévaux et Modernes*, eds. J. Burnouf, J. P. Bravard, & G. Chouquer. Sophia Antipolis: Éditions APDCA, pp. 577–99.

Davidson, D., & C. Tasker, 1982. Geomorphological evolution during the Late Holocene, in *An Island Polity, The Archaeology of Exploitation in Melos*, eds. C. Renfrew & M. Wagstaff. Cambridge: Cambridge University Press, pp. 82–94.

Davidson, D. A., & S. P. Theocharopoulos, 1992. A survey of soil erosion in Viotia, Greece, in *Past and Present Soil Erosion, Archaeological and Geographical Perspectives*, eds. M. Bell & J. Boardman. Oxford: Oxbow, pp. 149–54.

Davis, J. L. & S. E. Alcock 1998. *Sandy Pylos: An Archaeological History from Nestor to Navarino*. Austin: University of Texas Press.

Dawson, H., 2011. Island colonisation: settling the Neolithic question, in *The First Mediterranean Islanders: Initial Occupation and Survival Strategies*, ed. N. Phoca-Cosmetatou. Oxford: David Brown Book Company, pp. 31–53.

de Beaulieu, J.-L., 1977. *Contribution pollenanalytique à l'histoire tardiglaciaire et holocène des Alpes méridonales françaises*. Unpublished PhD thesis, Université Aix-Marseille III, France.

de Beaulieu, J.-L., Y. Miras, V. Andrieu-Ponel, & F. Guiter, 2005. Vegetation dynamics in north-western Mediterranean regions: Instability of the Mediterranean bioclimate. *Plant Biosystems – An International Journal Dealing with all Aspects of Plant Biology*, 139(2), 114–26.

De Boer, J. Z., & J. R. Hale, 2000. The geological origins of the oracle at Delphi, Greece. *Special Publication – Geological Society of London*, 171, 399–412.

de Haas, T., 2011. *Fields, farms and colonists: Intensive field survey and early Roman colonization in the Pontine region, central Italy.* Unpublished PhD thesis, Rijksuniversiteit Groningen.

De Lange, G. J., J. Thomson, A. Reitz, C. P. Slomp, M. Speranza Principato, E. Erba, & C. Corselli, 2008. Synchronous basin-wide formation and redox-controlled preservation of a Mediterranean sapropel. *Nature Geosci*, 1(9), 606–10.

De Meo, A., G. Espa, S. Espa, A. Pifferi, & U. Ricci, 2003. A GIS for the study of the mid-Tiber valley. Comparisons between archaeological settlements of the Sabine Tiberine area. *Journal of Cultural Heritage*, 4(3), 169–73.

De Pascale, A., R. Maggi, C. Montanari, & D. Moreno, 2006. Pollen, herds, jasper and copper mines: Economic and environmental changes during the 4th and 3rd millennia BC in Liguria (NW Italy). *Environmental Archaeology*, 11(1), 115–24.

de Wrachien, D., R. Ragab, & A. Giordano, 2006. Climate change, land degradation, and desertification in the Mediterranean environment. *Desertification in the Mediterranean Region. A Security Issue*, 3, 353–71.

Delano-Smith, C., 1996. Where was the 'wilderness' in Roman times, in *Human Landscapes in Classical Antiquity*, eds. G. Shipley & J. Salmon. London: Routledge, 154–79.

Delhon, C., S. Thiébault, & J.-F. Berger, 2009. Environment and landscape management during the Middle Neolithic in southern France: Evidence for agro-sylvo-pastoral systems in the Middle Rhone Valley. *Quaternary International*, 200(1–2), 50–65.

Di Castri, F., 1981. Mediterranean-type Shrublands of the World, in *Mediterranean-Type Shrublands*, eds. F. Di Castri, D. W. Goodall, & R. L. Specht. Amsterdam: Elsevier, pp. 1–52.

di Pasquale, G., P. di Martino, & S. Mazzoleni, 2004. Forest history in the Mediterranean region, in *Recent Dynamics of the Mediterranean Vegetation and Landscape*, eds. S. Mazzoleni, G. di Pasquale, M. Mulligan, P. di Martino, & F. Rego. Chichester: John Wiley, pp. 13–20.

Di Rita, F., A. Celant, & D. Magri, 2009. Holocene environmental instability in the wetland north of the Tiber delta (Rome, Italy): Sea–lake–man interactions. *Journal of Paleoliminology*, 44(1), 51–67.

Di Rita, F., & D. Magri, 2009. Holocene drought, deforestation and evergreen vegetation development in the central Mediterranean: A 5,500 year record from Lago Alimini Piccolo, Apulia, southeast Italy. *The Holocene*, 19(2), 295–306.

Diodato, N., G. Bellocchi, N. Romano, & G. B. Chirico, 2011. How the aggressiveness of rainfalls in the Mediterranean lands is enhanced by climate change. *Climatic Change*, 108(3), 591–9.

Dixon, J. E., & A. H. F. Robertson, 1996. *The Geological Evolution of the Eastern Mediterranean* (Geological Society Special Publication). London: Geological Society of London.

Drake, D., & T. Hunt, 2009. Invasive rodents on islands: Integrating historical and contemporary ecology. *Biological Invasions*, 11(7), 1483–7.

Drews, R., 1993. *The End of the Bronze Age: Changes in Warfare and the Catastrophe ca 1200 BC*. Princeton: Princeton University Press.

Driessen, J., 1998. *The Troubled Island: Minoan Crete Before and After the Santorini Eruption*. Liège: Université de Liège.

    2002. Towards an archaeology of crisis: Defining the long-term impact of the Bronze Age Santorini eruption, in *Natural Disasters and Cultural Change*, eds. R. Torrence & J. Grattan. London: Routledge, pp. 250–63.

Dubar, M., F. Damblon, S. Nichol-Pichard, J. L. Vernet, L. Chaix, J. Cataliotti, F. Irr, & J. F. Babinot, 1986. L'environnment côtier des Alpes Maritimes à la fin de la transgression versilienne d'après l'étude biostratigraphique du site de l'Etoile à Nice (France). *Revue de Paléobiologie*, 5(2), 289–310.

Duchêne, H., R. Dalongeville, & P. Bernier, 2001. Transformations du Paysage Naturel et évolution du Littoral dans l'Archipel délien, in *Le Paysage Portuaire de la Délos Antique: Recherches sur les Installations Maritimes, Commerciales et Urbaines du Littoral Délien*, eds. H. Duchêne, P. Fraisse, R. Dalongeville, & P. Bernier. Athens/Paris De Boccard: École Française d'Athènes.

Duclos, J. C., 2006. La Pratique de la transhumance d'hier à aujourd'hui, in *Aux Origines de la Transhumance: Les Alpes et la Vie Pastorale d'Hier à Aujourd'hui*, eds. C. Jourdain-Annequin & J. C. Duclos. Paris: Picard, pp. 17–23.

Dufaure, J. J., 1976. Le terrasse Holocène d'Olympie et ses équivalents méditerranéens. *Bulletin de l'Association Géographique Française*, 433, 85–94.

Dusar, B., G. Verstraeten, B. Notebaert, & J. Bakker, 2011. Holocene environmental change and its impact on sediment dynamics in the Eastern Mediterranean. *Earth-Science Reviews*, 108(3–4), 137–57.

Dusar, B., G. Verstraeten, K. D'Haen, J. Bakker, E. Kaptijn, & M. Waelkens, 2012. Sensitivity of the Eastern Mediterranean geomorphic system towards environmental change during the Late Holocene: A chronological perspective. *Journal of Quaternary Science*, 27(4), 371–82.

Eastwood, W. J., J. Tibby, N. Roberts, H. Birks, & H. F. Lamb, 2002. The environmental impact of the Minoan eruption of Santorini (Thera): Statistical analysis of palaeoecological data from Golhisar, southwest Turkey. *The Holocene*, 12(4), 431–44.

Efstratiou, N., P. Biagi, P. Elefanti, P. Karkanas, & M. Ntinou, 2006. Prehistoric exploitation of Grevena highland zones: Hunters and herders along the Pindus chain of western Macedonia (Greece). *World Archaeology*, 38(3), 415–35.

Ejarque, A., 2010. *Génesis y configuracion microregional de un paisaje cultural pirenaico de alta monta a durante el Holoceno: estudio polínico y de otros indicadores paleoambientales en el valle del Madriu-Perafita-Claror (Andorra)*, Institut Catalan d'Arqueologia Clàssica. Unpublished PhD thesis, Universitat Rovira i Virgili.

Ejarque, A., R. Julia, S. Riera, J. M. Palet, H. A. Orengo, Y. Miras, & C. Gascon, 2009. Tracing the history of highland human management in the eastern Pre-Pyrenees: An interdisciplinary palaeoenvironmental study at the Pradell fen, Spain. *The Holocene*, 19(8), 1241–55.

Ejarque, A., Y. Miras, S. Riera, J. M. Palet, & H. Orengo, 2010. Testing microregional variability in the Holocene shaping of high mountain cultural landscapes: A palaeoenvironmental case-study in the eastern Pyrenees. *Journal of Archaeological Science*, 37(7), 1468–79.

Engel, T., 1993. Charcoal remains from an Iron Age copper smelting slag heap at Feinan, Wadi Arabah (Jordan). *Vegetation History and Archaeobotany*, 2(4), 205–11.

Eriksen, T. H., 1993. In which sense do cultural islands exist? *Social Anthropology*, 1, 133–47.

Erlandson, J. M., & S. M. Fitzpatrick, 2006. Oceans, islands, and coasts: Current perspectives on the role of the sea in human prehistory. *Journal of Island and Coastal Archaeology*, 1, 5–32.

Evans, J. D., 1973. Islands as laboratories for the study of culture process, in *The Explanation of Culture Change: Models in Prehistory*, ed. C. Renfrew. London: Duckworth, pp. 517–20.

   1977. Island archaeology in the Mediterranean: Problems and opportunities. *World Archaeology*, 9(1), 12–26.

Evelpidou, N., P. Pirazzoli, A. Vassilopoulos, G. Spada, G. Ruggieri, & A. Tomasin, 2012. Late Holocene sea level reconstructions based on observations of Roman fish tanks, Tyrrhenian coast of Italy. *Geoarchaeology*, 27(3), 259–77.

Evershed, R. P., S. Payne, A. G. Sherratt, M. S. Copley, J. Coolidge, D. Urem-Kotsu, K. Kotsakis, M. Ozdogan, A. E. Ozdogan, O. Nieuwenhuyse, P. M. M. G. Akkermans, D. Bailey, R.-R. Andeescu, S. Campbell, S. Farid, I. Hodder, N. Yalman, M. Ozbasaran, E. Bicakci, Y. Garfinkel, T. Levy, & M. M. Burton, 2008. Earliest date for milk use in the Near East and southeastern Europe linked to cattle herding. *Nature*, 455(7212), 528–31.

Excoffon, P., C. Landuré, & M. Pasqualini, 2004. Habitat et risque fluvial dans le delta du Rhône au Ier s. av. J.- C. Les habitats de la Capelière et du Grand Parc en Camargue, in *Fleuves et Marais, une Histoire au Croisement de la Nature et la Culture: Sociétés Préindustrielles et Milieux Fluviaux, Lacustres et Palustres: Pratiques Sociales et Hydrosystèmes*, eds. J. Burnouf & P. Leveau. Paris: CTHS, pp. 213–34.

Fairbairn, A., E. Asouti, J. Near, & D. Martinoli, 2002. Macro-botanical evidence for plant use at Neolithic Catalhoyuk, southcentral Anatolia, Turkey. *Vegetation History and Archaeobotany*, 11(1/2), 41–54.

Farinetti, E., 2009. *Boeotian landscapes. A GIS-based study for the reconstruction and interpretation of the archaeological datasets of ancient Boeotia.* Unpublished PhD thesis, Leiden University.

Farjon, P., 2007. *Enregistrements sédimentaires des changements climatiques et des activités anthropiques depuis 3000BP dans le lac de la Roche-de-Rame,* Université Paul Cézanne, master's SET.

Faust, D., C. Zielhofer, R. Baena Escudero, & D. del Olmo, 2004. High-resolution fluvial record of late Holocene geomorphic change in northern Tunisia: Climatic or human impact? *Quaternary Science Reviews*, 23(16–17), 1757–75.

Fedele, F., 1992. Steinzeitliche Jäger in den Zentralalpen: Piano dei Cavalli (Splügenpass). *Helvetia Archaeologica*, 89, 2–22.

Fenech, K., 2007. *Human-Induced Changes in the Environment and Landscape of the Maltese Islands from the Neolithic to the 15th Century AD.* Oxford: Archaeopress.

Figueiral, I., L. Bouby, L. Buffat, H. Petitot, & J. F. Terral, 2010. Archaeobotany, vine growing and wine producing in Roman southern France: The site of Gasquinoy (Béziers, Hérault). *Journal of Archaeological Science*, 37(1), 139–49.

Finné, M., & K. Holmgren, 2010. Climate variability in the Eastern Mediterranean and the Middle East during the Holocene, in *The Urban Mind: Cultural and Environmental Dynamics*, eds. P. Sinclair, G. Nordquist, F. Herschend, & C. Isendahl. Uppsala: African and Comparative Archaeology, Department of Archaeology and Ancient History, pp. 29–60.

Finné, M., K. Holmgren, H. S. Sundqvist, E. Weiberg, & M. Lindblom, 2011. Climate in the Eastern Mediterranean, and adjacent regions, during the past 6,000 years – A review. *Journal of Archaeological Science*, 38(12), 3153–73.

Fischer, M., 2005. Peter the Iberian at Yavneh-Yam: Calamities in context, in *Concepts, Pratiques et Enjeux Environnemetaux dans l'Empire Romain*, eds. R. Bedon & E. Hermon. Limoges: Pulim, pp. 267–84.

Flemming, A., 2006. Post-processual landscape archaeology: A critique. *Cambridge Archaeological Journal*, 16(3), 267–80.

Fletcher, W. J., T. Boski, & D. Moura, 2007. Palynological evidence for environmental and climatic change in the lower Guadiana valley, Portugal, during the last 13,000 years. *The Holocene*, 17(4), 481–94.

Fletcher, W. J., & M. F. Sánchez Goñi, 2008. Orbital- and sub-orbital-scale climate impacts on vegetation of the Western Mediterranean basin over the last 48,000 yr. *Quaternary Research*, 70(3), 451–64.

Florido, E., R. Auriemma, S. Faivre, I. Radić Rossi, F. Antonioli, S. Furlani, & G. Spada, 2011. Istrian and Dalmatian fishtanks as sea-level markers. *Quaternary International*, 232(1–2), 105–13.

Follieri, M., D. Magri, & L. Sadori, 1989. Pollen stratigraphical synthesis from Valle di Castiglione (Roma). *Quaternary International*, 3–4, 81–4.

Forbes, H., 2000. Landscape exploitation via pastoralism, in *Landscape and Land Use in Postglacial Greece*, eds. P. Halstead & C. Frederick. Sheffield: Sheffield Academic Press, pp. 95–109.

Forenbaher, S., & P. Miracle, 2005. The spread of farming in the Eastern Adriatic. *Antiquity*, 79, 514–28.

Forman, R. T. T., 1995. *Land Mosaics: The Ecology of Landscapes and Regions*. Cambridge: Cambridge University Press.

Forsyth, T., 1998. Mountain myths revisited: Integrating natural and social environmental science. *Mountain Research and Development*, 18(2), 107–16.

Fouache, E., 1999. *L'Alluvionnement Historique en Grèce Occidentale et au Péloponnèse: Géomorphologie: Géomorphologie, Archéologie, Histoire*. Athens: École Francaise d'Athènes.

Fouache, E., & R. Dalongeville, 2003. Recent relative variations in the shorelines: A contrastive approach of the shores of Croatia and southern Turkey, in *The Mediterranean World Environment and History*, ed. E. Fouache. Paris: Elsevier, pp. 467–78.

Foxhall, L., 1996. Feeling the earth move: Cultivation techniques on steep slopes in classical antiquity, in *Human Landscapes in Classical Antiquity: Environment and Culture*, eds. G. Shipley & J. Salmon. London: Routledge, pp. 44–68.

2007. *Olive Cultivation in Ancient Greece: Seeking the Ancient Economy*. Oxford: Oxford University Press.

Franco Mugica, F., M. Garcia Anton, & O. Sainz, 1998. Vegetation dynamics and human impact in the Sierra de Guadarrama, Central System, Spain. *The Holocene*, 8(1), 69–82.

Frayn, J. M., 1979. *Subsistence Farming in Roman Italy*. London: Centaur Press.

Frederick, C., & A. Krahtopoulou, 2000. Deconstructing agricultural terraces, in *Landscape and Land use in Postglacial Greece*. Sheffield: Sheffield Academic Press, pp. 79–94.

French, E. B., 1996. Evidence for an earthquake at Mycenae, in *Archaeoseismology*, eds. S. C. Stiros & R. E. Jones. Athens: Institute of Geology and Mineral Exploration & The British School at Athens, pp. 51–4.

French, R., 1994. *Ancient Natural History*. London: Routledge.

Frenzel, B., & L. Reisch, 1994. *Evaluation of Land Surfaces Cleared from Forests in the Mediterranean Region During the Time of the Roman Empire*. Stuttgart: Gustav Fischer Verlag.

Fretwell, S. D., & H. L. Lucas, 1969. On territorial behavior and other factors influencing habitat distribution in birds. *Acta biotheoretica*, 19(1), 16–36.

Friedrich, W. L., 2004. *Fire in the Sea: The Santorini Volcano: Natural History and the Legend of Atlantis.* Cambridge: Cambridge University Press.

Frisia, S., A. Borsato, C. Spotl, I. Villa, & F. Cucchi, 2005. Climate variability in the SE Alps of Italy over the past 17,000 years reconstructed from a stalagmite record. *Boreas*, 34(4), 445–55.

Frisone, F., 2012. Rivers, land organization, and identity in Greek Western Apoikíai. *Mediterranean Historical Review*, 27(1), 87–115.

Frost, H., 1995. *Harbours and Proto-harbours: Early Levantine Engineering*, eds. V. Karageorghis & D. Michaelides. Nicosia: University of Cypurs/Cyprus Ports Authority, pp. 1–22.

Frumkin, A., 2009. Stable isotopes of a subfossil Tamarix tree from the Dead Sea region, Israel, and their implications for the Intermediate Bronze Age environmental crisis. *Quaternary Research*, 71(3), 319–28.

Fuchs, M., A. Lang, & G. A. Wagner, 2004. The history of Holocene soil erosion in the Phlious Basin, NE Peloponnese, Greece, based on optical dating. *The Holocene*, 14(3), 334–45.

Fuller, B. T., N. Márquez-Grant, & M. P. Richards, 2010. Investigation of diachronic dietary patterns on the islands of Ibiza and formentera, Spain: Evidence from carbon and nitrogen stable isotope ratio analysis. *American Journal of Physical Anthropology*, 143(4), 512–22.

Fuller, I. C., M. G. Macklin, D. G. Passmore, P. A. Brewer, J. Lewin, & A. G. Wintle, 1996. Geochronologies and environmental records of Quaternary fluvial sequences in the Guadalope basin, northeast Spain, based on luminescence dating. *Geological Society, London, Special Publications*, 115(1), 99–120.

Fuller, I. C., M. G. Macklin, J. Lewin, D. G. Passmore, & A. G. Wintle, 1998. River response to high-frequency climate oscillations in southern Europe over the past 200 k.y. *Geology*, 26(3), 275–8.

Galili, E., B. Rosen, A. Gopher, & H. Kolska, 2002. The emergence and dispersion of the Eastern Mediterranean fishing village: Evidence from submerged Neolithic settlements off the Carmel Coast, Israel. *Journal of Mediterranean Archaeology*, 15(2), 167–98.

Galili, E., D. Zviely, & M. Weinstein-Evron, 2005. Holocene sea-level changes and landscape evolution on the northern Carmel coast (Israel). *Méditerranée*, 104(1.2), 79–86.

Galili, E., M. Weinstein-Evron, I. Hershkovitz, A. Gopher, M. E. Kislev, O. Lernau, L. Kolska-Horwitz, & H. Lernau, 1993. Atlit-Yam: A prehistoric site on the sea floor off the Israeli coast. *Journal of Field Archaeology*, 20 (2), 133–57.

Galop, D., 1998. *La Foret, L'Homme et le Troupeau dans les Pyrénées Toulouse.* Toulouse: GEODE – Université de Toulouse–Le Mirail.

Garcia, D., 2002. Dynamique territoriales en Gaule M,ridionale durant l'âge du Fer, in *Territoires Celtiques: Espaces Ethniques et Territoires des Agglomerations*

Protohistoriques d'Europe Occidentale, eds. D. Garcia & F. Verdin. Paris: Éditions Errances, pp. 88–102.

Garcia, D., F. Mocci, & K. Walsh, 2007. Archéologie de la vallée de l'Ubaye (Alpes-de-Haute-Provence, France): Présentation des premiers résultats d'un Projet collectif de Recherche. *Preistoria Alpina*, 42, 23–48.

Gasco, J., 1994. Development and decline in the Bronze Age of southern France: Languedoc and Provence, in *Development and Decline in the Mediterranean Bronze Age*, eds. C. Mathers & S. Stoddart. Sheffield: Continuum – Sheffield Academic, pp. 99–128.

Gassends, J. M., & B. Maillet, 2004. Structures immergées dans l'anse Saint-Gervais (Fos-sur-Mer, Bouches-du-Rhône), in *Delta du Rhône Camargue Antique, Médiévale et Moderne*, eds. C. Landur, M. Pasqualini, & A. Guilcher. Aix-en-Provence: Service Régional de l'Archéologie, pp. 151–63.

Gerasimidis, A., & N. Athanasiadis, 1995. Woodland history of northern Greece from the mid Holocene to recent time based on evidence from peat pollen profiles. *Vegetation History and Archaeobotany*, 4(2), 109–16.

Ghilardi, M., A. Genç, G. Syrides, J. Bloemendal, D. Psomiadis, T. Paraschou, S. Kunesch, & E. Fouache, 2010. Reconstruction of the landscape history around the remnant arch of the Klidhi Roman Bridge, Thessaloniki Plain, North Central Greece. *Journal of Archaeological Science*, 37(1), 178–91.

Gifford, J. A., 1995. The physical geology of the Western Mesara and Kommos, in *Kommos: An Excavation on the South Coast of Crete. Volume I: The Kommos Region and Houses of the Minoan Town*, eds. J. W. Shaw & M. C. Shaw. Princeton: Princeton University Press, pp. 30–90.

Gifford, J. A., G. Rapp, & V. Vitali, 1992. Paleogeography of Carthage (Tunisia): Coastal change during the first millennium BC. *Journal of Archaeological Science*, 19, 575–96.

Giguet-Covex, C., F. Arnaud, D. Enters, J. Poulenard, L. Millet, P. Francus, F. David, P.-J. Rey, B. Wilhelm, & J.-J. Delannoy, 2012. Frequency and intensity of high-altitude floods over the last 3.5 ka in northwestern French Alps (Lake Anterne). *Quaternary Research*, 77(1), 12–22.

Gilbertson, D., 1996. Explanations: Environment as agency, in *Farming the Desert: The UNESCO Libyan Valleys Archaeological Survey*, ed. G. Barker. London: Society for Libyan Studies, pp. 291–317.

Gilbertson, D., C. O. Hunt, & P. A. Smithson, 1996. Quaternary geomorphology and palaeoecology, in *Farming the Desert: The UNESCO Libyan Valleys Archaeological Survey*, ed. G. Barker. London: Society for Libyan Studies, pp. 49–82.

Gili, S., V. Lull, R. Mico, C. Rihuete, & R. Risch, 2006. An island decides: Megalithic burial rites on Menorca. *Antiquity*, 80(310), 829–42.

Gilman, A., 1976. Bronze Age dynamics in southeast Spain. *Dialectical Anthropology*, 1, 307–19.

Gilman, A., & J. Thornes, 1985. *Land-Use and Prehistory in South-East Spain.* London: G. Allen and Unwin.

Giono, J., 1979. *Batailles dans la Montagne.* Paris: Gallimard.

Giraudi, C., 1998. Late Pleistocene and Holocene lake level variations in Fucino Lake (Abruzzo – Central Italy) inferred from geological, archaeological and historical data. *Paläoklimaforschung, Palaeoclimate Research*, 25, 1–17.

   2004. Le oscillazioni di livello del lago di Mezzano (Valentano-VT): variazioni climatiche e interventi antropici. *Il Quaternario*, 17, 221–30.

   2005. Late-Holocene alluvial events in the Central Apennines, Italy. *The Holocene*, 15(5), 768–73.

Giraudi, C., C. Tata, & L. Paroli, 2009. Late Holocene evolution of Tiber river delta and geoarchaeology of Claudius and Trajan Harbor, Rome. *Geoarchaeology*, 24(3), 371–82.

Giraudi, C., M. Magny, G. Zanchetta, & R. N. Drysdale, 2011. The Holocene climatic evolution of Mediterranean Italy: A review of the continental geological data. *The Holocene*, 21(1), 105–15.

Gkiasta, M., 2010. Social identities, materiality and connectivity, in *Material Connections in the Ancient Mediterranean*, eds. P. Van Dommelen & B. Knapp. London: Routledge, pp. 85–105.

Goalen, M., & D. Fortenberry, 2002. The Villa del Discobolo at Castelporziano on the Tyrrhenian coast of central Italy. *Antiquity*, 76(291), 29–30.

Goiran, J.-P., U. Collalelli, F. Salomon, H. Djerbi, & H. Tronchère, 2009. Découverte d'un niveau marin biologique sur les quais de Portus: Le port antique de Rome. *Méditerranée. Revue Géographique des Pays Méditerranéens*, 112, 59–67.

Goldberg, P., 1994. Interpreting late Quaternary continental sequences in Israel, in *Late Quaternary Chronology and Paleoclimates of the Eastern Mediterranean*, eds. O. Bar-Yosef & R. S. Kra. Arizona: University of Arizona Press: Radiocarbon, pp. 89–102.

Goldberg, P., & O. Bar-Yosef, 1990. The effect of man on geomorphological processes based upon evidence from the Levant and adjacent areas, in *Man's Role in the Shaping of the Eastern Mediterranean Landscape*, eds. S. Bottema, G. Entjes Nieborg, & W. van Zeist. Rotterdam: AA Balkema, pp. 71–85.

Goldin, O., 1997. Ecology of Critias and Platonic metaphysics, in *The Greeks and the Environment*, eds. L. Westra & T. M. Robinson. Oxford: Rowman & Littlefield, pp. 73–80.

Gómez Bellard, C., 1995. The first colonization of Ibiza and Formentera (Balearic Islands, Spain): Some more islands out of the stream? *World Archaeology*, 26(3), 442–55.

   2008. Ibiza: The making of new landscapes, in *Rural Landscapes of the Punic World*, eds. P. Van Dommelen & C. G. Bellard. Sheffield: Equinox, pp. 44–75.

González-Sampériz, P., P. Utrilla, C. Mazo, B. Valero-Garcés, M. C. Sopena, M. Morellón, M. Sebastián, A. Moreno, & M. Martínez-Bea, 2009. Patterns of human occupation during the Early Holocene in the Central Ebro Basin (NE Spain) in response to the 8.2 ka climatic event. *Quaternary Research*, 71(2), 121–32.

Gopher, A., 1993. Sixth–fifth millennia BC settlements in the coastal plain in Israel. *Paléorient*, 19(1), 55–63.

Gophna, R., 1979. Post-Neolithic settlement patterns, in *The Quaternary of Israel*, ed. A. Horowitz. London: Academic Press, pp. 319–21.

Gourley, B., & H. Williams, 2005. The fortifications of ancient Stymphalos. *Mouseion*, 49, 213–59.

Gorokhovich, Y., 2005. Abandonment of Minoan palaces on Crete in relation to the earthquake induced changes in groundwater supply. *Journal of Archaeological Science*, 32(2), 217–22.

Goy, J. L., C. Zazo, & C. J. Dabrio, 2003. A beach-ridge progradation complex reflecting periodical sea-level and climate variability during the Holocene (Gulf of Almeria, Western Mediterranean). *Geomorphology*, 50(1–3), 251–68.

Grattan, J. P., & D. D. Gilbertson, 2000. Prehistoric 'settlement crisis', environmental changes in the British Isles, and volcanic eruptions in Iceland: An exploration of plausible linkages. *Special Publication – Geological Society of America*, 345, 33–42.

Greaves, A. M., 2000. Miletos and the sea: A stormy relationship, in *The Sea in Antiquity*, eds. G. J. Oliver, R. Brock, T. J. Cornell, & S. Hodkinson. Oxford: Archaeopress, pp. 39–61.

Green, S., & M. Lemon, 1996. Perceptual landscapes in agrarian systems: Degradation processes in north-western Epirus and the Argolid Valley, Greece. *Ecumene*, 3(2), 181–99.

Greenfield, H. J., 2010. The secondary products revolution: The past, the present and the future. *World Archaeology*, 42(1), 29–54.

Grima, R., 2008. Landscape, territories, and the life-histories of monuments in temple period Malta. *Journal of Mediterranean Archaeology*, 21(1), 35–56.

Grmek, M., & D. Gourevitch, 1998. *Les Maladies dans l'Art Antique*. Paris: Fayard.

Grove, A. T., 2001. The 'Little Ice Age' and its geomorphological consequences in Mediterranean Europe. *Climatic Change*, 48(1), 121–36.

Grove, A. T., & O. Rackham, 2001. *The Nature of Mediterranean Europe: An Ecological History*. Yale: Yale University Press.

Groves, C. P., 1990. Feral mammals of the Mediterranean islands: Documents of early domestication, in *The Walking Larder: Patterns of Domestication, Pastoralism, and Predation*, ed. J. Clutton-Brock. London: Unwin Hyman, pp. 46–58.

Guerrero-Ayuso, V. M. G., 2001. The Balearic Islands: Prehistoric colonization of the furthest Mediterranean islands from the mainland. *Journal of Mediterranean Archaeology*, 14(2), 136–58.

Guglielmin, M., N. Cannone, & F. Dramis, 2001. Permafrost-glacial evolution during the Holocene in the Italian central alps. *Permafrost and Periglacial Processes*, 12(111), 124.

Guidoboni, E., & J. E. Ebel, 2009. *Earthquakes and Tsunamis in the Past. A Guide to Techniques in Historical Seismology.* Cambridge: Cambridge University Press.

Guilaine, J., 1994. *La Mer Partagée: La Méditerranée avant l'Écriture, 7000–2000 avant Jésus-Christ.* Paris: Hachette.

Guilaine, J., 2003. *De la Vague à la Tombe: La Conquéte Néolithique de la Méditerranée.* Paris: Seuil.

Guillaume, B., H. Pilar, K. Bouchaib, D. Gabriel, & S. Vincent, 2011. Genomic profiling of plastid DNA variation in the Mediterranean olive tree. *BMC Plant Biology*, 11.

Guillet, D., 1983. Toward a cultural ecology of mountains: The central Andes and the Himalayas compared. *Current Anthropology*, 24(5), 561–74.

Gulchard, F., S. Carey, M. A. Arthur, H. Sigurdsson, & M. Arnold, 1996. Tephra from the Minoan eruptions in sediments in the Black Sea. *Nature*, 363, 610–12.

Gunderson, L. H., & C. S. Holling, 2002. *Panarchy: Understanding Transformations in Human and Natural Systems.* Washington: Island Press.

Gvirtzman, G., & M. Wieder, 2001. Climate of the last 53,000 years in the Eastern Mediterranean, based on soil-sequence stratigraphy in the coastal plain of Israel. *Quaternary Science Reviews*, 20(18), 1827–49.

Hadjidaki, E., 1988. Preliminary report of excavations at the harbour of Phalsarna in west Crete. *American Journal of Archaeology*, 92(4), 463–79.

Halstead, P., 2008. Between a rock and a hard place: Coping with marginal colonisation in the Later Neolithic and Early Bronze Age of Crete and the Aegean, in *Escaping the Labyrinth: The Cretan Neolithic in Context*, eds. V. Isaakidou & P. Tomkins. Oxford: Oxbow Books, 229–57.

Halstead, P., & G. Jones, 1989. Agrarian ecology in the Greek islands: Time stress, scale and risk. *Journal of Hellenic Studies*, 109, 41–55.

Hamilakis, Y., 1996. Wine, oil and the dialectics of power in Bronze Age Crete: A review of the evidence. *Oxford Journal of Archaeology*, 15(1), 1–32.

Hamilton, S., R. Whitehouse, K. Brown, P. Combes, E. Herring, & M. S. Thomas, 2006. Phenomenology in practice: Towards a methodology for a subjective approach. *European Journal of Archaeology*, 9(1), 31–71.

Hancock, P. L., & E. Altunel, 1997. Faulted archaeological relics at Hierapolis (Pamukkale), Turkey. *Journal of Geodynamics*, 24(1–4), 21–36.

Harding, A., J. Palutikof, & T. Holt, 2009. The climate system, in *The Physical Geography of the Mediterranean*, ed. J. C. Woodward. Oxford: Oxford University Press, pp. 69–88.

Harfouche, R., 2007. *Histoire des Paysages Méditerranéens Terrassés: aménagements et Agriculture*. Oxford: Archaeopress.

Harris, W. V., 2005a. The Mediterranean and ancient history, in *Rethinking the Mediterranean*, ed. W. V. Harris. Oxford: Oxford University Press, pp. 1–38.

2005b. *Rethinking the Mediterranean*. Oxford: Oxford University Press.

Harrison, R. J., 1994. The Bronze Age in northern and northeastern Spain, in *Development and Decline in the Mediterranean Bronze Age*, eds. C. Mathers & S. Stoddart. Sheffield: Continuum – Sheffield Academic, pp. 73–97.

Hay, P., 2006. A phenomenology of islands. *Island Studies Journal*, 1(1), 19–42.

Heiken, G., F. McCoy, & M. Sheridan, 1990. Palaeotopographic and palaeogeologic reconstruction of Minoan Thera, in *Thera and the Aegean World III. Vol. 2: Earth Sciences*, eds. D. A. Hardy, J. Keller, V. P. Galanopoulos, N. C. Flemming, & T. H. Druitt. London: Thera Foundation, pp. 370–6.

Heiken, G., R. Funiciello, & D. De Rita, 2005. *The Seven Hills of Rome*. Princeton: Princeton University Press.

Heinz, C., I. Figueiral, J. F. Terral, & F. Claustre, 2004. Holocene vegetation changes in the northwestern Mediterranean: New palaeoecological data from charcoal analysis and quantitative eco-anatomy. *The Holocene*, 14(4), 621–7.

Heinz, C., & S. Thiebault, 1998. Characterization and palaeoecological significance of archaeological charcoal assemblages during late and post-glacial phases in southern France. *Quaternary Research*, 50(1), 56–68.

Henry, D. O., 1994. Prehistoric cultural ecology in southern Jordan. *Science*, 265, 336–41.

Henry, F., 2009. *Origine et dynamique long terme d'un écosystème herbacé, pseudo steppique, le cas de la plaine de La Crau (Bouches du Rhône, France)*. Unpublished PhD thesis, Université Paul Cézanne Aix-Marseille III.

Henry, F., B. Talon, & T. Dutoit, 2010. The age and history of the French Mediterranean steppe revisited by soil wood charcoal analysis. *The Holocene*, 20(1), 25–34.

Herva, V. P., 2006. Flower lovers, after all? Rethinking religion and human–environment relations in Minoan Crete. *World Archaeology*, 38(4), 586–98.

Hieke, W., & F. Werner, 2000. The Augias megaturbidite in the central Ionian Sea (Central Mediterranean) and its relation to the Holocene Santorini event. *Sedimentary Geology*, 135(1–4), 205–18.

Higginbotham, J. A., 1997. *Piscinae: Artificial Fishponds in Roman Italy*. Chapel Hill: University of North Carolina Press.

Higgins, C., 1966. Possible disappearance of Mycenean coastal settlements of the Messenian Peninsula. *American Journal of Archaeology*, 70(1), 23–9.

Higgs, E., 1978. Environmental changes in northern Greece, in *Environmental History of the Near and Middle East*, ed. W. G. Brice. London: Academic Press, pp. 41–9.

Hitchner, R. B., 1988. The Kasserine archaeological survey, 1982–1986. *Antiquités Africaines*, 24, 7–41.

1990. The Kasserine archaeological survey, 1987. *Antiquités Africaines*, 26, 231–60.

Hodge, A. T., 1995. *Roman Aqueducts and Water Supply*. London: Gerald Duckworth.

Hoekstra, A. Y., & M. M. Mekonnen, 2012. The water footprint of humanity. *Proceedings of the National Academy of Sciences*, 109(9), 3232–7.

Hoffman, G., & H. D. Schulz, 1988. Coastline shifts and Holocene stratigraphy on the Mediterranean coast of Andalucia (southeastern Spain), in *Archaeology of Coastal Changes*. Proceedings of the First International Symposium 'Cities on the Sea. Past and Present', ed. A. Raban. Oxford: B.A.R., pp. 53–70.

Höghammar, K., 2010. Long-term resilience: The reconstruction of the ancient Greek polis of Kos after earthquakes in the period c. 200 BCE to c. 200 CE, in *The Urban Mind: Cultural and Environmental Dynamics*, eds. P. Sinclair, G. Nordquist, F. Herschend, & C. Isendahl. Uppsala: African and Comparative Archaeology, Department of Archaeology and Ancient History, pp. 261–75.

Hohlfelder, R. L., 1976. The ports of Roman Baetica: A preliminary reconnaissance. *Journal of Field Archaeology*, 3, 465–8.

Holtvoeth, J., H. Vogel, B. Wagner, & G. Wolff, 2010. Lipid biomarkers in Holocene and glacial sediments from ancient Lake Ohrid (Macedonia, Albania). *Biogeosciences*, 7(11), 3473–89.

Hooke, J. M., 2006. Human impacts on fluvial systems in the Mediterranean region. *Geomorphology*, 79(3–4), 311–35.

Horden, P., & N. Purcell, 2000. *The Corrupting Sea: A Study of Mediterranean History*. Oxford: Blackwell.

Howard, A. J., & M. G. Macklin, 1999. A guide for archaeologists investigating Holocene landscapes. *Antiquity*, 73(281), 527–41.

Hughes, J. D., 1994a. Ecology in ancient Mesopotamia, in *Green History: A Reader in Environmental Literature, Philosophy and Politics*, ed. D. Wall. London: Routledge, pp. 33–5.

1994b. *Pan's Travail: Environmental Problems of the Ancient Greeks and Romans*. Baltimore: Johns Hopkins University Press.

2005. *The Mediterranean: An Environmental History*. Santa Barbara: ABC-CLIO.

Hunt, C., 1995. The natural landscape and its evolution, in *A Mediterranean Valley: Landscape Archaeology and Annales History in the Biferno Valley*, ed. G. Barker. London: Leicester University Press, pp. 62–83.

Iakovidis, S., 2001. Gla and the Kopais in the 13th century BC. *Library of the Archaeological Society at Athens*, 221.

Isoardi, D., 2010a. Découverte récente à Arles d'aménagements de berge du Rhône datés du Haut-Empire, in *Seminaire d'Antiquités Nationales, Centre Camille Jullian.*

    2010b. *Rapport de Fouille de Sauvetage au Lieu-dit 5, Place Jean-Baptiste Massillon (Arles) – 2009. Rapport de Fouille.* Aix-en-Provence: S.R.A. – P.A.C.A.

Issar, A. S., Y. Govrin, M. A. Geyh, E. Wakshal, & M. Wolf, 1992. Climate changes during the Upper Holocene in Israel. *Israel Journal of Earth-Sciences,* 40(1–4), 219–23.

Jackson, J. B. C., M. X. Kirby, W. H. Berger, K. A. Bjorndal, L. W. Botsford, B. J. Bourque, R. H. Bradbury, R. Cooke, J. Erlandson, J. A. Estes, T. P. Hughes, S. Kidwell, C. B. Lange, H. S. Lenihan, J. M. Pandolfi, C. H. Peterson, R. S. Steneck, M. J. Tegner, & R. R. Warner, 2001. Historical overfishing and the recent collapse of coastal ecosystems. *Science,* 293(5530), 629–37.

Jacob, J., J. R. Disnar, F. Arnaud, E. Gauthier, Y. Billaud, E. Chapron, & G. Bardoux, 2009. Impacts of new agricultural practices on soil erosion during the Bronze Age in the French Prealps. *The Holocene,* 19(2), 241–9.

Jahns, S., 1993. On the Holocene vegetation history of the Argive Plain (Peloponnese, southern Greece). *Vegetation History and Archaeobotany,* 2, 187–203.

Jalut, G., A. Esteban Amat, L. Bonnet, T. Gauquelin, & M. Fontugne, 2000. Holocene climatic changes in the Western Mediterranean, from south-east France to south-east Spain. *Palaeogeography Palaeoclimatology Palaeoecology,* 160(3–4), 255–90.

James, P., C. Mee, & J. G. Taylor, 1994. Soil erosion and the archaeological landscape of Methana, Greece. *The Journal of Field Archaeology,* 21(4), 395–416.

Jeftic, L., S. Keckes, & J. C. Pernetta, 1996. *Climatic Change and the Mediterranean: Environmental and Societal Impacts of Climate Change and Sea Level Rise in the Mediterranean Region.* London: Edward Arnold.

Jenny, H., 1994. *Factors of Soil Formation: A System of Quantitative Pedology.* New York: Dover.

Jiménez-Brobeil, S. A., P. du Souich, & I. Al Oumaoui, 2009. Possible relationship of cranial traumatic injuries with violence in the south-east Iberian Peninsula from the Neolithic to the Bronze Age. *American Journal of Physical Anthropology,* 140(3), 465–75.

Joffre, R., S. Rambal, & J. Ratte, 1999. The dehesa system of southern Spain and Portugal as a natural ecosystem mimic. *Agroforestry Systems,* 45(1), 57–79.

Johnson, M., 2007. *Ideas of Landscape.* Oxford: Blackwell.

Jolivet, L., J.-P. Brun, B. Meyer, G. Prouteau, & Collectif, 2008. *Géodynamique Méditerranéenne.* Paris: Vuibert.

Jones, R. E., & S. C. Stiros, 2000. The advent of archaeoseismology in the Mediterranean. *Special Publication – Geological Society of London,* 171, 25–32.

Jorda, M., & F. Mocci, 1997. Sites protohistoriques et gallo-romains du massif Sainte-Victoire dans leur contexte morphodynamique, in *La Dynamique des Paysages Protohistoriques, Antiques, Médiévaux et Modernes*, eds. J. Burnouf, J. P. Bravard, & G. Chouquer. Sophia Antipolis: APDCA, pp. 211–30.

Jorda, M., & M. Provansal, 1989. Le site de Glanum et l'histoire de l'environnement. *Les Dossiers de l'Archéologie*, 140(juillet–août), 2–7.

Jorda, M., & M. Provansal, 1996. Impact de l'anthropisation et du climat sur le detritisme en France du sud-est (Alpes du sud et Provence). *Bulletin – Société Géologique de France*, 167(1), 159–68.

Jost, M., 1996. The distribution of sanctuaries in civic space in Arkadia, in *Placing the Gods: Sanctuaries and Sacred Space in Ancient Greece*, eds. S. Alcock & R. Osborne. Oxford: Clarendon Press, pp. 217–30.

Judson, S., 1963. Stream changes during historic time in east-central Sicily. *American Journal of Archaeology*, 67(3), 287–9.

Judson, S., & A. Kahane, 1963. Underground drainageways in southern Etruria and northern Latium. *Papers of the British School at Rome*, 31, 74–99.

Jusseret, S., 2010. Socializing geoarchaeology: Insights from Bourdieu's theory of practice applied to Neolithic and Bronze Age Crete. *Geoarchaeology*, 25(6), 675–708.

Kaniewski, D., V. De Laet, E. Paulissen, & M. Waelkens, 2007. Long-term effects of human impact on mountainous ecosystems, western Taurus Mountains, Turkey. *Journal of Biogeography*, 34(11), 1975–97.

Kaniewski, D., E. Paulissen, E. Van Campo, H. Weiss, T. Otto, J. Bretschneider, & K. Van Lerberghe, 2010. Late second–early first millennium BC abrupt climate changes in coastal Syria and their possible significance for the history of the Eastern Mediterranean. *Quaternary Research*, 74(2), 207–15.

Katsouras, G., A. Gogou, I. Bouloubassi, K.-C. Emeis, M. Triantaphyllou, G. Roussakis, & V. Lykousis, 2010. Organic carbon distribution and isotopic composition in three records from the Eastern Mediterranean Sea during the Holocene. *Organic Geochemistry*, 41(9), 935–9.

Keay, S. J., M. Millett, L. Paroli, & K. Strutt, 2006. *Portus: An Archaeological Survey of the Port of Imperial Rome*. Rome: British School at Rome.

Keller, J., T. Rehren, & E. Stadlbauer, 1990. Explosive volcanism in the Hellenic arc: A summary and review, in *Thera and the Aegean World III. Vol. 2: Earth Sciences*, eds. D. A. Hardy, J. Keller, V. P. Galanopoulos, N. C. Flemming, & T. H. Druitt. London: Thera Foundation.

Keys, D., 1999. *Catastrophe: An Investigation into the Origins of the Modern World*. London: Arrow.

Kislev, M. E., A. Hartmann, & E. Galili, 2004. Archaeobotanical and archaeoentomological evidence from a well at Atlit-Yam indicates colder, more humid climate on the Israeli coast during the PPNC period. *Journal of Archaeological Science*, 31(9), 1301–10.

Knapp, A. B., 2008. *Prehistoric and Protohistoric Cyprus: Identity, Insularity, and Connectivity*. Oxford: Oxford University Press.

2010. Cyprus's earliest prehistory: Seafarers, foragers and settlers. *Journal of World Prehistory*, 23(2), 79–120.

Knappett, C., T. Evans, & R. Rivers, 2011. The Theran eruption and Minoan palatial collapse: New interpretations gained from modelling the maritime network. *Antiquity*, 85(229), 1008–23.

Knauss, J., 1985. Die Melioration des Kopais-Beckens im Altertum und heute. The reclamation of the Copais basin in the antiquity and today. *Wasser und Boden*, 37(12), 611–14.

Kolstrup, E., 1994. Late Holocene pollen records from the Segermes valley, NE Tunisia. *Historical Biology: An International Journal of Paleobiology*, 9(1), 131–6.

Kontogianni, V. A., N. Tsoulos, & S. C. Stiros, 2002. Coastal uplift, earthquakes and active faulting of Rhodes Island (Aegean Arc): Modeling based on geodetic inversion. *Marine Geology*, 186(3–4), 299–317.

Kosmas, C., N. Danalatos, F. Lopez-Bermedez, & M. A. Romero Diz, 2002. The effect of land use on soil erosion and land degradation under Mediterranean conditions, in *Mediterranean Desertification: A Mosaic of Processes and Responses*, eds. N. Geeson, C. J. Brandt, & J. B. Thornes. New York: John Wiley, pp. 58–70.

Kotthoff, U., U. C. Muller, J. Pross, G. Schmiedl, I. T. Lawson, B. van de Schootbrugge, & H. Schulz, 2008. Lateglacial and Holocene vegetation dynamics in the Aegean region: An integrated view based on pollen data from marine and terrestrial archives. *The Holocene*, 18(7), 1019–32.

Krahtopoulou, A., 2000. Holocene alluvial history of northern Pieria, Macedonia, Greece, in *Landscape and Land Use in Postglacial Greece*, eds. P. Halstead & C. Frederick. Sheffield: Sheffield Academic Press, pp. 15–27.

Kristiansen, K., & T. B. Larsson, 2005. *The Rise of Bronze Age Society: Travels, Transmissions and Transformations*. Cambridge: Cambridge University Press.

Kuniholm, P. A., 1990. Archaeological evidence and non-evidence for climatic change. *Philosophical Transactions of the Royal Society of London. Series A, Mathematical and Physical Sciences*, 330(1615), 645–55.

1996. Anatolian tree rings and the absolute chronology of the Eastern Mediterranean 2220–718 BC. *Nature*, 381(27), 780–3.

Kuzucuoglu, C., W. Dörfler, S. Kunesch, & F. Goupille, 2011. Mid- to Late-Holocene climate change in central Turkey: The Tecer Lake record. *The Holocene*, 21(1), 173–88.

Laborel, J., 1986. Vermetid gastropods as sea-level indicators, in *Sea Level Research, A Manual for Collection and Evaluation of Data*, ed. O. Van de Plassche. Norwich: Geo Books, pp. 28–310.

Laborel, J., & F. Laborel-Deguen, 1994. Biological indicators of relative sea-level variations and of co-seismic displacements in the Mediterranean region. *Journal of Coastal Research*, 10(2), 395–415.

Lamb, H. F., F. Damblon, & R. W. Maxted, 1991. Human impact on the vegetation of the Middle Atlas, Morocco, during the last 5,000 years. *Journal of Biogeography*, 18, 519–32.

Lamb, H. F., & S. Van der Kaars, 1995. Vegetational response to Holocene climatic change: Pollen and palaeolimnological data from the Middle Atlas, Morocco. *The Holocene*, 5(4), 400–8.

Lamb, H. F., U. Eicher, & V. R. Switsur, 1989. An 18,000-year record of vegetation, lake-level and climatic change from Tigalmamine, Middle Atlas, Morocco. *Journal of Biogeography*, 16(1), 65–74.

Lambeck, K., F. Antonioli, A. Purcell, & S. Silenzi, 2004. Sea-level change along the Italian coast for the past 10,000yr. *Quaternary Science Reviews*, 23(14–15), 1567–98.

Lambeck, K., F. Antonioli, M. Anzidei, L. Ferranti, G. Leoni, G. Scicchitano, & S. Silenzi, 2011. Sea level change along the Italian coast during the Holocene and projections for the future. *Quaternary International*, 232(1–2), 250–7.

LaMoreaux, P. E., 1995. Worldwide environmental impacts from the eruption of Thera. *Environmental Geology*, 26(3), 172–81.

Lanfranchi, F. d., & M. C. Weiss, 1973. *La Civilisation des Corses: Les Origines.* Ajaccio: Éditions Cyrnos.

Lanfranchi, F. d., & M. C. Weiss, 1997. *L'Aventure Humaine Préhistorique en Corse.* Ajaccio: Éditions Albiana.

Laskaris, N., A. Sampson, F. Mavridis, & I. Liritzis, 2011. Late Pleistocene/ Early Holocene seafaring in the Aegean: New obsidian hydration dates with the SIMS-SS method. *Journal of Archaeological Science*, 38(9), 2475–9.

Latour, B., 1997. *Nous N'avons Jamais Été Modernes.* Paris: La Découverte.

Laurens, H. 2010. *Le Rêve Méditerranéen: Grandeurs et Avatars.* Paris: CNRS.

Laval, H., J. Medus, & M. Roux, 1991. Palynological and sedimentological records of Holocene human impact for the Etang de Berre, southeastern France. *The Holocene*, 1(3), 269–72.

Le Gall, J., 1953. *Le Tibre: Fleuve de Rome dans l'Antiquité.* Paris: Presses Universitaires de France.

Leighton, R., 1999. *Sicily Before History: An Archaeological Survey from the Palaeolithic to the Iron Age.* London: Duckworth.

Leroy, S. A. G., S. Marco, R. Bookman, & C. S. Miller, 2010. Impact of earthquakes on agriculture during the Roman-Byzantine period from pollen records of the Dead Sea laminated sediment. *Quaternary Research*, 73(2), 191–200.

Lespez, L., 2003. Geomorphic responses to long-term land use changes in eastern Macedonia (Greece). *Catena*, 51(3–4), 181–208.

Leveau, P., 1977. L'opposition de la montagne et de la plaine dans l'historiographie de l'Afrique du Nord antique. *Annales de Géographie*, 86, 201–5.

1986. Occupation du sol, géosystème et systèmes sociaux. Rome et ses ene-
    mis des montagnes et du desert dans le Maghreb antique. *Annales ESC*, 6,
    1345–58.

1995. *Les moulins romains de Barbegal, les ponts-aqueducs du vallon des Arcs
    et l'histoire naturelle de la vallé des Baux (Bilan de six ans de fouilles pro-
    grammées)*. Paris: Comptes Rendus de l'Académie des Inscriptions et Belles
    Lettres, pp. 115–44.

Leveau, P., 2008a. La ville romaine alpine dans son contexte environnemental:
    Géoarchéologie et histoire du climat dans les Alpes, in *La Ville des Alpes
    Occidentales à l'Époque Romaine*, eds. P. Leveau & B. Rémy. Grenoble: Les
    Cahiers du CRHIPA, pp. 47–99.

Leveau, P., 2008b. Les inondations du Tibre à Rome: Politiques publiques et
    variations climatiques à l'époque romaine, in *Vers une Gestion Intégrée de
    l'Eau dans l'Empire Romain. Actes du Colloque International Université
    Laval Octobre 2006–290 p*, ed. E. Hermon. Rome: L'Erma di Bretschneider,
    pp. 137–46.

2009. Les conditions environnementales dans le nord de l'Afrique à l'époque
    romaine. Contribution historiographique à l'histoire du climat et des rela-
    tions homme/milieu, in *Sociétés et Climats dans l'Empire Romain. Pour
    une Perspective Historique et Systémique de la Gestion des Ressources en Eau
    dans l'Empire Romain*, ed. E. Hermon. Naples: Editoriale Scientifica,
    pp. 308–48.

Leveau, P., & J. M. Palet-Martinez, 2010. Les Pyrénées romaines, la frontière,
    la ville et la montagne. L'apport de l'archéologie du paysage. *Pallas*, 82,
    171–98.

Leveau, P., K. Walsh, G. Bertucchi, H. Bruneton, & B. Tremmel, 2000. Le
    Troisieme siècle dans la Valle des Baux: Les fouilles de la partie basse et
    de lemissaire oriental des moulins de Barbegal. *Revue d'Archéologie
    Narbonnaise*, 33, 387–439.

Leveau, P., P. Sillières, & J. P. Vallat, 1993. *Campagnes de la Méditerranée
    Romaine*. Paris: Hachette.

Lewin, J., & J. C. Woodward, 2009. Karst geomorphology and environmental
    change, in *The Physical Geography of the Mediterranean*, ed. J. C. Woodward.
    Oxford: Oxford University Press, pp. 287–317.

Lichardus, J., M. Lichardus-Itten, G. Bailloud, & J. Cauvin, 1985. *La Protohistoire
    de l'Europe: Le Néolithique et le Chalcolithique*. Paris: Presses Universitaires
    de France.

Lillios, K. T., 1997. The third millennium BC in Iberia: Chronometric evidence
    for settlement histories and socio-cultural change, in *Third Millenium BC
    Climate Change and Old World Collapse*, eds. H. N. Dalfes, G. Kukla, &
    H. Weiss. Berlin: Springer, pp. 173–91.

Lippi, M. M., C. Bellini, C. Trinci, M. Benvenuti, P. Pallecchi, & M. Sagri,
    2007. Pollen analysis of the ship site of Pisa San Rossore, Tuscany, Italy: The

implications for catastrophic hydrological events and climatic change during the late Holocene. *Vegetation History and Archaeobotany*, 16(6), 453–65.

Llobera, M., & T. J. Sluckin, 2007. Zigzagging: Theoretical insights on climbing strategies. *Journal of Theoretical Biology*, 249(2), 206–17.

Lolos, Y. A., 1997. The Hadrianic aqueduct of Corinth (with an Appendix on the Roman aqueducts in Greece). *Hesperia*, 66(2) 271–314.

López-Bermudez, F., A. Romero-Diaz, & J. Martinez-Fernandez, 1998. Vegetation and soil erosion under a semi-arid Mediterranean climate: A case study from Murcia (Spain). *Geomorphology*, 24(1), 51–8.

López de Heredia, U., J. S. Carrión, P. Jiménez, C. Collada, & L. Gil, 2007. Molecular and palaeoecological evidence for multiple glacial refugia for evergreen oaks on the Iberian Peninsula. *Journal of Biogeography*, 34(9), 1505–17.

López-Merino, L., & J. A. López-Sáez, 2009. 2,000 years of pastoralism and fire shaping high-altitude vegetation of Sierra de Gredos in central Spain. *Review of Palaeobotany and Palynology*, 158(1–2), 42–51.

Lowe, J. J., C. Davite, D. Moreno, & R. Maggi, 1994. Holocene pollen stratigraphy and human interference in the woodlands of the northern Appennines, Italy. *The Holocene*, 4, 153–64.

Lucas, G., 2005. *The Archaeology of Time*. London: Routledge.

Lumaret, R., & N. Ouazzani, 2001. Plant genetics: Ancient wild olives in Mediterranean forests. *Nature*, 413(6857), 700.

MacArthur, R. H., & E. O. Wilson, 1967. *Island Biogeography*. Princeton: Princeton University Press.

Macklin, M. G., I. C. Fuller, J. Lewin, G. S. Maas, D. G. Passmore, J. Rose, J. C. Woodward, S. Black, R. H. B. Hamlin, & J. S. Rowan, 2002. Correlation of fluvial sequences in the Mediterranean basin over the last 200 ka and their relationship to climate change. *Quaternary Science Reviews*, 21(14–15), 1633–41.

Macklin, M. G., & J. C. Woodward, 2009. River systems and environmental change, in *The Physical Geography of the Mediterranean*, ed. J. C. Woodward. Oxford: Oxford University Press, pp. 319–52.

Macklin, M. G., S. Tooth, P. A. Brewer, P. Noble, & G. A. Duller, 2010. Holocene flooding and river development in a Mediterranean steepland catchment: The Anapodaris Gorge, south central Crete, Greece. *Global and Planetary Change*, 70(1), 35–52.

Maggi, R., 1999. *Coast and Uplands in Liguria and Northern Tuscany from the Mesolithic to the Bronze Age*, eds. R. H. Tykot, J. Morter, & J. Robb. London: Accordia Research Institute University of London, pp. 48–65.

Magny, M., B. Vanniere, G. Zanchetta, E. Fouache, G. Touchais, L. Petrika, C. Coussot, A. V. Walter-Simonnet, & F. Arnaud, 2009. Possible complexity of the climatic event around 4300–3800 Cal. BP in the Central and Western Mediterranean. *The Holocene*, 19(6), 823–33.

Magny, M., C. Miramont, & O. Sivan, 2002. Assessment of the impact of climate and anthropogenic factors on Holocene Mediterranean vegetation in Europe on the basis of palaeohydrological records. *Palaeogeography Palaeoclimatology Palaeoecology*, 186(1–2), 47–59.

Magny, M., D. Galop, P. Bellintani, M. Desmet, J. Didier, J. N. Haas, N. Martinelli, A. Pedrotti, R. Scandolari, A. Stock, & B. Vanniere, 2009a. Late-Holocene climatic variability south of the Alps as recorded by lake-level fluctuations at Lake Ledro, Trentino, Italy. *The Holocene*, 19(4), 575–89.

Magny, M., J.-L. de Beaulieu, R. Drescher-Schneider, B. Vannière, A.-V. Walter-Simonnet, Y. Miras, L. Millet, G. Bossuet, O. Peyron, & E. Brugiapaglia, 2007. Holocene climate changes in the central Mediterranean as recorded by lake-level fluctuations at Lake Accesa (Tuscany, Italy). *Quaternary Science Reviews*, 26(13), 1736–58.

Magny, M., & J. N. Haas, 2004. A major widespread climatic change around 5300 Cal. yr BP at the time of the Alpine Iceman. *Journal of Quaternary Science*, 19(5), 423–30.

Magny, M., O. Peyron, L. Sadori, E. Ortu, G. Zanchetta, B. Vannière, & W. Tinner, 2012. Contrasting patterns of precipitation seasonality during the Holocene in the South- and North-Central Mediterranean. *Journal of Quaternary Science*, 27(3), 290–6.

Magri, D., 1995. Some questions on the Late-Holocene vegetation of Europe. *The Holocene*, 5(3), 354–60.

Magri, D., & L. Sadori, 1999. Late Pleistocene and Holocene pollen stratigraphy at Lago di Vico, central Italy. *Vegetation History and Archaeobotany*, 8(4), 247–60.

Mahoney, T. A., 1997. Platonic ecology, deep ecology, in *The Greeks and the Environment*, eds. L. Westra & T. M. Robinson. Oxford: Rowman & Littlefield, pp. 45–54.

Malone, C., 2003. The Italian Neolithic: A synthesis of research. *Journal of World Prehistory*, 17(3), 235–312.

Malone, C., S. Stoddart, & A. Bonanno, 2009. *Mortuary customs in prehistoric Malta: Excavations at the Brochtorff circle at Xagħra (1987–94)*. Cambridge: McDonald Institute for Archaelogical Research.

Malone, C., S. Stoddart, G. Barker, G. Clark, M. Coltorti, L. Costantini, J. Giorgi, J. Harding, C. Hunt, T. Reynold, & R. Skeates, 1992. The neolithic site of San Marco, Gubbio (Perugia), Umbria: Survey and excavation 1985–87. *Papers of the British School at Rome*, LX, 1–69.

Mangini, A., C. Spötl, & P. Verdes, 2005. Reconstruction of temperature in the Central Alps during the past 2000 yr from a δ18O stalagmite record. *Earth and Planetary Science Letters*, 235(3–4), 741–51.

Manning, J. G., & I. Morris, 2007. Introduction, in *The Ancient Economy: Evidence and Models*, eds. J. G. Manning & I. Morris. Stanford: Stanford University Press, pp. 1–44.

Manning, S. W., 1999. *A Test of Time: The Volcano of Thera and the Chronology and History of the Aegean and East Mediterranean in the Mid Second Millennium BC.* Oxford: Oxbow.

2008. Protopalatial Crete and formation of the palaces, in *The Aegean Bronze Age*, ed. C. W. Shelmerdine. Cambridge: Cambridge University Press, pp. 105–20.

Manning, S. W., C. B. Ramsey, C. Doumas, T. Marketou, G. Cadogan, & C. L. Pearson, 2002. New evidence for an early date for the Aegean Late Bronze Age and Thera eruption. *Antiquity*, 76(293), 733–44.

Manning, S. W., C. McCartney, B. Kromer, & S. Stewart, 2010. The earlier Neolithic in Cyprus: Recognition and dating of a Pre-Pottery Neolithic A occupation. *Antiquity*, 84(325), 693–706.

Marchetti, M., 2002. Environmental changes in the central Po plain (northern Italy) due to fluvial modifications and anthropogenic activities. *Geomorphology*, 44(3–4), 361–73.

Mariotti Lippi, M., M. Guido, B. I. Menozzi, C. Bellini, & C. Montanari, 2007. The Massaciuccoli Holocene pollen sequence and the vegetation history of the coastal plains by the Mar Ligure (Tuscany and Liguria, Italy). *Vegetation History and Archaeobotany*, 16(4), 267–77

Marriner, N., & C. Morhange, 2006. Geoarchaeological evidence for dredging in Tyre's ancient harbour, Levant. *Quaternary Research*, 65(1), 164–71.

Marriner, N., & C. Morhange, 2007. Geoscience of ancient Mediterranean harbours. *Earth Science Reviews*, 80(3–4), 137–94.

Marriner, N., C. Morhange, & M. Saghieh-Beydoun, 2008. Geoarchaeology of Beirut's ancient harbour, Phoenicia. *Journal of Archaeological Science*, 35(9), 2495–516.

Marriner, N., C. Morhange, & N. Carayon, 2008. Ancient Tyre and its harbours: 5,000 years of human–environment interactions. *Journal of Archaeological Science*, 35(5), 1281–310.

Marriner, N., J. P. Goiran, & C. Morhange, 2008. Alexander the Great's tombolos at Tyre and Alexandria, eastern Mediterranean. *Geomorphology*, 100 (3–4), 377–400.

Marsh, B., 1999. Alluvial burial of Gordion, an Iron-Age City in Anatolia. *Journal of Field Archaeology*, 26, part 2, 163–76.

Martinez-Fernandez, J., F. Lopez-Bermudez, & A. Romero-Diaz, 1995. Land use and soil–vegetation relationships in a Mediterranean ecosystem: El Ardal, Murcia, Spain. *Catena*, 25(1/4), 153.

Mastronuzzi, G., & P. Sansò, 2000. Boulders transport by catastrophic waves along the Ionian coast of Apulia (southern Italy). *Marine Geology*, 170(1–2), 93–103.

Mastronuzzi, G., & P. Sansò, 2004. Large boulder accumulations by extreme waves along the Adriatic coast of southern Apulia (Italy). *Quaternary International*, 120(1), 173–84.

Mather, A. E., 2009. Tectonic setting and landscape development, in *The Physical Geography of the Mediterranean*, ed. J. C. Woodward. Oxford: Oxford University Press, pp. 5–32.

Mathers, C., & S. Stoddart, 1994. *Development and Decline in the Mediterranean Bronze Age*. Sheffield: Continuum – Sheffield Academic.

Mattingly, D., 1996. Explanations: People as agency, in *Farming the Desert: The UNESCO Libyan Valleys Archaeological Survey*, ed. G. Barker. London: Society for Libyan Studies, pp. 319–42.

Mauquoy, D., B. Van Geel, M. Blaauw, & J. van der Plicht, 2002. Evidence from northwest European bogs shows 'Little Ice Age' climatic changes driven by variations in solar activity. *The Holocene*, 12(1), 1–6.

Mazier, F., D. Galop, M. J. Gaillard, C. Rendu, C. Cugny, A. Legaz, O. Peyron, & A. Buttler, 2009. Multidisciplinary approach to reconstructing local pastoral activities: An example from the Pyrenean Mountains (Pays Basque). *The Holocene*, 19(2), 171–88.

McClure, S. B., M. A. Jochim, & C. M. Barton, 2006. Human behavioral ecology, domestic animals, and land use during the transition to agriculture in Valencia, eastern Spain, in *Behavioral Ecology and the Transition to Agriculture*, eds. D. J. Kennett & B. Winterhalder. Berkeley: University of California Press, 197–216.

McClure, S. B., O. Garcia, C. Roca de Togores, B. J. Culleton, & D. J. Kennett, 2011. Osteological and paleodietary investigation of burials from Cova de la Pastora, Alicante, Spain. *Journal of Archaeological Science*, 38(2), 420–8.

McCoy, F., & G. Heiken, 2000a. The Late-Bronze Age explosive eruption of Thera (Santorini), Greece: Regional and local effects, in *Volcanic Hazards and Disasters in Human Antiquity*, eds. F. McCoy & G. Heiken. Boulder: Geological Society of America, pp. 43–70.

McCoy, F., & G. Heiken, 2000b. *Volcanic Hazards and Disasters in Human Antiquity*. Boulder: Geological Society of America.

McGovern, P. E., 2003. *Ancient Wine: The Search for the Origins of Viniculture*. Oxford: Princeton University Press.

McIntosh, R. J., J. A. Tainter, & S. K. McIntosh, 2000. Climate, history, and human action, in *The Way the Wind Blows: Climate, History, and Human Action*. New York: Columbia University Press, pp. 1–42.

McNeill, J. R., 1992. *The Mountains of the Mediterranean World*. Cambridge: Cambridge University Press.

Meiggs, R., 1982. *Trees and Timber in the Ancient Mediterranean World*. Oxford: Oxford University Press

Mercuri, A. M., M. Mazzanti, P. Torri, L. Vigliotti, G. Bosi, A. Florenzano, L. Olmi, & I. N'siala, 2012. A marine/terrestrial integration for mid–late Holocene vegetation history and the development of the cultural landscape in the Po valley as a result of human impact and climate change. *Vegetation History and Archaeobotany*, 1–20.

Mercuri, A. M., C. A. Accorsi, & M. Bandini Mazzanti, 2002. The long history of cannabis and its cultivation by the Romans in central Italy, shown by pollen records from Lago Albano and Lago di Nemi. *Vegetation History and Archaeobotany*, 11(4), 263–76.

Mercuri, A. M., C. A. Accorsi, M. B. Mazzanti, G. Bosi, A. Cardarelli, D. Labate, M. Marchesini, & G. T. Grandi, 2006. Economy and environment of Bronze Age settlements – Terramaras – on the Po plain (Northern Italy): First results from the archaeobotanical research at the Terramara di Montale. *Vegetation History and Archaeobotany*, 16(1), 43–60.

Messina, F., G. Scorrano, C. M. Labarga, M. F. Rolfo, & O. Rickards, 2010. Mitochondrial DNA variation in an isolated area of central Italy. *Annals of Human Biology*, 37(3), 385–402.

Meyer, W. J., & C. L. Crumley, 2012. Historical ecology: Using what works to cross the divide, in *Atlantic Europe in the First Millennium BC: Crossing the Divide*, ed. T. Moore & X.-L. Armada. Oxford: Oxford University Press, pp. 109–34.

Mikhailova, M. V., 2002. The hydrological regime and the peculiarities of formation of the Po river delta. *Water Resources*, 29(4), 370–80.

Mikhailova, M. V., P. Bellotti, P. Valeri, & P. Tortora, 1998. The Tiber river delta and the hydrological and morphological features of its formation. *Water Resources*, 25(5), 572–82.

Minoura, K., F. Imamura, U. Kuran, T. Nakamura, G. A. Papadopoulos, T. Takahashi, & A. C. Yalciner, 2000. Discovery of Minoan tsunami deposits. *Geology*, 28(1), 59–62.

Mitsch, W. J., & J. G. Gosselink, 1993. *Wetlands*. New York: Van Nostrand Reinhold.

Mocci, F., K. Walsh, S. Richer, M. Court-Picon, B. Talon, S. Tzortzis, J. M. Palet-Martinez, & C. Bressy, 2009. Archéologie et paléoenvironnement dans les Alpes méridionales françaises. Hauts massifs de l'Argentièrois, du Champsaur et de l'Ubaye (Hautes-Alpes et Alpes de Haute Provence) (Néolithique final – début de l'Antiquité). *Cahiers de Paléoenvironnement*, 6, 235–54.

Moe, D., & F. G. Fedele, 1997. Pollen analytical study on the early use of a present-day trail in the Central Alps. *Preistoria Alpina*, (33), 171–5.

Moe, D., F. G. Fedele, A. E. Maude, & M. Kvamme, 2007. Vegetational changes and human presence in the low-alpine and subalpine zone in Val Febbraro, upper Valle di Spluga (Italian central Alps), from the Neolithic to the Roman period. *Vegetation History and Archaeobotany*, 16(6), 431–51.

Moffett, L., 1992. Cereals from a Bronze Age storage vessel at Torralba D'En Salort, Menorca, Spain. *Vegetation History and Archaeobotany*, 1(2), 87–91.

Monaghan, J. J., P. J. Bicknell, & R. J. Humble, 1994. Volcanoes, tsunamis and the demise of the Minoans. *Physica D*, 77, 217–28.

Monna, F., D. Galop, L. Carozza, M. Tual, A. Beyrie, F. Marembert, C. Chateau, J. Dominik, & F. E. Grousset, 2004. Environmental impact of early Basque mining and smelting recorded in a high ash minerogenic peat deposit. *Science of the Total Environment*, 327(1–3), 197–214.

Moody, J., 1997. The Cretan environment: Abused or just misunderstood?, in *Aegean Strategies: Studies of Culture and Environment on the European Fringe*, eds. P. N. Kardulias & M. T. Shutes. Lanham: Rowman & Littlefield, pp. 61–77.

2000. Holocene climate change in Crete: An archaeologist's view, in *Landscape and Landuse in Postglacial Greece*, eds. P. Halstead & C. Frederick. Sheffield: Sheffield Academic Press, pp. 52–61.

Moody, J., & L. Nixon, 2006. *The Sphakia Survey: Internet Edition*. Oxford: University of Oxford.

Moore, A. M. T., & G. C. Hillman, 1992. The Pleistocene to Holocene transition and human economy in southwest Asia: The impact of the younger Dryas. *American Antiquity*, 57(3), 482–94.

Morales, J. A., J. Borrego, E. G. San Miguel, N. Lopez-Gonzalez, & B. Carro, 2008. Sedimentary record of recent tsunamis in the Huelva Estuary (southwestern Spain). *Quaternary Science Reviews*, 27(7–8), 734–46.

Morelli, C., A. Carbonara, V. Forte, R. Giudice, & P. Manacorda, 2008. The landscape of the Ager Portuensis, Rome: Some new discoveries, 2000–2002, in *Archaeology and Landscape in Central Italy. Papers in Memory of John Lloyd*, eds. J. A. Lloyd, G. R. Lock, & A. Faustoferri. Oxford: School of Archaeology, pp. 213–31.

Morelli, C., L. Paroli, & P. A. Verduchi, 2006. Summary of other recent fieldwork at Portus, in *Portus: An Archaeological Survey of the Port of Imperial Rome*, eds. S. J. Keay, M. Millett, L. Paroli, & K. Strutt. Rome: British School at Rome, pp. 241–68.

Morey, M., & M. Ruiz-Perez, 2008. The Balearic Islands, in *Mediterranean Island Landscapes: Natural and Cultural Approaches*, eds. I. N. Vogiatzakis, G. Pungetti, & A. M. Mannion. Dordrecht: Springer, pp. 271–96.

Morfis, A., H. Zojer, T. Harum, J. Zötl, & International Working Group on Tracer Methods in Hydrology, 1985. Karst hydrogeology of the Central and Eastern Peloponnesus (Greece), in *Steirische Beiträge zur Hydrogeologie*. Berlin: Kommission Springer-Verlag, pp. 1–301.

Morhange, C., C. Vella, M. Provansal, M. Hesnard, & J. Laborel, 1999. Human impact and natural characteristics of the ancient ports of Marseille and Fos, in Provence, southern France, in *Environmental Reconstruction in Mediterranean Landscape Archaeology*, eds. P. Leveau, F. Tremant, K. Walsh, & G. Barker. Oxford: Oxbow, pp. 145–53.

Morhange, C., F. Blanc, S. Schmitt-Mercury, M. Bourcier, P. Carbonel, C. Oberlin, A. Prone, D. Vivent, & A. Hesnard, 2003. Stratigraphy of

Late-Holocene deposits of the ancient harbour of Marseilles, southern France. *The Holocene*, 13(4), 593–604.

Morhange, C., J. P. Goiran, M. Bourcier, P. Carbonel, J. Le Campion, J. M. Rouchy, & M. Yon, 2000. Recent Holocene paleo-environmental evolution and coastline changes of Kition, Larnaca, Cyprus, Mediterranean Sea. *Marine Geology*, 170(1–2), 205–30.

Morhange, C., N. Marriner, G. Bony, N. Carayon, C. Flaux, & M. Shah-Hosseini, 2013. Coastal geoarchaeology and neocatastrophism: A dangerous liaison? *BYZAS, DAI, Istanbul.*

Morhange, C., P. A. Pirazzoli, N. Evelpidou, & N. Marriner, 2012. Late Holocene tectonic uplift and the silting up of Lechaion, the western harbor of ancient Corinth, Greece. *Geoarchaeology*, 27(3), 278–83.

Morris, M. W., 2002. *Soil Science and Archaeology: Three Test Cases from Minoan Crete.* Philadelphia: Institute for Aegean Prehistory Academic Press.

Morton, J., 2001. *The Role of the Physical Environment in Ancient Greek Seafaring.* Leiden: Brill.

Naveh, Z., 2004. The evolution of the cultural Mediterranean landscape in Israel as affected by fire, grazing and human activities, in *Evolutionary Theory and Processes: Modern Horizons: Papers in Honour of Eviatar Nevo*, eds. E. Nevo & S. P. Vasser. Dordrecht: Kluwer Academic, pp. 337–409.

Neboit, R., 1984. Érosion des sols et colonisation grecque en Sicile et en Grande-Grèce. *Bulletin de l'Association des Géographes Français*, 499, 5–21.

Neboit-Guilhot, R., & L. Lespez, 2006. Alluvionnement et creusement sur la rive nord de la Méditerranée: Vers une lecture systémique des rythmes historiques de la morphogenèse, in *L'Érosion entre Société, Climat et Paléoenvironnement*, eds. P. Alle & L. Lespez. Clermont-Ferrand: Presses Universitaires Blaise-Pascal, pp. 335–52.

Newell, W. L., B. Stone, & R. Harrison, 2004. Holocene alluvium around Lefkosia (Nicosia), Cyprus: An archive of land-use, tectonic processes, and climate change, in *Geo-Environment*, eds. J. F. Martin-Duque, C. A. Brebbia, A. E. Godfrey, & J. R. Diaz de Teran. Southampton: WIT, pp. 71–80.

Nir, Y., 1997. Middle and Late Holocene sea levels along the Israel Mediterranean coast – Evidence from ancient water wells. *Journal of Quaternary Science*, 12(2), 143–52.

Nixon, I. G., 1985. The volcanic eruption of Thera and its effect on the Mycenean and Minoan civilisations. *Journal of Archaeological Science*, 12, 9–24.

Nixon, L., J. Moody, V. Niniou-Kindelis, S. Price & O. Rackham, 1990. Archaeological survey in Sphakia, Crete. *Classical Views*, XXXIV(9), 213–20.

Nixon, L., & S. Price, 2005. Ancient agricultural terraces: Evidence from texts and archaeological survey. *American Journal of Archaeology*, 109(4), 665–94.

Nowicki, K., 1999. Economy of refugees: Life in the Cretan mountains at the turn of the Bronze and Iron Ages, in *From Minoan Farmers to Roman Traders: Sidelights on the Economy of Ancient Crete*, ed. E. Chaniotis. Stuttgart: Franz Steiner Verlag, pp. 145–71.

Ntinou, M., 2002. Vegetation and human communities in prehistoric Greece, in *El paisaje en el Neolitic mediterráneo: Neolithic Landscapes of the Mediterranean*, eds. E. Badal, J. Bernabeu, & B. Martí. Valencia: Universitat de Valencia, Papeles del Laboratoria de Arqueolgia de Valencia, Saguntum, pp. 91–103.

Nur, A., & D. Burgess, 2008. *Apocalypse: Earthquakes, Archaeology, and the Wrath of God*. Princeton: Princeton University Press.

Nur, A., & E. H. Cline, 2000. Poseidon's horses: Plate tectonics and earthquake storms in the Late Bronze Age Aegean and Eastern Mediterranean. *Journal of Archaeological Science*, 27(1), 43–64.

Obando, J. A., 2002. The impact of land abandonment on regeneration of semi-natural vegetation: A case study from the Guadalentín, in *Mediterranean Desertification: A Mosaic of Processes and Responses*, eds. N. Geeson, C. J. Brandt, & J. B. Thornes, London: John Wiley, pp. 58–70.

Oleson, J. P., C. Brandon, S. M. Cramer, R. Cucitore, E. Gotti, & R. L. Hohlfelder, 2004. The ROMACONS project: A contribution to the historical and engineering analysis of hydraulic concrete in Roman maritime structures. *International Journal of Nautical Archaeology*, 33(2), 199–229.

Ollivier, V., J. L. Guendon, A. Ali, P. Roiron, & P. Ambert, 2006. Postglacial evolution of travertine environments in the French Alps and Provence: New chronology, facies, and morphosedimentary dynamics. *Quaternaire*, 17(2), 51–68.

Olszewski, D. I., 1993. Subsistence ecology in the Mediterranean forest: Implications for the origins of cultivation in the Epipaleolithic Southern Levant. *American Anthropologist*, 95(2), 420–35.

Orengo, H., 2010. *Impacto humano en un medio altimontano pre-pirenaico durante los últimos 1500 años. Análisis paleoambiental de una turbera alcalina*. Unpublished PhD thesis, Institut catalan d'arqueologia classica.

Orland, I. J., M. Bar-Matthews, N. T. Kita, A. Ayalon, A. Matthews, & J. W. Valley, 2009. Climate deterioration in the Eastern Mediterranean as revealed by ion microprobe analysis of a speleothem that grew from 2.2 to 0.9 ka in Soreq Cave, Israel. *Quaternary Research*, 71(1), 27–35.

Ortu, E., S. Brewer, & O. Peyron, 2006. Pollen-inferred palaeoclimate reconstructions in mountain areas: Problems and perspectives. *Journal of Quaternary Science*, 21(6), 615–27.

Osborne, R., & B. Cunliffe, 2005. *Mediterranean Urbanization 800–600 BC*. Oxford: Oxford University Press/British Academy.

Packard, R. M., 2007. *The Making of a Tropical Disease: A Short History of Malaria*. Baltimore: Johns Hopkins University Press.

Paget, R., 1968. The ancient ports of Cumae. *The Journal of Roman Studies*, 58, 152–69.

Pagnol, M., 1988. *Jean de Florette*. New York: Andre Deutsch, North Point.

Palet, J. M., A. Ejarque, Y. Miras, S. Riera, I. Euba, & H. Orengo, 2007. *Formes d'ocupació d'alta muntanya a la vall de la Vansa (Serra del Cadí – Alt Urgell) i a la vall del Madriu-Perafita-Claror (Andorra): estudi diacrònic de paisatges culturals pirinencs.* Barcelona: Generalitat de Catalunya, pp. 229–53.

Palmer, C., S. Colledge, A. Bevan, & J. Conolly, 2010. Vegetation recolonisation of abandoned agricultural terraces on Antikythera, Greece. *Environmental Archaeology*, 15(1), 64–80.

Pantaleon-Cano, J., E. I. Yll, R. Perez-Obiol, & J. M. Roure, 2003. Palynological evidence for vegetational history in semi-arid areas of the Western Mediterranean (Almeria, Spain). *The Holocene*, 13(1), 109–20.

Papanastassiou, D., K. Gaki-Papanastassiou, & H. Maroukian, 2005. Recognition of past earthquakes along the Sparta fault (Peloponnesus, southern Greece) during the Holocene, by combining results of different dating techniques. *Journal of Geodynamics*, 40(2–3), 189–99.

Pareschi, M. T., M. Favalli, & E. Boschi, 2006. Impact of the Minoan tsunami of Santorini: Simulated scenarios in the Eastern Mediterranean. *Geophysical Research Letters*, 33(18), L18607-L.

Pasquinucci, M., & G. Rossetti, 1988. The harbour infrastructure at Pisa and Porto Pisano from ancient times until the Middle Ages, in *Archeology of Coastal Changes.* Proceedings of the First International Symposium 'Cities on the Sea. Past and present', ed. A. Raban. Oxford: B.A.R., pp. 137–55.

Pasquinucci, M., & S. Menchelli, 1999. The landscape and economy of the territories of Pisae and Volaterrae (coastal North Etruria). *Journal of Roman Archaeology*, 12(1), 122–41.

Patterson, H., F. di Gennaro, H. di Giuseppe, S. Fontana, V. Gaffney, A. Harrison, S. J. Keay, M. Millett, M. Rendeli, & P. Roberts, 2000. The Tiber Valley project: The Tiber and Rome through two millennia. *Antiquity*, 74(284), 395–403.

Patterson, H., H. di Giuseppe, & R. Witcher, 2004. Three south Etrurian 'crises': First results of the Tiber Valley project. *Papers of the British School at Rome*, 1–36.

Patton, M., 1996. *Islands in Time*. London: Routledge.

Pedley, M. A. R. T., 2009. Tufas and travertines of the Mediterranean region: A testing ground for freshwater carbonate concepts and developments. *Sedimentology*, 56(1), 221–46.

Pèlachs, A., J. Nadal, J. Soriano, D. Molina, & R. Cunill, 2009. Changes in Pyrenean woodlands as a result of the intensity of human exploitation: 2,000 years of metallurgy in Vallferrera, northeast Iberian Peninsula. *Vegetation History and Archaeobotany*, 18(5), 403–16.

Peltenburg, E. J., 2003. Conclusions: Mylouthkia 1 and the early colonists of Cyprus, in *The Colonisation and Settlement of Cyprus: Investigations at Kissonerga-Mylouthkia, 1976–1996*, ed. E. J. Peltenburg. Uppsala: P. Åström's Vörlag, pp. 83–103.

Peltenburg, E. J., S. Colledge, P. Croft, A. Jackson, C. McCartney, & M. A. Murray, 2000. Agro-pastoralist colonization of Cyprus in the 10th millennium BP: Initial assessments. *Antiquity*, 74(286), 844–53.

Pereira, P. M., & M. P. da Fonseca, 2003. Nature vs. nurture: The making of the montado ecosystem. *Conservation Ecology*, 7(3).

Pèrez, R. M., 2005. Towards a definition of politico-ideological practices in the prehistory of Minorca (the Balearic Islands): The wooden carvings from Mussol Cave. *Journal of Social Archaeology*, 5(2), 276–99.

Pèrez-Obiol, R., G. Jalut, R. Julià, A. Pèlachs, M. J. Iriarte, T. Otto, & B. Hernández-Beloqui, 2011. Mid-Holocene vegetation and climatic history of the Iberian Peninsula. *The Holocene*, 21(1), 75–93.

Pèrez-Obiol, R., & L. Sadori, 2007. Similarities and dissimilarities, synchronisms and diachronisms in the Holocene vegetation history of the Balearic Islands and Sicily. *Vegetation History and Archaeobotany*, 16(4), 259–65.

Pèrez-Obiol, R., & R. Julià, 1994. Climatic Change on the Iberian Peninsula recorded in a 30,000-yr pollen record from Lake Banyoles. *Quaternary Research*, 41(1), 91–8.

Perlès, C., 1999. The distribution of Magoules in eastern Thessaly, in *Neolithic Society in Greece*, ed. P. Halstead. Sheffield: Sheffield Academic Press, pp. 42–56.

   2001. *The Early Neolithic in Greece: The First Farming Communities in Europe*. Cambridge: Cambridge University Press.

Pescatore, T., M. R. Senatore, G. Capretto, & G. Lerro, 2001. Holocene coastal environments near Pompeii before the AD 79 eruption of Mount Vesuvius, Italy. *Quaternary Research*, 55(1), 77–85.

Pessina, A. & V. Tin, 2008. *Archeologia del Neolitico: l'Italia tra VI e IV secolo a. C.* Rome: Carocci.

Peyron, O., S. Goring, I. Dormoy, U. Kotthoff, J. Ç. Pross, J. L. De Beaulieu, R. Drescher-Schneider, B. Vannière, & M. Magny, 2011. Holocene seasonality changes in the Central Mediterranean region reconstructed from the pollen sequences of Lake Accesa (Italy) and Tenaghi Philippon (Greece). *The Holocene*, 21(1), 131–46.

Phillips, J. D., 2007. The perfect landscape. *Geomorphology*, 84(3–4), 159–69.

Phoca-Cosmetatou, N., 2011a. *The First Mediterranean Islanders: Initial Occupation and Survival Strategies*. Oxford: David Brown Book Company.

   2011b. Island occupation of the Cycladic islands in the Neolithic: Strategies for survival, in *The First Mediterranean Islanders: Initial Occupation and Survival Strategies*, ed. N. Phoca-Cosmetatou. Oxford: David Brown Book Company, pp. 77–97.

Piccarreta, M., M. Caldara, D. Capolongo, & F. Boenzi, 2011. Holocene geo-morphic activity related to climatic change and human impact in Basilicata, southern Italy. *Geomorphology*, 128(3–4), 137–47.

Pini, R., 2004. Late Neolithic vegetation history at the pile-dwelling site of Palu di Livenza (northeastern Italy). *Journal of Quaternary Science*, 19(8), 769–82.

Pirazzoli, P. A., 1976. Sea level variations in the Northwest Mediterranean dur-ing Roman times. *Science*, 194(4264), 519–21.

Pirazzoli, P. A., J. Ausseil-Badie, P. Giresse, E. Hadjidaki, & M. Arnold, 1992. Historical environmental changes at Phalasarna Harbor, west Crete. *Geoarchaeology*, 7(4), 371–92.

Piva, A., A. Asioli, F. Trincardi, R. R. Schneider, & L. Vigliotti, 2008. Late-Holocene climate variability in the Adriatic Sea (Central Mediterranean). *The Holocene*, 18(1), 153–68.

Planchais, N., 1982. Palynologie lagunaire de l'étang de Maugio. Paléoenvironnement végétal et évolution anthropique. *Pollen et Spores*, 24(1), 93–118.

Planchais, N., D. Duzer, & M. Fontugne, 1991. Palynologie de dépôts holocènes de Lattes (Hérault). *Comptes Rendus de l'Academie des Sciences Paris*, 313(2), 1357–60.

Pliny the Elder, 2009. *The Natural History of Pliny*, trans. J. Bostock & H. T. Riley. Charleston: BiblioBazaar.

Polio, M. V., 2005. *The Ten Books on Architecture*. Boston: Adamant Media Corporation.

Pons, A., & P. Quézel, 1998. A propos de la mise en place du climat méditer-ranéen. *Comptes. Rendus de l'Academie des Sciences Paris – Series IIA – Earth and Planetary Science*, 327(11), 755–60.

Powell, J., 1996. *Fishing in the Prehistoric Aegean*. Jonsered: Åström Editions.

Primavera, M., O. Simone, G. Fiorentino, & M. Caldara, 2011. The palae-oenvironmental study of the Alimini Piccolo lake enables a reconstruc-tion of Holocene sea-level changes in southeast Italy. *The Holocene*, 21(4), 553–63.

Pross, J., U. Kotthoff, U. C. Müller, O. Peyron, I. Dormoy, G. Schmiedl, S. Kalaitzidis, & A. M. Smith, 2009. Massive perturbation in terrestrial eco-systems of the Eastern Mediterranean region associated with the 8.2 kyr BP climatic event. *Geology*, 37(10), 887–90.

Provansal, M., 1995a. Holocene sedimentary sequences in the Arc River delta and the Etang de Berre in Provence, southern France, in *Mediterranean Quaternary River Environments: Refereed Proceedings of an International Conference University of Cambridge/United Kingdom/28–29 September*, eds. J. Lewin, M. G. Macklin, & J. C. Woodward. Rotterdam: AA Balkema, pp. 159–65.

1995b. The role of climate in landscape morphogenesis since the Bronze Age in Provence, southeastern France. *The Holocene*, 5(3), 348–53.

2006. *Seminaire – Hommages* ... Philippe Leveau, Centre Camille Jullian, Aix-en-Provence, France.

Pucci, S., D. Pantosti, P. M. De Martini, A. Smedile, M. Munzi, E. Cirelli, M. Pentiricci, & L. Musso, 2011. Environment–human relationships in historical times: The balance between urban development and natural forces at Leptis Magna (Libya). *Quaternary International*, 242(1), 171–84.

Purcell, N., 1995. Eating fish: The paradoxes of seafood, in *Food in Antiquity*, ed. J. Wilkins, D. Harvey, & M. Dobson. Exeter: University of Exeter Press, pp. 132–49.

1998. Alla scoperta di una costa residenziale romana: Il litus Laurentinum e l'archeologia dell' otium. *Castelporziano*, III, 11–32.

2005. Statics and dynamics: Ancient Mediterranean urbanism, in *Mediterranean Urbanization 800–600 BC*, eds. B. Cunliffe & R. Osborne. Oxford: Oxford University Press/British Academy, pp. 249–72.

Pustovoytov, K., 2006. Soils and soil sediments at Gobekli Tepe, southeastern Turkey: A preliminary report. *Geoarchaeology*, 21(7), 699–719.

Quézel, P., 2004. Large-scale post-glacial distribution of vegetation structures in the Mediterranean region, in *Recent Dynamics of the Mediterranean Vegetation and Landscape*, eds. S. Mazzoleni, G. di Pasquale, M. Mulligan, P. di Martino, & F. Rego. Chichester: John Wiley, pp. 3–12.

Raban, A., 1988. Coastal processes and ancient harbour engineering, in *Archaeology of Coastal Changes*. Proceedings of the First International Symposium 'Cities on the Sea. Past and Present', ed. A. Raban. Oxford: B.A.R., pp. 185–208.

1992. Sebastos: The royal harbour at Caesarea Maritima – A short-lived giant. *International Journal of Nautical Archaeology*, 21(2), 111–24.

Rackham, O., 2001. *Trees, Wood and Timber in Greek History*. Oxford: Leopard's Head Press.

2008. Holocene history of Mediterranean island landscapes, in *Mediterranean Island Landscapes: Natural and Cultural Approaches*, eds. I. N. Vogiatzakis, G. Pungetti, & A. M. Mannion. Dordrecht: Springer, pp. 36–60.

Rackham, O., & J. Moody, 1996. *The Making of the Cretan Landscape*. Manchester: Manchester University Press.

Raible, C., M. Yoshimori, T. Stocker, & C. Casty, 2007. Extreme midlatitude cyclones and their implications for precipitation and wind speed extremes in simulations of the Maunder Minimum versus present day conditions. *Climate Dynamics*, 28(4), 409–23.

Rainbird, P., 2002. A message for our future? The Rapa Nui (Easter Island) ecodisaster and Pacific island environments. *World Archaeology*, 33(3), 436–51.

Ramis, D., 2010. From colonisation to habitation: Early cultural adaptations in the Balaeric Bronze Age, in *Material Connections in the Ancient*

Mediterranean: Mobility, Materiality and Identity, ed. P. v. Dommelen. Abingdon: Taylor & Francis.

Ramis, D., J. A. Alcover, J. Coll, & M. Trias, 2002. The chronology of the first settlement of the Balearic Islands. *Journal of Mediterranean Archaeology*, 15(1), 3–24.

Ramis, D., & P. Bover, 2001. A review of the evidence for domestication of Myotragus balearicus Bate 1909 (Artiodactyla, Caprinae) in the Balearic Islands. *Journal of Archaeological Science*, 28(3), 265–82.

Reale, O., & J. Shukla, 2000. Modeling the effects of vegetation on Mediterranean climate during the Roman classical period: Part II. Model simulation. *Global and Planetary Change*, 25(3–4), 185–214.

Reale, O., & P. Dirmeyer, 2000. Modeling the effects of vegetation on Mediterranean climate during the Roman classical period. Part I: Climate history and model sensitivity. *Global and Planetary Change*, 25(3–4), 163–84.

Redman, C. L., 1999. *Human Impact on Ancient Environments*. Tucson: University of Arizona Press.

  2005. Resilience theory in archaeology. *American Anthropologist*, 107(1), 70–7.

Redman, C. L., & A. P. Kinzig, 2003. Resilience of past landscapes: Resilience theory, society, and the *longue durée*. *Conservation Ecology*, 7(1), 14.

Reille, M., & A. Pons, 1992. The ecological significance of sclerophyllous oak forest in the western part of the Mediterranean basin: A note on pollen analytical data. *Vegetatio*, 99–100, 13–17.

Rendell, H. M., A. J. Claridge, & M. L. Clarke, 2007. Late Holocene Mediterranean coastal change along the Tiber delta and Roman occupation of the Laurentine Shore, central Italy. *Quaternary Geochronology*, 2(1–4), 83–8.

Rendu, C., 2003. *La Montagne d'Enveig*. Canet: Éditions Trabucaire.

Renfrew, A. C., 1976. Megaliths, territories and populations, in *Acculturation and Continuity in Atlantic Europe*, ed. S. DeLaet. Ghen: De Tempel, pp. 198–220.

Renfrew, C., & M. Wagstaff, 2005. *An Island Polity: The Archaeology of Exploitation in Melos*. Cambridge: Cambridge University Press.

Retallack, G. J., 2008. Rocks, views, soils and plants at the temples of ancient Greece. *Antiquity*, 82(317), 640–57.

Richer, S., 2009. *From pollen to people: The interaction between people and their environment in the mid- to high- altitudes of the Southern French Alps*. Unpublished PhD thesis, University of York.

Riehl, S., & E. Marinova, 2008. Mid-Holocene vegetation change in the Troad (W Anatolia): Man-made or natural? *Vegetation History and Archaeobotany*, 17(3), 297–312.

Riera-Mora, S., J. A. Léspez, & J. B. Argilagés, 2004. Premières traces d'anthropisation à l'est de la péninsule ibérique et les Îles baléars, in *Néolithisation Précoce. Premières Traces d'Anthropisation du Couvert Végétal à Partir des Données Polliniques*, ed. H. Richard. Besançon: Presses Universitaires Franche-Comté, pp. 195–219.

Robb, J., 2001. Island identities: Ritual, travel and the creation of difference in Neolithic Malta. *European Journal of Archaeology*, 4(2), 175–202.

2007. *The Early Mediterranean Village: Agency, Material Culture and Social Change in Neolithic Italy*. Cambridge: Cambridge University Press.

Robb, J., & D. Van Hove, 2003. Gardening, foraging and herding: Neolithic land use and social territories in Southern Italy. *Antiquity*, 77(296), 241–54.

Roberts, N., 1990. Human-induced landscape change in south and south-west Turkey during the later Holocene, in *Man's Role in the Shaping of the Eastern Mediterranean Landscape*, eds. S. Bottema, G. EntjesNieborg, & W. van Zeist. Rotterdam: AA Balkema, pp. 53–67.

2002. Did prehistoric landscape management retard the post-glacial spread of woodland in Southwest Asia? *Antiquity*, 76(294), 1002–10.

Roberts, N., & A. Rosen, 2009. Diversity and complexity in early farming communities of Southwest Asia: New insights into the economic and environmental basis of Neolithic Çatalhöyük. *Current Anthropology*, 50(3), 393–402.

Roberts, N., D. Brayshaw, C. Kuzucuoğlu, R. Perez, & L. Sadori, 2011. The mid-Holocene climatic transition in the Mediterranean: Causes and consequences. *The Holocene*, 21(1), 3–13.

Roberts, N., P. Boyer, & R. Parish, 1996. Preliminary results of geoarchaeological investigations at Çatalhöyük, in *On the Surface: Çatalhöyük 1993–95*, ed. I. Hodder. Cambridge: McDonald Institute for Archaeological Research, pp. 19–40.

Roberts, N., W. J. Eastwood, C. Kuzucuoğlu, G. Fiorentino, & V. Caracuta, 2011. Climatic, vegetation and cultural change in the Eastern Mediterranean during the mid-Holocene environmental transition. *The Holocene*, 21(1), 147–62.

Robinson, S. A., S. Black, B. W. Sellwood, & P. J. Valdes, 2006. A review of palaeoclimates and palaeoenvironments in the Levant and Eastern Mediterranean from 25,000 to 5000 years BP: Setting the environmental background for the evolution of human civilisation. *Quaternary Science Reviews*, 25(13–14), 1517–41.

Rockman, M., 2003. Knowledge and learning in the archaeology of colonization, in *Colonization of Unfamiliar Landscapes: The Archaeology of Adaptation*, eds. M. Rockman & J. Steele. London: Routledge, pp. 3–24.

Rodriguez-Ariza, M. O., & S. Ruiz, 1996. Paleobotany of a Bronze Age community, Castellon Alto (Galera, Granada, Spain). *Revue d'Archéométrie*, 191–6.

Rodriguez-Vidal, J., L. M. Caceres, J. C. Finlayson, F. J. Gracia, & A. Martinez-Aguirre, 2004. Neotectonics and shoreline history of the Rock of Gibraltar, southern Iberia. *Quaternary Science Reviews*, 23(18–19), 2017–29.

Rohling, E. J., R. H. Abu-Zied, J. S. L. Casford, A. Hayes, & B. A. A. Hoogakker, 2009. The marine environment: Present and past, in *The Physical Geography of the Mediterranean*, ed. J. C. Woodward. Oxford: Oxford University Press, pp. 33–67.

Roiron, P., A. A. Ali, J. L. Guendon, M. E. Migueres, S. D. Muller, & V. Ollivier, 2006. New data on the Holocene vegetation in the southern Alps: The fossil flora of the Serre de Montdenier travertine (Alpes de Haute Provence, France). *Quaternaire*, 17(2), 69–78.

Rosen, A. M., 1995. The social response to environmental change in Early Bronze Age Canaan. *Journal of Anthropological Archaeology*, 14(1), 26.

2005. Phytolith indicators of plant and land use at Çatalhöyük, in *Inhabiting Çatalhöyük: Reports from the 1995–99 Seasons (Çatalhöyük Research Project S.)*, ed. I. Hodder. Cambridge: MacDonald Institute for Archaeological Research, pp. 203–12.

2007. *Civilizing Climate: Social Responses to Climate Change in the Ancient Near East.* Plymouth: AltaMira.

Rosser, Z. H., T. Zerjal, M. E. Hurles, M. Adojaan, D. Alavantic, A. Amorim, W. Amos, M. Armenteros, E. Arroyo, G. Barbujani, G. Beckman, L. Beckman, J. Bertranpetit, E. Bosch, D. G. Bradley, G. Brede, G. Cooper, H. B. S. M. Côrte-Real, P. de Knijff, R. Decorte, Y. E. Dubrova, O. Evgrafov, A. Gilissen, S. Glisic, M. Gölge, E. W. Hill, A. Jeziorowska, L. Kalaydjieva, M. Kayser, T. Kivisild, S. A. Kravchenko, A. Krumina, V. Kucinskas, J. Lavinha, L. A. Livshits, P. Malaspina, S. Maria, K. McElreavey, T. A. Meitinger, A. V. Mikelsaar, R. J. Mitchell, K. Nafa, J. Nicholson, S. Nørby, A. Pandya, J. Ç. Parik, P. C. Patsalis, L. Pereira, B. Peterlin, G. Pielberg, M. J. Prata, C. Previderé, L. Roewer, S. Rootsi, D. C. Rubinsztein, J. Saillard, F. R. Santos, G. Stefanescu, B. C. Sykes, A. Tolun, R. Villems, C. Tyler-Smith, & M. A. Jobling, 2000. Y-chromosomal diversity in Europe is clinal and influenced primarily by geography, rather than by language. *The American Journal of Human Genetics*, 67(6), 1526–43.

Rossignol-Strick, M., 1999. The Holocene climatic optimum and pollen records of sapropel in the Eastern Mediterranean, 9000–6000 BP. *Quaternary Science Reviews*, 18(4/5), 515–30.

Ruiz, M., R. Risch, M. Gonzalez, P. Castro, V. Lull & R. W. Chapman, 1992. Environmental exploitation and social structure in prehistoric southeast Spain. *Journal of Mediterranean Archaeology*, 5(1), 3–38.

Ruiz del Árbol, M., F. J. Sánchez-Palencia, J. A. López-Sáez, P. López, R. Macías, & O. López, 2003. A geoarchaeological approach to the study of Roman terraces: Landscape transformations in a mining area in the north-western Iberian Peninsula, in *The Mediterranean World Environment and History*, ed. E. Fouache. Paris: Elsevier, pp. 331–9.

Russo Ermolli, E., & G. di Pasquale, 2002. Vegetation dynamics of south-western Italy in the last 28 kyr inferred from pollen analysis of a Tyrrhenian Sea core. *Vegetation History and Archaeobotany*, 11(3), 211–20.

Ryan, W., & W. C. Pitman, 2000. *Noah's Flood: The New Scientific Discoveries about the Event that Changed History*. London: Touchstone.

Ryan, W. B. F., W. C. Pitman, C. O. Major, K. Shimkus, V. Moskalenko, G. A. Jones, P. Dimitrov, N. Goruer, M. Sakinc, & H. Yuece, 1997. An abrupt drowning of the Black Sea shelf. *Marine Geology*, 138(1/2), 119–26.

Sabbatani, S., R. Manfredi, & S. Fiorino, 2010. Malaria infection and the anthropological evolution. *Sao Paulo Medical Journal*, 19(1), 64–83.

Sadori, L., & B. Narcisi, 2001. The postglacial record of environmental history from Lago di Pergusa, Sicily. *The Holocene*, 11(6), 655–72.

Saez, J. A. L., P. L. Garcia, & M. M. Sanchez, 2002. Palaeoecology and Holocene environmental change from a saline lake in south-west Spain: Protohistorical and prehistorical vegetation in Cadiz Bay. *Quaternary International*, 93/94, 197–206.

Sagona, C., 2004. Land use in prehistoric Malta. A re-examination of the Maltese 'cart ruts'. *Oxford Journal of Archaeology*, 23(1), 45–60.

Sainz-Elipe, S., J. M. Latorre, R. Escosa, M. Masià, M. V. Fuentes, S. Mas-Coma, & M. D. Bargues, 2010. Malaria resurgence risk in southern Europe: Climate assessment in an historically endemic area of rice fields at the Mediterranean shore of Spain. *Malaria Journal*, 9.

Sallares, R., 2002. *Malaria and Rome: A History of Malaria in Ancient Italy*. Oxford: Oxford University Press.

Salowey, C. A., 1994. Herakles and the waterworks: Mycenean dams, classical fountains, Roman aqueducts, in *Archaeology in the Peloponnese: New Excavations and Research*, ed. K. A. Sheedy. Oxford: Oxbow, pp. 77–94.

Sampson, A., 1996. Causes of earthquakes at Mycenean and pre-Mycenean Thebes, in *Archaeoseismology*, eds. S. C. Stiros & R. E. Jones. Athens: Institute of Geology and Mineral Exploration & The British School at Athens, pp. 113–17.

Sangiorgi, F., L. Capotondi, N. C. Nebout, L. Vigliotti, H. Brinkhuis, S. Giunta, A. F. Lotter, C. Morigi, A. Negri, & G. J. Reichart, 2003. Holocene seasonal sea-surface temperature variations in the southern Adriatic Sea inferred from a multiproxy approach. *Journal of Quaternary Science*, 18(8), 723–32.

Schiffer, M. B., 1985. Is there a 'Pompeii Premise' in Archaeology? *Journal of Anthropological Research*, 41(1), 18–41.

Schlumbaum, A., M. Tensen, & V. Jaenicke-Després, 2008. Ancient plant DNA in archaeobotany. *Vegetation History and Archaeobotany*, 17(2), 233–44.

Schmidt, R., C. Kamenik, & M. Roth, 2007. Siliceous algae-based seasonal temperature inference and indicator pollen tracking ca. 4,000 years of climate/land use dependency in the southern Austrian Alps. *Journal of Paleoliminology*, 38(4), 541–54.

Schonfeld, J., & R. Zahn, 2000. Late glacial to Holocene history of the Mediterranean outflow. Evidence from benthic foraminiferal assemblages and stable isotopes at the Portuguese margin. *Palaeogeography Palaeoclimatology Palaeoecology*, 159(1–2), 85–111.

Schuele, W., 1993. Mammals, vegetation and the initial human settlement of the Mediterranean islands: A palaeoecological approach. *Journal of Biogeography*, 20(4), 399.

Schulte, L., 2002. Climatic and human influence on river systems and glacier fluctuations in southeast Spain since the Last Glacial Maximum. *Quaternary International*, 93/94, 85–100.

Schwab, M. J., F. Neumann, T. Litt, J. F. Negendank, & M. Stein, 2004. Holocene palaeoecology of the Golan Heights (Near East): Investigation of lacustrine sediments from Birkat Ram crater lake. *Quaternary Science Reviews*, 23(16–17), 1723–31.

Seager, R. B., 2000. *Excavations on the Island of Pseira*. Crete: Borgo Press.

Segard, M., 2009. *Les Alpes Occidentales à l'Époque Romaine: Développement Urbain et Exploitation des Ressources des Régions de Montagne. (Italie, Gaule Narbonnaise, Provinces Alpines)*. Aix-en-Provence: Éditions Errance: Centre Camille Jullian.

Shackleton, J. C., & T. H. van Andel, 1986. Prehistoric shore environments, shellfish availability, and shellfish gathering at Franchthi, Greece. *Geoarchaeology*, 1(2), 127–43.

Shaw, B. D., 2006a. *At the Edge of the Corrupting Sea*. Oxford: University of Oxford.

Shaw, J. W., 2006b. *Kommos: A Minoan Harbor Town and Greek Sanctuary in Southern Crete*. Princeton: American School of Classical Studies at Athens.

Shaw, J. W., & M. C. Shaw, 1993. Excavations at Kommos (Crete) during 1986–1992. *Hesperia*, 62, 129–90.

Sheffer, N. A., M. Rico, Y. Enzel, G. Benito, & T. Grodek, 2008. The palaeoflood record of the Gardon River, France: A comparison with the extreme 2002 flood event. *Geomorphology*, 98(1–2), 71–83.

Sherratt, A., 1981. Plough and pastoralism: Aspects of the secondary products revolution. *Pattern of the Past Studies in Honour of David Clarke*, eds. I. Hodder, G. L. Isaac, & N. Hammond. Cambridge: Cambridge University Press, pp. 261–305.

Shillito, L. M., 2011. Simultaneous thin section and phytolith observations of finely stratified deposits from Neolithic Çatalhöyük, Turkey: Implications for paleoeconomy and Early Holocene paleoenvironment. *Journal of Quaternary Science*, 26(6), 576–88.

Sigurdsson, H., S. Carey, M. Alexandri, G. Vougioukalakis, K. Croff, C. Roman, D. Sakellariou, C. Anagnostou, G. Rousakis, C. Ioakim, A. Gogou,

D. Ballas, T. Misaridis, & P. Nomikou, 2006. Marine investigations of Greece's Santorini volcanic field. *EOS, Transactions, American Geophysical Union*, 87(34), 337–42.

Silva, P. G., M. Sintubin, & K. Reicherter, 2011. New advances in studies of earthquake archaeology and palaeoseismology. *Quaternary International*, 242(1), 1–3.

Simeoni, U., & C. Corbau, 2009. A review of the Delta Po evolution (Italy) related to climatic changes and human impacts. *Geomorphology*, 107(1–2), 64–71.

Simmons, A. H., 1991. Humans, island colonisation and Pleistocene extinctions in the Mediterranean: The view from Akrotiri Aetokremnos, Cyprus. *Antiquity*, 65, 857–69.

   1998. Of tiny hippos, large cows and early colonists in Cyprus. *Journal of Mediterranean Archaeology*, 11(2), 232–41.

Sivan, D., S. Wdowinski, K. Lambeck, E. Galili, & A. Raban, 2001. Holocene sea-level changes along the Mediterranean coast of Israel, based on archaeological observations and numerical model. *Palaeogeography Palaeoclimatology Palaeoecology*, 167(1–2), 101–17.

Skeates, R., 1999. *Unveiling Inequality: Social Life and Social Change in the Mesolithic and Early Neolithic of East Central Italy*, eds. R. H. Tykot, J. Morter, & J. Robb. London: Accordia Research Institute University of London, pp. 15–45.

Soles, J. S., 1992. *The Prepalatial Cemeteries at Mochlos and Gournia and the House Tombs of Bronze Age Crete*. Princeton: American School of Classical Studies at Athens.

Soloviev, S. L., 2000. *Tsunamis in the Mediterranean Sea 2000 BC–2000 AD*. Dordrecht: Kluwer Academic.

Sondaar, P. Y., P. L. DeBoer, M. Sanges, T. Kotsakis, & D. Esu, 1984. First report on a Palaeolithic culture in Sardinia, in *Early Settlement in the West Mediterranean Islands and the Peripheral Areas*, eds. W. H. Waldren, R. W. Chapman, J. Lewthwaite, & R. C. Kennard. Oxford: B.A.R., pp. 29–59.

Soren, D., 2003. Can archaeologists excavate evidence of malaria? *World Archaeology*, 35(2), 193–209.

Souyoudzoglu-Haywood, C., 1999. *The Ionian Islands in the Bronze Age and Early Iron Age*. Liverpool: Liverpool University Press.

Spanò Giammellaro, A., F. Spatafora, & P. Van Dommelen, 2008. Sicily and Malta: Between sea and countryside, in *Rural Landscapes of the Punic World*, eds. P. Van Dommelen & C. G. Bellard. Sheffield: Equinox, pp. 129–58.

Spondilis, I., 1996. Contribution to a study of the configuration of the coast of Pylia, based on the location of new archaeological sites, in *Archaeoseismology*, eds. S. C. Stiros & R. E. Jones. Athens: Institute of Geology and Mineral Exploration & The British School at Athens, pp. 119–28.

Stanley, D. J., & F. C. Wezel, 1985. *Geological Evolution of the Mediterranean Basin: Raimondo Selli Commemorative Volume.* New York: Springer.

Stefaniuk, L., C. Morhange, P. F. Blanc, S. Francou, & J. P. Goiran, 2005. Évolution des paysages littoraux dans la dépression sud-ouest de Cumes depuis 4,000 ans. La question du port antique. *Méditerranée*, 104(1.2), 49–59.

Sternberg, M., 2004. Le rôle des fleuves dans la pêche du Ier au VIe siècle: État des connaissances, in *Fleuves et Marais, Une Histoire au Croisement de la Nature et la Culture*, eds. J. Burnouf & P. Leveau. Paris: CTHS, pp. 185–99.

Stevenson, A. C., 2000. The Holocene forest history of the Montes Universales, Teruel, Spain. *The Holocene*, 10(5), 603–10.

Stevenson, A. C., & R. J. Harrison, 1992. Ancient forests of Spain. A model for land-use and dry forest management in south west Spain from 4000 AD to 1900 AD. *Proceedings of the Prehistoric Society*, 58, 227–47.

Steward, J. H., 1955. The concept and method of cultural ecology, in *Theory of Culture Change: The Methodology of Multilinear Evolution*, ed. J. H. Steward. Urbana: University of Illinois Press.

　2005. The concept and method of cultural ecology, in *Anthropology in Theory: Issues in Epistemology*, eds. H. L. Moore & T. Sanders. Oxford: Wiley Blackwell, pp. 100–6.

Stewart, I., & C. Morhange, 2009. Coastal geomorphology and sea-level change, in *The Physical Geography of the Mediterranean*, ed. J. C. Woodward. Oxford: Oxford University Press, pp. 385–413.

Stiros, S. C., J. Laborel, F. Laborel-Deguen, S. Papageorgiou, J. Evin, & P. A. Pirazzoli, 2000. Seismic coastal uplift in a region of subsidence: Holocene raised shorelines of Samos Island, Aegean Sea, Greece. *Marine Geology*, 170(1–2), 41–58.

Stoddart, S., 1999. Long-term dynamics of an island community: Malta 5500 BC–2000 AD, in *Social Dynamics of the Prehistoric Central Mediterranean*, eds. R. H. Tykot, J. Morter, & J. Robb. London: Accordia Research Institute, University of London, pp. 137–47.

Stoddart, S., A. Bonanno, T. Gouder, C. Malone, & D. Trump, 1993. Cult in an island society: Prehistoric Malta in the Tarxien period. *Cambridge Archaeological Journal*, 3(1), 3–19.

Strasser, T. F., E. Panagopoulou, C. N. Runnels, P. M. Murray, N. Thompson, P. Karkanas, F. W. McCoy, & K. W. Wegmann, 2010. Stone Age seafaring in the Mediterranean: Evidence from the Plakias region for Lower Palaeolithic and Mesolithic habitation of Crete. *Hesperia: The Journal of the American School of Classical Studies at Athens*, 79(2), 145–90.

Strasser, T. F., C. Runnels, K. Wegmann, E. Panagopoulou, F. McCoy, C. Digregorio, P. Karkanas, & N. Thompson, 2011. Dating Palaeolithic sites in southwestern Crete, Greece. *Journal of Quaternary Science*, 26(5), 553–60.

Strauss, S., & B. Orlove, 2003. Up in the air: The anthroplogy of weather and climate, in *Weather, Climate, Culture*, ed. S. Strauss & B. Orlove. Oxford: Berg, pp. 3–14.

Sutton, M. O., & E. N. Anderson, 2004. *Introduction to Cultural Ecology.* Oxford: Berg.

Terral, J. F., & X. Mengual, 1999. Reconstruction of Holocene climate in southern France and eastern Spain using quantitative anatomy of olive wood and archaeological charcoal. *Palaeogeography Palaeoclimatology Palaeoecology*, 153(1–4), 71–92.

Terrell, J. E., 1999. Comment on Paul Rainbird, 'Islands Out of Time: Towards a Critique of Island Archaeology'. *Journal of Mediterranean Archaeology*, 12(2), 240–5.

Terrenato, N., 1998. Tam Firmum Municipium: The romanization of Volaterrae and its cultural implications. *The Journal of Roman Studies*, 88, 94–114.

Terrenato, N., & A. J. Ammerman, 1996. Visibility and site recovery in the Cecina Valley survey, Italy. *Journal of Field Archaeology*, 23(1), 91–110.

Thiebault, S., 1997. Early-Holocene vegetation and the human impact in central Provence (Var, France): Charcoal analysis of the Baume de Fontbrégoua. *The Holocene*, 7(3), 343.

Thomas, M. G., I. Barnes, M. E. Weale, A. L. Jones, P. Forster, N. Bradman, & P. P. Pramstaller, 2007. New genetic evidence supports isolation and drift in the Ladin communities of the South Tyrolean Alps but not an ancient origin in the Middle East. *European Journal of Human Genetics*, 16(1), 124–34.

Thomas, R. B., 1979. Effects of change on high mountain human-adaptive patterns, in *High-Altitude Geoecology*, ed. P. J. Webber. Boulder: Westview Press, pp. 139–88.

Thorndycraft, V., & G. Benito, 2006. The Holocene fluvial chronology of Spain: Evidence from a newly compiled radiocarbon database. *Quaternary Science Reviews*, 25(3), 223–34.

Thornes, J. B., 1987. The palaeoecology of erosion, in *Landscape and Culture*, ed. J. M. Wagstaff. Oxford: Blackwell, pp. 37–55.

2009. Land degradation, in *The Physical Geography of the Mediterranean*, ed. J. C. Woodward. Oxford: Oxford University Press, pp. 563–81.

Tilley, C., 1994. *A Phenomenology of Landscape: Places, Paths and Monuments.* Oxford: Berg.

2004. *The Materiality of Stone: Explorations in Landscape Phenomenology.* Oxford: Berg.

Tomaselli, R., 1981. Main physiognomic types and geographic distribution of shrub systems related to Mediterranean climates, in *Mediterranean-Type Shrublands*, eds. F. Di Castri, D. W. Goodall, & R. L. Specht. Amsterdam: Elsevier, pp. 95–106.

Touflan, P., B. Talon, & K. Walsh, 2010. Soil charcoal analysis: A reliable tool for spatially precise studies of past forest dynamics: A case study in the French southern Alps. *The Holocene*, 20(1), 45–52.

Tozzi, P., 1993. *Il libro del Po: Storie di acque, di terre, di uomini.* New York: New Press.

Traveset, A., M. Nogales, J. Alcover, J. Delgado, M. López-Darias, D. Godoy, J. Igual, & P. Bover, 2009. A review on the effects of alien rodents in the Balearic (Western Mediterranean Sea) and Canary Islands (Eastern Atlantic Ocean). *Biological Invasions*, 11(7), 1653–70.

Trément, F., 1993. Le secteur des etangs de Saint-Blaise: Pour une approche archéologique et paléoecologique d'un milieu de vie, in *Archéologie et Environnement de la Sainte-Victoire aux Alpilles*, eds. P. Leveau & M. Provansal. Aix-en-Provence: Publications Université de Provence, pp. 83–108.

Trifonov, V. G., & A. S. Karakhanian, 2004. Active faulting and human environment. *Tectonophysics*, 380(3–4), 287–94.

Trousset, P., 1986. De la montagne au désert. Limes et maitrise de l'eau. *Revue de l'Occident Musulman et de la Méditerranée*, 41(1), 90–115.

Turner, R., N. Roberts, W. J. Eastwood, E. Jenkins, & A. Rosen, 2010. Fire, climate and the origins of agriculture: Micro-charcoal records of biomass burning during the last glacial–interglacial transition in Southwest Asia. *Journal of Quaternary Science*, 25(3), 371–86.

Tykot, R. H., 1997. Characterization of the Monte Arci (Sardinia) obsidian sources. *Journal of Archaeological Science*, 24(5), 467–80.
  2004. Neolithic exploitation and trade of obsidian in the Central Mediterranean: New results and implications for cultural interaction. *BAR International Series*, 1303, 25–36.

Tzedakis, P. C., 2009. Museums and cradles of Mediterranean biodiversity. *Journal of Biogeography*, 36(6), 1033–4.

Tzortzis, S., & F. Mocci, K. Walsh, B. Talon, M. Court-Picon, V. Dumas, V. Py, & S. Richer, 2008. Les massifs de l'Argentièrois du Mésolithique au début de l'Antiquité: Au croisement des données archéologiques et paléoenvironnementales en haute montagne (Hautes-Alpes, parc national des Ecrins), in *Le Peuplement de l'Arc Alpin*, eds. D. Garcia & H. Richard. Paris: CTHS, pp. 123–48.

Unkel, I., C. Heymann, O. Nelle, & E. Zagana, 2011. Climatic influence on Lake Stymphalia during the last 15,000 years, in *Advances in the Research of Aquatic Environment*, eds. N. Lambrakis, G. Stournaras, & K. Katsanou. Berlin: Springer, pp. 75–82.

Urbainczyk, T., 2008. *Slave Revolts in Antiquity.* Berkeley: University of California Press.

Vallianou, D., 1996. New evidence of earthquake destruction in Late Minoan Crete, in *Archaeoseismology*, eds. S. C. Stiros & R. E. Jones. Athens: Institute of Geology and Mineral Exploration & The British School at Athens, pp. 153–67.

Valsecchi, V., W. Tinner, W. Finsinger, & B. Ammann, 2006. Human impact during the Bronze Age on the vegetation at Lago Lucone (northern Italy). *Vegetation History and Archaeobotany*, 15(2), 99–113.

van Andel, T. H., 1987. The Landscape, in *Landscape and People of the Franchthi Region*, eds. T. H. van Andel & S. B. Sutton. Bloomington: Indiana University Press, pp. 1–62.

van Andel, T. H., & C. Runnels, 1987. *Beyond the Acropolis: A Rural Greek Past*. Stanford: Stanford University Press.

van Andel, T. H., C. Runnels, & K. O. Pope, 1986. Five thousand years of land use and abuse in the Southern Argolid, Greece. *Hesperia*, 55, 103–28.

van Andel, T. H., & E. Zangger, 1990. Land use and soil erosion in prehistoric and historical Greece. *Journal of Field Archaeology*, 17, 379–96.

van Andel, T. H., & J. C. Shackleton, 1982. Late Paleolithic and Mesolithic coastlines of Greece and the Aegean. *Journal of Field Archaeology*, 9(4), 445–54.

van Andel, T. H., K. Gallis, & G. Toufexis, 1992. *Early Neolithic Farming in a Thessalian River Landscape, Greece*, eds. J. Lewin, M. G. Macklin, & J. C. Woodward. The Netherlands: AA Balkema, pp. 131–44.

van Andel, T. H., K. Gallis, & G. Toufexis, 1995. Early Neolithic farming in a Thessalian river landscape, Greece, in *Mediterranean Quaternary River Environments: Refereed Proceedings of an International Conference University of Cambridge/United Kingdom/28–29 September*, eds. J. Lewin, M. G. Macklin, & J. C. Woodward. Rotterdam: AA Balkema, pp. 131–43.

van der Leeuw, S., 2003. Une étude des causes de la dégradation des terres et la désertification, in *Archéologie et Systèmes Socio-environnementaux: Études Multiscalaires sur la Vallée du Rhône dans le Programme ARCHEOMEDES*, eds. S. van der Leeuw, F. Favory, & J. L. Fiches. Paris: CNRS, pp. 11–19.

van der Leeuw, S., F. Favory, & J. L. Fiches, eds., 2003. *Archéologie et Systèmes Socio-environnementaux: Études Multiscalaires sur la Vallée du Rhône dans le Programme ARCHEOMEDES*. Paris: CNRS.

Van Der Veen, M., 1996. Romano-Libyan agriculture: Crops and animals, in *Farming the Desert: The UNESCO Libyan Valleys Archaeological Survey*, ed. G. Barker. London: Society for Libyan Studies, pp. 227–63.

Van Dommelen, P., 1999. Islands in history. *Journal of Mediterranean Archaeology*, 12(2), 246–51.

Van Geel, B., & B. E. Berglund, 1997. A causal link between a climatic deterioration around 850 Cal BC and a subsequent rise in human population density in NW-Europe? *Alfred-Wegener-Stiftung*, pp. 126–30.

Van Strydonck, M., 2004. Radiocarbon and archaeological evidence for a possible climate-induced cultural change on the Balearic Islands around 2700 BP, in *Radiocarbon and Archaeology*, eds. T. Higham, C. Bronk Ramsey, & C. Owen. Oxford: Oxford University School of Archaeology, pp. 247–62.

Van Strydonck, M., M. Boudin, E. Ervynck, J. Orvay, & H. Borms, 2005. Spatial and temporal variation of dietary habits during the prehistory of the Balearic Islands as reflected by ^{14}C, d15N and d13C analyses on human and animal bones. *Mayurqa*, 30(2), 525–41.

van Zeist, W., H. Woldring, & D. Stapert, 1975. Late Quaternary vegetation and climate of southwestern Turkey. *Palaeohistoria*, 17, 53–143.

Vannière, B., M. J. Power, N. Roberts, W. Tinner, J. Carrión, M. Magny, P. Bartlein, D. Colombaroli, A. L. Daniau, W. Finsinger, G. Gil-Romera, P. Kaltenrieder, R. Pini, L. Sadori, R. Turner, V. Valsecchi, & E. Vescovi, 2011. Circum-Mediterranean fire activity and climate changes during the mid-Holocene environmental transition (8500–2500 Cal. BP). *The Holocene*, 21(1), 53–73.

Vaudour, J., 1994. Évolution Holocène des travertins de vallée dans le Midi Méditerranéan français. *Géographie Physique Quaternaire*, 48, 315–26.

Veggiani, A., 1994. I deterioramenti climatici dell'età del ferro e dell'alto medioevo. *Bollettino della Società Torricelliana di Scienze e Lettere, Faenza*, 45, 3–80.

Vermoere, M., E. Smets, M. Waelkens, H. Vanhaverbeke, I. Librecht, E. Paulissen, & L. Vanhecke, 2000. Late Holocene environmental change and the record of human impact at Gravgaz near Sagalassos, southwest Turkey. *Journal of Archaeological Science*, 27(7), 571–96.

Vermoere, M., S. Bottema, L. Vanhecke, M. Waelkens, E. Paulissen, & E. Smets, 2002. Palynological evidence for Late-Holocene human occupation recorded in two wetlands in SW Turkey. *The Holocene*, 12(5), 569–84.

Vernet, J.-L., 1997. *L'Homme et la Forêt Méditerranéenne de la Préhistoire à nos Jours*. Paris: Éditions Errance.

Vigne, J. D., & H. Valladas, 1996. Small mammal fossil assemblages as indicators of environmental change in northern Corsica during the last 2,500 years. *Journal of Archaeological Science*, 23(2), 199–216.

Vita-Finzi, C., 1969. *The Mediterranean Valleys: Geological Changes in Historical Times*. Cambridge: Cambridge University Press.

Vita-Finzi, C., & E. Higgs, 1970. Prehistoric economy in the Mount Carmel area of Palestine. Site catchment analysis. *Proceedings of the Prehistoric Society*, 36(1), 37.

Vitali, V., J. A. Gifford, F. Djindjian, & G. R. Rapp, Jr., 1992. A formalized approach to analysis of geoarchaeological sediment samples: The location of the early punic Harbor at Carthage, Tunisia. *Geoarchaeology*, 7(6), 545–81.

Vogel, S., & M. Märker, 2010. Reconstructing the Roman topography and environmental features of the Sarno River Plain (Italy) before the AD 79 eruption of Somma-Vesuvius. *Geomorphology*, 115(1–2), 67–77.

Vogel, S., M. Märker, & F. Seiler, 2011. Revised modelling of the post-AD 79 volcanic deposits of Somma-Vesuvius to reconstruct the pre-AD 79 topography of the Sarno River plain (Italy). *Geologica Carpathica*, 62(1), 5–16.

Vogiatzakis, I. N., & G. H. Griffiths, 2008. Island biogeography and landscape ecology, in *Mediterranean Island Landscapes: Natural and Cultural*

Approaches, eds. I. N. Vogiatzakis, G. Pungetti, & A. M. Mannion. Dordrecht: Springer, pp. 61–81.

Vogiatzakis, I. N., G. Pungetti, & A. M. Mannion, 2008. Introduction to the Mediterranean island landscapes, in *Mediterranean Island Landscapes: Natural and Cultural Approaches*, eds. I. N. Vogiatzakis, G. Pungetti, & A. M. Mannion. Dordrecht: Springer, pp. 3–14.

Vogiatzakis, I. N., & O. Rackham, 2008. Crete, in *Mediterranean Island Landscapes: Natural and Cultural Approaches*, eds. I. N. Vogiatzakis, G. Pungetti, & A. M. Mannion. Dordrecht: Springer, pp. 245–70.

Waelkens, M., E. Paulissen, M. Vermoere, P. Degryse, D. Celis, K. Schroyen, B. De Cupere, I. Librecht, K. Nackaerts, & H. Vanhaverbeke, 1999. Man and environment in the territory of Sagalassos, a classical city in SW Turkey. *Quaternary Science Reviews*, 18(4/5), 697–710.

Wagner, B., A. Lotter, N. Nowaczyk, J. Reed, A. Schwalb, R. Sulpizio, V. Valsecchi, M. Wessels, & G. Zanchetta, 2009. A 40,000-year record of environmental change from ancient Lake Ohrid (Albania and Macedonia). *Journal of Paleoliminology*, 41(3), 407–30.

Wagstaff, J. M., 1992. Agricultural terraces: The Vasilikos Valley, Cyprus, in *Past and Present Soil Erosion, Archaeological and Geographical Perspectives*, eds. M. Bell & J. Boardman. Oxford: Oxbow, pp. 155–61.

Wagstaff, M., & C. Gamble, 1982. Island resources and their limitations, in *An Island Polity: The Archaeology of Exploitation in Melos*, eds. C. Renfrew & M. Wagstaff. Cambridge: Cambridge University Press, pp. 95–105.

Wagstaff, M., & J. F. Cherry, 1982a. Settlement and population change, in *An Island Polity: The Archaeology of Exploitation in Melos*, eds. C. Renfrew & M. Wagstaff. Cambridge: Cambridge University Press, pp. 136–55.

Wagstaff, M., & J. F. Cherry, 1982b. Settlement and resources, in *An Island Polity: The Archaeology of Exploitation in Melos*, eds. C. Renfrew & M. Wagstaff. Cambridge: Cambridge University Press, pp. 246–63.

Wagstaff, M., & S. Augustson, 1982. Traditional land use, in *An Island Polity: The Archaeology of Exploitation in Melos*, eds. C. Renfrew & M. Wagstaff. Cambridge: Cambridge University Press, pp. 106–33.

Wainwright, J., 1994. Anthropogenic factors in the degradatation of semi-arid regions: A prehistoric case study in Southern France, in *Environmental Change in Drylands: Biogeographical and Geomorphological Perspectives*, eds. A. C. Millington & K. Pye. London: John Wiley, pp. 285–304.

2004. A review of European Union funded research into the history and evolution of Mediterranean desertification. *Advances in Environmental Monitoring and Modelling*, 1(4), 1–87.

Wainwright, J., & J. B. Thornes, 2004. *Environmental Issues in the Mediterranean: Processes and Perspectives from the Past and Present*. London: Routledge.

Waldren, W., 1997. The definition and duration of the Beaker Culture in the Spanish Balearic Islands: A radiocarbon survey. *Oxford Journal of Archaeology*, 16(1), 25–48.

Walker, B. H., & D. A. Salt, 2006. *Resilience Thinking: Sustaining Ecosystems and People in a Changing World.* Washington: Island Press.

Walker, B. H., C. S. Holling, S. R. Carpenter, & A. Kinzig, 2004. Resilience, adaptability and transformability in social-ecological systems. *Ecology and Society,* 9(2).

Wallace, S., 2010. *Ancient Crete: From Successful Collapse to Democracy's Alternatives, Twelfth to Fifth Centuries BC.* Cambridge: Cambridge University Press.

Walsh, K., 2004. Caring about sediments: The role of cultural geoarchaeology in Mediterranean landscapes. *Journal of Mediterranean Archaeology,* 17(2), 223–45.

2005. Risk and marginality at high altitudes: New interpretations from field-work on the Faravel Plateau, Hautes-Alpes. *Antiquity,* 79, 289–305.

Walsh, K., & F. Mocci, 2003. Fame and marginality: The archaeology of Montagne Sainte Victoire (Provence, France). *American Journal of Archaeology,* 107(1), 45–70.

Walsh, K., & F. Mocci, 2011. Mobility in the mountains: Late third and second millennia alpine societies' engagements with the high-altitude zones in the Southern French Alps. *European Journal of Archaeology,* 14(1–2), 88–115.

Walsh, K., F. Mocci, J. Court-Picon, J. M. Palet-Martinez, & S. Tzortzis, 2005. Dynamique du peuplement et activités agro-pastorales durant l'âge du Bronze dans les massifs du haut Champsaur et de l'Argentièrois (Hautes-Alpes). *Documents d'Archéologie Méridionale,* 28, 25–44.

Walsh, K., & S. Richer, 2006. Attitudes to altitude: Changing meanings and per-ceptions within a 'marginal' Alpine landscape – The integration of palaeo-ecological and archaeological data in a high altitude landscape in the French Alps. *World Archaeology,* 38(3), 436–54.

Walters, B. B., & A. P. Vayda, 2009. Event ecology, causal historical analysis, and human–environment research. *Annals of the Association of American Geographers,* 99(3), 534–53.

Warren, P., 1996. The Aegean and the limits of radiocarbon dating. *Acta Archaeologica,* 67, 283–90.

Watrous, L. V., 1982. *Lasithi. A History of Settlement on a Highland Mountain Plain in Crete.* Princeton: American School of Classical Studies at Athens.

Watrous, L. V., D. Chatzi-Vallianou, K. O. Pope, N. Mourtzas, J. Shay, C. T. Shay, J. Bennet, D. Tsoungarakis, E. Angelomati-Tsoungarakis, C. Vallianos, & H. Blitzer, 1993. A survey of the Western Mesara Plain in Crete: Preliminary report of the 1984, 1986, and 1987 field seasons. *Hesperia,* 62 (2), 191–248.

Watts, W. A., J. R. M. Allen, B. Huntley, & S. C. Fritz, 1996. Vegetation history and climate of the last 15,000 years at Laghi di Monticchio, Southern Italy. *Quaternary Science Reviews,* 15(2/3), 113–32.

Weiburg, E., M. Lindblom, B. Leppänen Sjöberg, & G. Nordquist, 2010. Social and environmental dynamics in Bronze and Iron Age Greece, in *The Urban*

Mind: Cultural and Environmental Dynamics, eds. P. Sinclair, G. Nordquist, F. Herschend, & C. Isendahl. Uppsala: African and Comparative Archaeology, Department of Archaeology and Ancient History, pp. 149–94.

Wengler, L., & J. L. Vernet, 1992. Vegetation, sedimentary deposits and climates during the Late Pleistocene and Holocene in eastern Morocco *Palaeogeography Palaeoclimatology Palaeoecology*, 94 (1–4), 141–67.

Weninger, B., E. Alram-Stern, E. Bauer, L. Clare, U. Danzeglocke, O. Jöris, C. Kubatzki, G. Rollefson, H. Todorova, & T. van Andel, 2006. Climate forcing due to the 8200 Cal yr BP event observed at Early Neolithic sites in the Eastern Mediterranean. *Quaternary Research*, 66(3), 401–20.

Weninger, B., L. Clare, E. Rohling, O. Bar-Yosef, U. Böhner, M. Budja, M. Bundschuh, A. Feurdean, H. G. Gebe, O. Jöris, J. Ç. Linstädter, P. Mayewski, T. Mühlenbruch, A. Reingruber, G. Rollefson, D. Schyle, L. Thissen, H. Todorova, & C. Zielhofer, 2009. The impact of rapid climate change on prehistoric societies during the Holocene in the Eastern Mediterranean. *Documenta Praehistorica*, 36, 7–59.

Westley, F., S. Carpenter, R. W. A. Brock, C. S. Holling, & L. H. Gunderson, 2002. Why systems of people and nature are not just social and ecological systems, in *Panarchy: Understanding Transformations in Human and Natural Systems*, eds. L. H. Gunderson & C. S. Holling. Washington: Island Press, pp. 103–19.

Whatmore, S., 2002. *Hybrid Geographies: Natures, Cultures, Spaces*. London: Sage.

Whitelaw, T. M., 1991. The ethnoarchaeology of recent rural settlement and land use in northwest Keos, in *Landscape Archaeology as Long-Term History: Northern Keos in the Cycladic Islands from the Earliest Settlement until Modern Times*, eds. J. F. Cherry, J. L. Davies, & E. Mantzourani. Los Angeles: Institute of Archaeology, University of California, pp. 403–54.

Whittle, A., 2002. Houses in context: Buildings as process, in *Neolithic Houses in Northwest Europe and Beyond*, eds. T. Darvill & J. Thomas. Oxford: Oxbow, pp. 13–26.

Wick, L., 1994. Vegetation development and human impact at the forest limit: Palaeoecological studies in the Splügen Pass area (north Italy), in *Highland Zone Exploitation in Southern Europe*, eds. P. Biagi & J. Nandris. Brescia: Museo civico di scienze naturali di Brescia, Monographie di 'Natura Bresciana' 20, pp. 123–32.

Wick, L., & A. Möhl, 2006. The mid-Holocene extinction of silver fir (*Abies alba*) in the Southern Alps: A consequence of forest fires? Palaeobotanical records and forest simulations. *Vegetation History and Archaeobotany*, 15(4), 435–44.

Wilkinson, T. J., 2005. Soil erosion and valley fills in the Yemen highlands and southern Turkey: Integrating settlement, geoarchaeology, and climate change. *Geoarchaeology*, 20 (2), 169–92.

Wilkinson, T. J., & S. T. Duhon, 1990. *Franchthi Paralia: The Sediments, Stratigraphy, and Offshore Investigations*, eds. T. J. Wilkinson & S. T. Duhon. Bloomington: Indiana University Press.

Willis, K. J., 1992. The Late Quaternary vegetational history of northwest Greece. III. A comparative study of two contrasting sites. *New Phytologist*, 121, 139–55.

1994. Altitudinal variation in the Late Quaternary vegetational history of northwest Greece. *Historical Biology: An International Journal of Paleobiology*, 9(1), 103–16.

Wilson, I., 2001. *Before the Flood*. London: Orion.

Winterhalder, B., 1994. Concepts in historical ecology: The view from evolutionary ecology, in *Historical Ecology: Cultural Knowledge and Changing Landscapes*, ed. C. L. Crumley. Santa Fe: School of American Research Press, pp. 17–41.

Wittenberg, L., H. Kutiel, N. Greenbaum, & M. Inbar, 2007. Short-term changes in the magnitude, frequency and temporal distribution of floods in the Eastern Mediterranean region during the last 45 years – Nahal Oren, Mt. Carmel, Israel. *Geomorphology*, 84(3–4), 181–91.

Wossink, A., 2009. *Challenging Climate Change: Competition and Cooperation Among Pastoralists and Agriculturalists in Northern Mesopotamia (c. 3000– 1600 BC)*. Leiden: Sidestone Press.

Wright, J. C., J. F. Cherry, J. L. Davis, E. Mantzourani, S. B. Sutton, & R. F. Sutton, 1990. The Nemea Valley archaeological project: A preliminary report. *Hesperia*, 59(4), 579–659.

Yalcner, A. C., B. Alpar, Y. Altnok, I. Ozbay, & F. Imamura, 2002. Tsunamis in the Sea of Marmara. *Marine Geology*, 190(1–2), 445–63.

Yaltrak, C., B. Alpar, M. Saknc, & H. Yuce, 2000. Origin of the Strait of Canakkale (Dardanelles): Regional tectonics and the Mediterranean-Marmara incursion. *Marine Geology*, 164(3–4), 139–56.

Yanko-Hombach, V., P. Mudie, & A. S. Gilbert, 2011. Was the Black Sea catastrophically flooded during the Holocene? – Geological evidence and archaeological impacts, in *Submerged Prehistory*, eds. J. Benjamin, C. Bonsall, & A. Fisher. Oxford: Oxbow Books, pp. 245–62.

Yasuda, Y., H. Kitagawa, & T. Nakagawa, 2000. The earliest record of major anthropogenic deforestation in the Ghab Valley, northwest Syria: A palynological study. *Quaternary International*, 73–4, 127–36.

YaSuouka, J. U. N. K., & R. I. C. H. Levins, 2007. Impact of deforestation and agricultural development on Anopheline ecology and malaria epidemiology. *American Journal of Tropical Medicine and Hygiene*, 76(3), 450–60.

Yener, K. A., C. Edens, T. P. Harrison, J. Verstraete, & T. J. Wilkinson, 2000. The Amuq Valley regional project, 1995–1998. *American Journal of Archaeology*, 104, PART 2, 163–220.

Yll, E. I., R. Perez-Obiol, J. Pantaleon-Cano, & J. M. Roure, 1997. Palynological evidence for climatic change and human activity during the Holocene on Minorca (Balearic Islands). *Quaternary Research*, 48(3), 339–47.

Zachos, K., 1996. Tracing a destructive earthquake in the southwestern Peloponnese (Greece) during the Early Bronze Age, in *Archaeoseismology*, eds. S. C. Stiros & R. E. Jones. Athens: Institute of Geology and Mineral Exploration & The British School at Athens, pp. 169–85.

Zangger, E., 1991. Prehistoric coastal environments in Greece: The vanished landscapes of Dimini Bay and Lake Lerna. *Journal of Field Archaeology*, 18, 1–15.

Zangger, E., 1994. Landscape changes around Tiryns during the Bronze Age. *American Journal of Archaeology*, 98(2), 189–212.

Zangger, E., 2001. *The Future of the Past*. London: Weidenfeld and Nicholson.

Zangger, E., M. E. Timpson, S. B. Yazvenko, F. Kuhnke, & J. Knauss, 1997. The Pylos regional archaeological project: Part II: Landscape evolution and site preservation. *Hesperia*, 66 (4), 549–641.

Zazo, C., J. L. Goy, L. Somoza, & C. J. Dabrio, 1994. Holocene sequence of sea-level fluctuations in relation to climatic trends in the Atlantic–Mediterranean linkage coast. *Journal of Coastal Research*, 10(4), 933–45.

Zielhofer, C., & D. Faust, 2003. Palaeoenvironment and morphodynamics in the mid-Medjerda floodplain (northern Tunisia) between 12,000 and 2000 BP: Geoarchaeological and geomorphological findings, in *Alluvial Archaeology in Europe*, eds. A. J. Howard, M. G. Macklin, & D. G. Passmore. Lisse: Swets & Zeitlinger, pp. 203–16.

Zielhofer, C., & D. Faust, 2008. Mid- and Late Holocene fluvial chronology of Tunisia. *Quaternary Science Reviews*, 27(5), 580–8.

Zielhofer, C., D. Faust, F. az del Olmo, & R. Escudero, 2002. Sedimentation and soil formation phases in the Ghardimaou Basin (northern Tunisia) during the Holocene. *Quaternary International*, 93–4, 109–25.

Zielhofer, C., D. Faust, & J. Linstädter, 2008. Late Pleistocene and Holocene alluvial archives in the Southwestern Mediterranean: Changes in fluvial dynamics and past human response. *Quaternary International*, 181(1), 39–54.

Zielhofer, C., D. Faust, R. B. Escudero, F. D. Del Olmo, A. Kadereit, K. M. Moldenhauer, & A. Porras, 2004. Centennial-scale late-Pleistocene to mid-Holocene synthetic profile of the Medjerda Valley, northern Tunisia. *The Holocene*, 14(6), 851–61.

Zielhofer, C., & J. Linstädter, 2006. Short-term mid-Holocene climatic deterioration in the West Mediterranean region: Climatic impact on Neolithic settlement pattern. *Zeitschrift für Geomorphologie NF*, 142, 1–17.

Zielinski, G. A., & M. S. Germani, 1998. New Ice-Core Evidence Challenges the 1620s BC age for the Santorini (Minoan) Eruption. *Journal of Archaeological Science*, 25, 279–89.

Zohary, D., & M. Hopf, 2001. *Domestication of Plants in the Old World*. Oxford: Oxford University Press.

Index

Acarnania, Greece, 77
Acheloös, river, Greece, 77
Actor Network theory (ANT)
  hybrids, 206
Adriatic, 33, 39, 40, 52, 152, 216
Aegean, 22, 25, 33, 38, 39, 41, 56,
  65, 137, 175, 210, 215, 217,
  230, 236
Aegila (Goat Island), 228
Aeolian Islands, 210
aeolian processes, 45, 49, 137, 189
Aetolia, Greece, 77
Agios Dimitrios (stream), 83
agro-sylvo-pastoral management, 190
Aguas river, Spain, 84
Albania, 250, 253
Algeria, 19, 137
alluvial geoarchaeology, 69, 85, 117
  alluvial 'stability' and 'instability',
  69
Almería, Spain, 132, 165, 182
Alpilles, France, 158, 203
Alps, 257–65
Alpujarra, Spain, 165
Amorgos, island, 227, 236
Amuq Plain, Turkey, 141
Amuq Valley, Turkey, 81
Anatolia, 24, 85, 127, 140, 142, 250,
  287
Andalucia, 60
Andorra, 266

Andros, island, 225
Aniene Valley, Italy, 276
anthracology, 21, 134, 192, 205, 259
  Alps, 258
  cultural choices of wood/plants,
  142, 205
Anthropic-Climatic Regime, 148
Antikythera, island, 224, 228–9
Apennines, Italy, 96, 97, 255–7
Apulia, Italy, 38, 129, 151
aqueducts, 108, 109, 201
Aquileia, Italy, 53, 58
arboriculture, 142, 168, 183, 185–7,
  252, 275
Arcadia, Greece, 109
archaeobotanical remains, 42
Argaric culture, Spain, 166, 168–70,
  183, 291
Argive, Greece, 47, 105, 118, 172
Argolid, Greece
  erosion and time, 207
  evidence for erosion, 178–80
Argos, Greece, 103, 172
arid landscapes, 136, 189
aridification, 5, 94, 126, 129, 132,
  133, 135, 144, 161
Arles, France, 115, 201, 204
Arno river, Italy, 57
Artemis (goddess), 109
Athens, Greece, 207
Atlantis, 15